Assessing

Language Ability

in the Classroom

Second Edition

Andrew D. Cohen
University of Minnesota

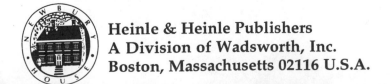

Heinle & Heinle Publishers
A Division of Wadsworth, Inc.
Boston, Massachusetts 02116 U.S.A.

The publication of *Assessing Language Ability in the Classroom*, Second Edition was directed by the members of the Heinle & Heinle ESL Publishing Team:

David C. Lee, *Editorial Director*
Kristin Thalheimer, *Production Editor*

Also participating in the publication of this program were:

Publisher: Stanley J. Galek
Editorial Production Manager: Elizabeth Holthaus
Project Manager: Judy Keith
Assistant Editor: Kenneth Mattsson
Manufacturing Coordinator: Mary Beth Lynch
Cover Design: Bortman Design Group
Illustrations: Kevin M. Flynn
Book Design and Composition: Matthew Dixon Cowles

Library of Congress Cataloging-in-Publication Data
Cohen, Andrew D.
    Assessing language ability in the classroom / Andrew D. Cohen,
        p.   cm.
    Includes bibliographical references (p.   ).
    ISBN 0–8384–4262–5
    1. English language—Study and teaching—Foreign speakers.
2. Language and languages—Ability testing. 3. English language—
Ability testing. I. Title.
PE1128.A2C6557 1994
428'.0076—dc20   93–41932
                                                          CIP

Heinle & Heinle Publishers is a division of Wadsworth, Inc.

Manufactured in the United States of America

ISBN 0–8384–4262–5

10 9 8 7 6 5 4 3

Contents

Acknowledgments

I would like to acknowledge those persons who assisted me in field testing this second version in four classrooms in three universities. My thanks first go to Neil Anderson and his students at Ohio University, who provided me with invaluable feedback regarding the pilot version of this textbook. Likewise, my deep appreciation goes to Rebecca Oxford and her students at the University of Alabama for their timely and extensive feedback. My thanks also go to my colleague Diane Tedick at the University of Minnesota and to her students. In addition, I would like to thank the students in my own graduate course in language testing for their helpful comments.

I also would like to acknowledge colleagues who have contributed to sections of the manuscript through feedback on specific chapters and through their answers to my queries. These people include Lyle Bachman, Charles Alderson, Liz Hamp-Lyons, Grant Henning, Dan Douglas, Elana Shohamy, Geoff Brindley, Jan Smith, and Thom Upton. I would also like to express my gratitude to Rupert Ingram, the founder of Newbury House Publishers, for his suggestion that I write the original edition of this book in the first place. It is through the encouragement of Doug Brown, Neil Anderson, and others that I have produced this second edition. I offer a special vote of thanks to Lee Searles for proofreading and for preparing the index.

I would also like to thank Alister Cumming (Ontario Institute for Studies in Education), Fred Davidson (University of Illinios), and LaVona Reeves (Eastern Washington University) for their helpful comments during the development of this book.

Finally, I wish to acknowledge my wife, Sabina, and my kids, Judy and Daniel, for their encouragement during the writing of this second edition, which for me involved nothing less than contending with a war in the Middle East, changing continents, and taking on a new academic position, all during the three years this book was being written.

Chapter 1:
Introduction

The assessment of students' language abilities is something on which teachers spend a fair amount of class time in one way or another. In the best of all possible worlds, such assessment is valuable for both the teachers and the learners. The assessment tasks are nonthreatening and are developmental in nature, allowing the learners ample opportunities to demonstrate what they know and do not know, and providing useful feedback both for the learners and for their teachers.

The intention of this book is as much to heighten readers' awareness of language assessment techniques and procedures with which they are already familiar as it is to teach new material. Ideally, the book will help language educators to be more systematic about their use of assessment procedures. We will explore a number of accessible and user-friendly assessment instruments and potential instruments throughout this book.

The first edition of this book was written primarily for teachers with no background in language assessment. This edition is written more for readers with some background in assessment—teachers, test constructors, other professionals engaged in assessment activities, and research students. In order to provide insights from research without losing the interest of those readers who are less interested in this area, the portions of the text that focus on research are set off and referred to as *Research Notes*. In this way, those readers who are interested in the research will know where to find summaries of relevant studies, and those who are not can go on to the next section.

Although some attention is still given to the "basics" of language testing and assessment, the focus of the book is now on going beyond basics. Also, whereas the focus of the earlier volume was on classroom tests, in this edition the focus shifts somewhat with regard to the types of assessment tasks described. While the main context for assessment continues to be the classroom, many of the issues to be discussed will involve the assessment of groups of learners beyond the individual classroom. However, we will not address the particulars of standardized tests such as TOEFL, the Cambridge First Certificate in English, and so forth. Descriptions of these and other assessment instruments can be found in publications such as Alderson, Krahnke, and Stansfield's *Reviews of English language proficiency tests* (1987).

This book constitutes far more than a revision of the 1980 volume. Most of the book is new, reflecting the many changes that have occurred over the last decade and a half. Not only have new chapters been added, but the other portions of the book have been rewritten or updated. The added chapters look at the testing of reading comprehension, listening and speaking, and writing.

Language Assessment: An Increasingly Popular Pastime

For many, traditional "testing" has been viewed as a somewhat unpopular area of language teaching and learning. Students have sometimes viewed tests as unfair measures of their language ability and have feared that they would not perform well on them. Teachers have sometimes felt reluctant to construct classroom tests and have not been altogether satisfied with their results when they have engaged in test construction. On occasion, teachers have also been suspicious of standardized, commercial tests when they have not been sure what these tests were actually trying to measure.

With regard to *standardized achievement tests*, a survey of over 1,200 second through eleventh graders in Michigan, California, Arizona, and Florida showed cumulative negative effects of repeated achievement testing, as the students—especially the low achievers—became increasingly suspicious and cynical about them (Paris, Lawton, Turner, & Roth, 1991). A large number of pupils reported becoming anxious about such tests, cheating, trying halfheartedly, or using poor test-taking strategies, such as not narrowing down the acceptable alternatives in multiple-choice items, not monitoring their time, not skipping items, and not checking answers. The authors concluded that these attitudes and behaviors undermined the validity of the test scores and discouraged genuine learning. They recommended a *developmental approach* to testing, whereby teachers and pupils would work collaboratively on authentic testing tasks that were *longitudinal* and *multidimensional*.

On the basis of a survey of English-as-a-foreign-language (EFL) teachers and students in Israeli public schools, Shohamy (1985) found a number of *classroom testing procedures* to be of questionable value (see Figure 1.1). The list of classroom testing procedures appearing in Figure 1.2 is substantially more positive. The main shift is from using assessment as a way to keep students in their place to using assessment as a way to help students *find* their place in school and in the world community of language users.

Fortunately, in the past few years there has been a growing interest in improving the language assessment situation. According to Bachman (1991), advances in language testing over the last decade have included

1. The development of a theoretical view that sees language ability as multi-componential and recognizes the influence of test-method and test-taker characteristics on test performance
2. The use of more sophisticated measurement and statistical tools
3. The development of communicative language tests commensurate with the increased teaching of communicative skills

3

Figure 1.1 Questionable Classroom Testing Procedures

- Using tests as punishment—for example, because no one did the homework
- Administering tests instead of giving instruction
- Using tests as the exclusive measure for grading
- Testing material that was not taught
- Returning tests to students without offering corrections or explanations
- Using only one testing method
- Giving tests that students did not know how to take
- Taking too long in returning tests

(based on Shohamy, 1985)

Figure 1.2 Promising Classroom Testing Procedures

- Broadening the scope of what is included in assessment from tests alone to a variety of formal and informal assessment techniques
- Viewing assessment as an opportunity for meaningful interaction between teacher and student
- Judging students on the basis of the knowledge they have, rather than on what they do not know
- Using assessment measures intended to help learners to improve their skills
- Making sure that the criteria for success on an assessment task are made clear to the respondents
- Having students' grades reflect their performance on a *set* of tests representing different assessment methods, rather than being based on just one measure
- Training the test takers in test-taking strategies if performance on the assessment task could benefit from such training
- Returning the evaluated tests promptly
- Discussing the results in class or in individual sessions

(based on Shohamy, 1985)

This interest in more innovative and sensitive measures of language ability, especially with regard to the productive skills of speaking (see Shohamy, 1988) and writing (see Hamp-Lyons, 1991a), has been an outgrowth of the wave of interest in communicative language teaching.

A Policy for Language Assessment

How readers relate to this book will depend in large part upon their needs and purposes with respect to language assessment. It is likely that the book will be used by both developers and users of assessment instruments. While developers are those who construct tests and other assessment tasks and set policies for particular assessment programs, users select assessment instruments, commission development of such instruments, or make decisions on the basis of assessment scores. Classroom teachers sometimes find themselves in both roles, as developer *and* user. For this reason, it is crucial for the classroom teacher to have a clear idea of how assessment will be conducted in the classroom.

The readers of this volume are invited to identify which assessment framework is meaningful or appropriate for them. Given that framework, they can make informed choices about what sections of this book to read when and how. They will be better able to deal with the various assessment approaches and techniques contained within these pages. They will be better able to deal with the basic assessment questions that are entertained in the volume: What? Why? How? When? Where? Who? Through what processes? For whom? Hence, readers need to make key decisions about how they use language assessment. The decisions that they make with respect to using this book may lead them to formulate a policy of language assessment for courses they are teaching or programs they are administering, or to enhance the policy they have already established.

Let us proceed to engage ourselves in this inquiry and see where it leads you, the reader, with respect to how to use this book. Fill out the following questionnaire. Try to focus on language assessment needs that you currently have or will have in the immediate future rather than on needs that you have had in the past. You may not have answers to some of the questions at present. Reading this book should assist you in providing answers to these questions. After completing the questionnaire, proceed to the discussion that follows it.

Language Assessment Needs Questionnaire

1. *What?* What language abilities would you like to assess? To what extent are you interested in assessing sociocultural and sociolinguistic ability? What interest do you have in grammatical ability? What about assessing the strategic ability to produce responses? To what extent are you interested in the different skill areas—reading comprehension, listening comprehension, speaking, and written expression? To what extent is your interest in assessment for administrative, instructional, or research purposes?

2. *Why?* Why are you choosing to measure these abilities and not others? What assessment approaches and techniques are you currently using, and what is your rationale for using these approaches and techniques?

3. *How?* If you are planning on developing new measures, how are you going to construct your assessment instruments? How are you going to validate these measures?

4. *When?* How often will assessment take place?

5. *Where?* What are the characteristics of the physical environment(s) in which the assessment will take place (e.g., adequate lighting, noise, ventilation, proper seating, and desks)?

6. *Who?* Who are your intended respondents? How might they be described in terms of their personal characteristics? What is their sociocultural background? What cognitive styles do they or might they display? How test-wise are they?

7. *Through what processes?* What processes do you think the respondents will go through in order to produce answers to items and procedures on the assessment measures that you give them?

8. *For whom?* For whom are the results on the language assessment measures intended? To what extent do you use a method for reporting the results and for giving feedback that benefits all concerned?

Discussion of Questionnaire Exercise

1. What? What language abilities would you like to assess and for what purposes? Chapter 2 includes a discussion of sociocultural, sociolinguistic, and grammatical ability. The later chapters of this book deal in some detail with specific applications for assessment: reading comprehension, listening comprehension, speaking, and written expression. The types of assessment possible given the purpose of the assessment—whether administrative, instructional, or research—are also discussed in Chapter 2.

Chapter 7 carefully examines the assessment of reading comprehension. It looks at types of reading, kinds of meaning, the skills that are involved in reading comprehension, and the methods available for assessment. Chapter 8 starts with a brief discussion of listening comprehension items and procedures, ranging from discrete-point items with a traditional focus on isolated language forms to more integrative assessment tasks. Then the chapter shifts to the assessment of speaking. Traditional interviews are considered, along with semi-direct tests and forms of role play to assess speech act performance. Chapter 9 considers the construction of instruments for assessing written expression, the taking of such instruments, and the rating of them. The nature of essay prompts and the processing of rating essays are also considered, along with alternatives to traditional essays, such as the portfolio approach. Finally, the interaction of reading and writing in the form of summary writing is explored.

2. Why? Why are you choosing to measure these abilities and not others? What is your rationale for taking this approach? Chapter 2 asks a series of basic questions about testing, starting off with "Why assess language ability?" If you are concerned about the benefits to students and to teachers, then you would want to run through that series of points in Chapter 2.

3. How? How will you construct and validate your assessment measures? This is a big question, deserving of a series of different and involved answers. The reader could start in Chapter 2, which includes a discussion of some of the basic procedural issues, such as choosing between norm-referenced and criterion-referenced assessment. The chapter also distinguishes quizzes from longer assessment instruments and calls attention to the role of quizzes in eliminating the fear syndrome that may accompany the notion of assessment in the minds of students and sometimes in the minds of teachers as well. In addition, Chapter 2 considers means for evaluating the results of the assessment instrument, including the issues of reliability and validity, which the informed may find useful as a review and the uninformed may want exposure to, since assessment measures that are neither reliable nor valid may be of questionable educational value.

Chapters 3, 4, and 6 provide extensive discussion of assessment items and their properties. Chapter 3 offers an analysis of formats for language assessment, while Chapter 4 looks at issues related to scoring of instruments, item analysis, instrument revision, and instrument evaluation. The analysis of an instrument's distinctive elements—that is, the item-elicitation and item-response formats, the response behavior being assessed, and scoring and evaluation procedures—is intended to provide valuable help in determining the validity of the assessment instrument.

Chapter 6 looks at the elements that constitute discrete-point and integrative assessment items and procedures. It emphasizes the notion that items may range from mostly discrete-point to mostly integrative in their format. Questions on assessment instruments are discussed in terms of the formats for item elicitation and for item response, respectively, in order to show that these two dimensions are separate and that a variety of items can result from varying the elicitation and response formats. Rather than listing all possible oral, written, or nonverbal formats for item-elicitation and item-response stimuli, the focus in the chapter is on a small number of sample formats. Throughout the discussion of specific assessment formats, we make an attempt to focus on results. This focus is based on our intent not only to present sample item-elicitation formats, but also to discuss possible answers, suggested scoring, and evaluation of the scores. The chapter also deals with the nature of the instructions that accompany assessment measures and with self-assessment procedures meant to shift some of the responsibility of evaluation onto the respondents themselves.

4. When? How often will assessment take place? Although this may seem like a minor issue, it is really quite important in that there is a delicate line between so little assessment that the learners wonder how they are doing and so much assessment that they wonder when they will just be allowed to learn without being assessed. Chapter 2 looks briefly at the issue of when to assess and the challenge associated with working out a series of ongoing, informal assessment techniques that get the job done, often unobtrusively. If the frequency of assessment is an issue that you are dealing with or would like to deal with, then you may want to read this discussion.

5. Where? What are the characteristics of the physical environment(s) in which the assessment will take place? We do not deal extensively with this issue, but Chapter 3 has a section that discusses administering standardized tests to large groups of respondents.

6. Who? Who are the intended respondents for the assessment? How might they be described in terms of their personal characteristics? Chapter 3 looks at how respondents' characteristics may influence their performance on assessment measures. If you are involved with nonhomogeneous groups in which individual differences may influence outcomes, then this section will be of interest to you.

7. Through what process? What processes will the respondents go through in order to produce answers to items and procedures on assessment instruments? Chapter 5 looks at the process of taking a language assessment measure. Even if both the assessor and the students are clear about what is being asked in a given item or procedure, the assessor may have little understanding of how the respondent is producing answers. This chapter looks at strategies used in the taking of language tests in order to identify some of the cognitive operations or processes involved in producing answers. It then looks at other means of determining the sources of difficulty in particular testing items and procedures.

8. For whom? Who will use the results? The end of Chapter 4 has a section on the reporting of results from assessment. Sometimes, the scores that respondents obtain on assessment instruments, especially on standardized tests, can have considerable influence on their further development and careers. Scores may be used as "gatekeepers" that let some students through and keep others back. Hence, the way that results are interpreted and reported is crucial, and teachers and administrators would want to put all student results in perspective in order to view the respondent in the fairest light possible.

At present, we are in the enviable position of having numerous textbooks that deal with a variety of issues in language testing. Bachman (1990), Brindley (1989), Davies (1990), Henning (1987), Hughes (1989), Shohamy (1985), and Weir (1990) are some of the more prominent ones. This was not the case when I wrote the first edition of this language testing book almost fifteen years ago. Now, more than ever before, the reader must be selective and discerning. Ideally, the current edition of this book can play a role in the field, whether as a textbook in language testing courses for teachers in training, as a reference book for the practitioner, or as a guide for the researcher.

Chapter 2: Key Questions in Language Assessment

When the first edition of this book appeared, the term *testing* was used throughout. In the intervening decade and a half, researchers in the field of language measurement have looked increasingly for means of evaluating language ability beyond the more traditional quizzes and tests. Consequently, this new edition will focus more on assessment rather than on testing. Thus, when we refer to *testing* in this volume, we will mean the broadest possible sense of the word—that is, the collection of any data that can be used to assess the language abilities of respondents.

In looking for the roots of change, we may be able to attribute a fair amount of the influence to work being done on second language acquisition (SLA). While SLA has taken a longitudinal view, concerning itself with the description and explanation of how second language proficiency develops, language testing has typically strived to capture a "slice of life"—that is, to describe language proficiency at a given stage of development (Bachman, 1989). SLA has put the emphasis more on the factors and processes that contribute to language development—on sequence in rule learning, on the influences of certain inputs on outputs, on learner characteristics such as age, gender, cognitive style, and so forth—while language testing has assessed the results of acquisition.

So the work in SLA has prompted those in language assessment to take a broader view of what assessment means—to include more variables when attempting to determine language proficiency and achievement. SLA research has also alerted assessment people to be more mindful of variability in grammatical accuracy, fluency, and other language elements in response to a given instrument and the context in which it is administered (Tarone, forthcoming).

Why Assess Language Ability?

There are numerous language acquisition contexts in which progress is not evaluated in any systematic way. The only "test" of performance might be the degree of success the language user has in speaking or writing the language sufficiently for the purpose of conducting some business transaction, such as bartering potatoes for oranges in a village marketplace. If the transaction is successfully completed as a direct result of the verbal (as opposed to the nonverbal) exchanges, then it might be considered that the language used was "adequate" for the purposes.

On the other hand, the language learning classroom marks a context in which progress can, and sometimes must, be evaluated in a systematic way. In fact, administrators, parents, teachers, and learners normally expect some form of evaluation of progress. Such systematic evaluation, however informal it may be (e.g., through journal writing, discussion groups, or portfolios), still constitutes assessment. Let us now look at some of the reasons for conducting language assessment in the classroom, but before we do so, let us make an important distinction between second-language and foreign-language testing, a distinction that we will come back to in a later chapter.

Unlike the environment created in the marketplace interaction mentioned above, the environment in which languages are often learned—especially in foreign-language contexts—is not exemplified by performance tasks—such as bartering—as a principal means for assessing ability. Plus, it may be impractical to set up such tasks in a language class (e.g., sending learners out to hotels to interview tourists and to return with five sets of responses to a questionnaire). In a *second-language assessment context*—i.e., where the language being assessed is one that is spoken in the community in which it is being learned—using community resources as part of the assessment process may be possible. In a *foreign-language assessment context*, on the other hand, the fact that the language being assessed is not spoken in the local community may create problems for assessment.

What adds further complexity to the situation is that the so-called foreign-language context sometimes has so much access to the target language that it really functions in many ways like a second-language context (e.g., learning Chinese as a foreign language while living in Chinatown in San Francisco and spending most of non-classroom time submersed in the Chinese-speaking community). Likewise, some second-language contexts can operate far more like foreign-language ones (e.g., the learning of Arabic by Hebrew speakers in Israel who have little or no contact with the Arabic-speaking community out of class). For our purposes, we will envision the theoretically simple models of the foreign-language context as implying little out-of-class contact and the second-language context as one with frequent exposure.

The Benefits for Learners

One of the primary reasons for conducting language assessment in the classroom is to promote **meaningful** involvement of students with material that is central to the teaching objectives of a given course. For this meaningful involvement to take place, the goals of the assessment tasks need to reflect the goals of the course, and these goals need to be made clear to the students. If students perceive a quiz or test as relevant to their needs in the course, they are probably going to be more motivated to deal with it. Quizzes may motivate students to pay closer attention to the material on a particular day, if the teacher announces at the outset of the class session that there will be a quiz on that material (Krypsin & Feldhusen, 1974). Of course, if there are too many such quizzes, or if the quizzes seem to be mindless exercises in order to amass numerical grades, such an approach may backfire. As with any technique, the teacher must use judgment and be sensitive to the students' needs and preferences.

Having students prepare for a test can serve as an inducement for them to review the material covered in the course. What does this mean in practice? First of all, it may mean that the students go to their notebooks and try to make order out of chaos. Notebooks usually reflect the chronological order in which material was presented in class. This may not be the best order for learning or review for tests. Instead, learners might rearrange their notebooks into some logical order, such as by organizing their vocabulary according to word classes (nouns, adjectives, adverbs, prepositions, connectors, etc.) and according to semantic categories (words expressing state of mind, weather, etc.). They may also want to use vocabulary and structures in functional practice (i.e., in communicative situations). For example, they might take a small stack of their flash cards, lay them out on a table, and engage a native speaker in a conversation by drawing on the words written on the flash cards. They could also sort out and classify grammatical rules according to type of rule, complexity, difficulty it causes them, and so forth (Cohen, 1990a:128-129). This would depend very much on the nature of the language learning. While some students thrive on rules, others attempt to keep a distance between themselves and formal rule learning.

Regular assessment of learning can provide learners with feedback about their language performance at various stages in the developmental process. While assessment is taking place, students are getting feedback on how well they perform on those tasks. Once the task has been scored and evaluated, students learn how well they did on what was assessed. Depending on the quality of the feedback and the attention the students give it, they may learn something about their areas of strengths and also about the areas in which they are weak, prompting further learning or review.

The Benefits for Teachers

Quizzes, tests, and other forms of assessment can also benefit teachers. The design and construction of a quiz or test acts as an incentive for a teacher to determine the goals of instruction with regard to

- *Subject matter:* for example, basic communicative skills such as greetings and leave taking, requests, refusals, apologies, complaints, and other speech acts; communicative grammar; pronunciation
- *Skills:* productive—speaking and writing; receptive—listening and reading
- *Desired level of achievement:* what the class as a whole and individual students are expected to attain

In theory, these goals should be clear to teachers before they prepare an assessment task, but in practice, preparation of an assessment instrument may cause teachers to ask themselves what their goals really are.

When the results are in, the teacher can see how well the students did on the material being assessed and check for any discrepancies between expectations and actual performance. This information may indicate how well the students are learning or if they have mastered the material, how well the teacher has put across the material, and also how well the item was written. Such feedback to the teacher can suggest areas for instruction, for review, or for improving future assessment.

Of course, this feedback is not automatically transferred to the teacher by virtue of the fact that a quiz or test is administered. Rather, teachers get value from the results if they invest time in their analysis. It may even be profitable to analyze the results of each item. For example, how many students got item 17 right? Was it a difficult item? It may be that an item answered correctly by more than 80% of the respondents or by fewer than 60% would be considered too easy or too difficult, respectively.

Was there any pattern to the wrong answers on this item? For example, supposing this item was a multiple-choice reading comprehension item where (b) was the correct answer and those who got the item wrong tended to choose the distractor, (c). What were some of the reasons students had for producing or selecting this wrong answer? Did those respondents who did better on the test as a whole also do better on this item? If not, then the item did not *discriminate* well on the test. Do the results point up a weakness in teaching, in learning, in item writing, or in a combination of all three?

Another beneficial approach to item analysis involves sitting with the student and going over a test individually, as time permits, in order to gain more precise insights into the student's strengths and weaknesses. Chapter 5 discusses having respondents report the strategies that they use in answering items and in making use of this information when analyzing test results. Teachers may even choose to organize students into small working groups to discuss the answers to particular questions. So for each item, some member of the group asks the others what the best answer is and why other answers are less desirable (a notion that is expanded in Chapter 3).

What to Assess?

In this section we will look briefly at the sometimes frustrating task of attempting to assess what students **really** know. Then we will address the issue of how to assess so-called *authentic* language, and, finally, we will consider the use of a modified theoretical framework of assessing oral communicative ability.

Assessing What Students Really Know

The current focus on the second-language learner (see, for instance, Ellis [1990] and Larsen-Freeman & Long [1991]) has brought attention to the fact that there is rarely a one-to-one correspondence between what is taught and what is learned in the language classroom. Students may not learn what is taught or may learn only partially or even incorrectly. Sometimes they learn incorrectly because they pay inadequate attention or because they do not have the proper **basis** for comprehending the material—a basis gained, for example, from coming to class regularly, doing the homework, or having exposure to the language out of class.

Assessment can provide an opportunity for learners to learn about what they know and do not know, but only if the feedback from assessment is intelligible to them.

Since language learners are continually formulating and reformulating hypotheses about the way language works, they can benefit from feedback about the degree to which the hunches, analogies, and generalizations that they have made are correct. It has been posited that learners progress in a target language by testing hypotheses about how the language works—using inferences based on previous knowledge (Schachter, 1983)—and that learners depend on *negative input* to verify hypotheses about whether their utterances are comprehensible, grammatically correct, or situationally appropriate (Schachter, 1984).

The problem is that no matter what approach is selected by the teacher, some experts (e.g., Allwright, 1975; Krashen, 1982; and others) would argue that corrective feedback on a test will probably have a limited or nonexistent effect if

1. The learners do not have enough knowledge of the area being corrected to benefit from the correction.
2. The learners do not have adequate proficiency to understand the teacher's explanation of what they did wrong (if the teacher writes an explanation on the test or explains the item in a student-teacher conference).
3. The learners have too little knowledge about how the language works to know what question to ask to get clarification.

Given that learners do not necessarily learn what is taught and that they may learn what the teacher did not intend to teach, teachers should check on the learning process rather frequently.

Sometimes it is poorly written textbooks or misguided teacher presentations themselves that induce what have been termed *cross-association* errors (George, 1972). Such errors result when a teacher or a textbook presents a pair of words or constructions too closely together and/or not thoroughly enough. The learner has not learned the formal and functional characteristics of the first form well enough to distinguish it correctly from the second form. Mutual interference results. For example, students cross-associate *I am* with *I go*, producing *I am go*, and *to the door* with *to the window* so that they confuse *door* and *window*. Other researchers have also called attention to teacher-induced errors, especially errors resulting from a teacher's incomplete presentation of some material (Stenson, 1974). Assessment may serve to pinpoint such areas of confusion, which result from incompletely taught and incompletely learned material.

Then again, if the **level** of assessment is too superficial, assessment may not serve to pinpoint the areas of confusion. For example, researchers have noted that the testing of both native- and second-language vocabulary often remains at too general a level to obtain an in-depth picture of how well the respondents really know the words in question (Curtis, 1987; Read, 1988; Wesche & Paribakht, 1993; see Chapter 7 for more on this point). The test constructor often has to make choices about the length of the test and the number of questions to include. As a result, follow-up probes are often not included and less is learned about what the respondent knows. The problem is probably more acute in the assessment of second- or foreign-language vocabulary. The tendency to assess vocabulary only superficially would then be a good reason for having a system of quizzes that allows for more ample probing of the areas that have been taught.

Assessing Authentic Language Use

Regarding what to assess for, there is an authenticity argument which holds that "only 'real' language use should be counted" when assessing language ability. According to Spolsky (1985:34), language testing does not assess *authentic* language behavior. He asserts that examination questions are not real, although they are possibly similar to real-life questions. Instead, respondents need to learn special rules of exams and are then asked to respond in an unnatural way—"to answer questions asked by someone who doesn't want to know the answers because he already knows them" (Spolsky, 1985:36). Therefore, Spolsky concludes that there is no such thing as a test of authentic or natural language use. For example, speaking tests are not intended for the purpose of making genuine conversation but instead to find out information about candidates in order to classify, reward, or punish them. Spolsky concludes that long-term, patient, and sympathetic observation of authentic language behavior is the only full solution to the problem of conducting natural language assessment.

Bachman (1991) identifies three alternate approaches that have been taken with regard to authenticity in testing: 1) to stipulate by definition that the language tests are measuring language ability **directly**, 2) to consider language tests to be assessing language use similar to that in **real life**, and 3) to consider language tests as authentic on the basis of face validity or **face appeal**. With regard to the first approach, Bachman notes that all language tests are indirect and that **inferences** are made about language ability since it is impossible to directly observe neurological programming that may account for language ability. With regard to the second approach, real life consists of an infinite set of unique and widely varied speech events, only a few of which are sampled in any test. With regard to the third approach, the purely subjective response of an evaluator about what is authentic, without criteria for appeal, is questionable; furthermore, what is appealing to experts in language assessment may be different from what is appealing to teachers, students, and their parents.

A new approach to language authenticity tries to capture the spirit of the above three approaches while avoiding their problems (Bachman, 1990; Bachman & Palmer, in press). Authenticity is seen to comprise (1) the relationship between test method characteristics and features of a specific language use situation and (2) the degree to which the test method invokes the test taker's language ability. Thus, the use of technical terms and topics from engineering would increase the authenticity of a test for specialists in engineering. But as Bachman (1991) points out, since test takers may have perceptions that differ from those of the test developers on the relevance of the test task to their target language use situations, the fit between test method and language use situation needs to be assessed from different perspectives.

In addition, test developers need to specify the extent to which the specific test task involves the test taker's language ability. Bachman suggests that this form of authenticity can be increased by adjusting the difficulty of the task. For example, the authenticity of writing tasks could be improved by means of some or all of the following:

1. Allowing a choice of topics and making sure the topics are interesting so that there is a purpose for writing
2. Stating in the prompt that planning is part of the task and perhaps requiring outlining
3. Encouraging the test takers to go back and revise their writing
4. Providing more explicit information in the prompts about the criteria for grading

Using Theoretical Frameworks for Assessment

Well over a decade ago, Canale and Swain provided a theoretical framework for communicative competence that has had a considerable impact on the design of assessment instruments over the intervening years. Before the framework appeared in the literature, much assessment focused on pronunciation and grammar. As a result of the Canale and Swain framework and other efforts, tests began to be seen as tapping one or more of the four components making up the construct of communicative competence, namely, sociolinguistic competence, discourse competence, grammatical competence, and strategic competence.

Sociolinguistic competence was seen to involve knowledge of the sociocultural rules of language and of discourse (Canale & Swain, 1980:29). *Discourse competence* as a separate dimension was added by Canale several years later (Canale, 1983) and was meant to reflect ability to connect sentences in stretches of discourse and to form a meaningful whole out of a series of utterances. *Grammatical competence* involved knowledge of lexical items and of rules of morphology, syntax, sentence-grammar semantics, and phonology. While discourse competence was meant to refer to intersentential relationships, grammatical competence concerned itself with sentence-level grammar (Canale, 1983). *Strategic competence* referred to the verbal and nonverbal communication strategies that might be called into action to compensate for breakdowns in communication due to performance variables or insufficient competence (Canale & Swain, 1980:30).

Efforts by this author to use the Canale and Swain framework for assessing oral communicative competence produced results that suggested the need for modifications in the framework. First, raters in a study by Cohen and Olshtain (1993) were found to have difficulty identifying clear examples of material that would be rated for discourse competence. There were some examples, such as ambiguous uses of cohesion (e.g., after hitting another car: "We didn't see you."), but not many. Hence, the discourse competence scale was dropped. Second, given the problems in rating discourse, instead of breaking the sociolinguistic competence scale out into sociocultural rules and discourse rules, two separate scales were created: sociocultural ability and sociolinguistic ability. This distinction was found to work in producing ratings that were relatively consistent over various groups of raters.

For the purposes of this volume, we will be using a modified version of the above theoretical framework for assessing what we will refer to as *communicative ability*.[1] In this chapter we will briefly describe the modified framework that we will cover in more detail in Chapter 8 with regard to the assessment of functional speaking ability during the performance of speech acts.

Sociocultural ability. The component of *sociocultural ability* relates to the appropriateness of the strategies selected for realizing communicative functions in given contexts, taking into account (1) the culture involved, (2) the age and sex of the speakers, (3) their social class and occupations, and (4) their roles and status in the interaction. This component also evaluates what is said in terms of the amount of information required in the given situation (i.e., not too much or too little; Grice, 1975) and the relevance and clarity of the information actually supplied.

Sociolinguistic ability. There is a separate component for *sociolinguistic ability*, which deals with the linguistic forms that respondents use to express the intent of the communicative act (e.g., regret in an apology, the grievance in a complaint, the objective of a request, or the refusal of an invitation). This category assesses the respondents' control over the actual language forms used to realize, for example, a speech act such as apologizing (e.g., "sorry" vs. "excuse me," "really sorry" vs. "very sorry"), as well as their control of register (e.g., an academic intervention during a symposium vs. a casual remark during a class break) or the formality of the utterance (from most intimate to most formal language).

Grammatical ability. This component deals with vocabulary, morphology, syntax, and phonology—that is, with how acceptably words, phrases, and sentences are formed and pronounced in the respondents' utterances. The focus is on both clear cases of errors in form, such as the use of the present perfect for an action completed in the past (e.g., "We have seen a great film last night.") as well as on matters of style (e.g., the learner uses a passive verb form in a context where a native would use the active form: "I lost your book." vs. "The book was lost."). Major errors might be considered those that either interfere with intelligibility or stigmatize the respondent. Minor errors would be those that do not get in the way of the listener's comprehension or annoy the listener to any extent.

Strategic ability. In an earlier version of this framework, the *strategic ability* component put the emphasis on "compensatory" strategies—that is, strategies used to compensate or remediate for a lack in some language area, as in the Canale and Swain (1980) framework. Piloting of the scales based on the framework demonstrated that strategic ability cannot be easily observed. Hence, strategic ability is now taking on a broader meaning—that suggested by Bachman (1990)—wherein it is broken down into three components. There is an assessment component whereby the respondents set communicative goals, a planning component whereby the respondents retrieve the relevant items from language ability and plan their use, and an execution component whereby the respondents implement the plan.

What Is the Purpose of Assessment?

In order to properly construct assessment instruments, it is helpful to have some explicit notion of what the instrument is assessing and how it might be labeled. One way to describe assessment instruments is according to their primary function—administrative, instructional, or research oriented (Jacobs, Zinkgraf, Wormuth, Hartfiel, & Hughey, 1981). In fact, the same instrument could conceivably be used for at least twelve different purposes (see Figure 2.1).

Figure 2.1

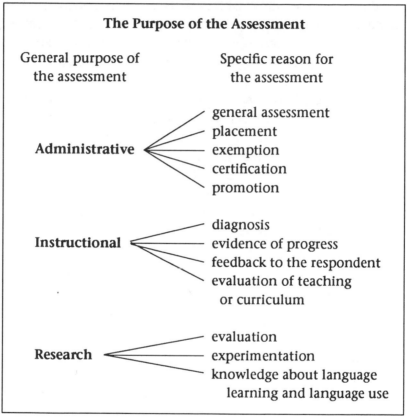

The Purpose of the Assessment

General purpose of the assessment	Specific reason for the assessment
Administrative	general assessment placement exemption certification promotion
Instructional	diagnosis evidence of progress feedback to the respondent evaluation of teaching or curriculum
Research	evaluation experimentation knowledge about language learning and language use

Assessing Language Proficiency and Language Achievement

The average assessment instrument is not used for more than several purposes, and the major split is often between *proficiency* tests intended for administrative purposes and *achievement* tests for assessment of instructional results. Sometimes teachers assess *language proficiency*, namely, the linguistic knowledge or competence students have in a language, or their ability to apply this knowledge functionally.[2] In many cases, students enroll in a class after already having taken some sort of proficiency test. Such a test may be locally developed, but it is more often a standardized, commercially marketed test.[3] Depending on the nature of the course, such a test may contain grammar items, reading comprehension items, and vocabulary items. Sometimes teachers do not have access to the actual test results by subtest; sometimes they do but do not review them. Occasionally, teachers review the test results at the outset to get a picture of the proficiency of incoming students. But as Shohamy (1990b) has noted, such test results may not be informative if they are too general. As she puts it, their purpose is often "to prove and not improve."

The other major type of assessment is motivated by the desire to determine what the student has learned: *achievement* testing. An achievement test assesses what has been "achieved" or learned from what was taught in a particular course or a series of courses. An achievement test may well include both items testing discrete points and those which assess language ability more integratively. (See Chapter 3 for more on item types.) It may well be that a layperson would be unable to determine whether certain types of achievement tests are meant to assess general proficiency or achievement. Sometimes there are clues in that the vocabulary or structures being elicited seem to concentrate on some area, signaling that they were covered in the course.

Actually, the same test given by a teacher at the beginning of a course to assess proficiency could be administered at the end of the course to assess students' achievement. Thus a general proficiency test could be used as an achievement test. But an achievement test cannot necessarily serve as a general proficiency test, particularly if it tests a certain syllabus that would not be expected to be common knowledge to all second-language learners at that level. It is worth noting that an achievement test does not automatically become above scrutiny just because it has been "standardized" through pretesting, norming (i.e., acquiring reference data from appropriate groups of examinees), and calculating its reliability and validity. In fact, Swain (1991) calls into question "the pursuit of psychometric respectability" when it ignores findings from both SLA research and second-language testing research that predict **variable** performance will be the norm rather than the exception. She suggests that inconsistencies in test results could derive from respondents having differential reactions to different testing tasks.

If teachers work with standardized tests, they may want to take a close look at the tests, subtest by subtest, item by item, in order to see what is really being tested (beyond the sometimes elegant-sounding labels that the test constructor gives each subtest). As will be discussed in Chapter 5, it can be useful to carefully examine the papers of several students, with the learners acting as informants, to see how good a job the test is actually doing. For instance, are the students getting items right for the wrong reasons and wrong for the right reasons? This exercise of scrutinizing the standardized test may call attention to some of the deficiencies of norm-referenced assessment for instructional and evaluational purposes (Popham, 1978:74-88).

Norm-Referenced and Criterion-Referenced Assessment

The distinction between *norm-referenced* and *criterion-referenced* assessment is getting ever greater emphasis in the assessment literature. Norm-referenced assessment provides a broad indication of relative standing, while criterion-referenced assessment produces information that is more descriptive and addresses absolute decisions with respect to the instructional goal (Davidson, Hudson, & Lynch, 1985). The norm-referenced approach results in an overall estimate of ability in the general field of knowledge or skill relative to other students or examinees.

For example, an assessment instrument can be used to compare a respondent with other respondents, whether locally (e.g., in a class), regionally, or nationally. Classroom, regional, or national *norms* may be established to interpret just how one student compares with another. If you are using norm-referenced tests, you should check the test manual to see what groups the test was normed on. Thirty years ago, in the early days of the bilingual education movement, for instance, the most common tests of Spanish listening and reading comprehension[4] were normed on Puerto Rican students, but those being tested included both Mexican American bilinguals and Anglo-Americans in the Southwest of the United States—pupils who had not been exposed to Puerto Rican Spanish.

In the criterion-referenced approach, *criterion* skills or behaviors are determined, and then test specifications are written. These test specifications delineate the operations called in order to measure the skill or trait. Thus, this approach produces information that is more descriptive and addresses absolute decisions with respect to the instructional goal (Davidson, Hudson, & Lynch, 1985). The criterion-referenced approach is used to see whether a respondent has met certain instructional objectives or criteria. In such a system of assessment, students presumably know exactly what knowledge has to be demonstrated and either demonstrate it and move on or cannot demonstrate it and check to see how their performance can be improved. Rivers has referred to this form of testing as "a revolution in the concept of testing" in that students become responsible for their own learning in a system where assessment becomes more closely linked to learning itself: "it may well lose the appearance of what we conceive of as a conventional test" (Rivers, 1983:143).

The challenge in constructing such criterion-based assessment instruments is not only in determining which objectives to assess, how to construct items for these objectives, and how to administer the items, but also in determining what constitutes *attainment of an objective*—that is, the percent of students who must answer a certain number of items of a given type correctly in order to say that this objective has been attained (Hambleton & Eignor, 1978). Let us say that we are interested in assessing the ability of our ESL university-level students to combine two sentences into one sentence that has a relativized subject, a relativized object, or a relativized object of a preposition. Here is what an item assessing ability to write a combined sentence with a relativized subject might look like:

> **Directions:** Combine the following sentences, attaching sentence (b) to sentence (a), using the words *who, whom, which,* or *that.*
>
> (a) Elaine wrote the book.
> (b) The book was a bestseller.
> *Correct answer:* Elaine wrote the book that/which was a bestseller.

First of all, we are assuming that this objective is worth assessing. We are then assuming that the format that appears above is an adequate way to assess for productive control of subject relativization. We also must determine how many items of a similar type would be necessary for us to determine that we were adequately assessing our respondents' ability to produce this kind of relative clause (e.g., three items for each type of relativization). If we were, in fact, interested in our respondents' ability to produce sentences with relativized objects or relativized objects of prepositions, then we would need to include a certain number of such items in our instrument as well.

We should note that any given item on a criterion-referenced test **may** look identical to a given item on a norm-referenced test. In other words, the above subject relativization item could appear on a norm-referenced test. In fact, the two tests could be identical, but the purposes for their use would be different. In the case of criterion reference, the item would be intended to give the respondent and the teacher feedback about the learner's control of that teaching objective: relative clauses. In the case of norm reference, the purpose would be to compare one learner with another, perhaps on a university basis or even nationally.

In practice, criterion-referenced and norm-referenced instruments **are** being constructed differently. In fact, some criterion-referenced assessment instruments do not look like tests at all—especially those oriented toward more general language proficiency. For example, Brindley (1989) reviews a number of such instruments that primarily reflect self-assessment and teacher-assessment inventories or checklists. With regard to the self-assessment inventories, learners rate, for example, their conversational skills and reading ability, possibly within a given domain (e.g., the health profession) or for a given set of functions (e.g., bookkeeping). For the language performance inventories, the teachers rate their learners' knowledge, comprehension, use, accuracy, and so forth on a series of communicative goals specified at the functional level (e.g., reading—getting information from a timetable; listening—getting details about a party from a recorded telephone message; writing—writing instructions on how to get to your house; speaking—making an arrangement involving time and place).

The array of instruments in Brindley's book is impressive, but he notes that the scales used are both imprecise and relativistic. He concludes as follows:

> Clearly we need information that is a great deal more precise—based on the observation and analysis of learners' actual language use—before valid criteria and levels of performance can be established. In addition, we need to collect data on the criteria exercised by native speakers when they are judging second-language learners' performance. (Brindley 1989:55)

As criterion-referenced instruments become more popular and as more of these nontraditional formats appear, teachers will probably need some guidance on when to use criterion-referenced and when to use norm-referenced assessment. In fact, criterion-referenced tests may be used in situations usually reserved for norm-referenced measures, such as that of administering a language exam across classrooms of nonnative students.

Research Notes

A study by Hudson and Lynch (1984) demonstrated the use of the criterion-referenced approach to assessment during the final examinations in the UCLA ESL service courses. While the typical norm-referenced instrument used in that situation would have given indications about a respondent's relative standing, the testers were interested in using criterion-referenced assessment in order to provide a measure of absolute standing with respect to the instructional goal. They wanted to answer the question "Who is qualified?"

In order to conduct statistical analysis of the test, they needed to compare a group receiving ESL instruction ($N = 57$) with an unstructed group ($N = 42$). Item analysis was then based on the difference between the proportion of uninstructed getting the item right and the proportion of instructed doing so (Hudson & Lynch, 1984:178). The results of item analysis demonstrated that the criterion-reference approach discriminated well between those who had mastery of the language objectives and those who did not, rather than dealing with items whose main purpose was to rank individuals without reference to mastery/non-mastery. With regard to reliability, the criterion-referenced approach provided information on the consistency of decisions about student mastery or non-mastery rather than focusing on psychometric properties of the test itself. Finally, the issues of content and construct validity, as opposed to criterion-related validity,[5] were found to be better addressed through the criterion-referenced approach than through the norm-referenced approach. The conclusion was that the criterion-referenced approach helped clarify what was being measured.

How to Assess Language Ability?

The best way to assess students' ability in a second language is still a matter of debate. Some people swear by one approach, some by another. Even the seemingly convincing reliability and validity statistics on one innovative testing approach may not convince those who stand by time-hallowed approaches. In other words, for assessment methods that have been around a long time, people may have reached a spoken or unspoken agreement that these methods look like the **right** way to assess whatever it is that needs to be assessed. In fact, teachers may choose methods that reflect the way they were assessed as students. It is always easier to continue to use a known quantity than to switch to a new approach. One debate has focused on the use of more *discrete-point* items, which are aimed at measuring one isolated language feature or structure, versus more *integrative* items and procedures, which are aimed at assessing a number of features or structures together (see Chapters 3 and 6 for more on this issue). Another debate has focused on the use of the *cloze* test as a means for assessing reading comprehension (wherein students are asked to supply words systematically deleted from a passage; see Chapter 7).

The criterion-referenced approach to item design and scoring described above is increasingly attractive in contexts where the main concern is for how well **individuals** have mastered the instructional content. In the early days of criterion-referenced testing, the approach was often characterized by careful planning of the intended student group, operations requested, and procedures for evaluation—that is, which students would perform what behavior with what results, under what conditions, judged by what standard (Green, 1975). For example, it would be stipulated that 70% of the students in the class would be expected to write a friendly letter in the target language (the behavior), consisting of 50 words or more (the results), within ten minutes (the conditions), with no more than three morphological errors (the standard). This objective was stated in terms of the "class minimal level of performance."

Today the general trend is to pay more attention to what was once referred to as the "individual student's minimal level" (Popham, 1973). For example, taking the example above, at what point is any individual student in the class said to have mastered the task of writing a friendly letter that is morphologically acceptable? What about the students who (1) cannot put fifty words on paper, (2) need twenty minutes to do so, (3) make more than three morphological errors per fifty words, or exhibit some combination of (1), (2), and (3)? For this reason, teachers who use criterion-referenced assessment in the classroom are probably more likely to set minimal performance standards for the individual student than to set performance standards for the entire class. Furthermore, these standards could vary according to students' strengths and weaknesses.

Given the wide variety of assessment methods available and the lack of consensus on the most appropriate means to use, the best way to assess language performance in the classroom may be through a multifaceted or eclectic approach, whereby a variety of methods are used. This book will give suggestions about some of these varied approaches.

How Are Quizzes to Be Used?

The concept of a quiz, as opposed to a test, is not usually developed in books dealing with language assessment (see Brooks [1967], and Valette [1977] for two exceptions). Perhaps the tacit assumption is that a quiz is not very rigorous or that it is only a short test. However, the quiz has certain distinctive and desirable features— not the least of which is that it tends to be more **informal** than a test and, as a result, may produce a more natural and accurate assessment of learners' language abilities than a test. While teachers may give a quiz without prior notice, they probably would not do so with a test. Especially if the activity is presented in a low-keyed and even informal manner, even test-shy students should be able to cope reasonably well with a quiz. Aside from possibly being informal, a quiz is usually brief and is therefore often easier to construct, score, administer, and evaluate than a test. The shortness of quizzes may serve as an incentive for teachers to look closely at how well the material was assessed. On a longer test, the teacher may feel overwhelmed by the work involved in evaluating the items.

If the quiz relates just to the highlights of the day's assignment and class activities, this can give it a timeliness and relevance that tests sometimes do not have. In addition, the focus of a quiz may be quite narrow, in terms of both the extent of coverage of what was taught/learned and the degree of variety of items and procedures. A quiz can also serve the important function of acquainting students with questions that will be on a test, so the quiz constitutes a form of training in taking that kind of test or in dealing with those kinds of items. Finally, quizzes can provide both teachers and learners with some useful feedback. Teachers can get feedback on the types of items or tasks that successfully meet the assessment needs of a given class. For students, the quiz can be a check on just how well they learned the latest material. Figure 2.2 summarizes differences in the characteristics of quizzes and tests.

Figure 2.2

Characteristics of Quizzes vs. Tests

Quizzes	Tests
informal	formal
possibly unannounced	announced
brief	lengthy
easy to score, administer, evaluate	take time to score, administer, and evaluate
timely, relevant	somewhat removed from time of instruction
narrow focus	broad focus
limited variety of items and procedures	variety of items and procedures
serve to familiarize or train students re item or task type	seen as the measurement itself—not training
immediate feedback for teachers on how items work	too late to do anything re poor items/tasks— just discount them
feedback for learners on how they did on that material	too late for learners to do anything about their weaknesses

There are times when even quizzes seem too formal, and there may also be teachers who resist giving them. Instead, a show of hands or a nod of the head is sometimes used to indicate that the material is understood (and hence learned?) before moving on. Allen and Valette (1977) conceded that teachers should not ask the question "Do you understand?" since those who do not understand usually remain quiet because they are too shy to show their ignorance, and others who have misunderstood are unaware that they have done so. Yet Allen and Valette still suggested that to check for student comprehension, for example, it might be helpful to ask questions or plan activities that allow students to demonstrate whether they have understood. They felt that the kind of informal feedback teachers get in normal classroom interaction may be sufficient:

> Teachers learn to tell from their students' reactions whether they have understood the meaning of a phrase. They can tell by the fluency and accuracy of the oral response whether the class has mastered a specified drill. (1977:49)

The problem is that assessment of learning based on such informal feedback may be impressionistic, intuitive, unsystematic, and even inaccurate. For one thing, cross-cultural differences among students and between students and teachers may result in teachers being unable to perceive whether students are having trouble learning. In certain cultures, the signals that learners send out regarding areas of difficulty may be not at all overt. Furthermore, teachers in typical frontal instruction may dominate sessions to a surprising degree—surprising if they were to know how little each individual student actually speaks during such a session. It may be because the class is large, because certain students dominate discussions, or simply because the teacher does much of the talking. The teacher's inadvertent tendency to talk extensively is clearly one of the many motivating factors behind instructional approaches such as the Silent Way (Gattegno, 1972, 1976) and Community Language Learning (Curran, 1976, 1978), which have attempted to put the teacher in a less frontal, more supportive, and even silent role (see also Larsen-Freeman [1986] and Richards & Rodgers [1986]).

As we will see in Chapter 5 when we take a close look at the process of test taking, it is not easy for teachers to be top-notch diagnosticians at the same time that their minds are focused on the task of teaching. In fact, the two activities—one to teach the language and the other to assess whether students are learning what is being taught—both demand a teacher's undivided attention. It is true that in some class activities there may be a fairly close fit between teaching and assessing (such as in teaching and assessing certain unknown vocabulary words), but in other activities (such as in the teaching and assessing of certain complex syntactic patterns) the two may be far apart. It would be an endless task for the teacher to check every student for current processing of what has been taught. Hence the quiz has a genuine role and explicit purpose in providing an opportunity to stop and take stock of what has been learned. The teacher who keeps a record of these periodic checks can not only provide diagnostic feedback along the way but also get an idea of student gains: when the gains took place, in what areas, and how extensive they were.

How Does a Test Differ from a Quiz?

A test may resemble a series of quizzes put together, particularly if quizzes consist of types of items that are to appear on a test. A test is announced in advance, is given every several weeks or at least at the end of each semester or trimester, and may take the whole class period or even longer to complete. If learners have had a series of *warm-up* exercises by means of quizzes, then the test need not pose any great threat but rather can be a welcome opportunity for them to demonstrate what they have learned and to check on what has still not been mastered.

While some tests of proficiency may be intended to be detached from any formal instruction, tests of achievement follow a period of teaching. In other words, there has usually been some teacher presentation, followed by explanation, and then practice or training **before** a quiz or test is introduced. Students may need some familiarization with an assessment technique even before it appears in a quiz. For example, before a cloze test is administered, it may first appear as a class exercise—for instance, a cloze task (see Chapter 7). This familiarization may serve both to reassure students and to improve their actual performance through the suggestion of possible test-taking strategies. (See Chapter 5 for more on test-taking strategies.)

When to Assess?

In the ideal situation, teachers are continually updating themselves about how much learning is going on in the classroom and the effects of what is taught on what is learned. While impressionistic data are useful and important, teachers, administrators, and others may want a more systematic measure of ability. While there are ongoing non-test-like means of collecting materials for assessment, such as through portfolios of written work or of speaking (i.e., selected writing samples or samples of speaking collected on cassette tapes), more formal quizzes and tests in the classroom may be helpful.

Frequency may mean the first or last five to ten minutes of almost every lesson. The advantage of having a quiz at the beginning of class is that it can serve as a review of what was covered in the last class. It also helps students settle in to the class session. An advantage of having the quiz at the end of class is that it helps to keep students' attention levels high. The particular moment for the quiz will depend on the given lesson. There are teachers who find that a short quiz during every class session (particularly at the beginning levels of instruction) or at least once every week or two is useful. One problem with having a series of quizzes (in addition to the usual tests) is that they require extra teacher time, both in preparation and in correction. The important notion here is that assessment can and should be interspersed with teaching as an interim activity, not just as a final one.

Whereas frequent quizzes can provide feedback to improve student mastery of a new language, an **overdose** of testing[6] can produce diminishing returns. An overdose arises when students receive more feedback than they are willing to process. The teacher must determine the necessary balance. Unlike quizzes, tests tend to be given at major intervals, such as halfway through the trimester, semester, or academic year, and at the end of the course. The use of tests to the exclusion of regular quizzes is easier for teachers because there is less need to prepare the assessment instruments and less frequent grading of them. However, the arrangement may be a bit less satisfactory in the students' eyes because they get less regular feedback on how they are doing.

How to Evaluate
the Assessment Instrument?

There are both more formal and less formal means of evaluating how effectively assessment instruments are doing their job. We will start by giving a brief overview of reliability and validity, and end by considering the ways in which classroom teachers can evaluate the instruments that they use.

Reliability

The *reliability* of a test concerns its precision as a measuring instrument. Reliability asks whether an assessment instrument administered to the same respondents a second time would yield the same results. Three different types of factors contribute to the reliability of language assessment instruments: test factors, situational factors, and individual factors.

Test Factors

Test factors include the extent of the sampling of the objective, the degree of ambiguity of the items and restrictions on freedom of response (e.g., being given more specific and thus constraining topics for compositions), the clarity and explicitness of the instructions, the quality of the layout, the familiarity that the respondents have with the format, and the length of the total test—with longer tests being more reliable (Hughes, 1989).

These test factors will contribute to the likelihood that performance on one item on a test will be consistent with performance on another item, producing a test with greater *internal consistency*. One measure of internal consistency is that of split halves reliability, which calls for correlating the odd-numbered items on the test with the even-numbered ones as a measure of inter-item consistency. Other measures of internal consistency, such as Kuder-Richardson Formulas 20 and 21, call for more complex calculations (see Bachman, 1990:172-178). For the purpose of classroom testing, a reliability coefficient of at least .70 is good. Higher reliability coefficients would be expected of standardized tests used for large-scale administration (.80 or better). A perfect coefficient is 1.0. Many years ago, Lado (1964:332) offered different reliability coefficients for tests of different skills. For example, he suggested that in general terms, acceptable reliability for a speaking test may be lower (.70 to .79) than for a listening test (.80 to .89) than for a reading test (.90 to .99). Today, uniformly higher reliability coefficients may be expected in all skills areas.

The reliability of **ratings** is also an important test factor. Considerations include the nature of the scoring key in terms of detail and clarity, the training of scorers, and the number of scorers (Bachman, 1990:178-183). In recent years, sophisticated statistical procedures using generalizability theory and multifaceted Rasch analysis have been employed to take into account the nature of the task being rated and the person doing the rating in determining the ratings' reliability (Bachman, Lynch, & Mason, 1993). Verbal protocol studies have also been conducted to determine the extent to which raters of compositions, for instance, adhere to the rating schedule that they have been provided (e.g., Hamp-Lyons, 1989).

Situational Factors

Along with test factors, test administrators need to be mindful of situational factors such as the manner in which the examiner presents the instructions, the characteristics of the room (e.g., comfort, lighting, acoustics), and outside noises. These factors may contribute to the lack of consistency of responses from the test takers.

Individual Factors

Transient factors include the physical health and psychological state of the respondent (motivation, rapport with the examiner, family matters, and so forth). *Stable factors* include mechanical skill, I.Q., ability to use English, and experience with similar tests.

Thus, to improve reliability, the teacher/test constructor would want to have clearer instructions, use more and better items, give the test in a more comfortable and less anxiety-provoking environment, and have the respondents be motivated to complete the tasks involved. As pointed out above, there may be assessment instruments for which the response patterns will be inconsistent, given the respondents' various reactions to different testing tasks

(Swain, 1991). In such cases, it would be up to the test developer or assessor to determine the extent to which low reliability or inconsistency of responses is a result of relatively stable individual factors, such as a predictably personal reaction to given testing tasks (for example, one individual finds a cloze task a real challenge while another is thoroughly frustrated by all the deletions).

Validity

Validity refers to whether the assessment instrument actually measures what it purports to measure. Thus, a test must be reliable in order to be valid. Assuming that the test is producing a reliable measure of something, the question is "What is that something? Is it what the test is supposed to be measuring?" A test can be considered as valid or invalid only with respect to some intended purpose. In other words, validity exists only in terms of specified criteria (Morrow, 1981). If the criteria selected are the wrong ones (i.e., not interesting or not useful), then the fact that the test is valid may be of little practical significance. Thus, a test with admirable characteristics may be invalid in that it is used for inappropriate purposes. For example, a test may be an adequate measure of general placement but be of limited utility or even worthless in the diagnosis of specific reading problems. It is still not uncommon to find a mismatch between what language educators want to test for and the instrument that they use, although instruments are becoming increasingly precise these days.

The assessment of test validity is conducted in different ways. The types to be described below are content validity, criterion-related validity, construct validity, systemic validity, and face validity.

Content validity. *Content validity* is determined by checking the adequacy with which the test samples the content or objectives of the course or area being assessed. Sometimes, even commercial tests developed by experts fail to state what objectives are being covered in the test and which items are specifically testing each of these objectives. For this reason, among others, teachers have been encouraged to look closely at what each test measures:

> For the language teacher, the degree of test validity is not derived from a statistical analysis of test performance, but from a meticulous analysis of the content of each item and of the test as a whole. (Valette, 1977:46)

In fact, content validation is ascertained by examining a copy of the test item by item, checking the table of specifications for the test, and reviewing the listing of content. The task includes looking for an operational definition of the constructs of the ability domain being assessed and a specification of test method characteristics. Bachman (1990) observes that since test developers seldom provide a domain definition that identifies the full set of language use tasks, it is difficult to demonstrate the content relevance of tests. He sees it as a problem of curricular or instructional validity; it would be nearly impossible for the test to take into account all classroom interactions.

Criterion-related validity. *Criterion-related validity*[7] calls for determining how closely respondents' performance on specific sets of objectives on a given assessment instrument parallels their performance on another instrument, or *criterion*, which is thought to measure the same or similar activities. If the instrument to be validated is correlated with another criterion instrument at the same time, then this is referred to as *concurrent validation*. If the correlation takes place at some future time, then the process is referred to as *predictive validation*.

As an example of concurrent validation, teachers may want to see how student performance on a test that they have constructed compares to student performance on some criterion measure of reading obtained from a commercial test. But even if there is a high correlation, the criterion measure may still not be an indicator of the ability in question. For one thing, the other test needs to have construct validity (see below) in order for this correlation to be of any value (Bachman, 1990). In addition, a high correlation between two tests does not indicate which is preferable, if either is any good for the given purpose, or whether one can be substituted for the other.

As an example of predictive validation, a language aptitude test may be validated by a test of a student's achievement in the language class in which the student was placed on the basis of the aptitude test. Here there is the problem that the placement or predictor test may be an inappropriate measure of the ability called for in a particular course. Bachman (1990) notes that there are actually a number of factors involved in predicting achievement in a language class.

Construct validity. *Construct validity* refers to the degree to which scores on an assessment instrument permit inferences about underlying traits. In other words, it examines whether the instrument is a true reflection of the theory of the trait being measured: language, in this case. These constructs may be at differing levels of abstraction. In conducting construct validation, we are empirically testing hypothesized relationships between test scores and abilities, an activity that requires both logical analysis (i.e., defining constructs theoretically and operationally) and empirical investigation. As noted above, concurrent and predictive validity are dependent to a certain degree on construct validity in that the *external criterion instrument* needs to have **construct** validation in order to be used in those two forms of criterion-related validation.

With regard to construct validation, teachers/test constructors need to keep asking themselves whenever they construct an assessment instrument whether the items and procedures on the instrument actually reflect what it means to know a language, as opposed to tasks that assess something different from actual language knowledge (Shohamy, 1985). Since validity in testing a given construct, such as listening comprehension, may be attained by assessing the same phenomenon in a variety of different ways, the classroom teacher can work towards this kind of validation simply through using multiple measures and comparing the results from each measure. The discussion of item types presented in Chapter 6 provides a number of techniques for assessing the same objectives differently. Varying the item-elicitation and item-response formats, as well as the discreteness and "integrativeness" of the items, can produce items that assess the same objectives in different ways. It may also be advisable to collect data on test-taking processes as well, to help determine what the test is actually assessing (Cohen, 1984; Anderson, Bachman, Perkins, & Cohen, 1991).

Systemic validity. In recent years, there has been an extension of the notion of construct validity to take into account the effects of instructional changes brought about by the introduction of the test into an educational system. This form has been referred to as *systemic validity* (Fredriksen & Collins, 1989). According to Frederiksen and Collins,

> A systemically valid test is one that induces in the education system curricular and instructional changes that foster the development of the cognitive skills that the test is designed to measure. Evidence for systemic validity would be an improvement in those skills after the test has been in place within the educational system for a period of time. (1989:27)

This concern of how assessment instruments affect educational practices and beliefs has also been referred to in the literature as the *washback* or the *backwash* effect (Morrow, 1986; Hughes, 1989; Weir, 1990). Alderson and Wall (1992) have found the notion of washback to be too simplistic. They suggest that the quality of the washback (positive or negative) may be independent of the quality of the test and recommend that truly considering the effect of the test on teaching and/or learning calls for looking at

1. The effect of the test on the instructional content
2. The process whereby the content is taught
3. The rate at which the material is covered
4. The nature of the sequencing of material
5. The quantity of material that the students actually learn and the depth at which they learn the given items or objectives

They also recommend looking at whether teachers and learners prepare for exams and, if so, how and why, and at whether the test has important consequences within the given context. Alderson and Wall conclude that if washback is to be considered, it is important to define its scope and to state explicitly the version of the washback hypothesis being used. Their recommendations actually constitute a useful set of guidelines for evaluating the systemic validity of assessment instruments.

Before leaving these three types of validity, we should point out that there are those who insist that validity really needs to be viewed as a unitary concept, subsuming the different types—content, criterion, and construct validity (Messick, 1988). Messick sees validity as an integrated evaluative judgment of the degree to which empirical evidence and theoretical rationales support the adequacy and appropriateness of inferences and actions, based on test scores. He also sees validity as involving ethical issues as well, namely, the educational or social consequences of using a given test. So, in order to do an adequate job of validating a test, he believes that convergent validation is called for—assessing the test from a number of perspectives.

Face validity. A final possible form of validity has often been excluded from discussions of validity for not having the same rigorous properties as the other forms. *Face validity* refers to whether the test **looks** as if it is measuring what it is supposed to measure. For example, a test that measures a respondent's own English pronunciation by assessing the respondent's rating of another's pronunciation of English may not be readily accepted as a valid measure, nor might filling in blanks on a cloze test in order to assess reading skill. Such measures may appear to be too indirect. The fact that they are indirect may confuse and distract the respondent. Also, a test's title may be misleading. For example, a test called "Pragmatic Syntax Measure" may deal more with morphology than with syntax and may use stilted grammar-book English rather than the language of everyday situational interactions, as a pragmatic measure would be expected to.

It has been suggested that the term *face validity* is unfortunate because of its derogatory overtones. Low (1985) would offer the term *perceived validity* instead. Other terms for this could be *surface credibility* or *test appeal* (Bachman, 1990). With respect to respondents, this form of validation would refer to

1. Their perceptions of any bias in test content (i.e., whether they perceive the content to favor a respondent with certain background knowledge or expertise).
2. Their understanding of the nature of the task that they are being requested to complete.

3. Their awareness of the nature of their actual performance on the test as a whole and on any particular subtests (for example, the test-taking strategies that they employed).

This concern for giving careful consideration to perceived validity comes at a time when verbal report measures are being called upon to gather from respondents data regarding the strategies that they are using during the process of taking tests (Dollerup, Glahn, & Rosenberg-Hanson, 1982; Cohen, 1984; Stemmer, 1991; Anderson, 1991). It has been demonstrated that verbal report protocols can yield empirical data that provide considerable information concerning how respondents perceive tests and how they actually deal with them in testing situations.

The Role of the Teacher in Evaluating Assessment Instruments

As any and all evaluation can help improve their future quizzes, tests, and other assessment instruments, teachers are encouraged to inspect certain aspects of the measures they construct. They may even wish to employ more formal, statistical means for determining if the instruments are reliable and valid. Whether through more formal item and test analysis (see Chapter 4) or through more informal inspection, teachers are likely to come up with suggestions that items or procedures should be excluded from scoring or that certain parts of the measures should be given greater prominence than originally intended because they function so effectively in the assessment process.

Teachers could pay attention to the following instrument evaluation categories:

1. The clarity of the instructions to the students—specifically, feedback from students regarding the clarity of the operations they were being asked to perform.
2. The appropriateness of time actually allotted—that is, if the students were pressed for time, was this consistent with the aims of the test?

3. The degree and type of student interest in the task—what parts of the quiz/test did the students enjoy doing, if any? Students could even be asked to evaluate the instrument anonymously (e.g., "I found this test helpful/not helpful because...," "I like/do not like this kind of test because...," and so forth).
4. The level of performance on a class basis and by individual students.
5. The meaningfulness of the data retrieved.
6. The appropriateness of the scoring procedures and weighting. (See Chapter 6 regarding testing for speed, accuracy, or quantity.)
7. The ease of interpretation and evaluation of the score. (See Chapter 4 for a discussion of scoring.)
8. The extent to which the instrument assesses what the teacher set out to assess.

Teachers who perform an ongoing analysis of the effectiveness of different types of quizzes may well have an advantage when it comes to designing a final course exam. They will have an idea about which approaches to assessment best tap the course goals towards which they have been teaching. If several teachers are teaching similar material, they could capitalize on this by designing, administering, and evaluating assessment instruments collaboratively.

Conclusion

In this chapter we have considered various basic issues in language assessment. We looked first at why we should assess language—at what teachers gain from learner feedback and at what learners gain from teacher feedback. We noted that language assessment can provide a valuable feedback mechanism. Testing and other forms of systematic assessment can serve as a check for the relationship between what is taught and what is learned. As learners are constantly formulating and reformulating hypotheses about the way the new language works, they need feedback on the accuracy of these hypotheses. The teacher also benefits from feedback on what is being learned. Language assessment constitutes a means of providing systematic feedback to both these interest groups.

Our next item of concern was what to test for. We started by considering the difficult challenge of tapping what learners really know. Then we looked at whether language tests need to assess authentic language, and we distinguished different kinds of authenticity. Next, we presented a theoretical framework for the assessment of language ability and described an approach using sociocultural ability, sociolinguistic ability, and grammatical ability. Purposes of language assessment instruments were then examined—administrative, instructional, and research. In the ensuing discussion, we looked at the distinction between achievement and proficiency testing and between norm-referenced and criterion-referenced assessment.

We then took a brief look at the choice of assessment method and noted that there is controversy regarding the formats to be used in assessing language abilities. We concluded that a safe compromise would be to use multiple means of assessment.

In terms of the vehicle for assessment, the quiz was then considered as a convenient tool for gathering information incrementally. Quizzes were compared with tests, and differences in length and frequency of administration were discussed. We then briefly dealt with the issue of when to assess language ability. Next, test reliability and validity were described in terms of content validity, criterion-related validity, construct validity, systemic validity, and face validity. Finally, we presented a checklist for teacher evaluation of assessment instruments.

Discussion Questions and Activities

1. Create three or four different assessment contexts: for example, an intermediate-level university course in French as a foreign language, a beginning high school class in Spanish, a Japanese full immersion class in fifth grade, and an adult ESL class. Form groups of three to four students and assign each group to one of these contexts. The task of each group is to plan in general terms the types of assessment they would like to conduct and to give their reasons for including each type of assessment. One person in each group plays the devil's advocate and offers reasons why **not** to use that type of assessment or why not to use any assessment at all.

Then have the groups compare their results, noting the similarities and differences in choices about assessment across the different assessment contexts.

2. You are a consultant to a school district in which there have been complaints from high school students that they do not get enough feedback about how they are doing in their foreign-language classes. You are called in to suggest that teachers use more quizzes. Make a case and then also prepare a reply to the remark one of the teachers has made about quizzes giving students an overdose of testing.

3. What is the difference between sociocultural ability and sociolinguistic ability? In your opinion, is this difference a genuine one? Would you use the terms presented in this chapter to describe this difference? If not, what terms would you use?

4. Can we actually achieve authenticity in language testing? What is Spolsky's view, and how is Bachman's view different? Take a stand one way or the other, and prepare a set of points to present your case at the next meeting of the teaching staff at the university department in which you work.

5. According to this chapter, what are some administrative, instructional, and research purposes for administering tests? Can you think of other purposes besides those mentioned in this chapter? Think of the purposes for which you need assessment carried out. To what extent does each of the three above purposes characterize your own use of assessment instruments?

6. In what ways have language achievement tests and proficiency tests differed in your own experience with language assessment? In what ways have they been similar? In your opinion, could the same test be used for both purposes? Give examples that relate to the language learning group(s) that you are interested in.

7. In what testing situations might you use a criterion-referenced test? Might the same test be used both for criterion-referenced assessment and for norm-referenced testing?

8. Suppose that you are teaching an advanced ESL conversation class at the university level and want your students to have a good working command of certain basic speech acts, such as requests, apologies, and complaints. Construct a criterion-referenced assessment task in which each of your students is called

upon to perform these three speech acts in three different situations. This will require setting up a situation in which the desired behavior is called for and then determining what behavior constitutes successful realization of each speech act. For example, you will want to establish what a student's performance needs to contain in each situation in order for it to be judged satisfactory. You will also need to determine whether students must perform the speech act correctly all three times in order to get credit for having control of this speech-act objective. Be sure to indicate what makes this task criterion-referenced and not norm-referenced in its approach. (Note that since Chapter 8 deals with the assessment of speech acts, you may want to refer to that section before doing this exercise.)

9. Using the eight test evaluation criteria offered in this chapter, evaluate a language test that you have recently constructed, administered, or taken. Compare the results you get with those of others in the class who evaluated the same or another test. Note similarities and differences, and see what conclusions (however tentative) you reach regarding possible strengths and weakness in test construction and use. You could also use the more detailed list of criteria at the end of Chapter 3.

10. The school district in which you work has heard of systemic validity, but the administrators do not really understand its value. Prepare a brief discussion in which you define systemic validity and illustrate its potential value in the assessment process. Propose a plan for assessing the systemic validity of a new test that your district has just started using for intermediate and advanced French as a foreign language. While you are at it, make a case for assessing face (or "perceived") validity as well, since your colleagues claim that it is not really assessing validity at all.

Notes

1 The term *ability* is used in place of *competence* in order to avoid the connotation that competence has come to have in the competence versus performance debate.

2 See Brindley (1989) for a three-way breakdown of proficiency into general proficiency, functional proficiency, and structural proficiency.

3 See Alderson, Krahnke, and Stansfield (1987) for a survey of English as a foreign language (EFL) language proficiency tests on the market. This survey is now somewhat in need of updating.

4 The Inter-American Tests of General Ability, Spanish and English Oral Comprehension, and Reading.

5 These terms are defined later in this chapter.

6 The term "overdose" is borrowed from Shohamy (1992).

7 Not to be confused with criterion-referenced assessment. In the case of criterion-related validity, *criterion* refers to another assessment instrument, while in criterion-referenced assessment, *criterion* refers to some instructional objective(s).

Chapter 3:
The Assessment Instrument, the Respondent, and the Assessment Process

In this chapter we take a close, analytical look at those features or elements which, when combined, result in a language assessment instrument. We will first define a set of terms for talking about assessment measures and then look at different assessment formats. Second, we will consider test-taker characteristics, since one or more of these characteristics may have a sizable influence on the results of assessment. Finally, we will take a brief look at procedures for administering assessment instruments.

The Nature of the
Assessment Instrument

Let us start with a few questions:

- If the purpose of the assessment is to measure achievement, is the primary concern to promote communicative ability, grammatical control, or some combination of the two?
- Are language structures selected and graded (e.g., on the basis of simplicity, regularity, frequency, or contrastive difficulty)?
- Are lessons constructed around language use situations (e.g., landing at the airport, finding a place to live, or interviewing for a job)?
- Is there a concern in the syllabus that learners have a working knowledge of certain speech act sets (e.g., apologizing, requesting, complaining, complementing, or showing gratitude)?
- Whatever syllabus or combination of various types is selected, how is the students' mastery of the material assessed?

It was suggested by Valette in the 1970s that teachers prepare a notebook of vocabulary and grammatical structures covered in the course and classify the vocabulary items according to grammatical function (e.g., noun, verb, preposition, adjective, and so forth) (Valette, 1977). Teachers were encouraged to add other categories besides grammatical function, such as topic groups, metaphors, idiomatic and non-idiomatic collocations, synonyms, and antonyms. Today that notebook might also list speech acts and other communicative functions covered in the course, and this information might well be stored in files on computer disks and accessed through a microcomputer. The existence of such a data base might be an incentive for the teacher to check periodically for the fit between the material covered in class and that covered in quizzes, tests, and other forms of assessment.

Some years ago a distinction was made between *skill-getting activities* (perception of language categories, functions, and the rules relating the two; practice in producing sound sequences and in formulating communication) and *skill-using activities* (composing an actual message, conveying personal meaning) (Rivers & Temperley, 1978; Rivers, 1981). It was even suggested that measures using skill-getting items could be designed to be "pseudo communication," thus leading naturally into spontaneous communication activities. This distinction still holds. There are those who for some years have been encouraging the assessment of communicative ability even in the early stages of language instruction (Oller, 1976; Shohamy, 1985). Again, the issue is one of whether such an approach to assessment supports the chosen curriculum, and if it does not, whether to change the approach or to change the curriculum.

Even in classrooms where teachers wish to avoid isolating linguistic elements into *discrete-point* items, some discrete-point teaching and testing is probably unavoidable.[1] Of course, a truly discrete-point item implies that only one element from one component of language is being assessed in one mode of one skill. For example, teachers would be testing a discrete point if they tested only for the past-tense morpheme *ed* (an element from the morphological component) in elicited speech (the productive mode, the speaking skill). In reality, most test items combine several elements. Perhaps it is for teachers to decide what kind of balance they desire, not just between items assessing *skill getting* and *skill using*, but also between those assessing discrete language points as opposed to more integrative ones.

Describing a Question on an Assessment Instrument

Inventory of Objectives

The place to start in assessment is by making an inventory of the objectives that are to be assessed. This involves distinguishing broad objectives from more specific ones. Examples of a broad and a specific listening comprehension objective are as follows:

> **Broad objective**: successful comprehension of academic lectures.

More specific objective: ability to identify connectors that function as markers of cohesion (for example, *furthermore*, *nevertheless*, *unless*, and *however*) in an excerpt from an academic lecture (in X field), to give their meaning, and to define their function in the lecture.

Important objectives are distinguished from marginal ones for the task at hand. This will vary by context, since the objective to assess for control of verb tense may be important for one instrument but relatively unimportant for another.

Items and procedures are then developed to assess these objectives separately or along with other objectives. Varying the type and difficulty of items or procedures assessing a particular objective helps the assessor distinguish one respondent's grasp of the area covered by the objectives from that of another. As said at the outset, a premium is currently being put on the use of multiple assessment techniques in order to obtain a more representative sampling of a learner's language behavior. In fact, the objectives to be assessed can also be assessed by means of a host of less formal or informal means as well. Hence, the teacher needs to be aware of how other options can complement or even replace the quiz or test. Some examples do not look very much like "items," although they may serve the same purpose:

- *Checklists*—the teacher checks off objectives that the learner has met. If the process is one of self-assessment, then the learner does the checking off. The following is an example for a college learner of Spanish as a foreign language:
  __ The learner can make polite requests at a formal dinner party.
  __ The learner uses the present subjunctive (in Spanish) with relative ease in discussion groups at academic seminars.
  __ The learner can carry out a friendly conversation with a Spanish-speaking student at the Student Union.
  __ The learner can get telephone directions in Spanish on how to get to a weekend retreat 200 miles away.
  __ The learner can speak in Spanish with a professor about changing a grade on an exam.

- *Rating scales*—a similar means of assessment would be to use a rating scale instead of a simpler checking procedure: The learner can make polite requests.
  always __   usually __   sometimes __   rarely __
- *Teacher observation*—the teacher determines that objectives have been met by observing the learners interacting in classroom situations, by reading their entries in dialogue journals (to be discussed in Chapter 9), and the like.
- *Homework assignments*—the teacher keeps an ongoing record of student performance from day to day by checking homework task sheets and by recording the results into a computer file; students' point scores are tallied on an ongoing basis; performance on each task is also converted into a percentage score (an activity that is common in certain high schools in the U.S., such as those in Minnesota and elsewhere).
- *Portfolios*—the teacher and learner collect samples of the learners' speaking and writing over time (see Chapters 8 and 9, respectively) in order to have an ongoing, incremental measure of performance, rather than relying on a one-shot measure, such as an oral interview or essay.

The number of items or procedures used to measure any given objective depends on several things. First, is the instrument intended to assess **mastery** of the objectives or simply **progress**? If mastery is being assessed, there should be a large enough sample of items to allow measurement of this. For example, including only one item on tag questions is unlikely to indicate to the teacher or any other assessor whether the respondent has a firm grasp of tag questions. But if the assessors do not have the testing time to allow for, say, three items on tag questions, then they should at least be aware that they are not really assessing mastery. A respondent's correct answer on one item could be the result of guessing. Teachers usually do not have the time to cover all the objectives that they would like to, so they must instead satisfy themselves with a sampling of these behaviors.

If the assessment instrument is designed for use in a course, then the objectives covered might be those most emphasized in the course and those of greatest utility value for the students as well. This means resisting the temptation to include difficult items of marginal importance simply because they differentiate between the better and poorer achievers.

Description of Items on an Assessment Instrument

Thorough description of the items and procedures used for assessment requires a set of terms that are clear and mutually exclusive. In practice, terms used to describe measurement instruments are sometimes vague and closely related, and they may overlap. One hears reference to "items," "questions," "points," "objectives," "activities," "tasks," and "procedures," and just what is being referred to may not be clear. For example, in lay terms, the general intent of an item may be referred to as the purpose of the item, its aim, its goal, or its objective.

For our purposes, one entry or question on an instrument will be referred to as an *item*, and a sizable task (e.g., writing a summary of an article) will be called a *procedure*.[2] An *objective* is the explicit intent of an item or procedure, which may be stated in terms of behavioral operations, such as a teaching objective. In other words, students are to draw on their knowledge of the language and perform some operation with that knowledge—for example, decode a word, read for comprehension, or listen to a dialogue, and then, say, produce a word or write a phrase. A *point* is defined as any feature or form that a given item elicits.

While the objective of an item may be to assess one point, the item may actually test one or more other points as well (with or without the teacher's awareness). This phenomenon therefore justifies our talking about intended objectives and the full range of points elicited by a given item. So let us consider the following item presented orally:

The music shop will
(a) circulate (b) show (c) inform (d) advertise
its special 24-hour electric guitar sale in all the local papers.

Let us assume that the respondents hear both the stimulus and the four response choices on an audiotape and then are to write the correct letter on the answer sheet. In this case, the objective might be to test for the listening skill of discriminating among similar verb meanings and identifying the correct one for the given context, which would be (d) advertise. The item may also be assessing other points or features—grammatical points such as the transitivity of verbs ("advertise a sale" but not "inform a sale") and verb + preposition combinations ("inform someone about," "circulate information about"), and points related to cognitive processing, such as aural memory for the four vocabulary words presented in sequence and the ability to remember the initial part of an utterance despite the insertion of a series of alternatives in the middle. These may be points that the tester wants to assess, or they may be extra points beyond the official objectives.

The explicit objective of a relatively simple vocabulary item may actually be to assess several points. For example, the student reads the word *ballot* and then *vote* and must indicate whether the latter is a synonym of the former. This item assesses decoding ability and the ability to recognize synonyms. Or the learner reads the word *ballot* and then must produce orally an appropriate synonym. In this case, the explicit intent of the item is to have the student (1) read a word, (2) choose an appropriate synonym, and (3) produce the synonym orally—three distinct points. If the objective of the item were to assess oral production of synonyms alone, the teacher would want to take into account that the reading of the stimulus would nonetheless constitute a point being tapped by that item.[3] If the students have limited reading ability and read *ballot* as *ballet*, they may say that *dance* is a synonym.

Two other terms to be aware of are *stem* and *distractor*. The stem of an item is the initial part—either a partial sentence to be completed, a question, or several statements leading to a question or an incomplete phrase (Valette, 1977). A distractor is an alternate-response choice that is intended to attract students who do not know the right answer (rather than to mislead students who do know the right answer).

Just as an item could assess more than one objective (e.g., an item assessing the reading of a word and the oral production of a synonym), so one objective (e.g., producing oral synonyms) can be assessed by more than one item and by more than one item type. In fact, some instruments include clusters of items intended to assess the same objective—for instance, three items all testing for control of tag questions in English. Items of a similar kind may also be grouped together to form *subtests* within a given instrument.

Perhaps the starting point in considering items or procedures for inclusion in a quiz or test is the enumeration of points that the item or procedure assesses. Such an analysis might suggest broadening the item so that it covers more points at once (e.g., the reading of the questions and then the morphological and syntactic accuracy when writing short paragraphs) or narrowing the item so that it covers fewer points (e.g., just the reading of the items and true/false questions about syntax). The important thing is to be aware of what the item or procedure is testing so that the results are meaningful and can be scored and evaluated appropriately.

The Intellectual Operation Required

Language items and procedures were once said to assess different levels of intellectual operation (Valette [1969], after Bloom et al. [1956]). They were purported to assess language ability at the following intellectual levels:

- *Knowledge*—bringing to mind the appropriate material
- *Comprehension*—understanding the basic meaning of the material
- *Application*—applying the knowledge of the elements of language and comprehension to how they interrelate in the production of a correct oral or written message
- *Analysis*—breaking down a message into its constituent parts in order to make explicit the relationships between ideas, including tasks such as recognizing the connotative meanings of words, correctly processing a dictation, and making inferences
- *Synthesis*—arranging parts to produce a pattern not clearly there before, such as in effectively organizing ideas in a written composition
- *Evaluation*—making quantitative and qualitative judgments about material

It was assumed that these levels demanded increasingly greater cognitive control as one moved from knowledge to evaluation. It was likewise construed that effective operation at more advanced levels, such as synthesis and evaluation, called for more advanced control of the second language.

Yet the construction of test items according to taxonomies of intellectual skills does **not** necessarily imply that the reading of texts requiring the use of so-called "higher-order" skills **necessarily** constitutes a more difficult task. In other words, interpreting complex relationships may not be any more difficult and perhaps easier than recognizing that two words are antonyms in a given context. Rather than viewing the taxonomy as hierarchic, Oxford (personal communication) suggests viewing these intellectual operations more as a matter of learning style. For instance, a *global* person (i.e., one who seeks the big picture right away) would use synthesis, a very high level in Bloom's taxonomy, in order to comprehend, which is a much lower-level function in the taxonomy. An *analytic* person (i.e., one who prefers detail rather than the overall picture) would use analysis to comprehend. In addition, the global and the analytic learners will use different forms of application and evaluation, but not in a hierarchical way (see Oxford, Hollaway, & Horton-Murillo, 1993).

Research Notes

With regard to a taxonomy of reading skills, Alderson and Lukmani (1989) reported on a study in which both weaker and more proficient Bombay university students had as much difficulty with *lower-order* questions as they had with *higher-order* ones. One explanation given was that whereas the lower-order questions measured language skills, the higher-order ones measured cognitive skills that the lower-proficiency students had no problem with. Another plausible explanation was that the lower- and higher-order distinction was faulty. Apparently, ten expert judges at Lancaster disagreed on what 27 out of the 40 reading items measured.

In another study looking at higher- and lower-order processing, twenty experts in applied linguistics were asked to rate 33 short-answer comprehension questions accompanying a short narrative text from an EFL listening comprehension test (Buck, 1991). The raters had to determine whether the items called for low-level or high-level processing and whether they were easy or difficult. The test was administered to 254 Japanese college EFL students, and the results showed full agreement on the ratings of the twenty lower-level items but only partial agreement on the higher-level items (seven out of thirteen). With respect to item difficulty, the expert raters did not agree with each other, nor did their ratings correlate significantly with the actual item difficulty coefficients. Two groups of Japanese raters who were familiar with the English ability of the respondents (twenty-one Japanese teachers of English and thirty-one college students of English) had closer agreement with each other but were still unsuccessful at predicting the actual difficulty of the items for the respondents involved. The conclusion was that the intuitions of experts may not be so helpful in investigating the causes of item difficulty.

Item-Elicitation and Item-Response Formats

Any given item or procedure has a format for eliciting data from a student and a format for the student to respond to the elicitation. The item *elicitation* may make use of an oral, written, or nonverbal medium or some combination of these.[4] The same is true for the item-response format. Thus, viewing the format as the joining of the medium for the item elicitation with the medium for the item response, we see that there are at least nine possible item-elicitation and item-response formats (even before considering combined formats such as an oral **and** nonverbal—i.e., gestural or pictorial— elicitation and a written response): an oral, written, or nonverbal *elicitation*, each with an oral, written, or nonverbal *response*. For an example of an oral elicitation with oral, written, and nonverbal responses, let us reconsider the following item:

The music shop will
(a) circulate (b) show (c) inform (d) advertise
its special 24-hour electric guitar sale in all the local papers.

Having the respondent produce the word that fits the utterance, *advertise*, would constitute an oral response. A written response could consist of having the respondent write down the word in full. A nonverbal response could call for circling or writing the letter or simply pointing to it on the page.

One basic format issue regarding a major assessment instrument is whether it progresses to increasingly more difficult items or whether easy and difficult items and procedures are interspersed. There are arguments on both sides. If items get increasingly more difficult, the respondents may give up after a while and not attempt items after encountering the first ones that stump them. Yet if respondents experience failure too frequently at the outset of a test because of difficult items, they may be discouraged from attempting the remainder of the items in a section. Thus, there may be a psychological advantage to pacing the items so that they become progressively more difficult. A compromise is to start the test with relatively easy items and then start interspersing easy and difficult ones.

The Skill Being Assessed

The language skills that we assess include listening and reading, the more receptive skills on a continuum, and speaking and writing, the more productive skills. Nonverbal skills can be both receptive (e.g., interpreting someone else's gestures) and productive (making one's own gestures). *Receptive* and *productive* are used instead of *active* and *passive* because it is misleading to think of listening, for example, as a passive activity. Listening actually calls for attentiveness and quick reflexes in identifying meaningful language elements, discriminating one from another, selecting those that are most important, and then ensuring that these elements remain in memory long enough to process them adequately.

Item Type

What emerges from the combination of an item elicitation and an item response is what will be referred to as an *item type*. For example, the item elicitation may be a reading passage followed by a series of statements about the passage. The item-response format may call for indicating whether each statement is true or false. In this section, several item types will be discussed, namely, those calling for alternate responses and multiple-choice item-response formats.

Alternate-Response Format

It is interesting that strong arguments have been advanced pro and con with regard to using a true/false, correct/incorrect, or yes/no item-response format. What emerges is the conclusion that this response format can be effective under certain conditions. The following are some of these conditions, based on Ebel and Frisbie (1986):

- The items test important structures or ideas.
- The items test more than rote memory.
- The correct answer is not obvious.
- For those lacking the knowledge, the wrong answer appears more plausible than the correct one.
- The item is expressed clearly and concisely (no tricky negatives).

Ebel and Frisbie also suggest having more false statements than true ones, since false statements tend to discriminate better between students of high and low achievement than do true statements. They also suggest avoiding the use of extreme determiners like *always* and *never* in false statements.

It has been noted that one major virtue of true/false items is that they are easier and quicker to construct for reading comprehension passages than are multiple-choice ones (Heaton, 1990). Also, the response format can be oral or pictorial so that the student is not required to read and interpret alternate responses. Thus, such a format can be used with students who have minimal or no reading skills. The true/false approach also allows the teacher to generate more items from the same material than in the multiple-choice item approach: "The number of independently scorable responses per thousand words of test or per hour of testing time tends to be considerably higher than that for multiple-choice items" (Ebel & Frisbie, 1986:141). For example, each of five statements that would be used as alternatives for a multiple-choice item could form a separate true/false item. Research has also shown that students can attempt three true/false items in the time required to attempt a pair of multiple-choice items (Ebel & Frisbie, 1986).

The following example is based on a portion of a Bertrand Russell (1950) text:

> We are all, whatever part of the world we come from, persuaded that our own nation is superior to all others. Seeing that each nation has its characteristic merits and demerits, we adjust our standard of values so as to make out that the merits possessed by our nation are the really important ones, while its demerits are comparatively trivial. The rational man will admit that the question is one to which there is no demonstrably right answer.

> Item:
> According to the author, the merits of one nation may sometimes be greater than those of another nation. T/F

The above item is presumably assessing the reader's careful reading of the text. The correct response (false) is not intended to be obvious—that is, to be answerable based on world knowledge alone or by matching the item with some material in the passage. A superficial reading or a reading based on lack of vocabulary knowledge might lead to accepting the item as plausible, especially given the use of *sometimes* in the item-elicitation prompt. The item is worded simply, as the item constructor resisted the urge to write "the merits of one nation may sometimes **exceed** those of another" out of the concern that the respondents may get the item wrong if they do not know the word *exceed*. And the word *merit* appears several times in the text (not that the weaker students will necessarily know what it means).

Regarding the response format, Rivers (1981) has suggested adding a third choice, "don't know," for answering true/false questions. If this approach were used, a heavier penalty for a wrong answer might be given to discourage guessing (Rivers, 1981:388). Perhaps the way for a classroom teacher to derive maximum benefit from true/false items is to require students to state a rationale for responding that an item is true or false. This rationale would be written either in the target language or in the native language.

For example, let us take a sentence testing skill in dealing with reference, with appositives, and with ellipsis:

> While John likes to eat ice cream in the winter even if it's cold out, Tim, his good friend, doesn't.

> Indicate whether the following statements about Tim are true or false:
> 1. Tim is a friend of John's.   T/F
> 2. Tim eats ice cream in all seasons.   T/F

Assuming the student gave the correct response to #1 (true), he or she would have to tell the group how he or she arrived at that response—for example, that the *his* in *his good friend* refers back to *John*, and that the appositive phrase (*his good friend*) modifies *Tim*. Then, with respect to #2, the students may simply complete the sentence out loud—that is, (Tim doesn't) "like to eat ice cream in the winter" (the part eliminated through ellipsis) to demonstrate that the item is false. Regardless of whether the students use the metalanguage of linguistic analysis to explain their reasoning (i.e., using terms like *reference* and *ellipsis*) or simply talk or write in simpler terms, they would be encouraged to indicate their awareness of the relationship described above in order to get the true/false answers correct.

Multiple-Choice Response Format

Because it takes time to design good multiple-choice items, the format is probably not used often by teachers for classroom quizzes and tests, and certainly not for more informal assessment activities as outlined above. In fact, this response format is sometimes viewed as a default choice rather than a preferred one if large numbers of students are being tested and there is not time to score open-ended responses. Multiple-choice items may turn up in classroom activities because such items are an integral part of commercial materials or of local materials produced independently of a particular teacher's class. In these instances, the items are not the teacher's own but reflect the philosophy of others.

The selection of distractors. Since multiple-choice items are still very much an option for assessment in class as well as outside it, we will discuss here a gray area with respect to constructing such items: the selection of distractors.[5] Often the teacher chooses distractors on the basis of intuition. The problem is that a teacher's intuitions about what will "distract" students from the correct answer are not always accurate. Dobson (1974) researched the possibility of obtaining distractors for grammar and vocabulary multiple-choice items from among high-frequency incorrect answers on completion items given to students. What Dobson's research suggested was that if a multiple-choice format is used, some empirical basis for choosing distractors is helpful—for example, the results of having students supply the missing vocabulary word. Actually, the classroom teacher has convenient sources for student-based distractors. For example, if a teacher has two parallel classes, or if two teachers have parallel classes, student answers to open-ended questions in one class can serve as material for distractors in the other.

Research Notes

In the study that Dobson (1974) conducted, a multiple-choice test with distractors obtained from analysis of answers to completion exercises was more reliable **and** more difficult when administered to 60 ESL students than was a test with distractors written by two professional item writers using standard rules of item writing. The latter test was also administered to 60 ESL students of comparable ability. Let us look at some of the similarities and differences between items based on student responses and those based on the judgment of professionals.

With regard to grammar items such as the following:

1) "I'm going to visit Ted today."
"You really_____to tell him first."

we see below that the item based on student responses included distractors related to the meaning of the stem, such as *must call*[6] and *had better*, which together attracted 16 people, whereas the professionals' item used only modals, two of which attracted only three people in all:

Student-Based Choices and Response Frequencies		Professionals' Choices and Response Frequencies	
(a) ought	40	(a) ought	43
(b) must call	6	(b) should	14
(c) might	4	(c) must	1
(d) had better	10	(d) might	2

Here is another example:

2) "That tree looks terrible."
"The man cut off all _____ branches yesterday."

Student-Based Choices and Response Frequencies		Professionals' Choices and Response Frequencies	
(a) of	13	(a) ones	1
(b) its	28	(b) of	16
(c) the leaves of	10	(c) its	31
(d) their	8	(d) their	12

On this item, the student-based and professionals' choices differ on only one distractor.[7] The professionals used the distractor *ones*, which distracted only one person, whereas the student-based distractor *the leaves of* distracted 10 students. It appears that this distractor attracted respondents because of its semantic relationship to the sentence, not because of its grammatical fit.

When gathering potential distractors through open-ended vocabulary items, it was found that students who answered incorrectly were prone to supply a word related semantically or associated syntagmatically (i.e., through a syntactic relationship with a word in the item stem).

The student-based distractor *bath*, in the item below, is an example of a syntagmatic associative (e.g., *sunbath*):

3) "The doctor told Penny that too much _____ to the sun is bad for the skin."

Student-Based Choices and Response Frequencies		Professionals' Choices and Response Frequencies	
(a) exhibition	3	(a) revelation	2
(b) exposure	42	(b) exposure	47
(c) bath	12	(c) exhibition	5
(d) disclosure	3	(d) illumination	5

The student-based distractor *disclosure* worked no better than the professionals' *revelation* or *illumination*, but the word *bath* attracted a fair number because of the syntagmatic relationship. Finally, one more example:

4) "The clothing store will _____ its hat sale in the local newspaper."

Student-Based Choices and Response Frequencies		Professionals' Choices and Response Frequencies	
(a) write	2	(a) advertise	55
(b) show	7	(b) circulate	3
(c) inform	7	(c) dispatch	2
(d) advertise	44	(d) petition	0

In this last item we see that the professionals' intuitively selected distractors were probably difficult to understand. Students might have avoided them for this reason alone. On the other hand, the student-based distractors *show* and *inform* attracted 14 respondents.

The Justification of Responses to Multiple-Choice Items

With respect to the processing of multiple-choice items by respondents, an approach by Munby (1978, 1979) to the careful wording of multiple-choice reading comprehension items deserves mention. In this approach, all or most of the distractors are somewhat appropriate, but only one is the best answer. And selecting this best answer calls for control of some particular "micro-skill" or combination of micro-skills. Actually, Munby saw this approach not as that of **testing** but as that of **developing** students' problem-solving abilities through multiple-choice reading comprehension questions. First, the students read a passage silently and answer a series of multiple-choice questions about it. Then they break up into groups of no more than five or six to discuss specific multiple-choice questions and to arrive at group answers through a majority vote. The participants in the groups must give reasons for rejecting the distractors for each item. Then there is a whole-class discussion of the items and of reasons for rejecting the key distractors.

Let us take one paragraph from a sample passage and a multiple-choice question that would be written for that paragraph:

> For those who have enough psychological imagination, it is a good plan to imagine an argument with a person having a different bias. This has one advantage, and only one, as compared with actual conversation with opponents; this one advantage is that the method is not subject to the same limitations of time and space. Mahatma Gandhi deplored railways and steamboats and machinery; he would have liked to undo the whole of the industrial revolution. You may never have an opportunity of actually meeting anyone who holds this opinion, because in Western countries most people take the advantages of modern technique for granted. But if you want to make sure that you are right in agreeing with the prevailing opinion, you will find it a good plan to test the arguments that occur to you by considering what Gandhi might have said in refutation of them. I have sometimes been led actually to change my mind as a result of this kind of imaginary dialogue, and, short of this, I have frequently found myself growing less dogmatic and cocksure through realizing the possible reasonableness of a hypothetical opponent. (Russell, 1950:137)

The sample question could be

> According to Russell, what is the advantage of having an imaginary conversation with someone else?
> a. It is sometimes easier than having an actual conversation with your opponent.
> b. Your choice of a conversational partner is not limited to a particular location or time period.
> c. It provides an opportunity to point out the dogmatic nature of your opponent's views.
> d. You will find that your conversational partner has many of the same biases as you.

Although distractor (a) may be true, it is not mentioned in the passage. Since there are respondents who do not read the passage carefully, they might select this distractor because it is plausible. As for (c) and (d), a careful reading of the paragraph suggests just the opposite—namely, that such an imaginary conversation provides an opportunity to question our own views and in particular to see the dogmatism in our views. Russell **does** state something equivalent to (b) in the second sentence of the above passage. One skill being assessed in this item is that of awareness of contextual meaning at the text level,[8] specifically, lexical cohesion across sentences. Respondents need to see that *the method* in the second sentence refers back to *imagine an argument* in the first sentence. They must make this cohesive link. They must also perceive that *location or time period* is a contextual paraphrase[9] for *time and space* in the second sentence. To avoid mindless matching of material on the part of the respondents, the test constructor did not use the exact same phrase.

It is the students' task in the Munby procedure to arrive at just these sorts of conclusions about why the distractors do not constitute the best answer. Regarding the matter of plausibility, it may also be useful, at least from time to time, to use totally implausible distractors, just to see which students are not actively engaged in the reasoning process of finding the "best" answer. Such items would be unlikely to attract a lot of students, but knowing which students are attracted may be useful.

The Use of Errors as Part of the Item-Elicitation Format

There appear to be two schools of thought with respect to purposely including grammatically incorrect items as part of the item-elicitation format. For example, the item elicitation could consist of a sentence for which the students have to identify the grammatically incorrect element or elements, or select from, say, four underlined parts the one that is incorrect. Here is an example (Ingram, 1974:320-321):

> Each sentence has four underlined parts, marked A, B, C and D. You are to identify the one underlined part which would **not** be accepted in formal, written English.
>
> A   B
>
> At first the old man seemed unwilling to accept
>
>   C   D
>
> anything that was offered by my friends and I.

Or the respondent is given a grammatically correct elicitation for which one or more of the distractors is not grammatically correct in the given context:

> Judy didn't see Harvey yesterday, did she?
>
> (a) No, she does.
> (b) Yes, she did.
> (c) Yes, she doesn't.
> (d) No, she don't.

In this example, distractor (d) is the only grammatically incorrect response out of context. In context, (a) and (c) both involve an incorrect reply to the tag questions plus a switch to present tense, but past tense is called for.

While the use of incorrect language by teachers in class may be accidental, its use in testing may be deliberate. For example, Ingram (1974) suggested that using incorrect forms in item elicitations was perfectly acceptable. She distinguished between teaching and testing, or between a "learning situation" and a "discrimination situation": "In the learning situation students may have a mental set to absorb everything that is presented to them, but in a discrimination or testing situation, they have a mental set to discriminate between right and wrong answers" (1974:323). Chastain (1976:491), on the other hand, warned that students make enough errors in the classroom without having teachers contribute some of their own. He went on to suggest that with some ingenuity, teachers can test the common errors without actually committing any errors themselves.

It is interesting to note that even in teaching materials, erroneous material has, in fact, been used from time to time. For example, in a section labeled "discrimination," Rutherford (1975) asked students to say "yes" if the question in a given list was grammatical and "no" if it was ungrammatical. If it was ungrammatical, they were to say it correctly:

1. What happened?
   Yes.
2. What did happened?
   No. What happened?
3. Who said that?
4. How do we get to the post office?
5. Where you can find a policeman?
6. When do we sit down?
7. Who did ask you?
   (Rutherford, 1975:31)

The thing that makes such items difficult is that nonnatives are not very proficient at spotting even the so-called glaring errors. It is for this reason that efforts at getting nonnatives to identify and correct their own errors in spoken language have not been very successful. For instance, over a ten-week period, Schlue (1977) found that intermediate college ESL students were able to spot only 40% of their errors at best.

The scoring of student compositions in class can be both a teaching and an assessment activity, depending on the circumstances under which the composition was written. Even if instructional emphasis is being placed more on what students do effectively rather than on their errors, the use of student errors may still have a role to play in such an exercise.

Various procedures have been proposed for the use of errors as a means of teaching students to write more grammatically correct compositions (Witbeck, 1976; Raimes, 1983). Perhaps the most traditional procedure calls for a total-class discussion of a single essay to determine its strengths and weaknesses. A second procedure consists of giving two students the paper of a third student and having them evaluate it with respect to certain points. A third procedure involves giving groups of two or three students a paper that the teacher has marked with guidelines about the areas to be considered. The paper will also contain clues for finding and correcting errors. In yet another procedure, the teacher selects approximately five essays and duplicates them, correcting all errors except those considered relevant for class correction. The students are divided up into the same number of groups as there are essays. The members of each group all get a copy of the same essay. The students individually evaluate that essay and then check with the other members of their group to see the areas in which they agree and disagree with respect to their evaluations.

There may be a genuine place for erroneous material in checking for students' awareness of the grammatical correctness of forms. However, performance on such tasks may vary according to the type of learner. It has been pointed out that while adults who learn a second language in a formal situation can call upon a conscious "monitor" to determine whether forms are correct or incorrect, not everyone uses this monitor. Or they just use the monitor with respect to certain rules. Even when learners are told to go back over their written work, they apparently do not catch more than a third of their errors (Krashen, 1977).

Research Notes

A systematic study regarding the effects of error correction on student written performance over time was conducted by Robbins (1977) as a follow-up to earlier work by Cohen and Robbins (1976). The small experimental group consisted of four university-level students of

English as a second language—speakers of Arabic, Japanese, Spanish, and Persian, respectively. For one hour per week, this group received special help on errors they had made in various writing tasks (e.g., speed writing in class, standard in-class compositions, and homework). A comparison group received training in other skills during that time. The four students receiving the special sessions were still only able to locate less than a fourth of their errors, on the average, and when they did, they were able to correct only somewhat more than half of these (57%).

Furthermore, just one of the four students—the Japanese speaker—made noticeably fewer errors over time as a result of these error-correction sessions. This student was 25 years old, had been in the United States for 6 months, was a nursery school teacher in Japan, and had studied English in Japan for 10 years. This was the study pattern that she used:

1. She repeated the corrected word or phrase and wrote down corrections for future reference.
2. She used her own corrections as guidelines for future reference.
3. She used grammar rules or formulations of grammar rules that she acquired from class, from the textbook, or elsewhere as guidelines.
4. She was interested in learning from her mistakes and anxious about making careless mistakes.

In addressing the issue of errors and error corrections, we see that while it is overly prescriptive to say that the teacher should refrain from using erroneous material in assessment, it is worth noting that the effects of such use will probably differ according to the type of learner. Available research studies mainly speak to the possible lack of **benefits** from using errors. They do not systematically investigate the issue of whether exposure to erroneous material actually **teaches** the erroneous forms instead of the correct ones. Once again, the effect probably varies according to the learner as well as according to the way that the material is presented.

Though Ellis (1990) has pointed up the inconclusiveness of research on the benefits of error correction, he would endorse a greater awareness of grammatical form on the part of learners.

Likewise, after studying his own informal and formal language learning as well as that of others, Schmidt (1990) concludes that paying attention to language form is probably helpful and may be necessary if adult learners are to acquire certain grammatical features, such as those that are redundant (e.g., the third person singular -s in "he drinks slowly"). Perhaps this concern for learners to be more aware of grammatical structures, regardless of whether they learn them, would speak in favor of having teachers use erroneous material in assessment, especially for classroom quizzes, which should then be discussed in-depth in order to avoid possible mislearning.

Item Banking

Henning (1987) suggested that potential items and procedures could be selected and stored in an item bank. Before the advent of computer applications and sophisticated statistical procedures for processing items, teachers and test constructors would keep file cards of items. Computers allow for more rapid and efficient handling of items that lend themselves to computer applications. Whether computerized or not, an item bank would benefit from descriptive information on each item or procedure, such as

1. The skill or combination of skills assessed
2. The language element(s) involved
3. The item-elicitation and item-response formats
4. Instructions on how to present the item
5. The section of the book or part of the course that the item relates to (if applicable)
6. The time it took to write the item (to give an estimate of the time needed to prepare a series of such items for an assessment instrument)

It is presumed that any item entered in the bank has been piloted on sample groups and reviewed. An item may seem easy or well written when it is generated but may exhibit glaring inadequacies upon later inspection.

It might be assumed that item banking is an activity reserved for the test constructor who is **not** a classroom teacher. However, in this age, when many teachers are keeping records of the vocabulary, structures, and communicative tasks that their students have covered and have some mastery over, it is not unreasonable to imagine that teachers would also store on disk certain items and procedures intended to assess those language elements. Then, too, these teachers could electronically file information on the progress of individual learners. Hence, the computer is storing information about what was taught and learned, how to test these things, and how well individual students are doing on these and other tasks.

In Chapter 7 we will return to the issue of computerized testing when we consider the developments in computerized testing of reading skills. At this point, we simply note that efforts at item banking can be combined with those of computerized testing so that items are both stored and delivered through computer technology. The goal would be to use computer technology so that the assessment instrument is more than simply a traditional instrument transmitted via the computer—through harnessing the special capabilities of the computer to do the following:

1. Randomly select items
2. Provide specialized feedback
3. Give options for a second and third try
4. Score and analyze the results

The Nature of the Respondent

Some students do well on measures of language ability, while others have more difficulty. What are the reasons for differences in achievement? A discrepancy between what students know and how they do on a given instrument may be a result of one-time performance factors, such as fatigue or apathy. A student may also temporarily lack the test sophistication necessary to do well on a certain type of assessment task. Such factors should be distinguished from more enduring learner characteristics—e.g., debilitating anxiety, which will be discussed in this section. Chapter 5 includes more about the test-taking process.

Personal characteristics have been hypothesized as the reason for the differential acquisition of language ability (Larsen-Freeman & Long, 1991). These and other test-taker characteristics could help explain differences in performance on assessment measures. Figure 3.1 displays such a set of characteristics, and the next section will briefly discuss each one in turn.

Figure 3.1

Test-Taker Characteristics

- Age
- Foreign-language aptitude
- Socio-psychological factors
- Personality
- Cognitive style
- Language use strategies
- Ethnolinguistic factors
- Multilingual ability

Age

Age may play a role in performance on assessment measures. Older respondents may be more patient than younger ones; they may be able to sit still longer. The older respondents may also be more methodical in their deliberations, more abstract in their thinking, more adept at solving problems, and better able to budget their time on a test. Younger respondents, on the other hand, may be more uninhibited in their performance, especially in measures of speaking ability, and better able to exercise their acquired language knowledge, rather than groping for bits and pieces of learned material. As Larsen-Freeman and Long put it, "While the ability to think abstractly might give adults a tremendous advantage in solving problems, the claim is that the trade-off is an inability to make use of the LAD (language acquisition device) for SLA" (1991:163). Additionally, older respondents (e.g., immigrants who must compete in educational institutions and in the job market) may have a more difficult time reading printed texts or texts on video screens, hearing taped material, and writing quickly.

Foreign-Language Aptitude

Many of the strengths and weaknesses that have been identified with respect to language-learning abilities are often subsumed under *foreign-language aptitude*. These abilities or aptitudes include the following:

1. *Verbal intelligence*—the knowledge of words and the ability to reason analytically when using verbal materials
2. *Short-term auditory and visual memory span*
3. *Phonetic coding ability*—the ability to identify distinct sounds, to form associations between these sounds and the symbols representing them, and to retain these associations
4. *Grammatical analysis skill*—the ability to recognize the grammatical functions of words (or other linguistic entities) in sentence structures (see Pimsleur [1966], Murakami [1974], and Skehan [1989])

For example, it appears that certain students have better visual memory than auditory memory, some are better at grammatical analysis than others, and so forth. This variation across students regarding language aptitude may have some effect on how individual students perform on particular types of language assessment.

Empirical work was conducted with the Modern Language Aptitude Test (MLAT) to determine whether performance on any of the subtests of the test could be improved through training (Carroll, 1979). It was found that training did not influence performance. For example, the MLAT was not found to assess grammatical knowledge that had already been acquired, but rather the ability to learn new grammatical forms in a language. More recently, Skehan (1989) reviewed the available research literature on measures of language aptitude and concluded that the results of training for improving language aptitude were not encouraging.

Socio-Psychological Factors

With respect to socio-psychological factors, motivation for learning languages has for many years been viewed in terms of *instrumental* and *integrative* motives. Instrumental motivation was seen as referring to utilitarian purposes such as furthering a career or improving one's social status, and integrative motivation as referring to identification with another ethnolinguistic group (Gardner & Lambert, 1972). A third orientation also exists, namely, a personal motivation—learning a language for the sake of self-enhancement. Also, it has been found that integrative motivation can actually entail a number of different factors, such as a desire to make friends, an interest in being more politically involved in the community of those who speak the language, or an interest in a foreign country for sociocultural reasons.

Thus, one respondent could have high motivation to do well on a language test out of a desire to get a summer job in a foreign-language pavilion at an international fair. This form of motivation would be considered *instrumental*. But a host of different motivations could all be subsumed under integrative—for example, wanting to travel abroad in the summer, wanting to know more about that language community's way of life, wanting to sing opera in that language, and wanting to improve one's GPA by getting good grades in the subject. Whether performance on assessment instruments would be of equal caliber with any of the above types of motivations is a question for research.

Research Notes

It has been found that a student's general attitude toward the learning of a language in a particular situation (as determined by an interviewer, using a 5-point scale) is a better predictor of success on language tests than are measures of instrumental (economic) or integrative (social) motivation (Naiman, Fröhlich, Stern, & Todesco, 1978:66-67). This study concluded that a brief but carefully designed interview with learners may indicate more about their overall attitude towards language learning, and therefore the probability of their success, than the results of an involved attitude battery (Naiman et al., 1978:67).

Subsequent work went even further by suggesting that the split between integrative and instrumental motivation was perhaps simplistic. Clement and Kruidenier (1983) found that while the meaning of *instrumental orientation* was relatively clear, *integrative orientation* could actually be defined in a number of ways. A factor analysis study with 871 students of Spanish in the 11th grade found nine separate factors—in opposition to the notion of a general integrative orientation. Four factors were general to all learners: instrumental, travel ("language facilitates travel"), friendship, and knowledge ("understanding of group"). The other factors were familiarity/involvement ("commitment to being like members of the L2 community"), dominance/recognition ("prestige," "respect"), pragmatic control ("influence-seeking," "social influence and dominance"), sociocultural ("interest in that way of life and the artistic side"), and curricular language ("studying the language at school for credit").

In addition to having specific, personal motivations for learning the language, respondents on a test can have a series of attitudes toward their learning situation, the specific curriculum, their teacher, their peers (e.g., degree of competition), and the nature of the test or subtest. In Chapter 5 we will be considering the attitudes that contribute to the face or perceived validity of the test, and to the respondents' subsequent success or failure on the instrument.

Personality

Personality variables may also influence how learners perform on language-learning tasks. In other words, respondents who are emotionally stable and assertive and possess an adventurous spirit may do better than those who are unstable, unassertive, and unwilling to take risks. It would also appear that being prone to anxiety could be counterproductive on a test. As for performance on specific types of assessment, the assessment of speaking may favor extroverts, especially if they are paired with other extroverts, and the taking of cloze tests may favor those with patience and a logical mind.

Research Notes

A four-trait factor comprising assertiveness, emotional stability, adventuresomeness, and conscientiousness affected students' success on a test of French speaking skills in a later (grade 7) French immersion program in Canada (Tucker, Hamayan, & Genesee, 1976). With specific regard to test taking, personality factors may work to the advantage of certain students in a language assessment situation and to the disadvantage of other students. For example, speaking fluency has been linked to extroversion among Chicano high school students in Los Angeles (Rossier, 1975). Some recent work with extreme introverts and extroverts suggests that there are patterned differences in their abilities on different types of subtests (Berry, 1991).

In a study with EFL students in Japan, for example, 21 extreme extroverts and 22 extreme introverts filled in 20 gaps in a text (maximum of four words per gap) through the viewing of two short video sequences (twice) (Berry, 1991). It was found that the introverts did significantly better—the extroverts just wrote down a key word from the phrase while introverts tried to be very accurate, confirming the researcher's hypothesis that extroverts would be more impulsive and less accurate. In a second study of Japanese EFL students, 18 extroverted and 18 introverted students were randomly assigned to one of three types of videotaped interviews: twelve individual interviews of introverts and extroverts, six homogeneously paired interviews (introverts with introverts, extroverts with extroverts), and six heterogeneously paired interviews. The interviews consisted of a warm-up, a picture stimulus for descriptions, the eliciting of comments on personal likes and dislikes, and role play prompted by a picture. It was found that the extroverts performed better in pairs than individually and best when in **homogeneous** pairs (i.e., with another extrovert rather than with an introvert).

With regard to test anxiety, earlier research suggested that certain students display *debilitating anxiety* at the moment of assessment—that is, their nervousness is counterproductive—whereas others might find that their anxiety actually facilitates their performance (Alpert & Haber, 1960; Kleinmann, 1977). A recent meta-analysis of 562 studies dealing with the nature, effects, and treatment of academic test anxiety suggested that there was no need to distinguish debilitating from facilitating anxiety because they were simply mirror images of each other (Hembree, 1988:74). In any event, the debilitating-facilitating anxiety distinction has not been pursued actively in the literature. For example, a study with 160 adult EFL learners in São Paulo did not attempt to distinguish facilitative nervousness or anxiety from the debilitative type. The study found that those who reported being nervous during the taking of an oral and written test battery also performed somewhat more poorly (Mary Lee Scott, 1986).

Young (1986) had 60 university students of French, German, and Spanish do a self-appraisal of their anxiety before doing the ACTFL Oral Proficiency Interview (OPI) and afterwards. She found a negative correlation between anxiety and the OPI, but this correlation was not significant when adjusting for individuals' language proficiency. However, anxiety levels may have been artificially low in that the learners knew that the OPI results would not affect their standing in their respective courses.

Certain subtests have been found to be more likely to provoke anxiety than others. For example, Oh (1992) found that a rational-deletion cloze test provoked significantly higher levels of anxiety among 18 freshman premed Korean ESL students than did two types of written recall tasks. In this case, the respondents had apparently not had experience with the cloze test format, whereas they had performed reading-recall tasks.

According to the meta-analysis by Hembree (1988), treatments have proven effective in reducing test anxiety. One major approach has been to deal with the emotional component of test anxiety through one or more of the following:

- Desensitization
- Relaxation training
- Modeling
- Covert positive reinforcement
- Hypnosis

Among other approaches, training in study skills and in test-taking skills has proved effective in reducing test anxiety (Hembree, 1988).

Cognitive Style

Cognitive style may also influence language performance. For example, cognitive measures such as word-order discrimination tasks, which measure the ability to *transfer* material appropriately from one situation to another, and category-width tasks, which measure skill at appropriate categorization or generalization, may ultimately help predict ease of learning a second language (Naiman et al., 1978). The dimension of *field independence*, the ability to break up an organized visual field and to keep a part of it separate from that field, has also been related to second-language learning. It is suggested that the field-independent learner pays more attention to relevant language details without being distracted by irrelevant ones. For example, students would say, "Quelqu'un nous avons raconté . . ." ("someone have told us") rather than "quelqu'un nous a raconté . . ." because of distraction caused by the *nous* in juxtaposition to *a* (Naiman et al., 1978:76).[10] Such dimensions may ultimately offer diagnostic information about language learners that language aptitude tests have not provided.

Language Use Strategies

Language use strategies are mental operations that learners consciously select when accomplishing language tasks. These strategies also constitute *test-taking strategies* when they are applied to the area of assessment. Language use strategies have been seen to play a key role in language performance (Oxford & Cohen, 1992). One area that has been the focus of both theoretical and empirical work on strategy use concerns *compensatory strategies*—that is, the use of alternate communicative resources (e.g., approximation, circumlocution, language transfer, and word coinage) when the learner is faced with a perceived communication difficulty (Faerch & Kasper, 1983; Tarone, 1977, 1983; Paribakht, 1985; Poulisse, 1989; Bialystock, 1990; Kellerman, 1991). Learners have been found to employ, among other things, strategies for simplifying communicative tasks—strategies often resulting in deviant forms on quizzes, tests, and other assessment measures.

Students may also use strategies for avoiding forms or rules over which they do not have complete mastery. Some of these strategies include avoiding, changing, or abandoning a communicative goal when faced with a perceived communication difficulty (Tarone, Cohen, & Dumas, 1983; Tarone, 1977; Bialystock, 1990; Paribakht, 1985). Such avoidance might or might not result in grammatical errors or inappropriate forms, given the particular context. Some of these strategies may be used more frequently and/or more effectively by more successful learners, but this is an area for more research. What research into language learning strategies has revealed is that learners differ somewhat in their choices of strategies but differ dramatically in the ways that they use the strategies and in the success that they have with them.

Ethnolinguistic Factors

Just as it may be possible to train respondents to adjust their test-taking behaviors to accommodate certain types of items, it is also possible to design items specifically to cater to populations with certain characteristics. For example, items may be written specially for certain ethnic or language groups (e.g., English-language items for Native Americans—or even more specifically for native speakers of Navajo). The justification for such item construction is that both intentional and unintentional cultural bias have been identified in the ways language assessment instruments are designed and administered (see, for example, Brière [1973], Messick & Anderson [1974], and Deyhle [1987]). For instance, language tasks designed with middle-class learners in mind may inadvertently cater to certain cognitive styles not characteristic of lower-class learners in a particular society.

As a case in point, the issue of *field dependence* (i.e., the inability to identify or focus on particular items without being distracted by other items in the background or context) has been raised as it relates to assessment. It has been stated that field dependence is more prevalent among lower-class Mexican-American learners in the United States than among middle-class Anglos (Ramírez & Castañeda, 1974). While subsequent research suggested that this was not the case (DeAvila & Duncan, 1978), there may still be a need to proceed with caution in using items or tests with respondents whose cognitive styles do not allow responses to such tasks. It may be worthwhile to assess the language learning styles of respondents (see Oxford, Hollaway, & Horton-Murillo, 1993) and to compare this with information regarding what the items and procedures are actually testing to see how good the match is.

Whereas it may be an unfeasible and even undesirable extreme to adjust forms of language assessment every year according to the particular constellation of characteristics found in the language classroom, the other extreme of continuing to give the same kinds of tests year after year without considering student characteristics may prove even less desirable. In fact, there may be a good reason to design tests, subtests, or test items that cater to a specific population with certain characteristics. (See Bachman, Purpura, & Cushing [1993], for more on determining the characteristics of test takers.)

Research Notes

In research conducted a number of years ago on nonnative speakers of English attending the University of California at Los Angeles, it was demonstrated that the results of testing traditional "foreign" students were markedly different from the results for the ever-increasing group of "minority" students (Cohen, 1975a). Five subtests were designed to measure foreign-like English (i.e., problem areas in English among foreign learners). These subtests included *grammar*—multiple-choice sentence completion; *cloze* —with every seventh word deleted; *reading comprehension*—a series of passages with multiple-choice questions; *listening comprehension*—short-answer items,[11] a mini-lecture, and a dialogue with multiple-choice responses; and *dictation*—with long phrase groups and punctuation given. The battery included three other subtests designed to tap minority-like English (i.e., an awareness of the difference between standard and nonstandard English). These subtests included *grammar*—underlining incorrect forms in a sentence; *modified cloze*—assessing regular and irregular verbs and modals; *dictation*—with short phrase groups (graded for spelling and punctuation) and structures, spelling, and punctuation employed in the dictation based on analysis of minority student essays.

As predicted, minority students had little difficulty with the foreign-English subtests but considerable difficulty with the minority-English subtests. The foreign students, on the other hand, had difficulty with the subtests for foreign English but did **better** on the minority-English subtests than did the minority students. The foreign students were generally more aware that certain forms were not acceptable in standard English than were minority students, probably because of the kind of English training, particularly in grammar, that the foreign students had received and their probable lack of exposure to minority forms. The students with minority-like English were found to have been in the United States for at least four years prior to the study, although some had in fact been born in the United States.

Multilingual Ability

There are other ways in which students differ that have not been discussed here, such as with respect to the number of languages that they have had contact with and the nature of contact. For example, a learner may be a **native** speaker of Spanish but actually be **dominant** in English. Thus, if the output on a composition task in a third language (e.g., Hebrew) reflects structures that can be attributed to interference from another language, this interference may come more, or exclusively, from the dominant language (English) and not from the native language (Spanish). One study actually found more negative transfer from the **second** language (English) than from the **first** (Jamaican Creole) in the learning of a third language (Spanish) among junior high and senior high pupils in Jamaica (Lewis, 1974). An explanation given in this case was that the first language had been denigrated to the extent that it was not the language of instruction at school; in fact, its use at school was prohibited.

Actually, interference from a second language in learning a third language could arise even if the second language is **not** the student's dominant language. For example, sometimes the interference results from accidental similarities between words in the two languages. For instance, although a native and dominant speaker of English, I once used a lexical item from Spanish (my third language) in speaking Hebrew (my sixth language). I chose the Hebrew word for *tickets*, *kartisim*, when I meant *mixtavim* (*letters*), because the word for *postal letters* in Spanish, *cartas*, interfered.

The Administration Process

Procedures for administering a more formal assessment instrument may vary. Whatever the arrangement is, it may have positive or negatives effects on the assessment experience itself and consequently on the reliability of the results. One issue concerns whether the measure has an open-book or closed-book format.

Open-Book Tests

In a language task, *open-book* could mean the use of dictionaries, vocabulary lists, student notebooks, and the like. It is noteworthy that several general books on testing speak disparagingly of open-book tests. On the plus side, such an approach may have a psychologically beneficial effect, as well as encourage students to put the emphasis in their studies on their ability to **use** knowledge rather than simply to remember it (Ebel & Frisbie, 1986). Furthermore, an open-book test may provide learners a useful incentive to organize their notebook so that, say, grammar rules and vocabulary will be easily retrievable for use during the test. Also, teachers might be encouraged in this format to use interpretation- and application-type questions, rather than ones assessing recall. On the minus side, open-book tests actually help the bright students more and have dubious long-term benefits for the poorer students (Green, 1975; Marshall & Hales, 1971). Furthermore, they may encourage students to study less and thus inadvertently encourage superficial learning (Ebel & Frisbie, 1986).

Take-Home Exams

A test may also be of a take-home variety, usually implying that it is "open-book"—i.e., students may consult class notes, articles, books, or whatever in completing the test. On the plus side is the removal of time pressure, which can defeat the purpose of a classroom open-book test in that anyone consulting notes or textbooks is losing valuable time in the process. On the minus side is the loss of assurance that the answers that students submit do in fact represent their own achievements. Hence, it is suggested that take-homes serve better as practice exercises for more formal assessment to follow. Students could even be encouraged to do these take-home exams in pairs or groups (Ebel & Frisbie, 1986).

Administering an Assessment Instrument

In administering an assessment instrument, the teacher has the option of giving a brief review of those elements that will appear on the instrument. For example, sample questions may have been given to the students before class or may be presented for the first time when the assessment begins. Sample items usually help allay test-taking anxieties. They can serve as a warm-up to get the learner into the task at hand, a matter that should not be minimized. Poor performance may be frequently traced to inadequate warm-up.

It is possible that the student is not required to answer all the items or procedures, but rather a subtest of these. This optional-choice approach may pertain to all of the test or just to one or more parts. Teachers and administrators contemplating using tests with formats of this kind need to be aware of the criticism leveled against the optional-choice approach: (1) such items and procedures introduce separate criteria for rating different students (according to the questions they answered), which is likely to reduce the reliability of the instrument; and (2) they may encourage students to learn only part of the material as well (Marshall & Hales, 1971:59).

The teacher may want to reserve a special affable-but-stern posture for assessment sessions in order to discourage copying. Perhaps the occurrence of unsolicited "group work" may not be a problem during a quiz, but it would be worth avoiding on an end-of-trimester test. On the other hand, the teacher may wish to encourage cooperation among students in testing sessions, depending on the nature of the task. Certain communicative speaking and writing tasks may benefit from such cooperative efforts.

Giving instructions and a sample item or two **before** students receive the measure itself may be advisable, to ensure that students will pay attention to the instructions. A graduate student of mine even recalled being asked to rewrite the instructions at the end of the grade-school exam as evidence that he **had**, in fact, read them (see Chapter 5 for a discussion on the nature of instructions). If there are instructions or questions to be read aloud, they should be read not only slowly but accurately as well—that is, with no departure from the chosen wording. If the teacher does change the wording, this should be noted, since it may well affect the nature of the responses and their subsequent scoring. If questions arise regarding items or procedures, the teacher may wish to paraphrase material on the test. The teacher should then be mindful of whether such paraphrasing adds any substantive clues regarding the answer to the item or procedure. If so, it is important to pay attention to whether the whole class received this paraphrase or just one or more of the students. Sometimes, out of "examiner fatigue," teachers may start feeding individual students the clues they need to answer the item.

The following checklist of administration tips applies primarily to the giving of classroom tests and is intended as suggestive, not prescriptive. The "shoulds" of test administration will vary according to the testing situation:

- The room should have adequate ventilation, heat, light, and acoustics.
- If a videotape or audiotape recorder is to be used, it should be set up and tested in advance to make sure that it works.
- The test administrator should assume an affable but stern posture. A few smiles help to put the respondents at ease, but the sternness is necessary to make it clear that cheating is not allowed—unless cooperative effort among respondents is an integral part of the particular test or a portion of it.
- If the instructions are read aloud, they should be read slowly with no departure from the established wording. If questions arise, the tester can use paraphrasing but should not add anything substantive to the instructions (Harris, 1969).
- The time that the exam begins and the total time remaining for the test and/or subtests should be written on the chalkboard.

Conclusion

This chapter notes an increasing trend away from assessing linguistic competence, or "skill getting," toward the assessment of the ability to communicate, or "skill using." As with any trend that has been in existence for some time, there are counter-movements back toward more traditional skill-getting assessment. The trick is to gracefully combine the two so that, for example, grammatical ability is assessed within a communicative framework.

We defined and contrasted terms for describing an assessment instrument, such as *objective, item, procedure, point, stem,* and *distractor.* It was noted that in order to discuss an assessment instrument, it is helpful to have a set of terms with which to state what the instrument is actually measuring. We discussed item-elicitation and item-response formats, and examined the value of alternate-response and multiple-choice response formats. We suggested that an alternate-response format can be effective under certain conditions. The multiple-choice approach will be more effective if the response choices are based on more than intuition—that is, on empirical analysis of results from open-ended questions and on the latest theoretical models in the field (e.g., basing reading comprehension items on discourse analysis). We also suggested that there may be some benefit in the use of errors as part of the item format.

We enumerated test-taker characteristics that may affect the results of assessment. Age; foreign-language aptitude, socio-psychological factors (motivation and attitudes), personality, cognitive style, language use strategies, ethnolinguistic factors, and multilingual ability were all shown to have a potential influence on the outcomes of assessment.

Finally, we briefly described how the format for administering a test, quiz, or other task may vary: through in-class or take-home tests, closed-book or open-book tests, and so forth.

Discussion Questions and Activities

1. You are a college ESL instructor and have designed a mid-term test that has your students read two passages with conflicting views on the issue of global warming. You have constructed ten short-answer questions that require the students to relate one text to the other. Half of your items call for "higher level" synthesis of ideas—such as through comparison and contrast—and the other half test for more "lower level" comprehension of concepts introduced to describe what global warming is or could be. Much to your surprise, some of the less proficient students in your class do well on the synthesis items and poorly on identifying the meanings for concepts, while truly proficient students do just the opposite. How would you explain this phenomenon, assuming the items themselves are well-constructed?

2. One of the reasons it is helpful to scrutinize carefully items on a language assessment measure is to make sure that no item is assessing factors beyond those which the instrument is intended to assess. Prepare to make such a case at a faculty meeting for foreign-language instructors where you work, and to explain to them what happens to the results of assessment when items **are** testing points other than those intended to be assessed.

3. What does it mean to derive distractors for multiple-choice items empirically? What advantages can you see in doing so?

4. As a group activity, take a multiple-choice reading comprehension test and have the participants respond to some or all of the items. Then divide up into small groups and have all the group members take turns giving their rationale for why they chose a particular alternative choice for each item. Be sure that all participants give their rationale for **not** choosing the other alternatives. This exercise has the potential of being an eye-opener for all participants, for they must examine the way in which they deal with multiple-choice items on a language test.

5. As part of a workshop you are giving to foreign-language teachers on language assessment, you are called upon to say a few words about purposely inserting errors into the assessment instruments. Under what circumstances might you suggest to the for-

eign-language teachers that they could use errors in the items that they construct? Under what circumstance might you reject such an option?

6. You are a high school teacher of French as a foreign language, and are very concerned about fair assessment. You make every effort to get multiple measures of each student's ability and endeavor to collect frequent measures of ability. While you would like your assessment to take into account the characteristics of your students, you have some doubts as to the **feasibility** of attempting to cater to different cognitive styles and personality variables when designing classroom assessment tasks. Nonetheless, you are called upon to present at the next faculty meeting the pros and cons of catering to respondents' characteristics. The issue at hand is whether to group extroverts and introverts for paired interaction tasks, with one student extracting information from the other. What would your case be, and what recommendation would you make?

Notes

1 In Chapter 6, we will look more extensively at the nature of discrete-point items.

2 For the purposes of this book, if *task* is used as a technical term, it will be referring to a procedure, such as dictation or writing an essay, as opposed to the answering of a single item.

3 For more on the distinction between item objectives and points, see Chapter 6.

4 Bachman (1990) and others refer to the format for item elicitation as the *input*. I prefer the term *item elicitation* because *input* can have a number of meanings. For example, we could think of the input as including the testing context, the student's background characteristics, and a host of other variables, whereas item elicitation refers specifically and exclusively to those features in the item that serve as a stimulus to obtain data.

5 Chapter 5 will look at strategies in taking multiple-choice items, and Chapter 7 will briefly summarize some of the pitfalls of multiple-choice items.

6 It may be that *must call* is perfectly acceptable and therefore should never have been included as a distractor (Eddie Levenston, personal communication). Thus care must be taken so that distractors related to the meaning of the stem could not possibly fit within the context for grammatical reasons, as in the case of *had better*.

7 We also note that this was a difficult item with both sets of choices in that only about half the students answered it correctly (see Chapter 2 regarding item difficulty).

8 As opposed to the more local word, phrase, or sentence level.

9 A synonymous phrase in that context.

10 Research with field-dependent and field-independent **native** speakers has also looked at linguistic behavior, such as the frequency of use of syntactic classes of lexical items in informal and formal written compositions. Among other things, it was found that field-dependent subjects are more inconsistent in their use of certain syntactic classes than are field-independent subjects. The investigator suggested that field-dependent persons have a greater need for "overt" syntactic structures (Henning, 1978:112).

11 The students heard ten questions and had to choose the appropriate response to each question from alternate responses appearing in the test booklet. Then they heard ten statements and had to choose, from alternate responses supplied, the statement that the same speaker would be most likely to make next.

Chapter 4: Scoring and Evaluating the Assessment Instrument

In this chapter we will start by considering different formats for scoring. We will then look at ways that the respondents themselves can become involved in the scoring process and we will also deal with the issue of what scores actually mean. Next we will consider two of the principal components of classical item analysis, namely, item difficulty and item discrimination. Finally, we will consider the process of revising assessment instruments, the criteria that can be used for evaluating instruments, and issues concerning the reporting of results.

Assigning Scores to Items

Scoring for Mastery of the Objectives

If an objective is assessed by means of more than one item—say, three to five items—then it is possible to speak of mastery of the objective, at least according to that method of measuring it. Ideally, these items or procedures reflect different assessment methods (e.g., the testing of reading comprehension not only through summaries and short-answer questions, but also through recall protocols, the use of cloze passages, and so forth). If Juan gets four of the five items or procedures right, he has displayed eighty percent mastery of that objective, according to the test. If Juan's test performance is stated only in terms of his mastery of the objectives rather than his relative standing in the class, then the test is being used for criterion-referenced assessment. What constitutes mastery of an objective is a difficult question to answer. Is it having four out of five items correct on that objective? What about three out of five? Further, what exactly constitutes achievement?

Weighting of Items

It could be that mastery of one objective reflects far more learning than mastery of another objective. For this and other reasons, items covering a certain objective may sometimes be weighted more than items covering other objectives. For example, a teacher may wish to give more weight to three questions asked after learners have viewed a videotaped lecture than to ten short-answer, multiple-choice reading or grammar items. Weighting also involves consideration of the ease of the task and the time spent on it. But the basic problem with weighting is that it may artificially distort the value of certain items or procedures. For this reason, Ebel and Frisbie suggest increasing the number of items meant to assess some area of greater importance rather than increasing the weight of the items (1986:220).

Objective Versus Subjective Scoring

The test constructor has to consider how long it will take to score particular types of items, as well as the easiest procedure for scoring (e.g., automated scoring by an optical scanner or computer scoring versus hand scoring). The more objective the scoring is for a particular item, the higher the scorer reliability is likely to be (i.e., the likelihood that two different scorers would come up with the same score for a particular respondent's test). For example, the scoring of a multiple-choice test would be considered more *objective* than that of an essay test, where the scorer's subjectivity would be expected to play a greater role. At times the most interesting items and procedures are precisely those that call for the most complex kinds of *subjective* scoring. For this reason, the scoring is time-consuming and may be unreliable, but the results are potentially richer in assessment information. We will deal with this issue, for example, when we consider four different formats for rating written essays—holistic, analytic, primary trait, and multitrait approaches—in Chapter 9.

The Value of the Score

Scoring is often taken for granted. The bulk of the concern is given to eliciting responses. Less attention is paid to determining the number of points that each item or procedure is to receive, and even less attention is paid to determining the value of the score. It is suggested in the testing literature that teachers develop a scoring key precisely in order to avoid the "I have a general idea what I'm looking for" approach (Krypsin & Feldhusen, 1974). One good way for teachers to derive their scoring key is to take the test themselves (Valette, 1977) and, if possible, to have another teacher take it as well. They can then poll themselves and their colleagues regarding what different items and sections should be worth. Another way to determine the value of scores is by having student respondents rate each item and procedure—for example, after they have completed a section or subtest. They can indicate how central to the course material or how difficult they perceived the item to be (see Roizen in Cohen, 1984). As Ebel and Frisbee (1986) point out, however, it is better to include **more** items of a type considered to be more valuable than to weight the given items more (see pages 97–98).

Scoring Formats

At the most objective end of the spectrum are items using the alternate-response format: true/false, correct/incorrect, yes/no, same/different, 1 or 2. For example, students hear one of two minimal-pair sentences (i.e., sentences which differ in only one phoneme) and must indicate whether they heard 1 or 2:

1 = The man *heats* the bottle.
2 = The man *hits* the bottle.

A slightly more complex scoring procedure involves having a group of students rate whether the student being tested said the first or the second sentence. The tested student's score in pronunciation is then based on this peer rating. For example, the student says **1** ("The man heats the bottle."). Out of a class of twenty-five students, nineteen indicate **1** and six indicate **2** (by raising their hands or in writing). The student's score would be 76% (19/25 of the students). This score thus reflects how easy it was for nonnative students to judge whether a fellow student produced the desired phoneme in a given context.[1]

The correct *ordering* of elements in a sentence could also be scored—for example, the correct ordering of elements in a question—as could correct *matching* between two sets of items. Scoring could also be checking for accurate *duplication* of material. For example, a teacher could score oral recitation in terms of the respondents' ability to stick to the text as it appears, that is, without insertions, omissions, substitutions, or changes in word order (see the discussion of *miscue analysis* in Chapter 5). A point could be given for every word recited correctly. Perhaps half a point would be taken off for a repetition, and if readers correct themselves, they get a point added on. The main purpose of applying such rigorous scoring procedures to an activity like oral recitation would simply be to help the teacher pay more attention to the student's actual performance.

Scoring could involve marking whether or not a blank has been **filled in** correctly. The scorer may want to mark a word as correct if it is in the proper form—tense, person, number, gender, and spelling—or may simply be concerned with whether the word conveys the semantic intent. For example, in:

Yesterday the girl _____*aks*_____ to be excused.

the desired form was *asked*. The given form lacks the past tense marker and is misspelled, but it does convey the notion of *asking*. So, when the teacher is scoring for functional language ability, *aks* may be acceptable to the extent that attention is paid more to contextual appropriateness than to grammar (e.g., inflectional endings) or to mechanics (e.g., spelling).

At the more subjective end of the spectrum, we find general, impressionistic scoring. For example, on a given composition or speech, the teacher could give a 1-to-5 rating on each of the following:

• Overall fluency/communicative efficacy
• Grammar
• Vocabulary
• Pronunciation (oral)
• Spelling (written)

Or on a composition, a teacher could simply give a "+" if the paper is good, a "✓" if it is acceptable, and a "–" if it needs to be rewritten.

In order to determine whether students are able to get the essentials from a lecture, a teacher could score the accuracy of students' lecture notes from a mock lecture conducted in class. The teacher might simply check whether the student has noted the main points. More generally, the teacher could check whether a student has understood any sort of message in the target language by evaluating student feedback (e.g., an oral summary, a written summary, oral or written answers to questions, or some combination of these) either in the target language or in the student's native language. In a class where the emphasis is on the students' reading comprehension in the target language (and not so much on speaking the target language) and where all students share the same native language, the teacher may obtain a more accurate measure of student comprehension by eliciting it in the students' native language.

Student Scoring

The students can do the scoring themselves, particularly if the teacher wants them to have immediate feedback. In fact, a part of students' grades could even be based on how well they score another student's paper. However, Valette (1977) cautioned that having students correct their own paper or exchange papers is "overly time-consuming" and that students make errors in scoring. She suggested that the teacher collect the papers and then review the quiz orally—by giving the students another blank copy of the quiz to take home and study. Of course, teachers may make mistakes in scoring as well, and students are usually quick to call such scoring errors to the teacher's attention.

In tasks like writing essays, students would need considerable direction on how to score each other's papers in order to do so accurately. In a study that had learners systematically correct each other's compositions, Madsen (1960) found that students needed more direction from the teacher. As indicated above, Witbeck (1976) looked comparatively at a series of three approaches to students' correction of compositions. In that study, the teacher/researcher first tried correction by the class as a whole. One essay was selected, and the teacher and the students corrected it together. Next, Witbeck tried having groups of from two to three students work together in correcting another student's composition. First, the group got two or three papers and had to correct certain points specified by the teacher. But even when they could decipher the handwriting, the students really did not know what to look for. As a variant, the papers had guidelines in the margin to help the students find and correct errors. Handwriting was still a problem.

In a third approach, Witbeck had the teacher select five or six compositions and then generate typed versions that were modified through the deletion of errors he or she judged to be irrelevant. Students within each small group were asked to correct the composition first individually and then with the other members of the group. Even in this approach, with a legible copy and only relevant errors present, the level of proficiency and native language background of the students sometimes interfered with successful correction. Witbeck concluded that this last approach was the most successful, but he pointed out that the method did not result in correction of all the students' compositions, just of those five or six selected. So such a technique would not eliminate teacher correction of compositions outside the classroom.[2]

The Meaning of the Score

We suggested above that **scoring** quizzes and tests is not the final step in the evaluation process, because the raw score in points does not have any inherent meaning. So first it is important to keep in mind what the score comprises. As an example, the score may be a composite of scores from several subtests or procedures. Some teachers may decide to weight different sections of the quiz or test differently. For example, they may use one of these two criteria: How difficult is it to get this item correct? How important is it to get this item correct? The teacher may feel intuitively that certain items or procedures are more difficult. Or perhaps the teacher had determined difficulty empirically by giving similar items to the same or other students. The teacher then gives the more difficult items or subtests a greater point value.

The teacher has to take into account that the more important material is sometimes actually easier for students to respond to. Then the dilemma is whether the teacher wants to distinguish among students through their ability to correctly answer difficult items—especially if these items are of marginal importance—or through their handling of *core* material. For example, a grammatical structure may be difficult because of its complexity but not very important within the context of the course. The same could be said about common verb tense forms and vocabulary items. Are they central to the course, or marginal?

A rather strong case can be made for not weighting items or subtests differently—i.e., for keeping to fixed-interval weighting (each item being assigned the same weight as every other item) and having the importance of the area reflected by the number of items assigned to that area rather than through weighting (Ebel & Frisbie, 1986). Thus, in a thirty-item test of vocabulary and grammar, the teacher may devote twenty items to vocabulary and ten to grammar if the former has twice the weight of the latter in terms of instructional goals. The result is that the more important areas are tested more reliably than the less important areas (because increased number of items in an area means greater reliability).

The important point is that scores themselves are arbitrary. The main concern is the interpretation of the scores. A score has meaning only in terms of some point of reference. Sometimes it is perfectly satisfactory to use the *raw score*, the score obtained directly as a result of tallying up all the items answered correctly on a test. But sometimes this number is not easy to interpret. One approach in such cases is to compute a percentage score, with the number of items on the test that the given student answered correctly divided by the total items on the test. For example, if a pupil receives a raw score of 28 out of 40 points, the percentage score is 28/40 x 100 = 70%.

One way to interpret a student's raw score so that it tells something about the performance in comparison with other students in the same classroom or across several classrooms is to report on a score's relative rank within the group. The group is referred to as the *norm group*, and in such cases, where the group is at the level of one or more classrooms, the norms are referred to as *local norms*.

A popular technique for comparing different individuals' test scores is to express them as a *percentile* (Popham, 1981; Ebel & Frisbie, 1986)—a number that tells what percent of individuals within the specified norm group scored lower than the raw score of a given student. The procedure for transforming a raw score into a percentile rank is as follows:

$$\text{Percentile rank} = \frac{\text{number of students below score} + \text{half the number of students at score}}{\text{total number of students}} \times 100$$

So let us assume that twenty-five pupils in the class got the following scores (ranked from lowest to highest):

59	62	67	78	87
60	63	68	78	90
60	65	70	80	92
61	65	71	84	92
61	66	72	85	93

We want to know the percentile rank of the student who scored 72. We then count fourteen students below the score and note that the student in question is the only one with a score of 72. The calculation is as follows:

$$\text{Percentile rank} = \frac{14 + 0.5}{25} \times 100 = 58$$

The percentile rank is 58.

We may also want to know what the mean score was, that is, the average score for a given group of students. To obtain the mean, we divide the student scores added together by the number of scores involved:

$$\text{Mean} = \frac{\text{sum of student scores}}{\text{total number of scores}}$$

The mean is as follows:

$$\text{Mean} = \frac{1829}{25} = 73.16$$

Thus, the average score was about 73 points.

Ultimately, the teacher evaluates the worth of a given raw score by affixing a grade to the numbers. One way is simply to use the raw scores, particularly if the course is based on number grades and the raw score is based on 100 points. Of course, a problem here is that teachers may feel that all classroom tests must be based on 100 points—an unnecessary prerequisite. A test can easily have whatever point total emerges after desired items and procedures have been included.

Another means for determining grades is by computing percentages as described above and by having the percentage be the grade, particularly in cases where the points on the test do not add up to 100. The grade could also be presented as a percentile rank. If letter grades are used, the teacher may want to determine what raw score, percentage, or percentile would constitute an A, B, C, etc. The decision on what letter grade to give could be based on a statistically derived normal curve, but other considerations enter into the picture as well (see Ebel & Frisbie [1986:243-264] for more on grading). One way is to tally scores by interval and assign the basic passing grade to the *median interval* (i.e., the interval that includes the point below and above which 50% of the scores occur). If we take the above data for twenty-five students, the median interval is 70 to 74; in a scoring system where a basic passing grade is 70, the scores from 70 to 74 would all be converted to 70. And then scores within each interval would be converted accordingly:

Interval	Frequency of scores	Grade
90–95	I I I I	90
85–89	I I	85
80–84	I I	80
75–79	I I	75
70–74	I I I	70
65–69	＋＋＋＋	65
59–64	＋＋＋＋ I I	60

In addition, the teacher may want to assess for whether or not the student has met one or more objectives. For example, a quiz or test may elicit five obligatory occurrences of a particular form. Then the teacher can decide how many of these forms the student must get right in order to be considered as having understood that form (e.g., 4 out of 5 or 3 out of 5). This is the criterion-referenced approach to scoring, wherein the score is mainly intended to indicate how many objectives each learner has mastered (Popham, 1978; Hambleton & Eignor, 1978; Davidson, Hudson, & Lynch, 1985).

Since the students' interest is highest during and immediately after tests and quizzes, they should receive prompt feedback on how they did (Chastain, 1976), regarding both their scores and what these mean. This feedback should not only be prompt but also intelligible. The teacher may also want to coach the learners in effective means for benefiting from the feedback. Especially in the area of feedback on compositions, teacher feedback is sometimes misunderstood by learners (see Cohen, 1987b).

Another area of concern for teachers, especially those working with younger learners, would be the impact that the reporting of scores has. The pupils will most likely check around the classroom in order to place themselves in relation to other students. This process has been referred to as a powerful social mechanism whereby pupils learn their place in the pecking order even though the teacher's intention may be to keep everyone equal (Poole, 1993). If the teacher goes over a test and asks students for the correct answers, those who got items **right** are the ones who tend to respond—so this activity also serves as a vehicle to learn who did well.

Classical Item Analysis

In recent years, classroom teachers, especially at the university level, have begun to use computerized analysis of language test data. Many universities have their own in-house programs.[3] There are also the commercial programs that are either part of large software packages, such as the reliability program within Statistical Packages for the Social Sciences (SPSS), or separate test analysis programs designed exclusively for that purpose. Given this panoply of available software, it is really no longer necessary for teachers to do their own statistical analyses for the types of activities to be described below.

These packaged programs often provide both classical test analysis and analysis based on the *item response theory* (IRT) model, wherein a latent "acquisition" continuum is inferred both for test items and for the ability level of the respondents. Since both respondents' ability and item difficulty are positioned along the same latent continuum, it is possible to make inferences from a respondent's performance that are referenced to the performances of other individuals or to the standards imposed by other tasks (Henning, 1987: Chapter 8). The power of using an IRT model is that it relates human performance to item performance in a more direct way than does classical item analysis.

IRT models such as Rasch are beyond the scope of this volume, so we will suffice with the classical approach to analyzing how students do on each item (item difficulty) and how well each item discriminates the better performers from the poorer ones (item discrimination). The various software packages also provide a variety of different reliability coefficients along with their analyses. For a discussion of language test reliability formulas, consult Henning (1987:80-85), Bachman (1990:168-177), and Hatch and Lazaraton (1991:531-538).

Item Difficulty

Item difficulty refers to the ratio of correct responses to total responses for a given test item. Hence, this index says something about how the items fared for this given group of students—whether the items were easy or difficult. A norm-referenced assessment instrument, which aims to differentiate among respondents, should have items that approximately 60% to 80% of the respondents answer correctly. (If ten out of twenty respondents answer an item correctly, the item difficulty is 50%.) If the assessment instrument is criterion-referenced, and aims to determine whether nearly all students have achieved the objectives of a course, then the assessor may wish to consistently obtain item difficulties of 90% or better. The first items on the test may be easier ones to give the respondents a feeling of success. (Of course, they could also be warm-up items that don't count at all.)

Item Discrimination

The *item-discrimination* index tells how well an item performs in separating the better students from the weaker ones. The index is intended to distinguish respondents who know the most or have the skills or abilities being tested from those who do not. Hence, while the item-difficulty index focuses on how the items fare, item discrimination looks at how the respondents fare from item to item. Teachers will sometimes just calculate the difficulty of items and on this basis alone make judgments about a test. The problem is that the item-difficulty rating alone does not tell the whole story—especially if the students getting the lowest scores on the instrument as a whole are the ones getting a given item right. In that case, something in the item is most likely misleading the better students, and it may be advisable to revise that item.

An item-discrimination level of .30 or above is generally agreed to be desirable. One way to calculate item discrimination is to distinguish the top 25% of the test papers and the bottom 25% (Ebel & Frisbie, 1986). For example, if there are twenty papers, the top five and bottom five are identified. These are labeled the "high" and the "low" groups, respectively. The others are called "middle."

There are three steps in the calculation. First, for any given item, the responses of the high and low groups are tabulated as "correct" or "incorrect." For example:

	Number of Respondents	Correct	Incorrect
High	5	4	1
Middle	(10)	(4)	(6)
Low	5	2	3

Second, the number of "lows" who answered correctly is subtracted from the number of "highs" who answered correctly. Third, the difference (here, 2) is divided by the number of papers in the high or low groups (here, 5). The result is the item-discrimination coefficient (here, 2/5 = .40). If there is an uneven number of papers in the high and low groups (e.g., 6 and 5), then the average (5.5) is used for calculations.

Another way to calculate item discrimination is by means of a point-biserial correlation, which measures an item's reliability. A correlation is made between all respondents' performance on a given item (a dichotomous variable—right or wrong) and their performance on some more general criterion, usually scores on the test as a whole (a continuous variable). The higher the point-biserial correlation for a given item, the more likely that the respondents getting a particular item right are also those who perform best on the total test (or other criterion measure). A correlation coefficient of .30 or better would make the item acceptable with respect to discrimination.

Piloting of Assessment Instruments

Ideally, an assessment instrument that is intended to perform an important function in an institution—such as a diagnostic placement test or an achievement test intended to serve as an exit test—would undergo *piloting* on a small sample of respondents similar to those for whom it is designed. The pilot administration provides the assessor feedback on the items and procedures. On timed subtests, the pilot group respondents could be instructed to mark how far they got when the time ran out and then to go ahead and complete the test so that there is feedback on all the items in the test. On the basis of piloting, the assessor can obtain some valuable insights about what part of the instrument needs to be revised before it is administered to a larger group.

Determining When to Perform Item Analysis

When and how often should classroom teachers sit down and actually calculate item difficulty, item discrimination, and test reliability? Clearly, this activity is going to be reserved for the results of specific assessment instruments and only after preordained administrations of those tests. Here are some suggestions:

1. Calculate item difficulty and item discrimination for items on mid-terms, final exams (with, say, ten or more respondents), and departmental tests when the tests are new and feedback on their effectiveness would be desirable.
2. Perform item analysis when you know that the assessment instruments are intended to be used again.
3. Calculate test reliability for groups of twenty or more students, and ideally only for major tests, such as departmental exams, and placement exams. Calculations should be made using the SPSS Reliability or some other test analysis program.

Revision of an Assessment Instrument

If an item on a norm-referenced assessment instrument has a difficulty coefficient of lower than 60% or higher than 80%, and if the discrimination coefficient is below .30, then the item should probably be eliminated or revised. The problem is what to do with the borderline items—those that do not quite fit your criteria. Especially if the item analysis is performed on a small sample, only one or two responses can change the index considerably. There may be good justification for leaving an easy item in the test if, for example, it is a leadoff item and its purpose is to give students encouragement to continue. Also, where an item appears in a test may affect performance on it. For example, students may do best on the items in the middle of an exam, after they have warmed up to the test and before fatigue sets in.

Multiple-choice items can be improved by examining the percent of respondents who selected each choice. If some distractors draw no responses or too many, then they should be omitted or altered. This task requires both rigor and intuition. For instance, it may be necessary to change the syntax or vocabulary of a distractor, or perhaps its semantic thrust. When piloting the test, the teacher can ask the respondents what their rationale was for choosing a particular distractor instead of the correct answer.

Ideally, the results of item analysis would be added to the information available on each item or procedure in the test constructor's item bank, if one has been established. If a particular test item comes under challenge by respondents or other examiners, being able to check the item-analysis information is useful. Perhaps it will turn out to be a borderline item that should probably not have been included in the test.

If the reliability of the test is low (.60–.70 or lower), then the following suggestions (based largely on Hatch and Lazaraton, 1991) may help to improve the coefficient:

1. Increase the length of the test (within reason).
2. Check to make sure that there are no items that are too easy or too difficult.
3. Make sure that there are items that discriminate well among students since these items boost the reliability of the test.
4. Make the items more homogeneous in nature (although this may conflict with a desire to use different testing methods).
5. Don't put time limits on performance.

Guidelines for Evaluating Assessment Instruments

The following are guidelines for evaluating an assessment instrument. You may wish to take a second- or foreign-language test— either your own or someone else's—and review it, using the review checklist of questions provided on the next page.

*Name of Assessment Measure*_____

*Class/Respondent Group*_____

*Date of Administration*_____

1. Instructions

    a. Are the instructions for each section clear?_____
    Would it be appropriate to include within the instructions
    some suggestions about how to do the tasks (i.e., how to
    read a text and how to prepare a written response)?_____

    _____

    Do all the items in each section fit the instructions for that
    section? _____

    b. Is the vocabulary used in the instructions and in the items
    at the desired level of difficulty? Are there any words in the
    instructions that the respondents might not know?

    _____

    c. Are there good examples of how to complete each section
    (where applicable)?_____

    _____

    d. In structured or open-ended sections, do the instructions
    indicate the approximate length of the desired response?

    _____

    _____

    e. If the test is timed—or timed in certain sections—is the
    timing realistic?_____

    _____

    f. Are the respondents informed in the instructions about
    whether the section is timed and how long they will have?

    _____

    g. Do the instructions indicate the value of the particular
    section with respect to the overall test score? _____

    _____

    Is the overall value of the assessment instrument clear to
    the intended respondents?_____

    _____

    What is the purpose of the instrument?_____

    _____

  h. Is the method of administering the quiz/test carefully established (i.e., so that someone else would administer it in exactly the same way)?_____

_____

2. Content
  a. (with reference to achievement tests) Is the assessment instrument doing an adequate job of evaluating the instructional objectives for the course?_____

_____

  Is it assessing material not taught/learned in the course? (Remember that a good instrument should reveal gaps in the instructor's teaching as well as in the students' learning.)_____

_____

  b. Is the instrument testing the desired receptive/productive language skills? _____

_____

  Has it adequately isolated the desired skill (if this is what it purports to do)?_____

_____

  c. Does the content of the instrument cover the intended aspects of communicative ability (sociocultural, sociolinguistic, and grammatical)?_____

_____

  Does the instrument intend to assess mastery of a set (or sample subset) of objectives, or simply some attainment of these objectives? Is the actual assessment instrument consistent with the expressed design for the instrument?

_____

  d. Is only one style (formal, casual, intimate) or dialect (standard or nonstandard) considered correct in one or all sections of the instrument? _____

_____

  Are the respondents aware of this (with reference to the "Instructions" section above)?_____

_____

If the intent is to keep the language "conversational" in, say, short-answer listening comprehension items, do the items reflect this intent? _____

_____

e. Might some or many items be assessing more points than you originally thought (if you constructed the test)?

_____

If so, would it then help to simplify these items or procedures in order to give greater prominence to the exact points intended to be measured? _____

_____

f. Are any of the sentences "linguistic curiosities" in an effort to test certain lexical and/or structural points?(See, "My brother has something beautiful and I have nothing ugly" in Rivers, 1981:376.)_____

_____

g. Does the instrument have the right title or might it mislead respondents, potential test administrators, and interpreters of the results? _____

_____

h. Is the content fair for test takers with different back-grounds (e.g., race, gender, ethnic background, or physical handicap)? _____

_____

Is there any insensitive content or language? (See Joint Committee on Testing Practices, 1988.) _____

_____

3. Item Format and Layout of the Assessment Instrument
   a. Is the assessment instrument as a whole too long or too short? (If too short, it may not be reliable.) _____

   _____

   b. Is one objective or another being tested too much or too little? (Over-testing may start giving away the answers, and under-testing may not give enough diagnostic information.)_____

   _____

   _____

c. Are the items that assess the same objective worded and spaced in such a way that one gives away the others?

_____

d. Are any items or sections clearly too difficult or too easy to answer? (Of course, item analysis helps answer this question. The difficulty of an item is often hard to determine on an a priori basis.)_____

_____

e. Have the correct true/false and multiple-choice responses been adequately randomized in order to avoid setting up a response pattern? (According to Ebel and Frisbie [1986], more T/F items should be "false" than "true" and M-C items should not all have either "b" or "c" as the correct answer.) _____

_____

f. Are the items paced so that even the poorest student will experience at least a modicum of success at the outset?

_____

g. Are the item response formats appropriate for what the instrument intends to assess? (For example, would matching be a more efficient means of testing vocabulary than completion or multiple-choice, or would the use of several formats be preferable?)_____

_____

h. Is the item-elicitation format appropriate? (For example, should the elicitation be audiotaped or videotaped, rather than written, or should both be used?)_____

_____

i. How good is the layout?
  1) Is the technical arrangement of the items on the page easy to follow? (For example, are the multiple-choice alternatives horizontal or vertical, in the sentence itself, or to one side?) _____

_____

  2) Is the spacing between and within items adequate?

_____

_____

3) If the test is dittoed, is the print legible? _____

_____

j. Have the items been adequately piloted and reviewed by nonnatives (if possible) and by other native speakers to eliminate poor distractors and deceptive or confusing items?_____

_____

4. Scoring
   a. Have the methods for scoring the instrument or grading a section been adequately determined? _____

   _____

   b. If items are weighted (and this may be undesirable), are the items and/or sections weighted appropriately in scoring? That is, do the weightings coincide with the assessor's notions about the most important objectives, are they the most useful ones, and are they the ones given the most emphasis in the instructional program? _____

   _____

Reporting Results

Since the results of a given assessment instrument may well have an impact on a learner's current and future academic career, teachers and other assessors should give careful thought to the reporting of results. In recent years there have been educational and political debates about language assessment practices, especially with regard to the notion of "gatekeeping"—the principle whereby language assessment instruments are expressly designed to let certain pupils through and to keep others out. (See Paris et al. [1991] on the political uses of test data.) For example, the case has recently been made for how tests of literacy may embrace one or another ideological model of what literacy means, often espousing one set of social values and judgments over other value systems (Hill & Parry, 1992). Thus, in reporting results, we need to place these results within the proper context. It may mean that we need to deemphasize the significance of certain standardized test scores by complementing them with a host of ongoing and comprehensive assessment measures, including portfolios, self-assessment, observations of student performance in class, student journals, and other forms of assessment.

Assuming that a formal assessment instrument was appropriate for the intended test-taking population and that it adhered to principles included in the above guidelines for instrument evaluation, then we could ask whether the results have been interpreted accurately and fairly. With regard to accuracy, we could ask whether the cutoff points used for assigning grades (if assignment of grades is on a curve) accurately reflect the relative standing of the students in the class. For example, do the resulting grades adequately represent each student's achievement on the given instrument? If people other than the students (e.g., parents or administrators) are going to be informed of these scores, will it be possible for them to interpret the scores, or would it pay to include written interpretation?

Sometimes, so much work goes into the design, construction, administration, and scoring of assessment instruments, that there doesn't seem to be enough time to adequately deal with the meaning of the results, both for the sake of the test takers and of others who may see the results. Yet this phase of the work is crucial. It is a bit like the case of the research paper that offers a copious review of the literature, an ample description of the study, and a clear presentation of the findings but that neglects to provide adequate interpretation of what those findings mean, including intuitive speculations. An experienced teacher may have valuable insights to add to particular scores.

In any event, the reporting of results needs to be handled in a fully professional manner so that the learners obtain maximum benefit. Even negative feedback to learners can be productive and have positive outcomes if it allows them to see the areas in which they need to develop their language skills. The final point to bear in mind is that multiple scores are better than lone scores in that they provide a more solid basis for assessment, especially if the assessment instruments are genuinely varied and are reliable and valid.

Conclusion

In this chapter, we discussed the concept of a score—that is, the format that it may take, who calculates it (e.g., teacher or student), and what it actually means. Then we presented item-analysis procedures, along with guidelines for test revision. The chapter ended with a checklist of issues to be considered in evaluating an assessment instrument, followed by a brief discussion on the reporting of the assessment results.

We devoted a full chapter to the scoring of tests and to the subsequent revision of tests because too frequently the emphasis in language testing books has been largely, or even exclusively, on the various formats for eliciting responses, with little or no attention given to the tasks awaiting the teacher or assessor once the instrument has been administered. These tasks are sometimes the most crucial and deserve not to be given short shrift. A perusal of the Guidelines for Evaluating Assessment Instruments should give the reader a sense of just how multifaceted and demanding instrument assessment can be. For this reason, any and all efforts to have teachers work in teams to construct and evaluate assessment instruments should be encouraged. This, in fact, is one of the benefits of using a portfolio model that calls for a committee of colleagues working together to screen material considered acceptable for inclusion. Members of this committee can then also serve as raters of the finished portfolio.

Discussion Questions and Activities

1. As a group task, identify a criterion-referenced assessment instrument that you or colleagues have used, are using, or may wish to use. Take a good look at its items. Can you determine which items are assessing which objectives? If so, take your analysis one step further and evaluate how well you think those objectives are being assessed by the given items. Then see if you can arrive at a consensus on how many of the items a respondent would need to get right in order for you to say that the learner has **mastered** that objective.

2. With the assistance of a partner, make a tally of the item-response formats and scoring procedures you tend to use in your teaching or would be partial to using if you were teaching. Then brainstorm the **possible** options for item-response formats and scoring formats for each. What alternatives, if any, might you want to add to your current assessment procedures?

3. You have been called on to do a workshop for your staff on item analysis, and although you have computerized programs available, you decide to indulge the group in number crunching in order to give them a better sense of what is actually being explored when item analysis is performed. You select a test that has been taken by a typical class of about twenty students and has already been scored. The instrument uses several item-elicitation and response formats—short-answer, summaries, and cloze. Have the participants calculate the median, the mean, and the standard deviation for the instrument (if possible). Next, calculate the item difficulty and discrimination for each item (based on comparing the top 25% of performers on the test with the bottom 25%). On the basis of the results, lead a discussion of the items that work and those in need of revision.

4. As a whole-class activity, take one language assessment instrument that is in use in your school. For instance, this could be an entrance test, exit test, mid-term, or final exam. Then each member of the class should use the Guidelines for Evaluating Assessment Instruments to evaluate this test according to its instructions, content, item format and layout, and scoring procedures. Compare the results category by category. Different students will probably identify different strengths and weaknesses. A modification of this exercise would be to have a group of students focusing just on the instructions, another group focusing just on the content, and so on. This approach sometimes results in a higher level of scrutiny and a greater number of insights than can be obtained from one person's efforts at analysis.

Notes

1   It is also a test of the other students' ability to distinguish between phonemes, but this is part of the reason for having the entire class do the rating. The average rating should serve as an estimate of pronunciation accuracy.

2   Since this section is on the notion of student scoring, not on the scoring of compositions per se, no attempt is made here to propose how best to score compositions. Chapter 9 discusses this issue.

3   At the University of Minnesota, for example, the program is called TESTAN and was developed by Philip Voxland at the Social Science Research Facilities Center.

Chapter 5:
The Process of Responding to an Assessment Instrument

Imagine that you need to pass an entrance exam in order to study at a university in another country. You have studied that country's language for several years but are not comfortable about your academic reading in the language. One of the subtests of the exam, "Reading Comprehension," requires you to read three texts (300-400 words each) and to respond in the target language to a series of five short-answer questions for each text. You know that your performance on the test will determine the course of your future studies. What do you do on this subtest?

Scenario A: You start by panicking. You then read each text through carefully, being sure not to miss a single word. You translate as many technical terms as you can into English. You sometimes find yourself reading the same sentence repeatedly. When you feel you understand the text, you then read each question and attempt to answer it by reading until you find related information. You try to answer each question that way, being sure to answer as much as possible in your own words in the target language. Unfortunately, time runs out when you are just starting to read the third text, and you have not even started answering the questions. About two-thirds of your responses to the questions on the first two texts turn out to be correct.

Scenario B: You start by carefully checking how much time you have and then quickly skim through the three texts and the questions, just so you have a general idea of the topics involved and the types of questions being asked. Then you read the questions for the first text carefully. You skim the first text until you find the material that is relevant to answering each question in turn. You do your best to use the language from the text as much as possible in your responses. This way you limit somewhat the number of discourse and grammar errors you are likely to make. When you are in doubt, you purposely use somewhat vague, general language so that the rater will be prone to give you the benefit of the doubt. You do not actually read each text in its entirety, and if you were asked to summarize the contents of a text, you would be hard-pressed to do so. Your focus is on answering each of the questions. You finish the subtest before your time is over, and you have time to check several items that you were not sure about. You end up getting most of the items right.

Which of our two imaginary respondents, if either, used test-taking strategies that you might employ under similar circumstances? Would your test-taking behavior vary depending on the nonnative language in which you were being tested (if you have studied more than one), or would the strategies you select be similar?

The purpose of this chapter is to focus on the process of responding to an assessment instrument, particularly those test-taking strategies that learners find beneficial in accomplishing assessment tasks. We give this attention to test-taking strategies since they constitute one potentially valuable means for validating language measures. A fair portion of this chapter will involve review of research studies, which should prove relevant for those either engaged in research on language assessment or concerned about the strategies used to process assessment items and procedures. On the other hand, some teachers or teacher trainees may find this material a bit too technical for their needs and may wish to skip over the research notes.

In order to better understand the test-taking strategy data, we will consider the nature of verbal report methods and their varying roles in obtaining test-taking data. We will take verbal report through its use in early investigation of foreign-language reading strategies, note its applications to other areas of language learning, and end with a focus on verbal report methods in better understanding language assessment processes. We will consider indirect and direct formats of assessment for which verbal report has provided test-taking strategy data. Next, we will discuss issues related to the following of instructions, and we will end with a look at the role of practice.

A Process Approach to Language Assessment

Responses to items on assessment instruments may not be very informative because the teacher is not sure where the student's difficulty lies—that is, what it was about the items that caused problems for the student in processing the information and/or in responding to it. For example, if learners are given a passage to read and then asked to respond to a series of questions, what is it that they use to pick a correct or incorrect answer? The fact that the learners got the items right or wrong may not provide much information concerning how well the students have comprehended the material.

Over the last twenty years, there has been increasing interest in approaching the assessment of language from the point of view of those who are responding to the assessment instrument. Bormuth (1970) was one of the first to register a plea for more attention to this area of investigation:

> There are no studies, known to the author, which have attempted to analyze the strategies students use to derive correct answers to a class of items. The custom has been to

accept the test author's claims about what underlying processes were tested by an item. And, since there were no operational methods for defining classes of items, it was not scientifically very useful to present empirical challenges to the test author's claims. (1970:72)

Bormuth's book outlined the objectives and major components of a theory for writing items for achievement tests, drawing on structural linguistics, semantics, and logic. Subsequently, studies began to appear that looked ethnographically at how learners at different age levels actually accomplish assessment tasks. For example, with respect to a teacher's oral questioning of young children, it was suggested that "the interrogator and respondent work together to jointly compose the 'social fact' we call an answer-to-a-question" (Mehan, 1974:44). On the basis of his research efforts, Mehan indicated that it may be misguided to conclude "that a wrong answer is due to a lack of understanding, for the answer may come from an **alternative**, equally valid interpretation."

Assessment instruments that are relied upon to indicate the comprehension level of readers may produce misleading results because of numerous techniques that readers have developed for obtaining correct answers on such instruments without fully or even partially understanding the text. As Fransson (1984) put it, respondents may choose **not** to proceed via the text but rather **around** it. Thus, whereas constructors and users of those tests may have certain assumptions about what processes are called for in order to produce responses on a given test, the actual processes that test takers go through to produce the responses may belie those assumptions. Students may get an item wrong for the right reasons or right for the wrong reasons.

In fact, it may be the case that some of the strategies that the respondents use are inappropriate for the given instances of test taking, or are potentially appropriate but are being used inappropriately in the given instance by the given respondents. For example, respondents may plod laboriously through a text to the multiple-choice questions, only to find that they have forgotten most of what they had read or that they did not focus adequately on those elements being assessed by the questions. For those respondents, the strategy of studying the questions carefully **before** reading the text may have been a more appropriate one.

The purpose of this section is to make a case for considering the processes involved in test taking. The main purpose is to determine the effects of test input upon the test taker—specifically, the processes that the test taker makes use of in order to produce acceptable answers to questions and tasks. There is a concomitant concern about determining the respondent's perceptions of tests before, during, and after taking them.

What Is Meant by Test-Taking Strategies?

Over the last decade, the role of *learner strategies* has gained increasing prominence in language research. Essentially, such strategies refer to mental operations that learners consciously select for use in accomplishing language tasks. The notion of strategy implies an element of selection. Otherwise, the processes would not be considered strategies. *Test-taking strategies* can be viewed simply as learner strategies applied to the area of assessment. Thus, test-taking strategies are instances of language use processes that the respondents have selected and that they are conscious of, at least to some degree.

As in the case of any language use strategies, test-taking strategies themselves are usually not inherently effective or ineffective. Their successful use depends first on whether they are appropriate for the given task. For example, some respondents may find that skimming a given passage to get the gist of it may not be an effective means for preparing a written summary of that text. It may be that the respondent does not have effective skimming skills or that the particular text is not conducive to skimming. Even if the strategy is appropriate for the task, the respondent needs to use it appropriately. So, effective skimming of a text **may** provide adequate preparation for a summary task, while unsystematic skimming of the same text may produce poor results.

At times the choice of strategies constitutes an opting out of the language task at hand (e.g., through a simple matching of look-alike information). At other times, the strategies may constitute shortcuts to arriving at answers (e.g., not reading the text as instructed but simply looking immediately for the answers to the given reading comprehension questions). In the majority of cases, test-taking strategies do not lead to opting out or to the use of shortcuts. Sometimes, quite the contrary holds true. One intermediate Hebrew second-language learner in a study of test-taking strategies in Israel actually produced a written translation into English of a Hebrew reading comprehension passage before he felt ready to respond to questions dealing with that text (Cohen & Aphek, 1979). Needless to say, this practice gave him less time to respond to the questions, so in that respect alone it was somewhat counterproductive.

While early work on *strategic competence* as a component of communicative language use (Canale & Swain, 1980) put the emphasis on "compensatory" strategies—that is, strategies used to compensate or remediate for a lack in some language area, Bachman's theoretical model (1990) for viewing strategic competence includes an assessment component (in our case, language assessment) whereby the respondent sets communicative goals, a planning component whereby the respondent retrieves the relevant items from language competence and plans their use, and an execution component whereby the respondent implements the plan. This framework is modified still further in Bachman and Palmer (in press) so that the assessment component now takes stock only of what is needed and what resources are available. This new framework has a separate goal-setting component that decides what to do and a planning component that decides how to use what there is (as above). In the revised model, the execution component is eliminated from the category of *metacognitive strategies*, since it is seen to involve neurological and physiological processes, not metacognitive ones.

Within this still developing and clearly broader framework for strategic competence, a fair number of test-taking strategies may still be, in fact, compensatory. Respondents often omit material because they do not know it when put on the spot, or produce different material from what they would like to with the hope that it will be acceptable in the given context. They may use lexical avoidance, simplification, or approximation when the exact word escapes them under the pressure of the test or possibly because they simply do not know the word that well or at all.

Thus, in theory, when respondents are asked to perform role play, they may first **assess** the situation, identifying the information that is needed in that context and what they have at their disposal. Then, they may **set goals** for what they will do and actually **plan** how to use what they have in their response. In the Bachman and Palmer model, the retrieval of grammatical, discourse, and sociocultural features from their language competence is part of the planning component.

As is the case with any theoretical model, test takers may make differential use of the components of this model when performing specific test-taking tasks. For example, respondents may assess the situation before starting the role play, or they may **not** do so—either as a general pattern, because of this specific situation, or due to some other factor. The lack of preliminary assessment may result in the violation of certain sociocultural conventions in their response. Likewise, some respondents make goals, and others do not. There are those who plan out their utterances before producing them while others would just start talking on an "on-line" basis. Recent research involving the use of verbal report directly after role-play interaction is beginning to obtain data regarding the extent of assessment and planning actually taking place before the execution of role-play tasks calling for apologies, complaints, and requests (Cohen & Olshtain, 1993).

Means for Investigating Test-Taking Strategies

Many of the strategies that learners use in responding to assessment instruments are the same strategies that they use for language learning in general. Numerous research methods have been used to access and describe these strategies. The methods have included

1. Questionnaires and interviews (e.g., Cohen & Robbins, 1976; Oxford & Crookall, 1989)
2. Observation schedules (e.g., FOCUS; Fanselow, 1977)
3. Performance analysis—for example, identification of communication strategies from speech protocols (Faerch & Kasper, 1983) and identification of reading strategies from miscue analysis (Goodman, 1988)
4. Language assessment instruments—for example, cloze testing for which completion of each blank presumes the use of a given strategy (Homburg & Spaan, 1981; Bachman, 1985; Jonz, 1990)

These methods have often produced indications or clues about the strategies that learners use rather than instances of actual strategy use, since what is usually obtained is some language **product** rather than information regarding the **processes** used to arrive at that product. Hence, researchers have relied to a certain degree on their own intuitions in their attempt to describe the strategies used by learners to accomplish such classroom tasks as producing an oral summary of a reading text or writing a written summary of that same text.

In an effort to gain greater access to strategy data, there has been an increased use of verbal report measures. Verbal report measures have been found to provide a viable means for obtaining empirical evidence regarding language learning and/or test-taking strategies in the areas of

1. Reading (Hosenfeld, 1977; Cohen, 1984, in press; Feldman & Stemmer, 1987; Stemmer, 1991; Gordon, 1987; Nevo, 1989; and Anderson, 1991)

2. Communication (e.g., Poulisse, Bongaerts, & Kellerman, 1986; Poulisse, 1989)
3. Translation (Borsch, 1986; Faerch & Kasper, 1986; Gerloff, 1987; Krings, 1987)

Early Verbal Report by Readers on their Reading Strategies

Before focusing on verbal report as it refers specifically to test-taking strategies, let us take a brief look at how this technique originally came into the second-language-acquisition field. It started with a growing interest in how reading strategies affect the successful or unsuccessful solution to problems of comprehension. Early process research done with adult native readers of English (Aighes et al., 1977) showed that the subjects only partially understood many words and phrases. They were found to form hypotheses about possible meanings, reread previous portions, jump ahead, consult outside sources, and make a written record in order to understand what they were reading.

Research on the reading strategies of **nonnative** readers was perhaps first conducted by Hosenfeld (1977). She developed a system for recording each strategy that the learners use as they read. The following are some of these strategies:

1. Analyzing
2. Translating
3. Attending to grammar
4. Using sentence-level context
5. Using passage-level context
6. Stopping at an unknown word
7. Skipping an unimportant/inconsequential word or phrase
8. Looking up a word in the back of the book or in a side gloss
9. Viewing the importance of words equally or differently
10. Going back
11. Sounding out a word

Hosenfeld found that, from this introspective, case-study type of analysis, a profile of successful foreign-language readers emerged. Such readers keep the content of the passage in mind as they read, read in broad phrases, skip words viewed as unimportant, skip unknown words and use the remaining words as clues to their meaning, and look up words only as a last resort (Hosenfeld, 1977).

In a subsequent study, Hosenfeld (1979) found that a ninth-grade student who had studied French since sixth grade and who was in the upper tenth of her class was nonetheless a surprisingly poor reader (as assessed through *introspective translation*[1] of a relatively simple text). The student was able to perform the typical classroom tasks, such as reading aloud, contributing to group discussion, and answering textbook questions, without ever having the need to read on her own. Hosenfeld had this reader compare her reading strategies to a protocol for a *contextual guesser* (a successful type of reader, according to Hosenfeld's findings). The ninth grader was then asked to list the differences between what she did and what the contextual guesser does (which is to keep the story or theme in mind while reading, check to see if words make sense in context, and not give up along the way). After this "discovery" phase of finding differences between the strategies that she used and that the idealized successful reader used, there was a practical phase in which the student tried out on a new passage strategies that she had not been using and that she thought might help her. The results showed marked improvement. In more recent years a number of other researchers have conducted studies of strategies used in reading in a second or foreign language (e.g., Block [1986], Serrano [1986], Cavalcanti [1987], and Sarig [1987]).

The Use of Verbal Report for Describing Test-Taking Strategies

Issues Regarding Verbal Report

In this section, let us look at some of the controversy surrounding the use of verbal report measures, since awareness of the problems can help us to avoid them.

The Choice of Language for the Verbal Report

Verbal reports are often collected in the native language of the respondents in order to eliminate the problem of the nonnatives' proficiency in the target language interfering with the reporting process. However, a potential problem could arise when respondents think through a task in the **target** (second or foreign) language but report on their cognitive processing in their **first** or yet another language. The respondents may well be *recoding* the information (i.e., having to translate their thoughts across languages). This recoding process may in turn cause information to get lost due to limits of memory capacity as well as other factors, such as accuracy at translation of thoughts. This reporting with recoding (especially in on-line self-revelation) may alter the original thought processes more than when no recoding takes place (Faerch & Kasper, 1987:19). A compromise approach would be to train the respondents to use whichever language feels most appropriate for verbal report at the given instant. In this case, it may be beneficial for the investigator to be bilingual as well because the respondents **may** refrain from using their native language if they feel that the investigator will not understand them.[2]

The Intrusive Nature of Verbal Report

Investigators also need to be wary of the intrusive effects that verbal report methods can have. In reading tasks, for instance, immediate retrospection may distort the process if the readers read more closely than normal, read sentence by sentence, or spend extra time concentrating on the additional cognitive and metacognitive tasks required by the verbal report itself (Mann, 1982). The type of instructions given, the characteristics of the participating subjects (some more informative than others), the types of material used in collecting protocols, and the nature of the data analysis may also influence the outcomes and should be carefully considered in the design of a study (Olson, Duffy, & Mack, 1984).

Countering the Intrusive Effects of Verbal Report

Steps can be taken to reduce the intrusive effects of the intervention. One is to streamline the reporting in the form of short answers or through a checklist, as Nevo (1989) did in a study of test-taking strategies used in the assessment of reading comprehension. She prepared a checklist of fifteen strategies, each appearing with a brief description and a label meant to promote rapid processing of the checklist. The following are the first three entries from that checklist:

1. *Background knowledge*: general knowledge outside the text called up by the reading in order to cope with written material
2. *Guessing*: blind guessing not based on any particular rationale
3. *Returning to the passage*: returning to the text to look for the correct answer after reading the questions and multiple-choice alternatives

Verbal Report as a Reliable Measure

Whereas the reliability of mentalistic measures has been questioned in comparison with behavioristic measures, research has demonstrated that verbal reports, elicited with care and interpreted with full understanding of the circumstances under which they were obtained, are in fact a valuable and a thoroughly reliable source of information about cognitive processes (Ericsson & Simon, 1980). In a recent study on test-taking strategies in listening comprehension tests, for example, Buck (1990) found that structured verbal reports elicited through an interview schedule were a more reliable means of obtaining immediate retrospective accounts of conscious test-taking processes than was unstructured verbal reporting. As to the validity of the method, Lieberman (1979) reports that in a number of settings, subjects' reports of their hypotheses and strategies have proved to be highly correlated with their subsequent behavior—and are often the most accurate predictors available.

Thus, while we could try to design assessment items and procedures that presumably **require** the use of certain strategies (e.g., cloze items calling for anaphoric reference) and then attempt to observe what respondents do during these assessment tasks, a potentially more effective means of describing test-taking strategies is through collecting verbal report data from the respondents, either while the items are being answered, just afterwards, or at some later time. Innovative research on test taking has helped to refine the research methodology for tapping such test-taking strategies.

For example, studies have found that it is possible to collect introspective and retrospective data from students just after they have answered each item on a multiple-choice reading comprehension instrument (e.g., Anderson, 1991). Several such studies will be discussed below. The approaches reported in previous work had involved at most a request of respondents after they had finished a subtest or group of items to reflect back on the strategies that they used in arriving at answers to those items, producing data of somewhat more questionable reliability and validity (Cohen, 1984).

Let us now consider research findings with respect to test-taking strategies on two more *indirect* assessment formats, namely, answering multiple-choice items and filling in a cloze test, and then consider strategies for three more *direct* formats, namely, summarizing, answering open-ended questions, and writing an essay. The focus will also be on tests of reading and writing skills. The purpose for reviewing the literature here is to help give the reader a sense of the empirical evidence regarding test-taking strategies. We will end with several suggestions that may lead to more effective test taking.

Indirect Assessment Formats

Indirect formats for assessment—that is, those formats which do not reflect real-world tasks—may prompt the use of strategies solely for the purpose of coping with the assessment format. Let us look at two such formats, multiple-choice and cloze, and at some of the research findings regarding strategies used in taking such assessment instruments, both in the native and the second language.

Multiple Choice

Given that the multiple-choice format is at best problematic (see Chapter 7), it can be helpful to learn more about what such items are actually assessing. Verbal report techniques can have a role in identifying test-taking strategies with respect to a given instrument in a given test administration with given respondents. For example, what was the role of guessing or simple matching of stems with alternatives? To what extent do items meant to assess one thing actually assess another (e.g., a grammar item that also tests lexical knowledge)? To what extent do respondents eliminate choices because their world knowledge tells them that those choices are absurd, impossible, or unlikely?

Research Notes

In this section, let us look at some of the studies that have considered multiple-choice items.

Studies with Young Native Speakers

An early investigation of a standardized test of English reading for native speakers, the Cooperative Primary Test Form 12A (Educational Testing Service, 1969), was conducted by MacKay (1974). By sitting down with individual first-grade learners and going over each item separately, MacKay found that learners did not necessarily link the stem and the answer in the same way that the test constructor assumed was correct. MacKay determined that the test had a somewhat arbitrary frame of reference. He found that real information about what children were using as reasoning was irretrievable from the test. For example, he noted that pictures were sometimes ambiguous. In an item requiring the student to link the expression "The bird built his own house" to a picture, MacKay illustrated how a student chose the right picture for the wrong reason. This student chose a nest of twigs with eggs in the middle over a wooden birdhouse because he claimed that some big birds could not fit in the hole of the birdhouse. The student missed the element that people, not birds, are responsible for building wooden bird houses with perches.

MacKay also gave an example of an item missed for the wrong reasons. The statement "The cat has been out in the rain again" had to be linked to one of three pictures that looked roughly like these:

The student perceived the dotted wallpaper as snow and decided that this picture was of the exterior of the house. Thus, he gave the dripping raincoat as the correct answer. Once the child had perceived the wallpaper as snow and thus had eliminated the third picture, his selection of the first picture, the dripping raincoat, rather than the second, was perfectly reasonable—even though cats do not wear raincoats.

Haney and Scott (1987) found patterns similar to those reported by MacKay with regard to the sometimes dubious fit between second- and third-grade children getting the item right or wrong and their verbal report on whether or not they had applied the skill meant to be assessed. For example, they produced unusual and perceptive interpretations of questions. One of these interpretations resulted in the wrong answer in the item "Which needs least water?" (followed by pictures of a cactus, a potted plant, and a cabbage). The respondent answered "cabbage" because it had been picked and therefore needed no water at all, while the expected correct answer was "cactus." A pupil's incorrect interpretation resulted in the right answer in an item asking why Eva liked to watch TV. The respondent reported personalizing the item and responding according to why **she** liked to watch TV, in this case producing the correct answer without relating to Eva at all.

Answering Items Through Shortcuts

With respect to older and nonnative respondents, the patterns are somewhat similar, as in a study of forty college ESL respondents using retrospective verbal report to gain insights about test-taking strategies (Larson [1981] in Cohen [1984]). The students were requested to describe how they arrived at answers during a ten-item multiple-choice test based on a 400-word reading passage. Seventeen students met with the author of the test in groups of two or three within twenty-four hours after the test, while twenty-three students met in groups of five or six four days after taking the test. The investigator found that the respondents used the following strategies:

1. They stopped reading alternatives when they got to the one that seemed correct to them
2. They matched material from the passage with material in the item stem and in the alternatives (e.g., when the answer was in the same sentence with the material used to write the stem)
3. They preferred a surface-structure reading of the text in their responding to items, rather than using an approach calling for more in-depth reading and inferencing (Larson [1981] in Cohen [1984]).

This superficial matching would sometimes result in the right answer. One example was as follows:

5. The fact that there is only one university in Filanthropia might be used to show why . . .
   a) education is compulsory through age 13.
   b) many people work in the fishing industry.
   c) 20 per cent of the population is illiterate.
   d) the people are relatively happy and peaceful.

Students were able to identify c as the correct answer by noticing that this information appeared earlier in the same sentence with the information that reappeared in the item stem:

> The investigating travel agency researchers discovered that the illiteracy rate of the people is 20 per cent, which is perhaps reflective of the fact that there is only one university in

Filanthropia, and that education is compulsory, or required, only through age 10.

They assumed that this was the correct answer without understanding the item or the word *illiterate*. They were right.

In another example, students did not have to look in the text for surface matches. They were able to match directly between the stem and the correct alternative:

2) The increased foreign awareness of Filanthropia has . . .
   a) resulted in its relative poverty.
   b) led to a tourist bureau investigation.
   c) created the main population centers.
   d) caused its extreme isolation.

Students associated *foreign* in the stem with *tourist* in option **b**, without understanding the test item.

It was also found that more reasoned analysis of the alternatives—e.g., making calculated inferences about vocabulary items—would lead to incorrect answers. The following item provided an example of this:

4) The most highly developed industry in Filanthropia is . . .
   a) oil.
   b) fishing.
   c) timber.
   d) none of the above.

This item referred to the following portion of the text:

. . . most [dollars] are earned in the fishing industry. . . . In spite of the fact that there are resources other than fish, such as timber in the forest of the foothills, agriculture on the upland plateaus, and, of course, oil, these latter are highly underdeveloped.

One student read the stem phrase *most highly developed industry* and reasoned that this meant "technologically developed" and so referred to the *oil industry*. He was relying on expectations based on general knowledge rather than on a careful reading of the text. The point is that his was a reasoned guess, not that of, say, surface matching, as in the previous example.

Answering Items Without Access to the Source Text

In an effort to investigate the extent to which multiple-choice questions are answered on the basis of prior knowledge of the topic and general vocabulary knowledge, thirty-two intermediate and twenty-five advanced Israeli EFL students were given a title and just the first paragraph of a passage appearing on the previous year's exemption examination, and were then asked to answer twelve questions dealing with the portion of text **not** provided. Two weeks later they were given the text in full, along with the questions, and were once again asked to respond (Israel [1982] in Cohen [1984]). The rate of success on the multiple-choice items was still surprisingly high—49% for the advanced group and 41% for the intermediates. These results were far better than the 25% success rate that would be expected on the basis of change alone. (These results are also consistent with those for native English readers, where the results were far better than chance alone; Tuinman, 1973-4; Fowler & Kroll, 1978). When the students were given the test with the complete passage and questions two weeks later, the advanced group now scored 77% and the intermediates 62%. The score necessary for exemption from further EFL study was 60%. The fact that the average performance on the test was low even when the passage was provided makes the results without the passage that much more striking.

Lower Proficiency Linked to More-Local Processing

In a research study by Gordon (1987) with thirty tenth-grade EFL students, of whom fifteen were high-proficiency and fifteen low-proficiency readers, respondents were asked to verbalize thoughts while finding answers to open-ended and multiple-choice questions. Gordon found that answers to test questions did not necessarily reflect comprehension of the text. Both types of reading comprehension questions were regarded by the respondents as "mini" reading comprehension tests. With respect to test-taking strategies, the low-proficiency students tended to process information at the local (sentence/word) level, not relating isolated bits of information to the whole text. They used such individual word-centered strategies as:

1. Matching words in the multiple-choice alternatives to words in the text
2. Copying words out of the text
3. Indulging in word-for-word translation
4. Formulating global impressions of text content on the basis of key words or isolated lexical items in the text or in the test questions

On the other hand, the high-proficiency students were seen to comprehend the text at a global level—predicting information accurately in context and using lexical and structural knowledge to cope with linguistic difficulties.

Checklist for Quick Report of Strategy Use

In an effort to provide immediate verbal report data, Nevo (1989) designed a testing format to allow for immediate feedback after each item. She developed a response-strategy checklist, based on the test-taking strategies that have been described in the literature and on her intuitions about strategies respondents were likely to select. A pilot study had shown that it was difficult to obtain useful feedback on an item-by-item basis without a checklist to jog the respondents' memories of possible strategies.

Nevo's checklist included fifteen strategies, each appearing with a brief description and a label meant to promote rapid processing of the checklist. She administered a multiple-choice reading comprehension test in Hebrew L1 and French as a foreign language to forty-two tenth graders, and requested that they indicate for each of the ten questions on each test the strategy that was most instrumental in their arriving at an answer as well as that which was the second most instrumental. The responses were kept anonymous to encourage students to report exactly what they did, rather than what they thought they were supposed to report.

Students were able to record the two strategies that they considered most instrumental in obtaining each answer. The study indicated that respondents transferred test-taking strategies from first language to foreign language. The researcher also identified the strategies that were selected in instances where the respondents got the items right. The selection of strategies that were inappropriate for the given item or the inappropriate use of potentially appropriate strategies was more prevalent in the taking of the foreign-language test than in the taking of the L1 version. The main finding in this study was that it was possible to obtain feedback from respondents about their strategy use after each item on an assessment instrument if a checklist was provided for quick labeling of the processing strategies employed. Furthermore, the respondents reported benefiting greatly from the opportunity to become aware of how they approached reading assessment instruments. They reported having been largely unaware of their strategies prior to this study.

The Effect of the Questions on the Choice of Strategy

Another study of test-taking strategies among nonnatives revealed that respondents used certain strategies differently, depending on the type of question that was being asked. For example, the strategies of "trying to match the stem with the text" and "guessing" were reported more frequently for inference-type questions than for the other question types, such as direct statement or main idea. Respondents reported using the strategy of "paraphrasing" more often in responding to questions involving a direct statement than those involving the main idea or inference (Anderson et al., 1991).

That study originated as a doctoral dissertation in which twenty-eight native speakers of Spanish studying at the Texas Intensive English Program in Austin took three measures of reading comprehension: a reading comprehension subtest from a test of language skills, a measure of ability to read college-level textbook prose (Textbook Reading Profile), and a second form of the standardized reading comprehension test (Anderson, 1991). After the first two tasks, the participants provided retrospective think-aloud protocols describing the strategies that they used while reading the textbook material and while answering the comprehension questions. The respondents also provided think-aloud protocols along with the final test. This was perhaps the first study of its kind to compare performance on equated forms of an exam, with one administered under standard test conditions and the other administered in conjunction with a verbal report.

The data were categorized into a list of forty-seven processing strategies, and these strategies were then grouped into five categories:

1. *Strategies for supervising strategy use*—for example, stating failure to understand a portion of text or confirming an inference
2. *Support strategies*—for example, skipping unknown words or skimming reading material for a general understanding
3. *Paraphrase strategies*—for example, translating a word or phrase into the L1 or breaking lexical items into parts
4. *Strategies for establishing coherence in text*—for example, reading ahead or using background knowledge
5. *Test-taking strategies*—for example, looking for the answers in chronological order in the passage or selecting an alternative answer through deductive reasoning

In the follow-up phase of the research, data from the participants' retrospective think-aloud protocols of their reading and test-taking strategies were combined with data from a content analysis and an item analysis to obtain a truly convergent measure of test validation (Anderson et al., 1991). The content analysis of the reading-comprehension passages and questions comprised the test designer's analysis and one based on an outside taxonomy, and the item-performance data included item difficulty and discrimination. This study was one of the first to combine both think-aloud protocols and more commonly used types of information on test content and test performance in order to examine the test validation in a convergent manner.

Another recent study corroborated earlier test-taking strategy research in that examinees were seen to focus on the search for answers to test questions. The respondents in the study paid little attention to strategies that provided an overall understanding of the native-language passage (Farr, Pritchard, & Smitten, 1990:223). The investigators concluded that a reading comprehension test is a special kind of reading task, one where skilled examinees do the following:

1. Contemplate answer choices
2. Use background knowledge
3. Weigh choices
4. Skim and reread portions of the reading selections
5. Hold off making choices until they feel confident about an answer choice

The researchers suggested that the types of questions following the passage will determine whether students' reading focuses only on the surface meaning of the text.

Test-Taking Strategies and Test-Wiseness

Emerging from the various studies on multiple-choice instruments of reading comprehension (presented in "Research Notes", pages 128–136) is a series of strategies that respondents may use at one point or another to arrive at answers to test questions. Whether these strategies are of benefit depends to a large extent upon when and how effectively they are used. Figure 5.1 provides a composite list of some of the more salient test-taking strategies that appear in one or more of the studies mentioned above.

Figure 5.1

Strategies for Taking a Multiple-Choice Reading-Comprehension Test

1. Read the passage first, and make a mental note of where different kinds of information are located.
2. Read the questions a second time for clarification.
3. Return to the passage to look for the answer.

(continues)

Figure 5.1 continued

4. Look for the portion of the text that the question refers to, and then look there for clues to the answer.

5. Look for answers to questions in chronological order in the text.

6. Read the questions first so that the reading of the text is directed at finding answers to those questions.

7. Try to produce your own answer to the question before you look at the options that are provided in the test.

8. Use the process of elimination—that is, select a choice not because you are sure that it is the correct answer, but because the other choices do not seem reasonable, because they seem similar or overlapping, or because their meaning is not clear to you.

9. Look for an option that seems to deviate from the others by being special, different, or conspicuous.

10. Select a choice that is longer/shorter than the others.

11. Take advantage of clues appearing in other items in order to answer the item under consideration.

12. Take into consideration the position of the option among the choices (a, b, c, or d).

13. Select the option because it appears to have a word or phrase from the passage in it—possibly a key word.

14. Select the option because it has a word or phrase that also appears in the question.

15. Postpone dealing with an item or selecting a given option until later.

16. Make an educated guess—for example, use background knowledge or extra-textual knowledge in making the guess.

17. Budget your time wisely.

18. Change your responses when appropriate—for example, in the case where new clues are discovered in another item.

For many years now, educational measurement texts have warned constructors of multiple-choice tests about writing items that are giveaways for test-wise students. For instance, Ebel and Frisbie have a section describing, among other things, multiple-choice items that are easy for the test-wise respondent (1986:170-176). However, regardless of how many warnings are given to test constructors regarding multiple-choice items, there will always be multiple-choice items that are giveaways for test-wise, native-speaking respondents.

While certain assumptions about test-wiseness have been made with respect to native speakers, little attention has been paid to nonnatives in this regard. For example, what extent are nonnatives familiar with the multiple-choice rubric? Methods of assessment that Americans take for granted may not be so widespread elsewhere in the world.[3]

Research Notes

A recent study sought to explicitly train ESL respondents in test-wiseness on multiple-choice tests and to assess the effects of such training. Allan (1992) developed a measure of test-wiseness for ESL students that included thirty-three items, with each item having only one test-wiseness cue and no items meant to be answerable on the basis of prior knowledge. The instructions specified that although the test contained vocabulary that the students might never have seen before, it was still possible to answer the questions successfully by using skill and initiative. There were four types of test-wiseness cues:

1. *Stem-option cues*—in which it was possible to match information from the stem with information in the correct option
2. *Grammatical cues*—where only one alternative matched the stem grammatically
3. *Similar option cues*—where several distractors could be eliminated because they essentially said the same thing
4. *Item giveaways*—where another item already gave away the information

The test was administered to fifty-one first-year polytechnic students in Hong Kong. One subgroup was asked to provide brief written explanations for their answers to each question. Since the mean was well above the chance level, the conclusion was that the test was measuring test-wiseness. But since there was apparently some guessing and since certain items proved not to be content free for all students, threats to the test's validity remained. Furthermore, the reliabilities for the stem-option and similar option items were low, suggesting that these cues were only sometimes recognized by respondents or that only some of the items in the subscales were measuring those test-wise phenomena. Despite the limitations of the study, it marks an important avenue for further investigation, both for improving test construction and for providing training in test-taking strategies.

Cloze Testing

Is Cloze Assessing
Macro-Level Language Processing?

The traditional format for the cloze test, namely, a passage with every *n*th word deleted, is probably more controversial than the traditional reading passage plus multiple-choice questions. (See Chapter 7 for more on the cloze test.) The controversy makes the instrument a perfect candidate for verbal report explorations that determine what the instrument is actually measuring. While the reliability of a given cloze test may be high because the individual items are interrelated, the test's validity as a measure of reading ability at the macro level has been questioned. While some researchers have claimed that completing the blanks successfully on a cloze passage does call for reading comprehension at the macro level (see, for example, Chihara, Oller, Weaver, & Chávez-Oller [1977], Chávez-Oller, Chihara, Weaver, & Oller [1985], Jonz [1990], Oller & Jonz [forthcoming]), other researchers have suggested that these claims are overstated. They contend that some or many of the blanks can be filled in successfully using micro, sentence/word-level reading skills rather than macro, discourse-level reading (Alderson, 1983; Klein-Braley, 1981; Bachman, 1985; Lado, 1986). Verbal report studies of respondents taking cloze tests have tended to corroborate the latter findings, with numerous items answerable by means of local, micro-level strategies (e.g., Cohen, 1984).

Intuiting Response Patterns on the Cloze

A few studies of strategies in filling in cloze tests have examined correct/incorrect completion of deletions explicitly intended to assess certain response patterns:

1. Processing within the clause
2. Processing across clauses within the same sentence
3. Processing across sentences within the text
4. Bringing in extra-textual material in order to respond

Research Notes

In order to indirectly investigate strategy use in completing a cloze passage, Homburg and Spaan (1981) administered a rational-deletion cloze with twenty-three blanks to thirty-nine EFL subjects from three levels. One of four strategies was intuited to be necessary in finding a correct word for each of the blanks: recognizing parallelism, being sentence-bound, reading ahead, or reading backward. Success at items calling for "forward reading" (cataphora) was significantly associated with success at understanding the main idea.

Verbal Report Studies of the Cloze Test

Verbal report studies on strategies for taking cloze tests have shown that perhaps only a quarter of nonnative respondents read the entire cloze passage before responding (Emanuel and Hashkes & Koffman in Cohen, 1984). Even if statistical analyses of a series of cloze tests demonstrate their macro-level potential (e.g., Jonz [1990], Oller & Jonz [forthcoming]), the verbal report research on strategies used in taking cloze tests would suggest that such assessment instruments may lend themselves to local-level reading as opposed to global reading, depending on the passage and the characteristics of the readers. Furthermore, such tests are more likely to assess local-level reading when they are in a foreign language (see, for example, MacLean & d'Anglejan, 1986).

Research Notes

A case study shed some light on the issue of how easy it is to read through a foreign-language cloze text before completing it, as is often requested in the instructions (Kleiman, Cavalcanti, Terzi, & Ratto, 1986). Verbal protocol data provided by a seventh-grade Brazilian girl filling in two cloze passages (one as a warm-up and the other as the exercise in Portuguese L1) indicated that the respondent was preoccupied with local clues from isolated elements of text for at least half the exercise. What emerged was that she did not use macro-level clues until she had completed a substantial number of blanks on the cloze. In other words, it is easier to read the cloze passage once it has been partially completed and the respondent has some idea of what it is about, much as a child may have an easier time of connecting numbered dots once the picture that the dots are forming becomes clearer.

In verbal report studies, it was found that nearly 20% of the EFL respondents did not use the preceding or following sentence for clues to blanks but rather guessed on the basis of the immediate context (Emanuel and Hashkes & Koffman in Cohen, 1984). Another study involved eleven Fijian sixth graders at three proficiency levels of EFL who provided verbal reports as they took three cloze passages representing different text types (Mangubhai, 1990). The researcher found that while the less skillful cloze takers did not check the appropriateness of the word in the passage, the more skillful cloze takers did the following:

1. They looked both at the immediate and at the larger context to help fill in the blanks.
2. They were more likely to evaluate choices for correctness.
3. They referred more often to prior knowledge.
4. They rephrased sentences more often to get at the meaning.
5. When necessary, they recalled knowledge of the passage and any other prior knowledge that could be of use.

A comparative study of native and nonnative respondents on the cloze test in English found that for natives, cloze taking was primarily executed at the whole-text level, while for nonnatives it was a more localized endeavor. Furthermore, cloze-taking ability was found to be **the** most important factor in taking a cloze test in a second language, thus indicating that there are skills to be learned in order to succeed at this kind of test (Turner, 1989).

Consistent with these findings for English-speakers in the U.S., a study involving eighteen Hebrew-speaking fifth graders at three levels of reading (high, intermediate, and low) found that the better readers were more likely to use macro-level schemata and strategies in completing the cloze (Kesar, 1990). Nonetheless, respondents at all three levels of reading proficiency were found to favor micro-level reading at the sentence level on a rational-deletion cloze test. An analysis of think-aloud protocols yielded at least twenty-six different strategies, which were then grouped:

1. Micro-level strategies
   a. word-level/part of sentence
   b. sentence-level
2. Discourse or macro-level categories
   a. intersentential level
   b. whole-text level
   c. extra-textual level
   d. metacognitive level
   e. other

More-Direct Assessment Formats

The test-taking strategies involved in the more direct formats, such as summarizing, open-ended responses to questions, and essay writing, have yet to be fully investigated through verbal report methods. Since the assessment of summaries and essays depends on judgments made by raters, there is a concomitant need for research on strategies used in doing the ratings, such as the recent work conducted by Hamp-Lyons (1989), Connor and Carrell

(1993), and Vaughan (1991). This section will discuss several of the verbal report studies that have been undertaken with direct formats.

Summarizing

Whereas more direct formats for assessment, such as text summarizing, allow for the use of more non-test-like language use strategies, results on such measures are still influenced by test-wiseness. As long as the task is part of a test, students are bound to use strategies they would not use under non-test conditions. In the case of a summary task, the respondent is most likely summarizing a text for a reader who already has a notion of what the summary should look like. In the real world, we usually summarize a text for our own future use or for the benefit of someone who has not read it. For example, it has been found that respondents spend more time reading the text to be summarized than they do in writing a careful, coherent summary. Furthermore, they lift material intact from the text, and when in doubt they prefer to be verbose rather than terse, hoping that they stand a better chance of covering the important points that way.

Research Notes

Test-Wise Shortcuts in the Writing of Summaries

Case-study research concerning the strategies used by respondents in producing summaries as assessment tasks found that respondents use various shortcut measures (Cohen, in press). One strategy was to lift material directly from the passage being summarized, rather than restating it at a higher level of abstraction or generality. In such cases, it was not clear whether the respondent understood the material or not. Furthermore, when respondents were in doubt about whether material should be included or deleted, they seemed to include it (particularly in the case of less proficient students), with the assumption that a summary that ran longer would probably be preferred by the raters to one that was too terse. The study found that the respondents spent more time on their strategies for reading the texts to be summarized than they did on producing their summaries. Not surprisingly, the summaries were not very coherent or polished. In her case study of an Israeli college student summarizing a series of L1 and EFL texts, Sarig (1993) also found her subject to spend more time (two thirds of the time) on the reading of the texts than on producing the summaries.

Supplying the Summarizers with Strategies

Another study on summarizing was conducted to determine the effects of a mini-training to promote the use of test-taking strategies (Cohen, 1993). The main purpose of the study was to determine the effects of specific guidelines in the taking and rating of tests of summarizing ability—tests in which respondents first read source texts and then provide written summaries as a measure of their reading comprehension level as well as of their writing ability. The study also looked at interrater agreement regarding the rating of specific ideas within the summaries. This study was designed on the basis of insights gained from previous verbal report research on summarization (Cohen, in press) and did not include verbal report measures.

The subjects for the study were sixty-three native-Hebrew-speaking students from the Seminar Hakibbutzim Teacher Training College in Tel Aviv. Twenty-six were from two high-proficiency EFL classes, and thirty-seven were from two intermediate EFL classes. Four raters assessed the students' summaries in the study. Five texts (two in L1 and three in EFL) were selected for the study, with each intermediate and advanced EFL student asked to write a Hebrew-language summary for two L1 and two EFL texts. Two sets of instructions were developed. One version was "guided" with specific instructions on how to read the texts and how to write the summaries. The other version had the typical "minimal" instructions (see Figure 5.2). The scoring keys for the texts were based on the summaries of nine Hebrew-speaking and nine English-speaking experts. All sixty-three respondents summarized the first Hebrew text, fifty-three summarized the second Hebrew text, and on the average, slightly more than a third of the students wrote Hebrew L1 summaries for the EFL texts.

The study demonstrated that whereas the guided instructions had a mixed effect on the summarizing of native-language texts, they had a somewhat positive effect on summarizing of foreign-language texts in the native language. In other words, supplying respondents with summarization strategies was seen to be more beneficial when the task was more difficult—that is, when the reading and the

Figure 5.2

Unguided and Guided Instructions for Summarization Tasks
Translation (from Hebrew) of the
Traditional Brief Instructions:
Reading the Text and Writing a Summary of It
Before you are four texts, two in Hebrew and two in English. You are to read each one so as to write a summary of it.
Instructions for Writing the Summary (in Hebrew)
1. Write briefly: the length of the summary is to be 80 words for the first passage and 120 words for the second.
2. Write a draft first, and then copy it over legibly.

Translation of the Elaborated Instructions:
Reading Text and Writing a Summary of the Text
Before you are four texts, two in Hebrew and two in English.
Instructions for Reading
Read each text so as to extract the most important points from it, that is, those points that contain the key sentences (for the given paragraph), or those points that the reader of the summary will be interested in reading.
Instructions for Writing the Summary (in Hebrew)
1. Reduce the information to main points only: avoid the inclusion of redundant information. Including this information will detract from your score.
2. Write briefly: the length of the summary is to be 80 words for the first passage and 120 words for the second.
3. Write the summary as a single passage: use connecting words to link the points together.
4. Do not translate literally: write the summary in your own words.
5. Write a draft first, and then copy it over legibly.

(from Cohen, 1993)

---

preparation of the summary were based on a foreign-language text. Actually, the guided instructions were seen to be both helpful and detrimental in the summarizing of texts: in some cases, they assisted respondents in finding the key elements to summarize, and in other cases they appear to have dissuaded the respondent from including details that in fact proved to be essential in the experts' opinion upon which the rating key was based. Thus, more empirical research is needed on the differential effects of explicit instructions on this kind of task.

Open-Ended Questions

Similar to the situation with summarization tasks, respondents may be prone to copy material directly from a text for use in an open-ended response. Hence, raters may not know whether the respondent in fact understands the material, and furthermore, such copying may produce linguistically awkward responses. This procedure of lifting material has been documented in verbal report research.

Research Notes

In a study of nineteen native, English-speaking, college-level learners of Hebrew L2, the learners provided retrospective verbal reports on how they had arrived at answers during their final exam, taken the previous week. The respondents reported having lifted material intact from an item stimulus or from a passage when producing their written responses (Cohen & Aphek, 1979).

This process of lifting material in an unanalyzed fashion resulted in two types of errors in this study. First, Hebrew verb forms were incorrectly inflected for (a) gender,[4] (b) person, (c) number, and/or (d) tense. Generally speaking, if students did not know the correct verb form, they would use the infinitive, take a form from a tense that they knew, take one inflectional ending and generalize it across person and gender, or take an inappropriate tense from the stimulus and simply add the personal prefix.

Secondly, verbs possessing the correct three-letter root were used, but they were part of an incorrect conjugation. Hebrew has five conjugations, in many cases the same root (often three letters) will be used to generate a verb in all of these conjugations. As an example of the respondents' confusion regarding conjugations, take the following: when given the form *metapsim* ("they climb") and asked to give the third-person plural past tense *tipsu* ("they climbed"), a fair number of students wrote *metapsu*. The students were, in fact, making erroneous visual and auditory analogies to some other conjugation, since the present-tense form (*metapsim*) is close to the *hitpael* conjugation in form. In other words, the learners may have thought the verb form was *mit-apsim*, the present tense prefix *mit* + root *a-p-as*, as opposed to the present tense prefix *me* + root *t-p-s* for *metapsim*.

Another strategy that these learners used in their efforts to get by on open-ended questions was simply to use prepackaged, unanalyzed material and combine it with analyzed forms. For example, given that Hebrew prepositions such as *mi* ("from") can be prefixed to the object of the preposition through elision (*mi* + *tsad* ["side"] = *mitsad* ["from a side"]), one respondent reported using this form as a prepackaged whole and then affixing another preposition to it: *bemitsad* ("on from a side") while intending "on a side" (Cohen & Aphek, 1979).

Essay Writing

The interpretation of essay topics is a problem that may be partly the result of students' inadequate attention to instructions. Usually, a prompt for the essay is presented in the form of a mini-text that the respondents need to understand and operationalize. Ruth and Murphy (1984) noted cases where students have misinterpreted words in the prompt, such as interpreting the word *profit* as *prophet*, thus shifting the meaning of the topic entirely. Perhaps of greater consequence are the strategies that respondents use or do not use to perceive the actual and sometime covert nature of the task. Ruth and Murphy give the example of a supposed friendly letter topic wherein what is **actually** called for is a response at a **higher** level of performance than would be reflected in an authentic friendly letter. In other words, the respondent is expected to write at a more formal level since the use of informal language and ungrammatical forms would be penalized.

The caution that Ruth and Murphy would have for the respondent is to be extra careful in interpreting topic-setting mini-texts. In the age of electronic mail, where writers may not have the ability on their e-mail system to go back and edit the texts that they have generated, informal letters are often letters that are devoid of any signs of editing and are replete with grammatical and mechanical errors.

Following Instructions

A crucial aspect of test taking for which strategy data have become available is the following of instructions. At issue is the extent to which respondents listen to or read the instructions on the test or subtest that they are taking and the extent to which they actually pay attention to them in completing the tasks. In investigating the process of test taking, we need to give careful consideration to the instructions the respondents attend to in accomplishing the particular testing tasks. The literature provides us with a list of "shoulds" associated with instructions:

1. **Brief**, but explicit; complete and unambiguous.
2. Specific about the form the answers are to take—if possible, **presenting a sample question and answer.**
3. Informative as to the **value of each item** and section of the assessment instrument, the **time** allowed for each subtest and/ or for the total instrument, and whether speed is a factor.
4. Explicit about whether guessing counts negatively (Krypsin & Feldhusen, 1974).

How Instructions Appear
and What Respondents Do with Them

In reality, classroom test items may not be accompanied by an explicit set of instructions. Sample questions are often lacking because the assumption is that the students know how to perform the tasks. And even if explicit instructions and examples are given, there is no certainty that students will read and understand them.

In fact, it may be beneficial to know just what part of oral or written instructions students actually do attend to and understand, and why. When the instructions are presented in the target language, nonnatives may have difficulty understanding them because of a lack of second-language proficiency.

It is possible that students may not read the instructions at all. Eugene Brière (personal communication) related that once in the middle of an American history test for eighth-grade native speakers of English, he inserted instructions to the effect that upon reaching that point in the test, the students were to pick up their test paper with their right thumb and index finger and give it to the instructor, while at the same time placing their left index finger on their nose. If they did so, they would get an automatic A on the test. Only one out of thirty-two students actually performed this act, and did so most cautiously. Thus, it is the teacher's/test constructor's task to make sure that the instructions have credibility. They must make sure that the students read and understand the instructions.

Sometimes instructions are too brief, sometimes too wordy. For certain students, the teacher's reading aloud of written instructions may be just so much static. Some students may have a basic disregard for instructions because they see them as a hindrance to getting the task done quickly. Unless trained to do otherwise, respondents may use the most expedient means of responding available to them—such as relying more on their previous experience with seemingly similar formats than on a close reading of the description of the task at hand. Thus, when given a passage to read and summarize, they may well perform the task the same way that they did the last summary task, rather than paying close attention to what is called for in the current one. This strategy often works, but on occasion the particular task may require subtle or major shifts in response behavior in order for the student to perform well.

Whereas the instructions for multiple-choice reading comprehension tasks may ask students to read the passage before answering the questions, a portion of the respondents report either reading the questions first or reading just part of the article and then looking for the corresponding questions (Cohen, 1984; Nevo, 1989; Farr, Pritchard, & Smitten, 1990). In the study by Farr et al. (1990), those who read the passage first were more likely to indicate that the passage was difficult because of unfamiliar vocabulary. In other words, reading the text first may in some cases invite respondents to get bogged down in analysis of individual vocabulary words, while reading the questions first may reduce the importance of individual words—at least ones that are not crucial in answering the questions.

Part of the reason for disregarding instructions may be that students have learned from previous experience that the instructions do not add any important information. This is partly the fault of the test constructor and can be remedied. Remember that in the study aimed at improving the taking of tests of summarization described above (Cohen, 1993), guided instructions assisted students in their native-language summaries of foreign-language texts, whereas such instructions had a mixed effect on the summarizing of native-language texts.

Suggestions for the Preparation of Instructions

It may be a good rule of thumb to include a sample item in sections of the assessment instrument where the format is not obvious or where there is a variation in that assessment format that should be called to the test takers' attention. It may also be reassuring to the students to know the point value of each section of an assessment instrument (and of individual items within the section if items receive different point values). Finally, suggesting the amount of time to spend on a section may help students budget their time better. A section may begin as follows:

> In the following section you are to write a question for each response presented. Example:
>
> The one in the blue jacket. (response)
>
> **Which of these boys is your son?**
> (possible question)
>
> (25 points, 15 minutes)

The introduction provides brief instructions, a sample item with an appropriate answer, the point value for the section, and a suggested amount of time to spend.

It may be useful to teach explicitly or at least check for students' comprehension of words and phrases that are used in instructions written in the second language. For example, students would need to perceive the precise function/meaning of *the best* as superlative if asked to select the best answer from a set of possible answers. This could be a classroom exercise in itself. The teacher provides a list of instructions, and students have to either explain what activity is to be performed or provide their own sample item.

It is always a good idea for teachers to take their own quiz or test—to put themselves in the role of the student respondent to check for any undesired problem areas. Sometimes they may be surprised to find that a question that seemed easy is actually complicated and perhaps even ambiguous. It can be helpful or even essential to have one or more other native speakers take the test, particularly if it is an end-of-course exam. Such native-speaker validation can serve several functions, such as identifying multiple-choice items where none of the alternatives sound good, identifying ambiguous items, and establishing the upper level of achievement. Although native speakers make errors from time to time, the teacher can assume that the occurrence of too many "errors" by natives in general or too many errors on a particular item means that something is wrong. It is also preferable that the native speakers be comparable in age and educational background to the second-language students for whom the assessment instrument is intended.

Although it is unlikely that a teacher would want to pilot a quiz or test on a large sample of native speakers, it should be mentioned in passing that unencouraging results with natives need not automatically indicate the test items or procedures are inappropriate for the nonnative population. For example, Clark (1977) researched the performance of eighty-eight native-English-speaking, college-bound high school students on the Test of English as a Foreign Language (TOEFL). He found that they had some difficulty with the test, primarily with two parts: Error Recognition (checking for basic points of grammar such as "parallelism of construction" and "verbal agreement") and Reading Comprehension (items dealing with "passage summarization or interpretation"). He concluded that such findings need not warrant eliminating from the examination either "structure" items that the test constructor thinks are at least "subjectively indispensable" to nonnatives for effective academic work at the undergraduate level, or reading comprehension items that developers of tests and reviewers deem important.

The implications of this research study for the classroom teacher are that if tests are piloted at all, pilot data from a group of native speakers on a test for nonnatives can be helpful in seeing how the test works. The issue is whether a teacher should reject, say, grammar items that some educated native speakers get wrong. It could be argued that these college-bound natives from the Educational Testing Service (ETS) study would be using English in the same university contexts as the foreign students. In any event, such piloting helps to focus attention on discrete points of grammar, for example, that can be controversial.

Practice in Test Taking

Results from Research

A commonly held attitude is that respondents who have a chance to practice taking different types of assessment instruments over time—especially assessment formats that are unfamiliar to them—will see their performance improve. While research findings with regard to practice on language tests have been mixed, at the time when those studies were conducted, training in test taking was limited to the taking of traditional discrete-point items (see Schulz, 1977). However, information is now available on strategies for taking cloze tests and other assessment instruments that have more unconventional formats. Hence, a replication of earlier studies on cloze (e.g., Kirn, 1972) using current insights about taking a cloze test might well produce better results for those receiving the training.

Research Notes

One study of the practice effect investigated whether nine weeks of biweekly practice in taking dictation (for listening comprehension purposes) and in completing cloze passages would produce a greater improvement rate in an experimental group of EFL students than in the control group (Kirn, 1972). Eighty-five university students in five classes at three levels of ESL at UCLA served as experimental students. Another 114 students served as a control. At each level, half the experimental students were given biweekly practice in taking dictations; the other half were given cloze passages to complete. The practice sessions were not found to produce significantly greater improvement among those receiving the sessions than among the control-group students.

In an exhaustive investigation of the cloze test, Klein-Braley (1981) found among other things that cloze tests in EFL for German-speaking university students could be tackled properly only by those who had had instruction in the cloze procedure. For example, she found that training in taking cloze tests eliminated the problem of "refusers" (i.e., respondents who leave cloze items blank rather than attempting to fill them in). When the cloze tests were administered to **trained** university groups, both in the middle and at the end of the semester, unfilled blanks involved less than 1% of all responses. However, this was not the case with untrained respondents. Furthermore, students reported feeling much more comfortable with the cloze procedure at the end of the semester than they did in their first confrontation with it.

Another study investigated whether there would be a practice effect from repeated administration of a standard EFL test, using different forms (Bowen, 1977). Five forms of the Michigan Test of English Language Proficiency were given to thirty-eight students, with eight days separating each form. It was found that there was no learning derived from having taken a previous form of the instrument.

On the other hand, a third study obtained evidence that learners could enhance their performance on discrete-point items assessing phonological, morphological, and syntactic elements of language (Schulz, 1977). One group of thirty-five learners of French at Ohio State University received only tests of simulated communication, and another group of forty-five students received only discrete-point tests over ten weeks of instruction. With respect to the discrete-point item test, listening comprehension and reading comprehension were assessed through multiple-choice questions (two or more alternatives—written, oral, or recalled from memory); writing and speaking were assessed through structural pattern drills. The simulated communication test called for making a spontaneous response (written, oral, or gestural) in a specified realistic situation. Here the emphasis was on meaning, not on linguistic correctness. Sample communication tasks included summarizing in the target language information heard or read in the native language, drawing pictures or following directions on a map according to directions in the target language, and asking and answering questions.

At the end of the time period, the two groups were given both a simulated communication test and a discrete-point item test. Those students who had received the discrete-point treatment performed significantly better on discrete-point items testing listening, reading, and writing, but **not** speaking. However, the students who had received the communication treatment did not, however, perform significantly better on communication tasks. Among other things, the author concluded that discrete-point items take special test-taking skills, the implication being that those who get exposure to such items over time will benefit.

Findings such as these by Schulz may encourage a teacher to teach to a particular discrete-point test if the teacher knows that success on the assessment instrument depends on training. This phenomenon has been referred to as the *washback effect* (see Chapter 2). In such cases, the instrument, not the instructional objectives and course syllabus, would be dictating the nature of instruction.

The results of the various research studies described above could be incorporated into classroom activities for helping students improve their test-taking skills. In this section we will discuss some of these applications.

Group Analysis of Multiple-Choice Distractors
One pre-assessment activity would require group analysis of multiple-choice distractors. One approach to locating errors in com-

prehension involves designing multiple-choice items so that each distractor is intended to attract readers who manifest a particular type of failure to comprehend. Following the suggestion of Munby (1978, 1979), the distractors could possibly tap failure to understand any of the following:

1. Explicit or implicit (inferred) meaning
2. Conceptual meaning—for example, quantity, comparison, means, cause
3. Communicative value of the text—for example, hypothesis, exemplification, disapproval
4. Relation between one part of a text and another through cohesive devices—for example, reference, ellipsis, apposition
5. Grammatical relationship between words

Munby's group-discussion approach to multiple-choice responses was discussed in full in Chapter 3 (under "Item Type"), so it will just be described briefly here. The technique calls for students working in small groups to determine what the best answer to a question is, based on a reasoned rejection of the distractors in each question. Having students work on their own and then in groups to find a rationale for eliminating distractors is intended to help the students and the teacher establish whether the students are comprehending correctly or falling prey to a type of reading failure.

This kind of activity is considered more as training in understanding reading material than as a testing activity. Through this problem-solving approach, students can become explicitly aware of what makes one answer right and another answer wrong. A sequel to the activity could then be a more formal testing of reading comprehension through multiple choice, and presumably these students would be able to perform in a more reasoned way on such a task.

A Practice Quiz Focusing on Test-Taking Strategies

The teacher could take the strategies summarized below and construct a short quiz where, for example, one or more of these strategies is crucial for successful completion of the quiz. These quizzes would be worked through in class as part of a procedure for training students in more effective test taking. Here are some test-taking strategies that respondents might consider employing for the appropriate task and at the appropriate time:

1. On multiple-choice reading comprehension instruments, read the questions **before** reading the text in order to have a better idea of what to look for.
2. On multiple-choice or open-ended items, read the instructions carefully and pay attention to the entire item stimulus. Deal with all material, both in the item stimulus and in the response options (if there are any), guessing where necessary.
3. In doing cloze tests, when not sure of the correct completion for a blank, read ahead as well as checking back, since clues may be in the next sentence. Also, look for clues in the larger context.
4. In performing summary tasks, determine whether it is necessary to restate ideas in the text in your own words. If so, make an effort to do this, drawing on the language of the text wherever necessary.
5. In writing compositions, pay careful attention to the language used in the statement of the topic so that you are sure to write the essay that is requested.

Conclusion

The processes that students use to complete an assessment instrument may say a great deal about the product. In an oral interview, the interviewer and respondent work together to compose the social fact referred to as an "answer." On written tests, students may get an item right for the wrong reasons, even though their reasoning is sound. The results on paper may not reflect the use or nonuse of reasoning. Students may have sophisticated shortcuts for doing exercises, but these may bypass activities that the teacher considers an essential part of the task.

If language testing is to be a more genuine means for helping the student to learn the language, attention should be paid to the process of test taking and to the specific test-taking strategies that respondents use. Teachers can collect verbal reports from the students while they are taking tests by having them answer test-processing questions inserted in between items and/or by having them refer to checklists of strategies. Students could also arrive at insights through working in small groups, as in the above-mentioned student scrutiny of multiple-choice distractors.

With respect to the instructions on assessment instruments, test constructors may not pay adequate attention to this important aspect of the assessment process. A teacher should know what the students actually understand their task to be and how they use instructions to perform the required task. It is suggested that a teacher provide a sample item in cases where the format may not be clear, indicate the value of each section (and possibly of each item on a test), and estimate the time to be spent on each section.

It is also valuable for teachers to spend a small amount of time in practice exercises to help learners familiarize themselves with test-taking strategies. Here the emphasis would be not on the test-wiseness strategies that help learners get by, but rather on those strategies that help them to demonstrate their true skills in the language.

Discussion Questions and Activities

1. You are a foreign-language teacher, and your department has become dissatisfied with the exit test at your level. For one thing, the reliability is not high enough. At a teachers' meeting where a departmental test is being discussed, you have been called on to explain how it is possible that "a respondent could be getting an item right for the wrong reasons or wrong for the right reasons." Prepare a brief discussion for your colleagues, indicating the importance of this issue both with respect to the reliability and the validity of the exit exam.

2. Define for yourself the term *test-taking strategy*. Now compare your definition with the one in this chapter. How do they compare? Give three examples of test-taking strategies that are

used as shortcuts or tricks to getting the answer. Then give three examples of test-taking strategies that reflect significant language-learning or language-using procedures.

3. What was the meaning of *strategic competence*, as Canale and Swain used it? In what ways did Bachman broaden the notion? As an activity, do a role-play interaction in pairs (e.g., where one is the interlocutor and the other the respondent: a request, an apology, a complaint, etc.). Then have the respondent recreate the stages of the role play, first using the notion of strategic competence in the Canale and Swain sense, and then using the categories from Bachman and Palmer's model of strategic competence. You will have noticed that in the Canale and Swain sense there may not have been clear instances of strategic competence. In the Bachman sense there had to have been. Why is this?

4. What are verbal reports? In what ways can such data be collected? Find a partner, and then work with this partner in listing three advantages and three potential disadvantages associated with the collection of these kinds of data.

5. As an assessment activity, work in pairs, with one partner thinking aloud as he or she fills in each blank in a short cloze test so that the other partner understands why he or she filled in the blank that way. At the end of the task, have the investigator summarize the cloze-taking patterns of the respondent. Next, switch roles and do the activity again.

6. What are some of the strategies respondents use to answer multiple-choice items on reading passages? Identify the ones that you have used over the years. Which ones would you consider the most useful?

7. How would you characterize test-wiseness strategies? What sets them apart from other types of test-taking strategies?

8. Repeated claims have been made that the cloze test measures macro- and not micro-level reading. From the evidence offered in this chapter, would you say that those claims are adequately substantiated? What do you think the cloze test measures? Refer back to Exercise 5 above. What results did you obtain? What percent of the items in that cloze test called for macro-level reading?

Notes

1   That is, students translated the passage out loud while providing an ongoing commentary regarding the procedures they were using to perform the translation. It is worth noting that a recent study (Buck, 1992) found psychometric evidence that translation can be both a reliable and valid means for assessing reading comprehension, contrary to earlier assertions (Klein-Braley, 1987).

2   The extent to which the language skills of the investigator determines the choice of language for verbal reporting is still an empirical matter for investigation. It would appear to depend on the nature of the assessment task, the nature of the verbal report, the training that the respondent has received, and other contextual variables.

3   The multiple-choice format is, in fact, referred to slightly pejoratively in Israel as "the American system."

4   Hebrew verbs are inflected according to the gender of the subject.

Chapter 6: Preparing an Assessment Instrument

In this chapter we start by providing the anatomy of an item, in order to help teachers prepare items and procedures for classroom tests in a second or foreign language. We will begin with a discussion of the more discrete-point and integrative items, and the continuum on which they can be placed. We will next consider formats for eliciting and responding to assessment items and procedures, and guidelines for giving instructions to respondents. Then we will describe the ability of multiple means of assessment over time to provide a richer data base of information on students. Last, we will consider student self-assessment measures, since these are at the cutting edge of language assessment. As part of that discussion, we will look at sample means for having students assess their own progress in language learning.

Discrete-Point/Integrative and Indirect/Direct Assessment

Since the 1960s, the notion of *discrete-point* assessment, that is, assessing one and only one point at a time, has met with some disfavor among theorists. The following is such an item, testing for verb tense in the auxiliary:

> (Written elicitation)
> "Did you go to the frisbee tournament last night?"
> (Written multiple-choice completion)
> "No, I _____."
>> (a) didn't go
>> (b) haven't gone
>> (c) hadn't gone

Critics of this approach raise several points of contention. They feel that such a method provides little information on the student's ability to function in actual language-use situations. They also contend that it is difficult to determine which points are being assessed. Even if we could assume that there was a list of important points to be assessed in a particular language, we would still need to select only a sampling of these points for any given assessment instrument and therefore would have to ask whether the items we chose were representative (Spolsky, 1968). Testing points have in the past been determined in part by a contrastive analysis of differences between the language being assessed and the native language of the learner. But this contrastive approach in itself was criticized for being too limiting and myopic. A rival philosophy of integrative testing then emerged, with the emphasis on testing more than one point at a time.

Whereas twenty years ago an *integrative* approach (i.e., consciously assessing more than one point at a time) might have been considered a bold step, today it is taken for granted that a test or quiz will have at least some items on it that assess a broad spectrum of features. As has become evident over the years, there is actually a continuum from the most discrete-point items on the one hand

Figure 6.1

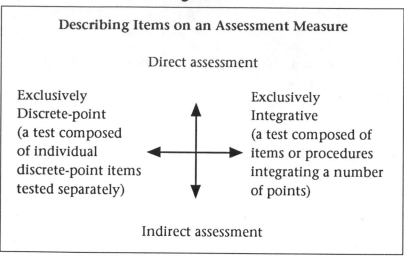

Describing Items on an Assessment Measure

Direct assessment

Exclusively
Discrete-point
(a test composed
of individual
discrete-point items
tested separately)

Exclusively
Integrative
(a test composed of
items or procedures
integrating a number
of points)

Indirect assessment

to the most integrative items or procedures on the other (see Figure 6.1). Most items fall somewhere in between, regardless of the label attached to them.

We should also point out that a discrete-point item need not be assessing just one isolated grammar or vocabulary point. Not only is it possible to use a discrete-point approach to test for grammatical knowledge within a sociolinguistic context, but it is also possible to use the discrete-point format to test for sociocultural knowledge. An item such as the following would be an example of one that tests for a specific discrete point regarding refusals:

> Your professor invites you over for dinner on Friday evening. You are most flattered and pleased at the invitation but must attend your parents' fiftieth wedding anniversary party that evening. Select the **least** appropriate response to your professor:
>
> (a) Thank you, Prof. Brown, but I'm sorry to say I'm unavailable that evening.
> (b) Oh, wow! What an honor to be invited. I would love to come, but I have a family engagement I can't break.
> (c) Sounds good, but no way! I'm tied up.
> (d) I can't do it because of a previous engagement, but perhaps maybe another time. Thanks for asking.

Figure 6.1 also shows the distinction between *direct* and *indirect* assessment. A direct measure samples explicitly from the behavior being evaluated, while an indirect measure is contrived to the extent that the task differs from a normal language-using task (Hughes, 1989). There is an increasing concern being voiced in the general testing literature that assessment instruments need to be developed that directly reflect the traits they are supposed to measure. For example, Frederiksen and Collins (1989) view direct-assessment measures as more systemically valid[1] than indirect measures because instruction that improves performance on such measures is likely to improve performance on extended tasks of a like nature. Davies (1990: Chapter 4) makes the distinction between direct and indirect assessment somewhat differently, referring to *test-like* instruments, such as vocabulary and grammar tests, and *test-unlike* instruments, such as oral interview tasks.

Referring to Figure 6.1, if students are assessed on their ability to give a talk in front of the class and at the same time are evaluated for their usage of specific verb tenses, we would say that the assessment instrument is a *direct* measure of a particular behavior—in this case, "giving a talk"—and is concentrating on discrete points, namely, verb tenses. If the same talk were rated more integratively for a whole range of items, say, in pronunciation, grammar, and lexicon, then we would call it a *direct integrative* measure. A traditional multiple-choice grammar test with specific items checking for points of grammar could be termed an *indirect discrete-point measure* in that it is a contrived situation and one in which the students are not displaying actual grammatical performance in normal classroom routines or even out of class. Finally, an example of an *indirect integrative measure* would be a cloze test, which will be discussed in more detail in Chapter 7. This is an indirect measure of integrative reading ability in that it is not assessing reading ability directly, but rather the ability to write words into randomly deleted or rationally deleted blanks as a measure of reading ability.

Close scrutiny of items at the more discrete-point end of the continuum reveals that **truly** discrete-point items are not easy to construct. A discrete-point item (as in the example above) implies that only one element (e.g., the contracted form of the negative, singular, past tense auxiliary: *didn't*) from one component of language (e.g., syntax) is being assessed in one skill (reading), which is a *receptive* or *perceptive* (as opposed to a *productive*) skill. In reality, so-called discrete-point items often assess more than one point at a time. For example, if an item calling for a speaker to convert a present tense form into past tense has an oral item elicitation (e.g., the teacher gives the cue "Did you go to the frisbee tournament last night?"), the item is also assessing the skill of listening. Or if the item is testing written syntax but the respondent must read the item first in order to know what response to write out, the item is also assessing reading. For example,

> Read the following sentence, underlining an incorrect form if one exits. Write the correct form at the right margin.

> The boys couldn't <u>found</u> their pants.   *find*

Such an item has been referred to as a *hybrid* test item in that it is assessing several things at the same time (Valette, 1977).

Of course, it may be that these other points included in the item do not cause difficulty and therefore are not considered as among the discrete points being assessed. For example, in the written syntax item above, although reading comprehension is a necessary condition for obtaining a correct answer, the teacher may be assuming that all the students will read and understand this elicitation without problems. Good assessment practice would, in fact, require that item writers confine source of difficulty **only** to what they want to assess. However, experience has demonstrated that the item writer's intentions are not always carried out. This is where verbal report can be of assistance (as discussed in the previous chapter): checking up on what the items actually tested for and on what gave respondents difficulty during the process.

For examples of more integrative items, let us turn to reading comprehension items, which are often based on *discourse analysis*[2] of texts. Such analysis of text has revealed different kinds of meaning in text, including grammatical meaning, informational meaning, discourse meaning, and the meaning conveyed by the writer's tone. So let us say we have the sentence "But your alligator is bigger than my crocodile!" We could use all four kinds of meaning in our analysis of this sentence and may need to do so in order to make any sense out of it.[3]

Grammatical Meaning

We may undertake a grammatical analysis of a text in order to determine the grammatical categories that words, phrases, and sentences fall into. We could consciously identify words by their grammatical function as nouns, adjectives, verbs, or adverbs. We could also analyze sentences for the syntactic role they play in the text. If we take the above sentence, we need to know that *your* is a pronoun, presumably referring to the addressee. *Alligator* must be identified as a noun and as the subject of the sentence, and *crocodile* as the object. We then identify *is* as a copula verb and *bigger* as a comparative adjective. In reading in a native language, much of this analysis is performed automatically, as needed. In a target language, such analysis may be quite conscious and even labored.

Informational Meaning

We normally read to extract information from the text—in other words, to determine the basic concepts or messages that the text tries to convey. To do this, we need to do enough analysis of vocabulary to distinguish known words from those which are possibly known and those which are unknown. In the given example, the information is that the addressee has an alligator and that the speaker believes that this alligator is bigger than the crocodile which he or she has. It is not known whether these are model animals or real animals, live or stuffed. It may help us to know that alligators and crocodiles are different reptiles with certain distinguishing features.

Discourse Meaning

Discourse meaning concerns the fit between portions of a text—that is, the grammatical and/or lexical relationships between the different elements of a text. The way in which different parts of the text are linked together (pronominal reference, ellipsis, substitution, connectors, and so forth) is referred to as *cohesion*. Thus, in the context "your alligator is bigger than my crocodile," *your* and *my* play important roles in linking the two reptiles together in the given text.

Also with respect to discourse meaning, we could look for the relationships that link the meanings of the sentences in a text in order to produce an intelligible text. This phenomenon is called *coherence*. The above sentence seems to be coherent. However, "your alligator is bigger than my pride" causes us more difficulty if we are without the benefit of context. Such a sentence could make sense with more context. In isolation it is incoherent. Another aspect of discourse concerns the function of the portion of text. "But your alligator is bigger than my crocodile!" could constitute a complaint—a feeling by a younger sibling that an older one had gotten a bigger model. It could also serve as a compliment, intended to indicate how clever or skilled the poacher was in bagging such a large alligator.

The Meaning Conveyed by the Writer's Tone

Finally, we have the meaning that is conveyed by the writer's attitude or tone. In an explicit, clearly written text, the writer's tone may be easy to determine. In other cases, the writer's tone may be quite subtle and require the ability to pick up on small cues to irony, for example, where the use of a certain word is ironic to the native and tends to be ignored by the nonnative reader (through lack of knowledge or awareness).

An accurate interpretation of the message about the alligator and the crocodile may depend upon awareness of whether the sentence was intended to be neutral, funny, sad, sarcastic, cynical, or angry. Punctuation sometimes helps out, such as exclamation points. Intensifiers (e.g., *too big*) or invectives (e.g., *your damn alligator*) can help indicate the tone. In order to appreciate the author's tone, the reader should have dealt with all or most of the other types of meaning in the text, however briefly, from recoding to decoding for grammar, information, and discourse.

In order to illustrate what several more-integrative reading comprehension items might look like, let us take two paragraphs from Russell (1950):

A good way of ridding yourself of certain kinds of dogmatism is to become aware of opinions held in social circles different from your own. When I was young, I lived much outside my own country—in France, Germany, Italy, and the United States. I found this very profitable in diminishing the intensity of insular prejudice. If you cannot travel, seek out people with whom you disagree, and read a newspaper belonging to a party that is not yours. If the people and the newspaper seem mad, perverse, and wicked, remind yourself that you seem so to them. In this opinion both parties may be right, but they cannot both be wrong. This reflection should generate a certain caution.

For those who have enough psychological imagination, it is a good plan to imagine an argument with a person having a different bias. This has one advantage, and only one, as compared with actual conversation with opponents; this one advantage is that the method is not subject to the same limitations of time and space. Mahatma Gandhi deplored railways and steamboats and machinery; he would have liked to undo the whole of the industrial revolution. You may never have an opportunity of actually meeting anyone who holds this opinion, because in Western countries most people take the advantages of modern technique for granted. But if you want to make sure that you are right in agreeing with the prevailing opinion, you will find it a good plan to test the arguments that occur to you by considering what Gandhi might have said in refutation of them. I have sometimes been led actually to change my mind as a result of this kind of imaginary dialogue, and, short of this, I have frequently found myself growing less dogmatic and cocksure through realizing the possible reasonableness of a hypothetical opponent.

Let us assume that this paragraph appeared in a text being read in class and that the teacher had prepared two integrative reading comprehension questions:

1. What kinds of newspapers does Russell suggest we read? Why? (Possible answer: "Newspapers written by political parties espousing views that differ significantly from our own because this may cause us to reflect on our opinions and perhaps be more cautious about the positions that we take.")

2. According to Russell, what is the advantage of having an imaginary conversation with someone else? (Possible answer: "Your choice of a conversational partner is not limited to a particular place or time.")

Both of the above questions could be considered integrative. Each has several specific features that it is assessing, and it is assessing these in consort. Let us look first at question 1. With respect to grammatical meaning, the question tests for an understanding of lexical items such as *disagree, mad, perverse*, and *wicked*. With regard to informational meaning, the item is checking for comprehension of phrases such as *a party that is not yours* and *they cannot both be wrong*. The question also assesses comprehension of discourse meaning. Respondents have to understand that the reference is to a **political** party. They also need to get the meaning of *so* in *you seem so to them*—that it refers anaphorically back to *mad, perverse, and wicked*. Thus, question 1 tests for grammatical, informational, and discourse meaning.

With regard to grammatical meaning, the second question refers respondents to a portion of the text that has far more lexical meanings to process: *bias, opponents, limitations, deplored, take . . . for granted, prevailing, refutation, dogmatic, cocksure*, and *hypothetical*. At the informational level, phrases such as *subject to the same limitations, take for granted, the prevailing opinion*, and *hypothetical opponents* could be difficult for an intermediate ESL student to interpret. With respect to discourse meaning, the question checks for an ability to perceive the cohesion in the text, specifically, that the initial *this* in the second sentence refers to an imaginary argument and that the *imaginary dialogue* referred to later in the paragraph is synonymous to this imaginary argument. Also, respondents have to perceive that *refutation of them* refers to *arguments* and that these arguments are those contained in the *prevailing opinion.*

The purpose of this elaborate example was simply to point out that reading comprehension items can assess understanding of various types of meaning within a text and that they can and usually do assess these types of meaning in an integrative fashion. If the respondents experience comprehension difficulties, the assessor may want to determine which type(s) of reading were being engaged at the point where comprehension broke down.

A Focus on Integrative Assessment

The main purpose here is to call attention to those *integrative* assessment techniques that are practical for use in the language classroom—on short notice and with a minimum of preparation. They are by no means representative of all the possible techniques to assess language items. Many other language-testing books have attempted to offer a comprehensive coverage of test items, so the reader is referred to one or more of these (e.g., Lado, 1964; Valette, 1977; Harris, 1969; Clark, 1972; Heaton, 1975, 1990; Shohamy, 1986; Hughes, 1989). This discussion will consider integrative items on the basis of their component parts: the item-elicitation format, the item-response format, and the tested response behavior. The more traditional means of categorizing items by means of skill being tested—for example, listening, speaking, reading, and writing—will not be adhered to in this discussion precisely because the same or similar elicitation and response formats are often used in assessing different skills. Thus the same or similar items seem to keep reappearing as the discussion moves from one skill to the next.

Although models have been developed for the exhaustive analysis of the distinctive elements of language tests (see, for example, Carroll [1968], and more recently, Bachman [1990] and Bachman & Palmer [in press], for categories of test method characteristics), our purpose here is to provide an analysis of just **some** of the elements that can be combined relatively easily to produce a variety of different integrative assessment measures for the classroom. It may be that students function best on assessment tasks if they are constantly challenged by a variety of item-elicitation and item-response formats. Of course, such variety means more teacher effort at test or quiz construction and also requires that students pay closer attention to the items and procedures with which they are dealing.[4]

What follows now with regard to the *elements of an assessment instrument* is meant to be practical for the classroom teacher. Describing item types in terms of elicitation and response formats is intended to highlight distinctive elements. If teachers are aware of such elements, they can not only produce items that assess distinctly different things, but also items that are variations on the same theme. It may help to keep students alert and to get a more rounded picture of their ability to vary the combination of formats for the *item elicitation* (i.e., oral, written, or nonverbal) (see Figure 6.2) and for the *item response* (likewise oral, written, or nonverbal) (see Figure 6.3). Rather than providing all possible item-elicitation and item-response formats, we include a sampling of formats that may be usable in class with a minimum of preparation.

In the previous edition of this book, Chapter 6 included a description of numerous item types for assessing listening skills (auditory identification and discrimination, listening as it relates to grammar and vocabulary, and auditory comprehension), reading (grammar: morphology and syntax; lexicon: vocabulary and idioms, pragmatics, mechanics, stylistics, and integrative items and procedures), speaking (pronunciation, grammar, vocabulary, and pragmatics), and writing (dictation, mechanics, grammar, vocabulary, and written composition). The emphasis was largely on the assessment of discrete language items. During the intervening years, greater emphasis has been put on more integrative assessment of language. The following discussion of item types is intended to reflect current thinking about assessment.

Just as in the previous edition of this book, the following discussion will not provide a cookbook listing of items by skill area (listening, speaking, reading, and writing). Taking the elicitation

Figure 6.2

Item-Elicitation Format

Oral Elicitation
    Contextualized minimal pairs
    Sentence with selected grammatical structures
    Conveying of information
    Questions in an interview
    Instructions

Written Elicitation
    Sentence as a means of elicitation
    Passage as a means of elicitation
    Instructions

Nonverbal Elicitation: Gestures or Pictures
    Type of picture
    Affective value of picture
    Presentation format
    Subject of picture
    Display format
    Purpose of picture

---

and response features and generating items is left up to the teacher. The approach here is of providing a "grab bag" of features to combine into a given assessment measure.

So let us say that teachers want to assess knowledge of the simple past tense in English. Then they might choose a written elicitation, such as a sentence (page 177), and a written response, such as rewriting (page 190), that is, transforming the verb in the sentence into past tense. Or teachers who want to measure the conversational ability of the whole class but do not have time to assess each student's speaking ability individually could choose as an item-elicitation format an oral set of instructions (pages 175–176) for how their students are to act out a given role play:

> You are to make a strong complaint to your friend over his inconsiderateness, but you also wish to maintain your close friendship with the person.

Figure 6.3

Item-Response Format

Oral Response
    Oral recitation
    Role play
    Interviewing

Oral or Written Response
    Distinguishing
    Ordering
    Combination
    Identification
    Completion
    Paraphrase
    Structured or free response
    Reporting

Written Response
    Matching
    Note taking
    Rewriting

Nonverbal Response
    Gestures
    Identification
    Responding to requests
    Pictorial response

Then, for the sake of expediency, the item-response format could be written. In other words, students would be requested to write out a script (pages 190–191) reflecting as much as possible the way that the respondent would say the lines when acting them out—thus constituting a projective measure of speaking.[5]

Item-Elicitation Format

Teachers can use one of three different formats to elicit language behavior: oral, written, and nonverbal (through gestures or pictures). They can also use some combination of these to assess language. Let us look at these in turn.

Oral Elicitation

An oral elicitation can involve a variety of formats. The following are questions you may want to ask yourself:

1. Is the oral elicitation the teacher's voice or that of one or more others? For example, the voice could be that of students, perhaps at varying levels of target-language proficiency. It could instead be the voice of a commentator or other professional.
2. Is the voice live—in person or over a telephone line, or is it recorded on audiotape or videotape?
3. Is the input clear or distorted—that is, is there noise (perhaps intentional) in the background?
4. Is the input natural speech, oral reading of material as if natural speech, or oral reading of material as formal oral recitation?
5. Is the pace fast or slow, natural or unnatural? Some recorded oral dialogues, for example, sound funny to native speakers because they immediately perceive that a native would never say it that way—with stilted, drawn-out pronunciation at an unusually slow speed.

The following are some suggested oral formats for item elicitation to be used in the classroom.

Contextualized minimal pairs. A teacher or a student says (reads) a sentence containing a target-language sound. The sound is contextualized in a sentence. The speaker then repeats the sentence, either substituting a word containing a sound that is a minimal pair for the target sound or leaving the original word as it was (Lado, 1964; Brière, 1967; Bowen, 1972). For example,

1. He's **heating** the fish.
2. He's **hitting** the fish.

With respect to EFL, there are books that provide vowel and consonant contrasts in initial, medial, and final position and that provide contextualized minimal pairs such as in the above example. The literature also offers examples of minimal pairs in English based on the phonemic discrimination problems of learners from a variety of different language backgrounds (see, for example, Nilsen & Nilsen [1973]; and Avery & Ehrlich [1992: Chapter 8]). Since the format is simply one of contextualized minimal pairs delivered orally, the content could also involve assessing awareness of, say, grammatical markers. For example,

1. He **hits** the ball.
2. He **hit** the ball.

Here again the speaker either gives sentence 1 twice, sentence 2 twice, or 1 and 2 in either order. (In this example and in the previous one, the *response* format could also be that of nonverbal identification or of oral distinguishing.)

Sentences with selected grammatical structure. Sentences containing tense, number, gender, a combination of these, or other elements of interest are read aloud. For example,

A boy's making the mess.
(singular subject + contracted copula + present progressive + definite article + object)

We note that even such a short sentence has a number of grammatical features that could be assessed. For example, despite the definite article *a*, students may interpret *boy's* as the plural *boys*. (One possible *response* format would be oral or written identification—e.g., singular or plural.) The item could also be assessing the ability to distinguish the contracted auxiliary forms of *is* and *has*—for example, "a boy is"/"a boy has." (Then a *response* format might be oral or written, distinguishing a boy has/a boy is/a boy's [possessive].)

Conveying of information. Students hear an informant talk, lecture, or discuss in person or through the media. They are then asked questions orally to assess their comprehension of content or form. The information can also be in written form so that students can follow along while they listen. If a simulated lecture is used, the teacher should see that it has the normal false starts, repetitions, and filled pauses[6] that give it normal qualities of redundancy. If a "lecture" is simply the reading of a printed text, it is really assessing the comprehension of a text read orally—not of a lecture.

Questions or interviews. Students are asked questions individually (e.g., to spot check a grammar point; Chastain, 1976:506). For example, the question is posed, and then a student is named. The teacher might even select the student randomly from a set of name cards to introduce the element of chance. Once students' names have been drawn, their cards are set aside so that they are not called again until the next activity, or perhaps their name cards are kept in the pack to keep them alert. For example,

> Teacher: "What happened to Harvey after he slipped on the banana peel? Carlos?"

The teacher may also ask a series of questions in the form of an interview and have this constitute all or part of an assessment task. For example,

> Teacher: What do you think actually triggered that riot?
> Teacher: Do you think the authorities handled it well?
> Teacher: What is the likelihood of similar riots in the future?

Instructions. A student is given instructions to interview someone else. For example,

> You are the host on an evening talk show and are now interviewing a man who teaches parrots, parakeets, and other birds how to talk. It is your task to ask a series of stimulating questions.

Students could also be given a situation and be asked to react, or more indirectly, could be asked to tell what they would say in that particular situation. For example,

> Your neighbor's dog was on the porch barking at the crack of dawn for the third day in a row. This time you're fed up. You go next door to complain.

Neighbor (opens the door with a big smile on his face and shakes his neighbor's hand): "Come in, pal."

Student: (The student role plays and responds directly.) Student (indirect approach): "If my neighbor's dog woke me up three days in a row and I were going next door to complain, I would. . . ."

Or students could be given secret instructions on how to play a particular role in a role-playing situation (Valette, 1977:155). For example,

One student is told in secret that he or she is to play the role of a plainclothes police officer who has just encountered the student activist responsible for starting a violent riot on campus last week. Another student is told to play the role of a withdrawn, serious student with no interest in politics. This student is told that a student prankster is running around, impersonating a plainclothes policeman/woman.

For a final suggestion, students are asked to describe the events that they are witnessing. What they witness could be acted out live by staging a dramatization in class or could be on videotape or film. For example,

A student comes into the room, pretending to be a robber. She is holding a banana in her hand as if it were a revolver. The teacher, in fright, hands over his money. The student exits rapidly with the money, eating the banana and dropping the peel in the wastebasket on her way out of the room.

These types of instructions could also be written so that students can follow along at the same time that they hear the instructions given orally.

Written elicitation

A sentence as a means of elicitation. The student is given fragments of a sentence out of order and must arrange them in the proper order. For example,

I   <u>had seen</u>   <u>immediately reminded me</u>
       A   B

<u>Albert's face</u>   <u>in a zoo</u>   <u>of a silly monkey</u>
     C   D   E

       Correct order: <u>C</u>   <u>B</u>   <u>E</u>   <u>A</u>   <u>D</u>

The student reads a sentence and is asked to perform a variety of functions—for example, correct it grammatically; transform it to another person, tense, or number; or paraphrase it. For example,

> Correct the grammar:
> "I have counselors which already finish the army."

> Paraphrase the following sentence so that it reflects the way a native speaker would say it:
> "I have counselors who already finished the army." (surface corrections).

> "The counselors working here have already finished their army duty." (the way a native would probably say it).

The student is given a sentence with a word or phrase missing, possibly preceded by a sentence or two to set the context. The student is to fill in the word. For example,

> Nobody seemed to know what had happened to Herbert's portable TV. He had set it down on the bench while he was playing basketball. He had no choice but to _____ the loss to the police.

Students are given two separate sentences that they are to combine into one. For example,

> That lemon meringue pie is hard to resist.
> I am on a strict diet.

A passage as a means of elicitation. The student is given a passage to read and then is asked to write answers to questions. These questions could be posed explicitly (e.g., a direct question about a structure) or implicitly (e.g., a general comprehension question involving the structure). Categories of questions could tap different types of meaning: semantic categories, the informational content of the passage, textual cohesion, the discoursal functions of the material (e.g., classification and definition), or the author's attitude. The students themselves could be responsible for writing their own questions to go with a given passage. These would serve as an elicitation if the students then answered them. If the writing of the questions were an end in itself or part of the "response" that the passage was the stimulus for, this activity would fall under oral or written response (below), specifically, structured or free response.

Instructions. The student is given written instructions to write a certain type of composition, for example, a narrative, a descriptive piece, or a comparative composition:

> Write a **narrative** discussing what you did last summer and what you intend to do this summer.

> Give a **description** of what you consider to be the basic requirements for a happy life.

> Make a **comparison** of the character of the people and pace of life in two major cities with which you are familiar.

Teachers may intend for the narrative to elicit past and future tenses, the "happy life" essay to elicit nouns, and the comparison of people in two cities to elicit adjectives. If so, they may want to stipulate that students use a certain number of words from the given form class and particular verb tenses to ensure that such forms appear in the students' essays. It has been demonstrated that assigning a particular topic does not automatically control the frequency of parts of speech (Brière, 1964).

Nonverbal Elicitation: Gestures or Pictures

Gestures can serve as the item-elicitation format, especially if knowledge of culture-specific nonverbal behavior is being assessed. In other words, the teacher performs a given gesture that is coupled with some item-response format through which the students indicate a knowledge or lack of knowledge of the particular gesture (see below). Numerous sources can be found regarding varieties of nonverbal behavior within and across language groups (see, for example, Key, 1977:136-138).

A more frequently used nonverbal elicitation is a picture. In fact, it could even be a picture of a gesture. However, there are some drawbacks to using pictorial stimuli. For example, preparing pictures takes teacher time. Finding ready-made pictures also takes time. Pictures may be interpreted in various ways, either because they are simply ambiguous (Valette, 1977:223) or because they presuppose a certain cultural background, educational level, socioeconomic status, or age (Harris, 1969; Heaton, 1975:74-75). In light of the difficulties in interpreting complex pictures, Clark (1972:52) recommended that pictures used in assessment measures be simple, stylized, and free of distracting background or superficial detail.

Despite the various reservations, well-designed pictures can serve useful functions. They can get elicitation information across to the students without the use of elaborate verbiage. In fact, pictures may be crucial if teachers do not want a supposed measure of their students' ability to write a composition to be actually an assessment of their ability to read and correctly interpret a set of instructions about what to write on. Furthermore, a pictorial-elicitation format helps eliminate the problem of students' simply lifting material verbatim from a verbal-elicitation prompt to use in the response (Heaton, 1975:133). Pictures can also be used to elicit conversation between a tester and a respondent (Heaton, 1990:61-65). Commercial tests of oral language actually rely heavily on pictures to elicit data.

In fact, pictures do not usually appear alone as an elicitation for language items (as they might in a nonverbal subtest of intelligence, e.g., an "analogy" or a "classification" subtest), but rather in conjunction with some oral or written material. So the item-elicitation format could consist of a written passage accompanied by four pictures, only one of which depicts what is described in the passage.

An appraisal both of commercially available formats and of the pictorial stimuli serving as examples in various books on language testing yielded the following breakdown into relevant dimensions: the type of picture, the affective value of the picture, the presentation format, the subject of the picture, the display format, and the purpose of the picture. We will deal with each of these in turn.

The type of picture. A picture may be a simple sketch (for example, stick figures), it may be a complete drawing, or it may even be a painting with full detail, as used in the Dailey Language Facility Test (Dailey, 1968; Silverman, Noa, & Russell, 1976). It may also be a photograph (see Figure 6.4). As mentioned above, detailed

Figure 6.4

Different Types of Pictures

pictures can present problems. The extent of detail may depend on the population. When the Dailey test of oral language, employing a photograph, a painting, and a sketch, was used with young bilingual children (K-3) in the Redwood City study (Cohen, 1975b), it appeared that in both languages the children most enjoyed describing the sketch. Perhaps it was because this format allowed them the most room for imagination in their stories.

The affective value of the picture. The picture can be serious or humorous. The element of humor is sometimes introduced through the use of exaggerated or imaginary elements (see Figure 6.5).

The presentation format. Pictures can be used individually, in a group, or in a series. There is an important difference between a group and a series. In a group, two or more pictures may be the

Figure 6.5

Depicting an ill-fated picnic

same except for one feature, and the student must choose which picture is being referred to (see Figure 6.6). Or the pictures in the group may be quite different from one another, and only a proper understanding of some oral or written input will lead the student to the correct choice (see Figure 6.7).

In a series of pictures, there can be a chronology from one picture to the next (see Figure 6.8).

The subject of the picture. The picture may be that of some object(s) or person(s). The object may be illustrated to stress size, shape, or color. With both people and objects, the picture may be intended to elicit some action, for instance, an action verb such as *push* (see Figure 6.9).

Part of the criticism of certain traditional pictorial measures is that they focus too much on objects and too little on people engaged in pictorially interesting events (Oller, 1979).

The display format. For assessment purposes, students must be able to see the pictures. One approach is to use transparencies and an overhead projector. The teacher could display a picture in front of the class (e.g., a picture from a magazine pasted on a board)

Figure 6.6

Locate the Missing Feature: A Tennis Match

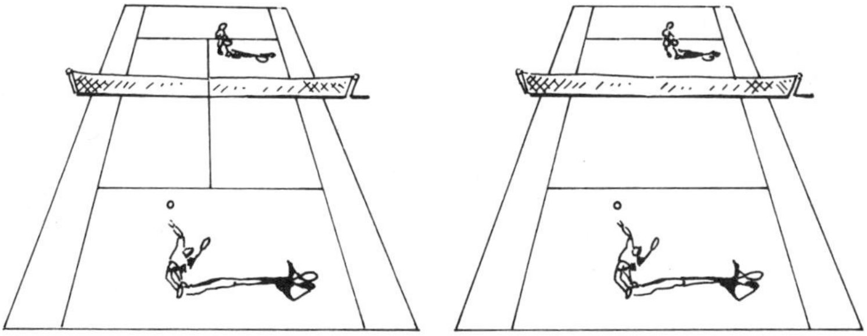

Figure 6.7

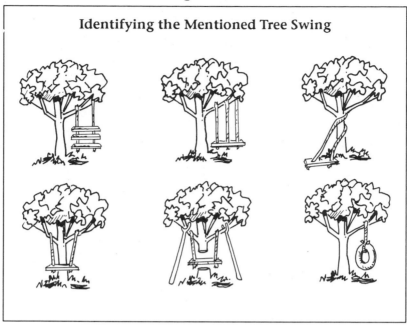

Identifying the Mentioned Tree Swing

Figure 6.8

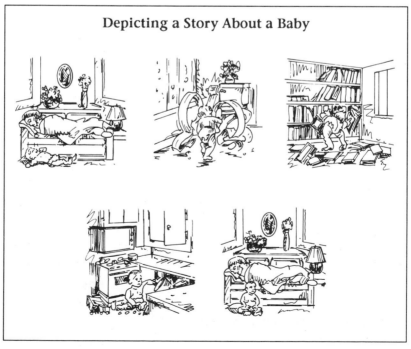

Depicting a Story About a Baby

Figure 6.9

Depicting Action Verbs: *Push!*

if all the students can view it well enough. Teachers may also copy the picture onto a ditto, but this calls for more preparation time on the part of the teacher, and unintentional imprecision may make the picture(s) difficult for students to interpret. Other possible media include video, where the videotape could be paused at a given scene or set of scenes. It may be possible to use a large video screen for display purposes (for example, in a language laboratory).

The purpose of the picture. Pictures can serve a variety of functions. For example, two or more pictures may be used to stimulate comparison across pictures, in search of the correct answer. A picture or series of pictures may elicit a narrative or discussion, or may be used to check for written or oral comprehension of a series of statements. The student indicates whether the statements are true or false, on the basis of the picture. A picture can also be used to recreate a situation under discussion. For example, a series of pictures can represent a purse-snatching incident. The student describes the incident and the outcome, based on the pictures (Hughes, 1989:84).

Item-Response Format

Teachers can have students respond to assessment items in one of three ways—orally, in writing, or nonverbally. The item-response format can be fixed, structured, or open-ended. Those items with a fixed format include true/false, multiple-choice, and matching. Those which call for a structured format include ordering (where, for example, respondents are requested to arrange words to make a sentence and several orders are possible); duplication, both written (e.g., dictation) and oral (e.g., recitation, repetition, and mimicry); identification (e.g., explaining the part of speech of a form); and completion. Those calling for an open-ended format include composition, both written (e.g., creative fiction, and expository essays) and oral (e.g., a speech), as well as other activities such as free oral response in role-playing situations.

Oral Response

Oral recitation. After students have had a chance to read a passage silently, they are asked to read it aloud. They can read aloud in several ways, depending on the material. The material can be written to be read as if spoken (e.g., lines from a play), to be read in an informational style (e.g., a news broadcast), or to be read as a recitation (adapted from Gregory, 1967).

Role play. Students participate in a *role-play interview*, in which they respond by playing the part of someone described in the prompt (e.g., an employee apologizing to the boss after forgetting an important meeting). Likewise, the students could physically act out a role-play situation, which sometimes reduces the inhibitions encountered in a sit-down interview. An adventuresome teacher may even be willing to have the students engage in *real play*—that is, role play out of class in the actual setting with a native speaker of the target language playing one major role (e.g., car dealer, furniture store manager, or pharmacist) (Jenks, 1979). This real play could be tape-recorded for later analysis and assessment.

Interviewing. Students are given a list of items (possibly appearing in the native language) about which they are to obtain information by interviewing someone in the target language. This could be combined with real play in that the interviewees could be native speakers encountered outside the classroom.

Oral or Written Response

Distinguishing. Students indicate that an item is true/false, correct/incorrect, one/two, yes/no, same/different orally or in writing. Or students select the correct answer from three or more alternatives.

Ordering. Students arrange fragments of a sentence, a set of paragraphs, and so forth in their proper order.

Combination. Students combine two sentences into a single one. In some cases the aim may be to produce a shorter, simpler sentence. In other cases it may be to produce one longer but more cohesive sentence. In still other cases, the aim may be to arrive at greater complexity. Here, the assessment process demonstrates how the combining of sentences can have different purposes.

Identification. Students indicate whether an utterance refers to past, present, or future tense by supplying *yesterday*, *today*, or *tomorrow* after hearing an utterance or reading some material that employs one of the three tenses. In like manner, students can indicate whether a verb is in the singular or plural form by supplying pronouns such as *he*, *she*, or *they*. Or the students could simply mark an X next to the appropriate picture (see Figure 6.10).

Completion. Students supply a word or phrase (e.g., a phrasal verb) missing from a sentence or passage. The cloze test is by now the best-known example of a multiple-completion task at the word level (see Chapter 7). Yet completion can entail parts of words (e.g., the C-test; see Chapter 7), phrases, and sentences as well.

Paraphrase. Students produce another sentence or set of sentences that has the same information contained in the elicitation sentence or sentences, but without using the same content words (except proper nouns). For example,

> **Elicitation:** Penelope construed from Dudley's remarks that he was intent on accomplishing his goal.
> **Student response:** Penelope took Dudley's comments to mean that he was set on achieving his aim.

Figure 6.10

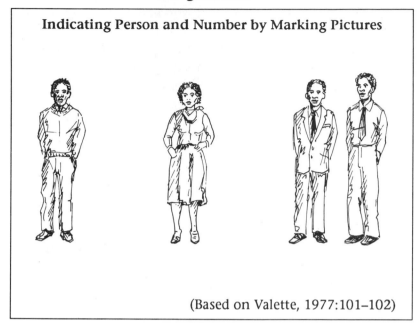

Indicating Person and Number by Marking Pictures

(Based on Valette, 1977:101–102)

Here, the surface structure of the paraphrase is similar to that of the original sentence. A paraphrase could also call for some transformation, such as from active to passive voice. But then the teacher should be mindful that the transformed sentence may be only a partial paraphrase. For example,

John took Mary home. ≠ It was John that took Mary home.

Structured or free response. Students answer questions about a news broadcast, lecture, casual talk, or passage in their native language or in the second language. Whereas in many situations it is taken for granted and even obvious that students are to write answers in the second language, under certain circumstances it may be more effective to have students respond in their native language (see Nation [1978], and TESOL [1978]). For example, Laufer (1978, 1983), reporting on an experiment that she conducted among university-level EFL students in Israel, noted that in a context where the course emphasis was on comprehension of specialized texts and where writing was not taught as a skill, there were problems in having students write open-ended answers in the foreign language (in this case, English) and advantages to having them write such answers in the native language (in this case, Hebrew).

Her research findings suggest that native-language answers may be preferable as an indicator of reading comprehension (given the nature of the course and the student population). She found that when nonnatives respond in the foreign language,

1. The answer may be copied from the text.
2. The writing may be of such poor quality that it is hard to know if the nonnatives understood the text.
3. The response may be terse in the foreign language—that is, it does not supply quite enough information for the scorer to judge whether the respondents know the answer or not.

The research findings of others, such as Zupnik (1985) and Gordon (1987), support the use of native-language responses. Actually, tight or rigorous paraphrase is in some ways a special skill—one that even natives may not necessarily be good at. But rough paraphrasing is something that second-language learners often do as a strategy for getting around material they do not know well (see Tarone, Cohen, & Dumas, 1983).

Assume that when students read a textbook in a foreign language, they take notes in their native language, use a bilingual dictionary, and translate excerpts for use in term papers and exams in the second language. In addition, let us suppose that when they listen to a lecture in a foreign language, they also take notes in their native language, translate sentences into the native language for use in papers and exams, and even ask questions in their native language. In such instances, assessment exercises that elicit student responses in their **native** language would appear not only natural but preferable. The real question would be, how effectively are students translating foreign-language material into their native language? Assuming this translation goes on anyway, it may be valuable to check how accurately it is being conducted.

There are various problems with target-language answers, such as

1. Uncertainty about whether the answer was simply copied from the text (sometimes with irrelevant material included)
2. Difficulties in deciphering ambiguous or incomprehensible answers due to problems in grammar, vocabulary, and punctuation
3. The real possibility of teacher distraction from the **content** of the answers because of the **form**—negatively affecting teachers' judgments about the information

Of course, there are problems with responses in the native language as well. Teachers have to be familiar with their students' first language so that they can evaluate whether answers are correct. Furthermore, students have to be able to find native-language equivalents for the vocabulary and grammatical patterns of the text with which they are working.

Reporting. Students describe events that they have witnessed. For example, students could be required to find a newsworthy event that took place in their community and to give an oral report on the event. This report could be tape-recorded at home or in the language lab. Likewise, students could be asked to describe in the target language the contents of a passage that they read in their native language. The use of the native-language text here would be intended to ensure maximal comprehension of the material to be reported on.

Written response

Matching. The student locates a match for a word or phrase—in other words, a word or phrase that is a contextual paraphrase (a synonymous phrase) for another phrase in the given context. For example,

> Read the following paragraph, and write out the contextual paraphrase for each of the underlined phrases appearing elsewhere in the test:

On the day before the voting took place, the politicians were still making <u>the kind of preposterous allegations</u> with which they had started their campaigns. The amazing thing was that many of the voters were wont to believe every word that they heard. Yet it was easy to identify the type of absurd accusations being made as just so much politicking before the <u>ballots were cast</u>.

Answers: <u>the kind of preposterous allegations</u> = the type of absurd accusations
<u>ballots were cast</u> = voting took place

Note taking. A student takes notes on a lecture, news broadcast, or talk. The notes may constitute the response, or the student may then be asked to summarize what was said or to provide structured or free responses to questions.

Rewriting. A student rewrites a passage, changing one or more elements—for example, from present to past tense, from first person to third person, from singular to plural, or from direct speech to indirect speech.

Written discourse as if oral. The respondents write down what they would say in such a situation. The following is the format for a discourse completion task where some elicitation has been given:

Your neighbor's dog in the next apartment was on the porch barking at the crack of dawn for the third day in a row. This time you're fed up. You go next door to complain.

Neighbor (opens the door with a big smile on his face and shakes his neighbor's hand): "Come in, pal."

(As a discourse-completion task)

Student: (The student is to perform written role play.)

Neighbor: "Well, dogs have to bark, you know! What can I do?"

Student: (Reply to the rejoinder)

Neighbor: "OK, I didn't realize it was that bad. I'll make sure he spends the night indoors and away from open windows."

Nonverbal Response

Identification by gestures. Classmates can be requested to hold up one finger if they hear the teacher or a fellow student say "They **hit** the bottle" and two fingers if they hear "They **heat** the bottle."

Responding to requests. Students can be asked to respond to imperative statements—for example, "Put your hands on your head after you've touched your toes." Or a student could be asked to find a place on a map from a description, arrange blocks or other items according to a description, or identify one of several pictures from a description.

Pictorial response. Like pictorial-elicitation formats, pictorial-response formats are problematic. In a response format, students are being called on to demonstrate some artistic ability—even if it is simply to draw an arrow between two objects or to complete some stick drawing. Also, such a format may encourage students to check what other students are doing, which may constitute cheating if this activity is not what the teacher had intended. All the same, partial and total drawing can constitute a change of pace for students and may be enjoyable.

If students are asked to draw, the possibilities are somewhat limited. The most reasonable type of picture to request would be stick figures or a simple sketch. Heaton (1975:73-74, 1990:48-49) suggested having students draw geometric shapes in various places on the page or, given a street scene, for example, having them supply a number of missing elements, provided orally or in a written list. Figure 6.11 presents such an example, aimed specifically at checking for comprehension of vocabulary frequently in instructions for homework assignments—for example, *to circle, to underline, to box in, to add, to delete,* and *to substitute.* Figure 6.12 involves completing a picture. Needless to say, the picture-completion exercise is meaningful only insofar as it assesses objects that have been taught in the course. For example, suppose the class has done extensive work on prepositional relationships. Picture completion would check for this.

Figure 6.11

Following Directions

Following Directions

You are to read this material <u>carefully</u> and to perform the <u>following</u> tasks:

1. Draw a circle around every <u>letter t</u> appearing in this exercise ↓
2. Underline any word with a double <u>letter</u> in it. ↓
3. Box in this one instruction ↓
4. <u>Add</u> an <u>arrow</u> pointing downward at the end of every numbered instruction. ↓ ✳
5. Delete the <u>arrow</u> added to the previous instruction and substitute an asterisk in its place. ↓

Figure 6.12

Completing the Picture

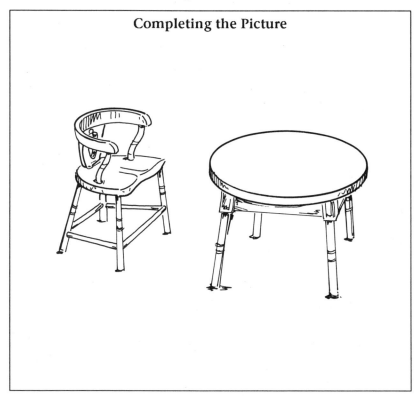

The Response Behavior Being Assessed

Similar items or procedures can be used to assess different response behaviors. For example, students who are asked to write with *accuracy* for twenty minutes about their best friend and who are told to pay attention to grammar and mechanics will approach the task differently from students who are told to write as much as they can about their best friend in ten minutes with the emphasis on *speed* and *quantity* of information. Almost invariably, the two tasks will produce different results.

Likewise, a reader may be given an hour to carefully read five pages of an article on energy conservation in order to answer ten questions calling for detailed responses. Or the student may be asked to read rapidly a few selected paragraphs from the article in order to indicate the main idea of each paragraph. Some items may call for a quick response to determine how effectively the respondent replies under time pressure. Since such tests are less reliable, there needs to be a good reason for using them. One such reason is to assess the ability to skim material rapidly. If respondents are given too much time, they may not skim. Providing a text that is too long to read intensively in the allotted time may help to promote the desired skill of skimming.

A student can be asked to listen closely to a reporter's question and a dignitary's answer at a press conference so that the student's accuracy of comprehension of the question and of the answer is tested, or to listen to the entire press conference in order to identify the major points that came up. When learners are tested for accuracy, they may (1) listen so intently to a part of the message that they miss the message in its entirety, (2) speak with repeated pauses, or (3) read with numerous regressions.

The constraint of timing a test or quiz may help to give the students added confidence by showing them that they are able to function quickly in the new language if they need to. For instance, practical suggestions have been provided regarding *quickwriting* tasks in class, whereby students get as many of their ideas on paper in a specific time without worrying about the form their writing takes. Thus, learners must write without editing and focus exclusively on expressing their thoughts (Scarcella & Oxford, 1992). In one version of quickwriting, the teacher writes a topic on the board and then leads a short, guided discussion about the topic, writing key points on the board in an organized fashion. Next, students write for seven minutes about some aspect of the topic that is of particular concern to them, at the end of which time the papers are collected (Celce-Murcia, 1974).

Preparing Instructions for Assessment Instruments

Let us return to the principles of good instructions, as presented in Chapter 4, and consider each in turn.

Be brief but explicit; be complete and unambiguous. This principle almost seems like a contradiction in terms, because when trying to be explicit, complete, and unambiguous, it is difficult to be brief. In fact, the results of a recent study of summarizing (Cohen, 1993) would suggest that explicit (lengthy) instructions may be more beneficial than traditional brief instructions, especially if the task is not an easy one. If students are not depending on the instructions but are functioning on the basis of prior knowledge, then it does not matter whether the instructions are anything but brief. On the other hand, if the instructions are the source of crucial pointers on how to perform the task, as in the case of the summarization research study (Cohen, 1993), then their extra length may be an asset rather than a liability. In fact, it may be beneficial to regard the instructions as an opportunity to provide an on-the-spot mini-training for the respondents to make sure that they all have certain common knowledge about how to respond to the given assessment measure(s).

Be specific about the form the answers are to take, providing a sample question and answer if possible. In general, this is good advice. The advantage of a sample answer is that the respondents will then know the form that their response is to take. However, there is a danger that the respondents may not read the instructions at all but may simply go on the basis of analogy to what they presumed the sample answer was requiring. If they have misinterpreted the function of the answer, then they may do poorly on the test or subtest. Another problem is that items and procedures may not easily lend themselves to the sample's question-and-answer format. This would be especially true for essay questions and for certain speaking tasks. Finally, it is important to give the respondents a chance to warm up. Particularly in tests of speaking, this may mean giving respondents several turns at saying the same thing, in a loop fashion (see Arevart & Nation, 1993), to ensure that their minds are as fully engaged in speaking the target language as possible. However, the assessment measure must not be too lengthy, so efforts at providing adequate warm-up need to be included in moderation.

Give sufficient information on the value of each item and section of the assessment instrument, the time allowed for each subtest and/or for the total measure, and whether speed is a factor. It can be most helpful to indicate at the outset the value of each item and section; otherwise, certain students may spend an inordinate amount of time working on items or sections that are of little value in their overall score. It could also be beneficial to provide criteria for the assessment of performance on a given test or subtest. For example, students could benefit from knowing the criteria to be used in evaluating an essay. If, for example, they are informed that grammar will not be weighted heavily, they may put more emphasis on the ideas that they wish to communicate and less on the structures that they use to communicate these ideas.[7] Ideally, the instrument should be constructed so that there is ample time to finish it within the time allotted. If it is a "speeded" test, then this needs to be made clear to the respondents; in such cases, instructions on how to proceed might be even more beneficial. For some assessment instruments, it may be beneficial to actually give the suggested number of minutes to spend on each item.

Multiple Means of Assessment Over Time

Not only is assessment reflecting more of an integrative approach in recent years, but it has also become increasingly clear that assessment of language benefits from the use of multiple means over time. So, with respect to the assessment of speaking and writing, *portfolios* are being used to obtain a set of tape recordings and essays from each student, rather than basing assessment on one single speaking or essay test score. With regard to writing portfolios, individuals are assessed on the basis of a collection of their writings that the individuals and a committee of teachers deem worthy of assessment (see Chapter 8 for more on writing portfolios).

Dialogue journals have also emerged as a technique for assessing over time the extent to which learners can genuinely communicate in the target language. While learners are preparing their written work on the right side of a notebook or "journal," they also write any comments or queries they have about their writing on the left side. Ideally, these are "on-line" remarks based on an immediate problem (e.g., deciding what word, phrase, or syntactic structure to use). The teacher periodically collects up a portion of the class's journals and goes over them, commenting in the space on the left side of the notebooks. While the rules of the game are such that teachers are not to correct any of the language in the journal portion of the notebook, they are certainly free to make holistic judgments on the general communicative ability of their students in this free-communication task.

The same type of journal can be used to record experiences while reading texts assigned in the course. Students are also encouraged to write comments about the course or about things happening in their lives, not just about problems arising during the preparation of assignments.

An approach to assessing spoken language over time might involve the teacher collecting snippets of tape-recorded speech (e.g., two minutes each) on each of, say, six occasions. This way the teacher would have twelve minutes of speech in order to chart the students' improvement in speaking. Ideally, these snippets of language would be on subjects with which the speakers feel comfortable and about which they get adequately involved, so that they focus on their message and not on its form (e.g., "an event that made me incredibly happy," with the focus on content).

Multiple means of assessment of speaking would also include varying the ways in which the speaking samples are evaluated. For example, oral presentations by nonnative students in the classroom could be rated in different ways. First, the students could rate themselves through viewing a videotape of their presentation and assessing themselves on a given set of criteria:

1. What did I do well?
2. Where could I have improved?
3. How could I have improved?
4. What did I learn from this presentation?[8]

Second, their peers could rate them, both during the presentation itself and in viewing the videotape. Third, the teacher could rate the presentation (Solé, 1991; Rolfe, 1990). The important thing is to work out criteria for assessment that are comprehensible, fair, and convenient.

Self-Assessment

The use of self-assessment has gained popularity, but it is also a source of some controversy. Self-assessment entails having the learners evaluate their own performance. At the non-language-specific level, learners could be asked to rate their performance in a small group. By now it is well-known that small groups are by no means a panacea in the classroom, since whole groups and individuals in those groups may, in fact, engage in little or no activity conducive to learning simply by virtue of being placed in the group. Figure 6.13 provides a sample self-assessment instrument intended to be used by elementary and secondary-school pupils in order to evaluate their own group participation.

With regard to the self-assessment of language abilities, learners could be asked to rate their ability to perform specified functional tasks or to indicate whether they would be able to

Figure 6.13

How Well Do I Help My Group Get the Job Done?:
Self-Assessment of Small-Group Participation

Observable behaviors that are indicators of how well I help my group get the job done	Often	Some-times	Seldom	Not yet
Contribute information.				
Take my turn.				
Complete the work assigned to me.				
Ask for the participation of others.				
Help the group follow the directions.				
Help the group understand the goal.				
Help the group make a plan.				
Help the group stick to the plan.				
Help the group use time well.				
Listen attentively.				
Ask helpful questions.				
Make sure all group members understand.				
Help to organize materials and supplies.				
Keep my attention on the task.				
Ask for help when I do not understand well enough.				

* *

Overall, how well do I help my group get the job done?
Circle one:

1	2	3	4	5	6	7	8	9	10
Not a help							A very good help		

This assessment schedule was developed in the last several years by Jayne Bischoff at Stoner Prairie Elementary School, Verona Area Public Schools, Fitchburg, Wisconsin, and Stephen Elliott at the Department of Psychology, University of Wisconsin-Madison.

respond successfully to given assessment items or procedures. As with any technique, the use of self-assessment may lead to abuse, depending on the circumstances under which it is used and the specific assessment materials involved. On the basis of a review of sixteen self-assessment studies, Blanche and Merino (1989) identified five factors that can threaten the validity of self-assessment methods:

1. Learners' lack of training in how to perform the types of self-assessment that are asked of them
2. A lack of common criteria for learner self-ratings and for teacher interpretations of these ratings
3. A conflict between the cultural backgrounds of the learners and the culture on which the self-assessment tasks are based
4. Any inabilities that the learners may have in monitoring their behavior (i.e., learners may not be able to report on what is subconscious behavior for them)
5. The intervening effects of subjective influences (past academic record, career aspirations, or expectations of others)

The first three of these factors are interrelated in that effective training would be intended to establish self-assessment criteria common to students and teachers, and presumably such training would take into account as much as possible the cultural backgrounds of the learners.

We might conclude that careful self-assessment by students in a classroom could be one of the means for multiple assessment, while the use of self-assessment for large-scale assessment might be more problematic, especially when administrative decisions of class-level placement are involved.

Research Notes

The earliest reports on self-assessment appeared in the late 1970s (Oskarsson, 1980). One of these studies found that in all language areas except for grammar, students' self-assessments were highly correlated with their actual performance (von Elek, 1982). Learners responded to a large number of items (1,500: sixty subtests, each with twenty-five items) assessing vocabulary, grammar, listening comprehension, reading comprehension, oral proficiency, and written proficiency. Students were to indicate if they absolutely knew the answer, thought so, or did not know the answer. The correlations between learner response and actual performance ranged from .60 to .97 on all the subtests except for grammar, where the range was lower (.45 to .65). The conclusion was that learners made most misjudgments with regard to grammar.

A more recent self-assessment project involved the development of a range of self-assessment tools and formats for a group of sixteen adult immigrant learners of mixed national groups and in the lower proficiency range (Lewis, 1990). The investigator found self-assessment to be a useful tool in encouraging learners to be more involved in planning their own learning and reflecting on their progress. Self-assessment increased the dialogue between teachers and learners. It was concluded that if learners were given adequate explanation and practice, self-assessment could become part of the teaching program as a means to see if learners are meeting their needs and if the tasks and situations rated are sufficiently specific.

Another investigation producing evidence in favor of self-assessment was conducted by Blanche (1990) at the Defense Language Institute in Monterey, California. The study involved forty-three adult learners of French and used examinations for both external assessment and self-assessment. The focus was on accuracy in speaking at the levels of grammaticality and proficiency, and the assessment was conducted over several months during an intensive language program. The results were considered promising in that the overall self-evaluations were found to be accurate, although the small sample size and the fact that it was a unique learning environment in which the learners demonstrated unusually high motivation were seen as limitations. Furthermore, several personal variables were not taken into account (age, sex, personality), and the nature of the assessment instrument itself was not analyzed closely.

A study by Rolfe (1990) looked at the relationship of self-assessment, peer assessment, and teacher assessment within a group of sixty adult ESL learners (five classes ranging from low to low-intermediate). Unlike the previously cited studies, in this case the researcher found considerable variation in self-ratings of proficiency. What Rolfe also found was that the correlations between the mean peer ratings and those by the teachers were consistently high, indicating that the peer ratings were as reliable as those of the teachers, if not more so. He suggested that since peers actually spend more time interacting with each other than with the teacher, they may be in better position to monitor their own and others' communicative performance.[9]

The final study to be noted here is that of Ready-Morfitt (1991), which took a second look at a self-assessment program started at the University of Ottawa in 1984 as the only means of placement in ESL and French-second-language classes. Students were asked to rate a series of statements on a five-point scale, from "I cannot do the task at all" to "I can do it all the time." As of 1987, students were also given the cutoff levels so that they could register themselves into courses by mail. A standardized placement test of reading and listening comprehension was developed, administered, and compared with the results from self-assessment. The results indicated that approximately 75% of the students were misplaced at the two lower levels and 40% at the higher levels.

One apparent reason for the misplacements was over-assessment, given the wide variation in students' previous learning experiences. Efforts to have learners rate their abilities by specific performance tasks did not produce an improvement in the relationship between self-assessment and objective assessment. One telling factor is that students who underassessed themselves were actually shown in Des Brisay's (1984) study to function well in the course, showing that the course met their needs. It was suggested that the self-assessment questionnaire did not make fine enough distinctions. Also, students may have wanted to avoid taking the two lower-level, non-credit courses. The researcher suggested using three types of self-assessment questions: (1) "How much English grammar do you know?" (knowledge); (2) "How many different kinds of grammar mistakes do you make in English?" (difficulty in use); and (3) "How often can you tell when someone makes a grammar mistake?" (recognition of trait). Even with modifications in place, Ready-Morfitt concluded that such a self-assessment instrument should not be used in place of an objective performance test.

Designing an Instrument for Self-Assessment in the Classroom

Let us now look at the design of an instrument for self-assessment in the classroom. As Brindley (1989) effectively illustrates, there is no single self-assessment instrument appropriate for all learners in all situations. Rather, instruments should be designed according to the areas of concern for the teacher and learners in the given language-learning context. The criteria for assessment would also have to fit the local needs.

Let us consider some examples of possible areas for rating the different language skills, bearing in mind that these are merely suggestive. Ideally, the students themselves would help to draw up an instrument that they would feel comfortable using, as a means of keeping tabs on their progress in their course of instruction. Whereas these suggestions offer particular areas for self-assessment, Lewis (1990) and others would be sure to include open-ended items such as "I think my strengths are the following . . .," "I think my weak points are the following . . .," and "I would like more work in class on the following . . . ."

Listening

Comprehension of questions asked. These questions could be further broken down by type of questions—for instance, questions about grammatical structures, questions about the content of newspaper articles, questions regarding literary texts, or questions about opinions. Here is a possible set of self-rating scales:

> 5—I can always understand the questions with no difficulty and without having to ask for repetition.
> 4—I can usually understand questions, but I might occasionally ask for repetition.
> 3—I have difficulty with some questions, but I generally get the meaning.
> 2—I have difficulty understanding most questions even after repetition.
> 1—I don't understand questions well at all.

Comprehension of instructions. Again, what the instructions deal with could be specified—for example, the teacher gives detailed instructions on how to do the homework or gives details about how to work some mechanical apparatus. Here is a possible self-rating scale of student comprehension:

My level of understanding:
5—all the instructions
4—most of the instructions
3—enough of the instructions to perform the task,
but various details not understood
2—some of the instructions, but not enough to perform
the task satisfactorily
1—a few of the instructions, but not enough to do anything

Comprehension of conversation in the classroom and/or out of class. The students could be asked periodically to rate themselves in terms of their success at understanding spoken language in the following situations, using this rating scale: 5 = excellent, 4 = good, 3 = fair, 2 = poor, 1 = minimal:

- Conventional greetings and farewells
- Invitations
- Compliments
- Someone else's personal information (name, address, phone number)
- Personal opinions of the teacher or of classmates
- Directions on how to get to somewhere a bit out of the way
- A radio news broadcast
- TV news
- Getting details from a telephone call or from a message recorded rapidly on an answering machine

Speaking

For self-rating of their success in speaking, students could select from among numerous criteria. The challenge is to find scales that are informative and user-friendly at the same time. This may call for some trial and error.

Grammatical problems get in the way. A possible rating scale is 5 = never, delivery is effortless in terms of grammatical structure; 4 = occasionally; 3 = a moderate number of grammatical problems get in the way; 2 = often; 1 = problems with grammatical structure make communication all but impossible.

Distinguishing different types of vocabulary knowledge. For example, for academic needs in my courses, basic interpersonal exchanges, or high-level interactions with friends, 5 = I feel I have all the words I need; 4 = I feel I have most of the words I need; 3 = I feel I have only about half of the words I need; 2 = I feel I have only a few of the words I need; 1 = I feel I don't have any of the words I need.

The use of appropriate style. 5 = always use the appropriate style; 4 = usually use the appropriate style; 3 = moderate use of the appropriate style; 2 = on occasion use the appropriate style; 1 = no sense of what style to use. For such a scale to function well, the students must have a good sense of what style means in terms of levels of formality. The following situations could be used for self-rating:

1. Giving directions
2. Expressing my political views
3. Describing to a doctor the symptoms of an ailment I have
4. Expressing important functions (speech acts) such as
   • apologies
   • complaints
   • requests (can I make these courteously?)
   • refusals
   • compliments
5. Summarizing a conversation I just had

There are other scales that could be used, such as those for sociocultural and sociolinguistic ability, which will be discussed in

Chapter 8. The problem is that scales such as these may be difficult if not impossible for the language learners to use in self-ratings.

Reading

For self-rating of reading ability, the most important scale would probably be that of *vocabulary knowledge*, again possibly indicating vocabulary control by general or specific domain. For instance, in academic subject matter areas or for common-language needs: 5 = complete control of vocabulary; 4 = knowledge of most of the words, but unknown words don't interfere with comprehension; 3 = knowledge of some key words lacking, which interferes with comprehension; 2 = frequent gaps in vocabulary knowledge, with comprehension poor; 1 = vocabulary totally inadequate, with very little comprehension.[10]

Another possible scale could be for *reading flexibility*: 5 = I always adjust my reading to the style of writing and pace myself accordingly; 4 = often; 3 = sometimes; 2 = rarely; 1 = never.

Other scales could deal with facility in recognizing discourse markers as signs of *cohesion*, ability to perceive the *author's tone* (serious, humorous, sarcastic, cynical), and so forth. The following are some sample reading activities that could be rated:

1. Headlines from the newspaper/front-page stories in the newspaper/a sports-section article
2. Reading a text in order to summarize it orally for somebody else
3. Finding and successfully using important material in a computer manual or other technical guide (e.g., to a car or appliance)
4. Using a dictionary to find necessary information
5. Using the classified section of a phone book
6. Reading a handwritten personal letter

Writing

The self-rating scales to measure writing ability could include some of the scales included above in the discussion of speaking—namely, *grammar*, *vocabulary*, *style* (e.g., 5 = I always have a sense of how to write something politely; 4 = usually; 3 = sometimes; 2 = rarely; 1 = never). Self-assessment of writing ability could also include scales for *organization* and *mechanics* (spelling, punctuation, and paragraphing). Some activities that could be rated include:

1. Writing an academic paper
2. Filling out a detailed questionnaire (e.g., preparing a curriculum vitae in questionnaire form)

How the use of self-assessment is defined in the given instructional setting will depend on the teacher and the learners. If the learners keep a diary or journal of their learning activities, then self-assessment could be built into this journal. Students would keep an ongoing record of how they are progressing in one or more of these areas over time. They could add comments that would help to clarify the meaning of given self-ratings. Teachers would perhaps have general class discussions from time to time in order to help clarify the rating system both for their benefit and for the students as well.

Conclusion

In this chapter we have noted that items on language assessment instruments in the 1990s tend to be of a more integrative than discrete-point nature than they were twenty years ago. We also provided a distinctive-element analysis of item-elicitation and item-response formats that might be combined successfully for the purposes of classroom assessment—often involving no more than short quizzes. The breakdown of items by skill—listening, speaking, reading, and writing—was purposely avoided since formats cut across skill boundaries and since such breakdowns are found in a number of books on language assessment. The approach taken here has rather been that of demonstrating to the teacher the advantage of scrutinizing the truly distinctive elements of test construction. In other words, with a few elements the teacher may construct a variety of classroom quizzes or tests.

We also looked at other dimensions related to assessment formats, namely, the response behavior being assessed and the nature of the instructions. The job of test construction does not end once items have been selected. It is important to determine the type of response behavior desired, in terms of speed, accuracy, and quantity, and the nature of the instructions.

We then considered the use of multiple means of assessment over time, such as through the use of speaking and writing portfolios, in an effort to provide richer information on students. Finally, we described self-assessment as a means whereby students can use self-ratings to determine their own progress in learning a second or foreign language.

Discussion Questions and Activities

1. You are teaching a basic conversation course for twenty-five adult ESL students at a community center. There is a syllabus for the course, which includes the basic structures of English and survival vocabulary for everyday needs. You and your students want feedback on how much learning is going on. Hence, you start to construct an assessment instrument. You want it to assess both overall speaking ability and the learning of specific vocabulary and grammatical structures. So you devise an instrument with tasks that measure communicative ability in an integrative fashion, using discrete-point items. Give the rationale for your instrument to a fellow colleague, and describe six sample items and procedures from your test.

2. Refresh your memory of the different types of meaning that can be assessed through reading comprehension questions. Then construct several short-answer reading comprehension questions based on a passage that you have available. Be sure that your questions require respondents to comprehend at least two types of meaning. Pilot your items with other students in the class, and then try them out on several nonnative readers, using verbal report to determine whether the items actually assess the types of meaning that you intended them to.

3. You are an intermediate-level teacher of Japanese as a foreign language. It has become clear to you that your students often copy material directly from the Japanese text when you ask them to respond to short-answer questions in Japanese on mid-terms and finals. Since your students are all native speakers of English, you decide to ask them reading comprehension questions about Japanese language texts in English. When your department head gets word that you are doing this, she reminds you that the course is not a course in translation and that you are expected to use Japanese as much as possible. What arguments do you pose to her regarding the advantages and disadvantages of having students respond in their native language rather than in the target language?

4. As a class activity for teacher trainees, have each students generate three items using three different item-elicitation formats and three different item-response formats. Then have the students exchange test items with a peer, respond to the items, and then discuss their reactions on an item-by-item basis. Finally, have the students share with the entire class any insights they have gained through constructing test items in this analytical way.

5. Again as an activity for teacher trainees, have each student find three assessment instruments, either from within the department or elsewhere. These could be mid-terms, finals, exit exams, or commercial tests. Their assignment is to scrutinize all the instructions for responding to every item and procedure. Then they are to share first with a small group and then with the whole class the strengths and weaknesses of the instructions that they evaluated. Let this exercise be the basis for producing a set of issues that test constructors need to consider when preparing instructions for test items and procedures.

6. You have for some time wanted to give students some say about the grade they get in your advanced ESL reading and composition course at the university. You decide to introduce self-assessment by having your pupils assess their own reading of selected texts. You let them know that their self-determined grade will form part of their course grade. What remains for you to do is to plan out a means by which your students actually self-assess their reading ability. Select one or more reading passages that you

feel would be appropriate for such an activity, and construct a self-assessment instrument around the passage(s). Share this instrument with several of your colleagues to get their reactions. Check over the list of factors threatening the validity of self-assessment instruments, and do your best to avoid these threats, both in the training that you provide the students before you pilot the instrument on them and in the criteria that you establish for the ratings (e.g., what do *excellent*, *good*, and *lacking* actually mean?).

Notes

1 In Chapter 2 we introduced the concept of *systemic validity* to take into account the effects of instructional changes brought about by the introduction of a test into an educational system.

2 That is, the study of how sentences in spoken and written language form larger, meaningful units.

3 This four-level model is adapted from Nuttall (1982) and appeared in Cohen (1990a) as well.

4 The author and a colleague found evidence with young children (third grade, for example) that tests with multiple item formats (in this case, sixteen formats on a criterion-referenced test) produced poorer results than tests using a single format (in a standardized test), particularly among children with limited cognitive flexibility and short attention span (Rodríguez-Brown & Cohen, 1979).

5 We need to bear in mind that using a projective or indirect measure of the skill (writing as if speaking) makes the assessment more susceptible to problems of reliability and validity.

6 Noises such as *uh* or *er*, which indicate that speakers are continuing but have stopped to choose what they will say next.

7 As noted in Chapter 4, it is usually considered better practice in assessment to provide more items for objectives that are of

greater importance on the test than to give differential weighting to items of a given type (e.g., giving greater weighting to inference questions and less weighting to items assessing control of prepositions).

8 The following section concentrates on self-assessment.

9 In keeping with this finding, Chapter 8 suggests that peer ratings of speaking ability could enter into the assessment of oral proficiency.

10 It might not even be necessary to have a scale for grammar since, as was mentioned in Chapter 4, grammatical control does not seem to play a major role in reading comprehension.

Chapter 7:
Assessing
Reading
Comprehension

In order to assess reading comprehension in a second or foreign language, it is necessary to have a working knowledge of what that process entails. In many ways, reading in a target language is like reading in the native language. For this reason, let us first take a brief look at reading in the native language. Then we will consider similarities and differences in second-language reading. From there we will look at types of reading, types of comprehension, and the skills involved. Finally, we will explore methods for testing reading comprehension: communicative tests, multiple-choice and alternative formats, the cloze test, the C-test, recall protocols, the testing of vocabulary, and computer-based testing.

Reading in the Native Language

First of all, L1 reading is not a **passive** activity as it has sometimes been labeled. Even in the 1960s, reading began to be referred to by psycholinguists as a most active **psycholinguistic guessing game**—

a process whereby readers predicted what would come next on the basis of what they had already sampled from the text[1] and then confirmed or corrected their hunches about the predicted meaning of the text, based on what the sampling provided (Goodman, 1967). Reading calls for the reader to actively supply meaning to text on a continual basis. Michael Scott (1986) pointed out some other mistaken notions regarding reading, aside from the false notion that reading is a passive skill:

1. Whereas readers may think that they remember sentences that they read, they most likely remember the meaning and not the exact words or grammar. This explains why they may have difficulty precisely identifying which sentence they have read when presented with a set of similar sentences.
2. Whereas readers may think that they are reading through a text without *regressions* (i.e., visual cycling back over words or phrases already read), they may actually be moving back and forth in the text more than they think—almost as they would do when observing a picture they have never seen.
3. Whereas readers may think they are reading in a smooth, linear, word-for-word fashion, their eyes actually jump from one fixation point to another. This helps explain why we do not necessarily notice repeated words or typing errors in a text. This is the "sampling" phenomenon referred to above in Goodman's description of reading as prediction, sampling, and confirmation.
4. Whereas readers may think that they cannot understand a text with a number of unknown words in it, they may well find that it is possible to understand the text without the use of certain unknown words and to make reasonable guesses about the other words on the basis of the context and possibly through analysis of the words themselves.

Among the more prominent theoretical frameworks for the reading process is that of the interactional model, where reading is viewed as an interaction between the text and the reader, with comprehension varying according to a number of *text features* and *reader characteristics* (see Barnett [1989], Bernhardt [1991], and Swaffar, Arens, & Byrnes [1991]). Text includes features of discourse and grammar, while reader characteristics include not only language proficiency, attitudes, and motivation, but also background knowledge. We could add to this *context* characteristics as well, namely, the physical surroundings (light, noise, comfort, and so forth) and the amount of time allowed for reading.

Reading for meaning involves the activation of networks of real-world and rhetorical information for the purpose of interpreting texts. These sources of background knowledge have been referred to more technically as *schemata* (Rumelhart, 1980; Anderson & Pearson, 1984; Carrell & Eisterhold, 1983; Carrell, 1988). Such schemata have been classified according to three basic types:

1. *Content schemata*—systems of factual knowledge, values, and cultural conventions
2. *Language schemata*—sentence structure, grammatical inflections, spelling and punctuation, vocabulary, and cohesive structures
3. *Textual schemata*—the rhetorical structure of different modes of text—for example, recipes, letters, fairy tales, research papers, and science textbooks

When readers approach text on the basis of the prior content, language, or textual schemata that they may have with regard to that particular text, this is referred to as *top-down* reading (Carrell, 1988). For example, readers may identify a given text as an article reporting on a piece of research in an academic journal. This realization would be likely to activate certain *textual schemata* regarding research papers. In other words, the readers would most likely apply their prior textual schemata to the reading of this research paper. They would also be likely to have certain expectations with respect to *language schemata*—types of terminology that appear in the article (e.g., *research hypotheses, stratified random sample,* and *analysis of covariance*) and patterns of cohesion that are likely to be found (e.g., the mention of key concepts in the abstract of the paper, elaboration of these concepts in the review of literature, reference to them in the findings section and in the discussion). Finally, they would notice that the article is, for example, a study of differences in the male and female brain. This topic would immediately signal either certain *content schemata* or an awareness of the lack of them. In other words, the readers could come to the realization that they are lacking the relevant content schemata necessary to understand what the text is about.

Although it may be convenient to assume that prior content knowledge simply means having the content schemata or not, the issue is more complex. Sometimes, having no content schemata is preferable to having only some of the schemata, since the accommodating of **existing** knowledge structures can be more problematic than dealing with new knowledge. At other times prior false concepts are seen to be so deeply fixed in the minds of the readers that they actually discard their accurate observations in order to maintain the integrity of these false concepts (see Pace, Marshall, Horowitz, Lipson, & Lucido, 1989).

When readers focus exclusively on what is present in the text itself, and especially on the words and sentences of the text, this is referred to as *bottom-up* reading. Such reading is also referred to as *text-based* or *data-driven*. Successful readers usually display a combination of top-down and bottom-up reading. In fact, it has been suggested that readers may use top-down reading to compensate for deficiencies in bottom-up reading, and vice versa (Stanovich, 1980). In other words, a reader who has poor word-recognition skills may rely on top-down reading.

Reading in a Second Language

What happens when the reading is in a second language? It appears that much of what the reader does is the same as when reading in the first language. However, L2 reading is often slower and less successful. A study done some years ago revealed that the slowness is not because L2 readers are making more fixations or *saccades*[2] per line, but rather because they are spending more time at each fixation (Tullius, 1971; Oller & Tullius, 1973). The difference between the eye movement of university-level ESL students and that of native readers was that the ESL students' eye fixations were almost three times as long.

Furthermore, when reading in a second language, we are usually confronted with far more unknown vocabulary words. Also, the sentence structure may pose an obstacle, but perhaps less than might be expected. Readers use various tricks for overcoming unfamiliar sentence structure. One such trick is to focus almost exclusively on vocabulary and to infer probable sentence structure based on the likely relationship of words.[3] In some ways it is like piecing together the syntax of a telegram on the basis of the few words provided (although the syntax of telegrams is usually not very complex).

When reading in a second or foreign language, readers may try a host of busy bottom-up reading activities—e.g., word analysis, use of a dictionary, and analysis of sentence structure—without coming away with a clue about what a word, phrase, sentence, or passage means. Such a situation can be avoided if the texts that are selected are not too far above the level of the readers' proficiency. And when a text that is clearly above an individual's reading level is being tackled, the reader must compensate for the lack of bottom-up knowledge by using top-down reading—invoking whatever content, textual, and language schemata can be of help in answering the question "What does this text mean?" At times, the use of such knowledge makes a positive contribution. At other times, the procedure will lead to distortions.

Let us consider the following example of distortion caused by top-down compensation for deficiencies in bottom-up vocabulary knowledge. The example is taken from research by Laufer and Sim (1983). Within a text by Margaret Mead that the reader had to interpret, there was the following sentence:

> This nurturing behavior, this fending for females and children instead of leaving them to fend for themselves, as the primates do, may take many different forms.

One reader read *nurturing* as *natural*, *fending* as *finding*, and *leaving* as *living*. The reader's interpretation of the sentence was as follows:

> Instead of living natural life, natural behavior, females and children find many different forms of life.

The reader substituted other words that were known instead of the unknown words and built meaning around these substitutions.[4]

Assessing Reading Comprehension Ability

For at least a decade now, experts in native and second-language reading assessment have recommended that reading comprehension be measured in less traditional ways. The basic argument is that assessment has been too limited in scope. For example, Johnston (1983) called for a series of new directions in the assessment of reading comprehension in a native language. He included the following suggested areas among what could be assessed:

1. Awareness and use of cues in text
2. Perception of the author's plan
3. Insights into the nature of the text
4. Strategies for retrieving information after reading
5. Schemata selection
6. Cognitive monitoring skills
7. The knowledge of summarization rules

He also suggested that these factors could be assessed by using verbal report as a way to get strategy information (Johnston, 1983).

What we see emerging is a concern that the testing of reading be more consistent with a strategic view of the reading process, as suggested by the preceding depiction of how readers actually read a text (Michael Scott, 1986)—a departure from viewing reading as a discrete skill. The traditional approach of using a number of short, unauthentic texts was seen to eliminate the need for calling on prior knowledge in order to answer items. In addition, such tasks were believed to rely on literal comprehension, to allow for only one correct answer, and to call for no more than the main idea (Valencia & Pearson, 1987). Furthermore, it was felt that the texts fragmented the reading process and that fluency was not assessed. Johnston (1983) asserted that the best assessment consisted of having teachers observe and interact with students who were reading authentic texts for genuine purposes, and of having teachers see how their students constructed meaning.

Reading comprehension items or procedures—however traditional or innovative—require that learners use a certain type or types of reading, comprehend one or more types of meaning, enlist a certain comprehension skill or skills, and do all of this within the framework of a certain testing method or methods. Let us now look at some of the choices available to the test constructor and at the concerns of the test user with respect to the types of reading, types of meaning, and types of comprehension skill to be assessed.

Types of Reading Assessed

Items and procedures can be written so that they implicitly or explicitly call for different types of reading.[5] For example, a respondent can be given such a lengthy passage to read in such a limited time frame that the only way to handle it successfully is either to *skim* it (i.e., inspect it rapidly with occasional periods of close inspection) or *scan* it (i.e., read in order to locate a specific symbol or group of symbols—e.g., a date or a name of a person or place). A distinction is also made between scanning and *search reading*, wherein the respondent is scanning without being sure about the form that the information will take (i.e., whether it is a word, phrase, sentence, passage, or whatever) (Pugh, 1978:53).

These three types of reading are quite common in everyday life, yet they do not often appear explicitly on reading comprehension tests—especially not on those involving the reading of short texts or single sentences. It may be that reading items and tasks are not always constructed with careful consideration of how the respondent is to read them. The test constructor may even want to indicate to the respondent the type of reading expected. For example, a certain item could be introduced by the following:

> Imagine that you are in your dentist's waiting room and you come upon a lengthy article of keen interest just several minutes before you are to be called in for your appointment. Since you are really anxious to get the gist of the article quickly, you read the text through rapidly (i.e., skim it) in order to get the main points. Do that now, and be aware that there will not be time to read the text

intensively. When you have completed this reading, answer the questions provided—without looking back at the text. You will have ten minutes for the exercise.

A respondent could also be given a passage to read *receptively* or *intensively*, a form of careful reading aimed at discovering exactly what the author seeks to convey. This form of reading is probably what respondents attempt to do as their "default" option, sometimes exaggerating by looking up too many words (if they are allowed to use a dictionary) or by trying to translate whole chunks of discourse.

Yet another approach is to have respondents read *responsively*, with the written material acting as a prompt to them to reflect on some point or other and then possibly to respond in writing. Testing formats in which questions are interspersed with running text may especially cater to such an approach, if the questions stimulate an active dialogue between the text and the reader. So if we take the Russell passage from Chapter 6, a small portion of responsive assessment might look like the following:

If you cannot travel, seek out people with whom you disagree, and read a newspaper belonging to a party that is not yours. If the people and the newspaper seem mad, perverse, and wicked, remind yourself that you seem so to them.

1. What does *so* in the second sentence refer to?

2. What is the tone of the writer at this point in the text?

In this opinion both parties may be right, but they cannot both be wrong. This reflection should generate a certain caution.

3. Paraphrase and explain the sentence that starts "In this opinion. . . ."

This approach of embedding questions eliminates time spent hunting for material during a test. On the other hand, the assessor may want to measure just this ability. Thus, one might use this format only in conjunction with other formats that do not signal so clearly the place in the text where the answer can be found.

Types of Meaning Assessed

A test item or procedure can tap at least four types of meaning, separately or simultaneously: grammatical meaning, informational meaning, discourse meaning, and the meaning conveyed by the writer's tone (adapted from Nuttall, 1982). These kinds of meaning were referred to in Chapter 6. Note that these categories are presented as a rough rule of thumb, rather than as four completely distinct types of meaning.

Assessing Grammatical Meaning: The Role of Syntax

The interest in types of meaning builds on earlier assessment approaches that focused heavily on the syntax of text and made assumptions about the difficulty of second-language text because of its syntax. Research over the last several decades has given evidence that somewhat downplays the role of syntax in reading comprehension (Ulijn, 1981; Ulijn & Strother, 1990) and therefore in its assessment. One approach to locating the source of errors in reading has been through analysis of syntactic patterns found in target-language text material that the learner is reading, as contrasted with patterns in similar material in the learner's native language. This technique has provided an opportunity to determine the importance of such contrasting syntactic patterns in the reading process.

According to theories concerning the effects of first-language interference on second language, learners could possibly misread a section simply because their expectations about the way the grammar conveys meaning in the target language are conditioned by their experience with grammar in their native language. Thus, they may be prone to misinterpret structures that are not like those they are used to.

Research Notes

Cowan (1976) gave examples of such contrastive reading difficulties—for example, native Persian speakers incorrectly processing relative clauses in reading English, and native English speakers incorrectly interpreting co-reference in reading Hindi or word order in reading German.[6] Cowan suggested that a priori contrastive analysis[7] may lead to correct predictions of reading difficulties. Teachers do not often verify native-language interference as a source of reading problems, because it calls for extra preparation on the teacher's part, particularly if several language groups are represented in a class.

Ulijn and Kempen (1976) conducted various types of empirical research to determine the extent to which parallelism of syntactic structures in the target language and the first language affect reading. In several studies, they found that success at reading in the target language (measured in words per second) was not necessarily affected by the presence of target-language syntactic structures different from those in the native language (Ulijn, 1977; Ulijn & Kempen, 1976). However, the researchers did identify a condition under which lack of parallelism of syntactic structures in the first language and in the target language could make a difference, namely, when conceptual and referential knowledge is limited. The experimenters hypothesized that under these conditions the readers would be forced to scrutinize the syntactic structure of each sentence and that differences in syntactic patterns between the first language and the target language would hamper comprehension.

A group of Dutch second-year psychology students was asked to read target-language (French) instructions for using an apparatus without actually seeing the apparatus. Then they were told to translate this set of instructions into their native language. In this case, the results indicated that target-language structures created more difficulty in translation when they were not parallel to the Dutch structures. This experiment was intended to demonstrate that subjects will revert to a syntactic reading strategy when they lack conceptual knowledge—in this case, using visual cues to infer the meaning of lexical items. And the researchers claimed that once a syntactic reading strategy is employed, there is more likelihood that degree of parallelism of structures between native and target language will play a role.

The importance of research such as that of Ulijn and Kempen (1976) is that it empirically addresses the issue of where errors or difficulties in reading a second language actually lie. Such research raises the issue that if learners encounter a lack of parallelism in structures between their native and target languages while reading target-language texts and if they are employing a syntactic reading strategy at that time, they may then have problems with comprehension.

We note that this line of research appeared at a time when contrastive analysis was still relatively popular but that in later years this issue has seemed to be eclipsed. Several investigators looked at the effects of syntax on reading, but no longer from a contrastive point of view. For example, Blau (1982) looked at the effect of "simple" sentences versus "complex" sentences with clues to underlying relationships left intact versus "complex" sentences without such clues. She found that for a group of eighty-five native, Spanish-speaking EFL students in Puerto Rico, it was the short and primarily simple sentences that were an obstacle to comprehension. Blau's explanation was that the relationships inherent in complex sentences were apparently lost through efforts to keep sentences short.

Berman's (1984) research suggested that sentence complexity was likely to be an impediment to grasping specific details, while confirming that core syntactic comprehension was enough for getting the gist. She called attention to problematic structures such as *heavy noun phrases* (i.e., phrases acting as subjects, objects, or objects of prepositions). In fact, the Cohen, Glasman, Rosenbaum-Cohen, Ferrara, and Fine (1979) study found that heavy noun phrases were predictably problematic for Hebrew readers of ESL texts at the college level, although lack of comprehension of these structures did not necessarily impair comprehension of the passage in which they appeared.

In recent years, reading studies have tended to place syntax low on the list of priorities in terms of readers' concerns (e.g., Laufer & Sim, 1985). Readers are seen to start with analysis of individual words and the semantic role of these words, then progress to an analysis of the discourse in which the words are found, and proceed to a syntactic analysis only if all else fails.

Research Notes

Strother and Ulijn (1987) investigated the effect of syntactic simplification of a technical text about computers. Their sample comprised forty-eight American students from the Florida Institute of Technology, half of them computer science majors and the other half humanities majors, and 139 Dutch ESL students with a similar split. One version of the text was revised to simplify the syntax (i.e., sentences containing nominalizations, passives, and participle constructions were rewritten in a syntactic form more suitable for what the authors called "a common language version"), but the meaning was not changed. The students were randomly assigned to reading one of two text forms and answering true-false questions about the text.

Strother and Ulijn found no significant effect. The students' principal strategy was apparently one of seeking content words. Neither their reading comprehension score nor their reading time was affected by simplification. The conclusion of the researchers was that thorough syntactic analysis was not needed. However, they did recommend lexical rewriting to increase readability—with a focus on semi-technical vocabulary because of the multiple meanings of some words.

Thus, a question for the teacher/assessor is whether it pays to determine when students are employing a syntactic reading strategy. If so, then how should the teacher go about determining what it is? Instead of asking students to write out a full translation, as in the traditional grammar-translation approach, teachers could ask them to choose which of two or more sentences in their native language is the best translation of a target-language sentence. The teacher could, for example, have the alternate-choice sentences differ in just one or more syntactic features. Another approach would be to have students translate just those several sentences from the text that contain the syntactic features of concern (see Buck, 1992). But these approaches may draw extra attention to the features in question and inadvertently simplify the task, and we would always want to return to the question of the purpose of assessment and the relevance to the curriculum and to the special needs of the students involved.

Assessing Informational Meaning

As indicated in Chapter 6, when we are reading for the informational meaning of the text, our purpose is to determine what the basic concepts or messages are that the text wishes to convey. To do this, we need to do enough analysis of vocabulary to distinguish known, possibly known, and unknown words, concepts, relationships, and the like. Some nonnative readers get stuck here. They have so much difficulty trying to determine the basic meanings of the idea units in a given text that they have no time or energy left to determine the relationships among these ideas, or to determine what the writer's attitude is towards these ideas.

Assessing Discourse Meaning

The kind of meaning that has gotten perhaps the most attention in the literature in recent years is *discourse meaning*, especially the perception of rhetorical functions conveyed by text. For example, an item may overtly or covertly require a respondent to identify where and how something is being defined, described, classified, exemplified, justified, or contrasted with something else. Often such rhetorical functions are signaled by connectors, or *discourse markers*. Nonetheless, uninformed or unalert readers may miss these signals—words or phrases such as *unless, however, thus, whereas*, and the like. Research has shown that such markers need not be subtle to cause reading problems. Simple markers of sequential points (*first, also,* and *finally*) may be missed by a reader, as well as more subtle markers (see Cohen, Glasman, Rosenbaum-Cohen, Ferrara, & Fine, 1979).

Assessing the Meaning Conveyed by the Writer's Tone

Actually, a kind of meaning that is worthy of more attention, especially at the advanced levels of assessment, is that of tone. This is an area that calls for advanced reading skills because the author's tone—be it sad, cynical, sarcastic, caustic, or humorous—may be signaled by the use of one word or phrase, possibly including a play on words. In addition, a reader does not have the cues that a listener might have when a speaker's intended meaning is also signaled by tone of voice and facial expression.

For example, it may be the case that nonnative respondents lack the language or content schemata to perceive humor. For instance, some years ago I inserted a humorous passage into the English-as-a-Second-Language Placement Test at the University of California at Los Angeles in order to assess perception of humor. The item turned out to be quite difficult. There was a short text about a man who turned to the woman sitting next to him at a fancy banquet and informed her that he thought the current speaker had nothing to say and should sit down. The woman replied, "My good man. Do you know who I am?" When he said "no," she informed him, "I am the speaker's wife!" "My good lady," he replied, "Do you know who I am?" When she said "no," he said, "Good!" and got up and left. The passage had a multiple-choice item inquiring whether the text was serious, sad, humorous, or cynical. Most of the 700 respondents responded that it was "serious." Regardless of whether a passage like this would be used today, the example would still suggest that test respondents may not be perceiving the writer's intent when they perform certain tasks.

Type of Comprehension Skill Assessed

Not only is it useful for test constructors and users of assessment instruments to be aware of types of meaning, but they should also be aware of the skills tested by reading comprehension questions that assess one or more types of meaning. There are numerous taxonomies of such skills. Alderson and Lukmani (1989) offer one (mentioned in Chapter 3) that reflects a compilation of other taxonomies and includes:

1. The recognition of words and phrases of similar and opposing meaning
2. The identifying or locating of information
3. The discriminating of elements or features within context; the analysis of elements within a structure and of the relationship among them—e.g., causal, sequential, chronological, hierarchical
4. The interpreting of complex ideas, actions, events, and relationships
5. Inferring—the deriving of conclusions and predicting the continuation
6. Synthesis
7. Evaluation

We note that this taxonomy omits the reader-writer relationship—for example, the author's distance from the text and the level of participation in the text that the author requires of the reader. With this taxonomy, as with others, the boundaries between skills are assumed to be discrete when, in reality, they may not be. Furthermore, as pointed out in Chapter 3, research has called into question whether this lower-order/higher-order distinction really holds, given that supposedly higher-order cognitive skills may pose no problem for the lower-proficiency students whereas so-called lower-order ones do (Alderson & Lukmani, 1989; Alderson, 1993).

Also, there may be a need for a test constructor to verify that the taxonomy of comprehension skills being used is socioculturally appropriate for the given respondents. For example, the American Council on the Teaching of Foreign Languages (ACTFL) guidelines for the assessment of language proficiency (to be discussed in the next chapter) call for a rating of the respondents' reading proficiency on "straightforward, familiar, factual material." But the issue has been raised of what constitutes straightforward, familiar, and factual material in a given language, and what background knowledge that respondents would be presumed to have (Child, 1988). It is necessary to establish local, relevant criteria for rating and to use raters who are familiar with those criteria.

Another issue regards the specificity of the information in the text. The current emphasis on language for specific purposes (LSP), especially at the tertiary education level, has prompted a concern for including interchangeable reading modules on tests to provide respondents with texts that are appropriate, given their academic backgrounds. However, research suggests that reading passages labeled "specific" vary greatly in specificity, some being too general and some too specific for their reading modules. Clapham (forthcoming) gives an example from her study of a text dealing with fuel on which Arts and Social Science students did better than the Physical Science and Technology students for whom the text was intended. The subject-specific texts in the two other major areas, Arts and Social Science and Life and Medical Science, were suitably specific. So there would appear to be a need to empirically validate the specificity of LSP texts.

Testing Methods

Besides considering the type of reading to be performed, the desired types of meaning, and the comprehension skills to be tapped, the test constructor or user of assessment instruments needs to give careful thought to the assessment method. The challenge is to maximize the measurement of the trait (i.e., the respondent's ability) while minimizing the reactive effects of the method. In order to do this, one should know the options for testing with each method and what these options yield. We will now look at some of the methods for testing reading: (1) communicative tests; (2) fixed-response formats: multiple-choice and alternatives to it; (3) structured-response formats: the cloze, the C-test, and recall protocols; (4) testing of vocabulary; and (5) computer-based testing. The assessment of summarization, which is both a measure of reading and of writing, will be discussed in Chapter 9.

Communicative Tests

For years much attention has been paid to so-called "communicative tests"—usually implying tests dealing with speaking. More recently, efforts have been made to design truly communicative tests of other language skills as well, such as reading comprehension. Canale (1984) pointed out that a good test is not just one that is valid, reliable, and practical in terms of test administration and scoring, but also one that is acceptable—in other words, one that is accepted as fair, important, and interesting by test takers and test users.[8] Also, a good test has *feedback potential*—rewarding both test takers and test users with clear, rich, relevant, and generalizable information. Canale suggested that acceptability and feedback potential have often been accorded low priority.

Some recent approaches to communicative assessment were in part an outgrowth of Canale and Swain's theoretical framework (Canale & Swain, 1980). The particular variety of communicative test that they dealt with has been referred to as a *storyline test*, which has a common theme running throughout in order to assess context effects. The basis for such an approach is that the respondents learn as they read on, that they double back and check previous content, and that the ability to use language in conversation or writing depends in large measure on the skill of picking up information from past discussion (hence, developing content schemata) and using this information in formulating new strategies (Low, 1986).

For example, Swain (1984) developed a storyline test of French as a foreign language for high-school French immersion students. The test consisted of six tasks around a common theme, "finding summer employment." There were four writing tasks (a letter, a note, a composition, and a technical exercise) and two speaking tasks (a group discussion and a job interview). The test was designed so that the topic would be motivating to the students and so that there would be enough new information provided in order to give the tasks credibility. Swain provided the respondents with sufficient time, suggestions on how to do the test, and clear knowledge about what was being tested. There was access to dictionaries and other reference materials, and opportunity for students to review and revise their work. Swain's main concern was to "bias for best" in the construction of the test—to make every effort to support the respondents in doing their best on the test.[9]

The following is an example of a storyline test of native-language reading and writing designed for thirty-two ninth-grade native Hebrew speakers (Brill, 1986). It involved five tasks about membership in a youth group. Here is a description of the tasks and of the general criteria for assessment:

1. Writing a letter as a response to a friend interested in the youth movement to which the writer belongs. The letter was assessed both for the respondents' ability to read from a flyer and relay detailed information concerning the youth movement, and for their use of an appropriate letter-writing register.
2. Presenting questions to the group leader to get more information on the movement. The task was assessed in terms of how well the respondents used the information in the flyer as a basis for asking questions beyond what was spelled out. The text describing the youth movement was purposely written with several ambiguous sections. The questions themselves were assessed in terms of how clear they would be to a group leader—that is, whether this leader would in turn have to ask questions in order to understand the questions.
3. Preparing an announcement about the movement to post on the bulletin board. The task was assessed according to the respondents' ability to comprehend the relevant points in the announcement and in the preparation of the announcement, according to the respondent's ability to be brief yet write something that would stimulate interest, inquiries, and enrollments.
4. Writing a telephone request for information about which activities of a local funding agency could aid the youth movement. On the level of comprehension, respondents were assessed according to whether they made a link between a theme of the movement ("love for the country") and the involvement of the funding agency. The request was to involve the appropriate presentation of self and of the issue so that it would be clear to the other party just what was being requested.

5. Writing a telephone response to an invitation by a political group to join its demonstration. The respondent had to comprehend the section in the flyer that related to the apolitical nature of the movement. The negative reply was to be written in such a way so that the movement's position could be explained without offending the representative of the political group.

After completing the tasks, the students were then asked to compare their experience on this test and on the traditional multiple-choice one they had taken previously. They almost unanimously endorsed the communicative test as preferable because it was more creative, allowed them to express their opinions, was more interesting, taught them how to make contact with others, and investigated communication skills in addition to reading comprehension. For these reasons, they felt that it provided a truer measure of their language ability than did the traditional test.

Communicative storyline tests have received criticism for various reasons (Jones, 1984; Liskin-Gasparro, 1984; Low, 1986; Weir, 1990). The following are some of the reservations voiced concerning such types of tests:

1. In order to better approximate real life, it is necessary to move away from mass administration and scoring in that tests which are acceptable (fair, important, and interesting) and give feedback are usually small-scale, classroom tests.
2. With a thematic organization, there is less efficiency because learners need to produce more text or respond to fewer items.
3. Such a test limits the variety of language material and thus leads to content bias, expressly because the focus of the test is narrow.
4. It is difficult to design such tests because of the need to have genuine links between sections without having them too interdependent.

5. There is the possibility of contamination—that a question relating to the first part of the test will be unintentionally answered in a later section. The fact that learners can use information from earlier parts of the test in answering subsequent questions may enhance the validity of the test, but it lowers the test's reliability. Weir (1990) refers to this as the problem of "muddied measurement" due to the local independence of items and tasks.

6. There is a potential shock effect if respondents have not been tested by this approach before.

7. Student performance on such tests is difficult to score, and consequently it is difficult to report the results of performance on the tests.

Despite the criticism that has been leveled at such tests, it is important to bear in mind what has given them theoretical and practical appeal in and out of the classroom. Canale (1985) viewed communicative tests such as the storyline version as "proficiency-oriented achievement tests" and offered five reasons supporting this view:

1. Such tests put to use what is learned. There is a transfer from controlled training to real performance.

2. There is a focus on the message and the function, not just on the form.

3. There is group collaboration as well as individual work, not just the latter.

4. The respondents are called upon to use their resourcefulness in resolving authentic problems in language use as opposed to accuracy in resolving contrived problems at the linguistic level.

5. The testing itself is more like learning, and the learners are more involved in the assessment.

So the practitioner has somewhat of a dilemma in determining whether to use a testing instrument that has a host of psychometric problems associated with it but meets a number of legitimate instructional and measurement needs and has an intuitive appeal to students.

Fixed-Response Formats

Multiple-Choice. Multiple-choice items are favored in many cases because their scoring can be reliable, rapid, and economical. The usual response format of four alternatives continues to be used widely in objective testing of reading comprehension. Although the literature has suggested numerous modifications of this format to assess for degree of certainty on the part of the respondent, the basic format remains that of simply selecting one of four options. There are also warnings in the literature regarding the pitfalls of using such items, primarily because of the difficulties associated with construction of good multiple-choice items. Testing books such as those of Hughes (1989) and Weir (1990) list the following shortcomings of multiple-choice items:

1. The techniques test only receptive knowledge, and not productive skills.[10]
2. Guessing may have a considerable but unknowable effect on test scores.
3. The technique severely restricts what can be tested.
4. It is very difficult to write successful items. Here are some examples of problem areas:
   * Items meant to assess grammar only may also test for lexical knowledge as well.
   * Distractors may be eliminated by respondents as being absurd.
   * Correct responses may be common knowledge.
   * Items are answerable on the basis of a perfunctory matching of material without comprehension (see also Cohen, 1984).
   * Items get encumbered with material meant to trick the careless respondent—for instance, the use of double negatives.
5. Multiple-choice items are used in tests where they are not appropriate.
6. Items are constructed with more than one correct answer or with clues to the correct alternative (i.e., differences in length or structure that would signal it as the correct answer).
7. Backwash (i.e., training in improving educated guesses rather than in learning the language) may be harmful.
8. Cheating may be facilitated.

Even though the list of weaknesses associated with the multiple-choice format may be long, there may well be a place for such items on a given test if the items are a product of adequate quality development rather than just turned out rapidly without being piloted. Chapter 3 provides a discussion of means for improving distractors, such as through obtaining the distractors empirically by having the respondents provide open-ended answers and using the best of the incorrect ones. Chapter 4 mentions an activity in which learners justify their elimination of each alternative and their selection of the one that they determine to be correct (Munby, 1978, 1979). This approach has been used more as a vehicle for improving test-taking awareness than as a format for testing, but it would be possible to leave a blank line next to each alternative and request that respondents write their rationale for selecting or rejecting that alternative on the test.

The fact that such items lend themselves to guessing is a drawback to the multiple-choice format, unless respondents are required to give their rationale for selecting each item. Using four alternatives instead of three decreases the likelihood of getting the item right by chance alone. There is a 33% chance of getting a three-choice item right by guessing and a 25% chance of guessing correctly on a four-choice item. Of course, this assumes that all choices are equally attractive to the respondent who does not know the answer, a condition that is not always met.

A rigorous way to determine the extent to which respondents guess on multiple-choice items would be to give them a means to indicate their certainty (Ben Simon, 1988). One way is through *elimination testing*. In this approach the respondents eliminate all the alternatives that they are sure are not correct. Another way is through *confidence marking*. In this approach the respondents pick the alternative considered to be correct and then indicate their level of certainty (i.e., 1 = intelligent guess, 2 = unsure, 3 = pretty sure, and 4 = absolutely sure). A third approach involves *ordering*, whereby the respondents rank all the choices by their likelihood of being correct. Yet another approach is referred to as *probability testing*, whereby the respondents indicate the percent of the likelihood that a response is correct.

Alternatives to multiple-choice. In an effort to suggest alternatives to the traditional multiple-choice approach to assessing reading comprehension in the native language, Valencia and Pearson (1987) suggested a series of tasks consistent with the process approach:

1. *Summary writing*—having students read three or four summaries by other students about a text they read and pick the best summary, possibly working from a list of summary features and having to check the reasons for their rating
2. *Metacognitive judgments*—having students determine which retellings of a text are appropriate for different audiences
3. *Question selection*—having students select from a set of twenty the ten questions that they think will best help a peer understand the important ideas in a text.
4. *Multiple acceptable responses*—either having students select all responses found plausible or having them grade the responses as "really complete," "on the right track," or "totally off base."
5. *Prior knowledge*—having students predict (no/maybe/yes) whether certain ideas are likely to be included in a text on a specified topic, or rate the relatedness of vocabulary terms to a central concept of the text (e.g., blood circulation), with both formats being machine scorable.

All these tasks could be adapted for use with second-language testing. The multiple-acceptable-response approach is similar to the approaches (described by Ben Simon, 1988) used to get at fine tuning of assessment of different alternatives. The summary-writing task is an exercise that involves both reading and writing and calls for skill in reconceptualizing the ideas expressed in the text. The "metacognitive judgment" task also calls for a form of summarizing through retelling, and emphasizes the issue of language style. Question selection is a beneficial task in that active processing of the text is required in order to generate good questions to ask about a text or, as in this case, select from a larger set those questions that best get at the text's important ideas. The prior-knowledge tasks of predicting the contents of a text or identifying meanings that vocabulary words will probably assume in relation to some central theme are common instructional activities. However, they are not so commonly used in assessment activities, but they can have a useful role in assessment that is more process oriented.

Structured-Response Formats

Cloze. The cloze test is extensively used as a completion measure, ideally aimed at tapping reading skills interactively, with respondents using cues from the text in a bottom-up fashion as well as bringing their background knowledge to bear on the task. As has become commonly known, the basic form of the cloze test is a passage from which a word is deleted after every certain number of words, according to a fixed-ratio procedure—for example, every fifth, sixth, or seventh word after one sentence of unbroken text (Oller, 1973, 1979). The following is an example of sixth-word deletion:

People today are quite astonished by the rapid

improvements in medicine. Doctors_____   1.___are___
                                        1
becoming more specialized, and_____drugs 2.___new___
                                 2
are appearing on the_____daily. At the   3.__market__
                       3
same time,_____are dismayed by the   4.__people__
          4
inaccessibility_____doctors when they are 5.___of___
                5
needed. _____doctors' fees are constantly 6._Whereas_
        6
on_____rise, the quality of medical   7.___the___
   7
_____has reached an abysmal low.   8.___care___
   8

Various multiple-choice approaches have appeared as modifications of the basic cloze test (Jonz, 1976; Ozete, 1977; Pikulski & Pikulski, 1977; Doherty & Ilyin, 1981). Generally, those who have recommended an alternate-choice format for the cloze suggest that the best distractors are those obtained from answers to the same cloze passage when administered in the basic way. Others (e.g., Porter, 1976) would generate distractors intuitively according to the reading level of the students—grammatically and semantically incorrect distractors for beginners, semantically incorrect distractors for intermediate students, and distractors that are incorrect because of serious problems in style or register in the case of advanced respondents. Whether distractors are derived from student answers or derived intuitively with some rationale in mind (like Porter's), the provision of choices changes the nature of the task. Students no longer have to make such sweeping, global decisions about the nature of the missing word (e.g., conjunction, adverb, auxiliary verb), the appropriate semantic choice, syntactic agreement in the context, its fit in the thread of discourse beyond the phrase level, and so forth.

Another type of modification of the basic cloze is not to delete words randomly, but rather to delete them rationally—on the basis of some linguistic criteria. Not so surprisingly, the multiple-choice cloze has been found to be easier than the fixed-ratio and the rational-deletion versions (Chapelle & Abraham, 1990).

The cloze has been used as a measure of readability, global reading skills, grammar, and writing, and its proponents have claimed it to be a projective measure of listening comprehension and speaking. Cloze tests can be scored according to an exact-word, acceptable-word, or multiple-choice approach.

Assumptions that have been made about the cloze as a measure of second-language ability include the following (Klein-Braley, 1981):

1. It is an integrative measure of discourse.
2. It is easy to construct.
3. Fixed-ratio deletion adequately samples the text.
4. The actual deletion rate does not affect the results very much.
5. The starting point can vary.
6. The choice of texts is not a key issue.
7. It ranks examinees in a consistent manner.
8. It is highly reliable and valid.

As was mentioned in the discussion of cloze test-taking strategies in Chapter 6, the extent to which cloze measures macro-level comprehension of written discourse is still a debated research issue. Oller and others (Oller, 1975; Chihara, Oller, Weaver, & Chávez-Oller, 1977; Chávez-Oller, Chihara, Weaver, & Oller, 1985; Jonz, 1990; Oller & Jonz, forthcoming) have continuously produced evidence that ability to fill in cloze items in a second language is not just a matter of perceiving local redundancy but rather involves an awareness of the flow of discourse across sentences and paragraphs (beyond five to eleven words on either side of a blank).

However, other researchers would argue that traditional fixed-ratio deletion is more of a micro-level completion test (a measure of word- and sentence-level reading ability) than a macro-level measure of skill at understanding connected discourse (Alderson, 1978, 1983; Klein-Braley, 1981; Markham, 1985). Their research has led them to the conclusion that performance on the cloze as a whole is not based on awareness of the larger context, but that only a small subset of items on a cloze with fixed-ratio deletion will tap the reader's ability to comprehend text rather than just isolated phrases.

Given the limitations of the fixed-ratio deletion, researchers began investigating the advantages of the rational-deletion cloze, whereby words are deleted according to predetermined, primarily linguistic criteria—often stressing the area considered to be underrepresented, namely, macro-level discourse links (Levenston, Nir, & Blum-Kulka, 1984). Research by Bachman (1985) with EFL university students found that the rational-deletion approach sampled much more across sentence boundaries and somewhat more across clause boundaries within the same sentence than did the fixed-ratio cloze. He concluded that the rational-deletion cloze was a better measure of the reading of connected discourse but that the question still remained of whether or not such tests "in fact measure the components of language proficiency hypothesized by the deletion criteria" (Bachman, 1985:550)—that is, the flow of discourse across sentences and paragraphs within a text.

Thus, while the cloze test was heralded as the answer to a tester's needs in the 1970s, it is probably fair to say that in the 1990s it has dropped in popularity. Perhaps the new book by Oller and Jonz, *Cloze and coherence* (forthcoming) will help to enhance the status of the instrument. To summarize the criticism that has been leveled at the cloze, we could include the following:

1. The *n*th-word cloze may actually amount to a micro-level fill-in (depending on the text selected, the nature of the deletions, and the characteristics of the respondents).
2. The fixed-ratio deletion approach may be unreliable.
3. There is a tendency in such tests to inadvertently overrepresent one word class.
4. Different deletion rates do make a difference.
5. It is an indirect and unnatural measure of reading ability on which it may be possible to do well without understanding the passage; it is not clear whether the respondent on a cloze test truly understands the mutilated text that is being restored.
6. Contrary to earlier claims that practice does not improve cloze test performance, it would now appear possible to improve performance on the cloze test through the use of selected test-taking strategies (described in Chapter 5).

With regard to criticism 5 above, some testers request that the respondents write a summary of the passage or answer open-ended reading comprehension questions about the text after they have completed the cloze task in order to help determine how well the passage as a whole was understood. With regard to criticism 6, Hughes provides a series of tips on how to take cloze tests and states that "the more practice [respondents] have had, the more likely it is that their scores will represent their true ability in the language" (1989:70). With regard to specific strategies to practice, Bachman would suggest practicing the strategy of skipping around, because after observing hundreds of individuals take cloze tests over the years, he concluded that test takers who skip around are likely to achieve higher scores than those who rigorously move through the passage, filling in the gaps in the order in which they occur (1990:121). Hence, results on the cloze may tap test-wiseness and not just micro- and some macro-level reading.

Furthermore, it would seem that rational-deletion cloze tests are preferable to fixed-ratio deletion tests. But there needs to be continued concern about the extent to which the test will measure macro-level reading.

The C-Test. A suggested alternative to the cloze test, the C-test, has been proposed by Klein-Braley and Raatz (Raatz & Klein-Braley, 1982; Klein-Braley & Raatz, 1984; Klein-Braley, 1985; Raatz, 1985). In this procedure the second half of every other word is deleted, leaving the first and the last sentence of the passage intact. A C-test has a number of short passages (a maximum of 100 words per passage) on a variety of topics. This alternative eliminates certain problems associated with cloze, such as choice of deletion rate and starting point, representational sampling of different language elements in the passage, and the inadvertent assessment of written production. With the C-test, a clue (half the word) serves as a stimulus for respondents to find the other half. The following is one passage within a C-test (from Raatz, 1985):

Pollution is one of the biggest problems in the world

today. Towns a_____ cities a_____ growing, indu_____

is gro_____, and t_____ population o_____ the

wo_____ is gro_____. Almost every_____ causes

poll_____ in so_____ way o_____ another. T_____ air

i_____ filled wi_____ fumes fr_____ factories a_____

vehicles, a_____ there i_____ noise fr_____ airplanes

a_____ machines. Riv_____, lakes, a_____ seas a_____

polluted b_____ factories and by sewage from our

homes.

It appears that the C-test may well be a more reliable and valid means of assessing what the cloze test assesses, but as suggested above, to what extent the C-test assesses more than micro-level processing is not clear (see, for example, Cohen, Segal, & Weiss Bar-Siman-Tov [1984], and Stemmer [1991]). Because half the word is given, students who do not understand the macro-context may still be able to mobilize their vocabulary skills adequately to fill in the appropriate discourse connector without indulging in higher-level processing.

In a review of a collection of articles on the C-test, Carroll (1987) expressed skepticism about this testing format, just as he and colleagues had voiced reservations about the cloze test thirty years previously (Carroll, Carton, & Wilds, 1959). He referred to the passages as constituting an incomplete and distorted message, and felt it was risky to presume that the strategies used in responding to such a test were accessing language ability. He felt that if the test stimulated creativeness, it was not in being effective users of language but rather in knowing how to fill in the blanks. In short, he felt that the C-test might serve as a useful supplement to more conventional language testing techniques but that it could not replace more informative, accurate, and diagnostic forms of assessment.

Given the reservations that have been raised both to the cloze and to the C-test, we would refrain from endorsing either one as clear measures of macro-level discourse. Rather, it would seem that at times they may tap an understanding of discourse meaning and at other times be limited to micro-level reading.

Recall protocols. The basic assumption behind the use of recall protocols as a measure of reading comprehension is that there is a direct relationship between what readers comprehend from a text and what they are able to recall. Consequently, all things being equal, those who comprehend a text better will recall it better.

Since the early 1980s, the use of recall protocols has been recommended not just as an instructional tool but also as a means for assessment of reading comprehension (see, for example, Johnston, 1983). Its proponents see it as a more valid method for assessing reading comprehension than most of the other current methods. With respect to foreign-language testing, Bernhardt (1991), for instance, views multiple-choice and true/false responses as not necessarily passage dependent, views cloze as a test of individual vocabulary words and not an assessment of reading of connected discourse, and views open-ended questions as possibly causing respondents to reject their view of a passage and shift their understanding. She considers the two main benefits of recall protocols as follows:

1. They show where a lack of grammar interferes with comprehension without focusing the reader's attention on linguistic elements.
2. They do not influence the reader's understanding of the text (whereas reading comprehension questions form another "text" for comprehension).

Bernhardt (1991:187) lists the basic procedures of the immediate-recall protocol as follows:

1. Select an unglossed text (perhaps 200 words).
2. Tell students that they may read the text as often as they wish, and that when they are finished you will ask them to write down everything that they remember from the text.
3. Give students sufficient time to read the text several times.
4. Ask the students to put the text out of sight and to write down (in English) everything that they remember.
5. Collect the protocols written by the students.

Bernhardt suggests that the protocols be written in the native language of the reader, although she notes that this admonition often goes unheeded.

With regard to scoring the protocols, whereas Meyer's (1985) recall protocol scoring system is frequently used, it takes from twenty-five to fifty hours to prepare a coding template for a 250-word text and up to an hour to score each respondent's recall protocol (perhaps even longer if the protocol is written in the students' L1 when it is not the L1 of the teacher). Bernhardt (1991) offers a more expedient scoring method, with each proposition in the text weighted by means of a method developed by Johnson (1970) for L1 recall protocols. After a text is divided into its pausal units, two fluent readers sort the propositions in the text into groups at four levels—the lowest level being the least important 25% of the propositions in the text, the next level being the next least important 25%, and so forth. The highest-level propositions—those that would maintain the thread of the text in a telegraphic style—receive a score of 4, the next highest a score of 3, and on down. Bernhardt found this system of scoring to correlate very highly with Meyer's system (1991:209), and it took approximately ten minutes to score a protocol rather than an hour.[11]

Bernhardt endorses the process of L1 recall of L2 texts as an effective means of assessing L2 reading comprehension.[12] She contends that performance on such measures is consistent with performance on other language proficiency measures (and hence concurrent validity can be claimed for the measure) and that scores from recall are useful and interpretable because they provide both quantitative and qualitative information (Bernhardt, 1991).

All the same, objections have been raised regarding the use of recall protocols for assessment purposes. For example, Swaffar, Arens, and Byrnes (1991) take issue with having the protocols in the native language of the respondents, since this is inappropriate for many ESL situations, where respondents would come from a host of language backgrounds. They also contend that if foreign-language students are tested predominantly in English, then "it may be done at the cost of incentive to practice cognitive bonding between comprehension and production of the second language" (1991:165). Their other objections to recall protocols concern grading. First, they raise the issue of whether to rate recall protocols as reader- or text-based organization, and if reader-based, then how to account for the readers' schemata (1991:164). Second, they see the assessment of protocols as demanding sophistication with regard to the weighting and analysis of propositions.

Another issue we might add to the queries about recall protocols concerns the instructions that the respondents are given regarding the completion of the task. Lee (1986) came to the conclusion that the lower the ability of the respondent, the more *orienting directions* aided comprehension. By orienting directions, Lee simply meant telling respondents before they read a text that afterwards they would be asked to recall as much of the passage as possible. While this is probably the usual approach, certain issues could be spelled out for the respondents in order to reduce anxiety about the task and possibly improve performance:

1. Whether respondents are to write the recall for a rater who is either fully familiar with the text or has never seen it before, since this could affect the nature of the recall protocol
2. Whether they are to produce the gist, or a complete recall with as many details as possible
3. Whether they are to reproduce the surface structure of the text

Giving respondents an opportunity to practice the recall task in a test-like situation may be useful. This would also be an opportunity for the teacher/assessor to experiment with different instructions to see which, if any, appear to contribute to improved performance.

Testing Vocabulary Knowledge

As noted in Chapter 2, vocabulary testing may not be very informative if vocabulary tests access a limited sampling of the learner's total vocabulary and if the level is too superficial for the depth of vocabulary development to be determined (Curtis, 1987; Read, 1988; Wesche & Paribakht, 1993). The challenge is to assess how well learners know specific vocabulary words. The tendency to assess vocabulary only partially and superficially might justify using more quizzes to probe for control of second- or foreign-language vocabulary. The following are three suggested approaches for assessing vocabulary recognition, and then one approach to assessing vocabulary production. This fourth approach is intended to assess increased knowledge about given words.

Identifying the meaning by multiple-choice. Probably the most common means of assessing vocabulary recognition directly in reading tasks at present is through asking respondents to indicate what a word means within the context of a given passage.

The format is either multiple-choice or open-ended.

What does *delinquent* mean in line 7?

(Multiple-choice response):

(a) naughty (b) haughty (c) sinful (d) irresponsible.
(Open-ended response): _____ .

This type of item, particularly in its multiple-choice format, is the kind of item that may give only a superficial measure of students' vocabulary control. Among other things, such items may test for knowledge of the distractors (in this case, *naughty* and *haughty*) or for the ability to make intelligent guesses rather than for the ability to identify the exact meaning of the target word.

Matching. In another approach, the respondents receive a list of words and a list of definitions, synonyms, or translations that has three or four fewer items than the list of words. They are to write the number of that word next to its meaning. Nation (1990) explains that this approach makes it easier for the test constructor to produce test items because it is not necessary to find three or more distractors for each correct answer. The following is an example:

1 apply
2 elect   ___ choose by voting
3 jump   ___ become like water
4 manufacture ___ make
5 melt
6 threaten

Checking off familiar words. In a third approach, respondents receive a long list of words (e.g., 100 or more) and are to indicate whether they know their meaning. To control for learners' overestimating their vocabulary, the list contains a mixture of words and non-words (Anderson & Freebody, 1983; Nagy, Herman, & Anderson, 1985). The following is an example from Meara and Buxton (1987):

Tick the words you know the meaning of.

gathering	forecast	wodesome	loyalment
flane	crope	dismissal	sloping
bluck	enclose	rehearsion	turmoil

The way the task is scored is by subtracting the number of non-words marked (erroneously, since they do not exist) from the number of real words marked and divide this by the quantity 1 minus the non-words marked. This produces a coefficient of words known. Nation (1990) notes that while this method has promise, there are problems, such as its unreliability for students who are poor at spelling.

Combining self-report with performance. A fourth approach would be through an instrument such as the Vocabulary Knowledge Scale (VKS) (Paribakht & Wesche, forthcoming). The instrument measures both recognition and recall knowledge of specific vocabulary items, and it is intended to represent gains on a self-report scale as well as changes in knowledge during relatively limited instructional periods. The VKS scale, which elicits both self-perceived and demonstrated knowledge of specific words in written form, includes the following options:

I.   I don't remember having seen this word before.
II. I have seen this word before, but I don't know what it means.
III. I have seen this word before, and I **think** it means _____.
     (synonym or translation)
IV. I **know** this word. It means _____. (synonym or translation)
V.   I can use this word in a sentence. _____. (If you do this section, please also do Section IV.)

The responses are scored as follows:

1— the word is not familiar at all.
2— the word is familiar, but its meaning is not known.
3— a correct synonym or translation is given.
4— the word is used with semantic appropriateness in a sentence.
5— the word is used with semantic appropriateness and grammatical accuracy in a sentence.

Wesche and Paribakht (1993) report that the scale succeeds in capturing progression in development of knowledge of particular words. However, the scale does not track knowledge of different meanings of the same word or different aspects of word knowledge (e.g., collocations or knowledge of derivative forms). In a study with seventeen ESL students using four texts and selected vocabulary words from the texts, the researchers found a high correlation between perceived and demonstrated scores (generally, r = .95 or better).

Computer-Based Testing

Modern technology has been employed in computer-based testing and in a subtype of computer-based testing, namely, computer-adaptive testing. *Computer-based testing* involves the use of the computer as a vehicle for assessment instead of paper and pencil, while *computer-adaptive testing* adds the dimension of having the computer program select test items according to how the respondent has done on previous items on that test. Computer-based tests require that scoring systems be objective in nature, since all possible answers need to be entered into the computer's memory if the computer program is to be responsible for scoring. It is also possible to have students write an essay that the teacher will score later.

Some of the advantages of computerizing assessment that have been noted in the literature (Larson & Madsen, 1985; Madsen, 1986, 1991; Alderson, 1987; Meagher, 1987; Alderson & Windeatt, 1991) include

1. Individual testing time may be reduced.
2. Frustration and fatigue are minimized.
3. Boredom is reduced.
4. Test scores and diagnostic feedback are provided immediately.
5. Respondents can be given a second chance to get an item right.
6. Test security may be enhanced (if respondents receive different items or the same items in a different sequence).
7. Accurate and consistent evaluation of results is provided.
8. Record-keeping functions are improved.
9. Teachers are provided with diagnostic information.
10. There is rapid access to banks of test items.
11. There is a potential for rapid editing of items.
12. Information is readily available for research purposes.

Alderson (1987) viewed computerized testing as a means for innovating in language testing and for breaking down distinctions between testing and teaching. He suggested that tests are potentially more user friendly on the computer.

At present, at least one set of computerized language-testing programs for widespread distribution is being developed, the Lancaster University Computer-Based Assessment System (LUCAS). LUCAS is intended to allow the authoring of a range of tests for IBM-compatible PCs, using a range of different item types and facilities (Alderson & Windeatt, 1992). LUCAS includes "Help," "Clue," and "Dictionary" facilities, and a series of item formats well beyond the multiple-choice format that such programs initially employed (Alderson and Windeatt, 1992):

1. *Multichoice*—each of four choices is displayed on a separate screen, with each screen showing text in which one section may or may not be correct. This format is intended to enable review of each option without the distraction of the other choices.
2. *Deletion*—a text has an extra word or phrase that is to be deleted.
3. *Insertion*—the location in the text that needs material inserted is to be identified, and then the insertion is to be made.
4. *Correction*—the respondent is to find the mistake in the text on the screen (misspelling, grammatical error, factual error, etc.) and correct it.
5. *Completion*—the text on the screen is incomplete, and the missing text is indicated by a dotted line. The respondent is to replace the missing text. The program allows for multiple correct answers.
6. *Transformation*—a top window contains text, and a bottom window contains incomplete text. The task is to complete the text in the bottom window so that it means the same as the text in the top window. The middle window is reserved for instructions.
7. *Reorganization*—the respondent is to rearrange four sections of text that are presented in jumbled order. The rearranging is done by highlighting the text to be moved and then by moving it to its appropriate location.
8. *Matching*—the respondent is to match each line in the right-hand column with each line on the left.

With computer-based testing, there can be access to at least five types of dictionary information: further examples, synonyms, an exploration of meaning in context, an explanation of all meanings of the word, and a translation of the word.

Research Notes

A study by Fletcher (1989) found that twenty ESL students enjoyed a computer-based test more than a paper-based one that used the same item types and had been matched for difficulty. However, the respondents tended to score lower on the computer-based form of the test. There was a high correlation between degree of anxiety about the test and poor performance on it. Interesting, those respondents who did poorest on the paper-based test did relatively better on the computer-based one.

The *multiple-choice* and *jumbled text* items were the most popular on the computer-based test. While *matching* was found to be the most useful on the paper-based test, *gap filling* was reported by the respondents to be the most enjoyable and useful in the computer-based form. They found it more useful in that they received immediate feedback, had a chance for a second try, and learned more vocabulary and grammar. In fact, candidates who used the dictionary option most often reported learning more vocabulary. On the negative side, the respondents reported feeling less relaxed on the computer-based test than on the paper-based one. Furthermore, the computer-based test results were influenced by past experience using computers, so the test was testing something other than just language performance—namely, the complexity of operations required to complete the test.

Computer-based testing has also begun to include efforts at scoring open-ended items, and at least one study has been reported in the literature (Henning, Anbar, Helm, & D'Arcy, 1993). Not so surprisingly, the investigators in this study found that programming the computer to recognize all correct open-ended responses according to degree of correctness was a difficult task, involving frequent piloting and debugging.

Research Notes

The study by Henning et al. (1993) actually involved both open-ended as well as traditional multiple-choice items in a computer-based instrument for assessing reading comprehension. Twenty-seven ESL students participated. The study used three reading passages from former TOEFL tests (averaging 100-250 words each). There were nineteen multiple-choice items and nineteen open-ended items requesting information identical to that requested by the multiple-choice items. Half the respondents received the multiple-choice items first and the open-ended items second and vice versa. The twenty-seven were from a larger group of forty-four, and comprised those who actually responded to all the items for the first three passages (there were eight passages in all). The reliability of the open-ended items improved, for the analysis incorporated degrees of correctness and not just correct/incorrect. The researchers reported that "programming the computer to recognize all correct open-ended responses according to degree of correctness is a nontrivial task involving frequent piloting and debugging" (1993:129).

Computer-adaptive testing. Computer-adaptive testing is both a subtype of computer-based testing and a subtype of general adaptive testing. *Adaptive tests* are measures that tailor the difficulty of the prompt or item elicitation in real time to an ongoing evaluation of the respondent's ability level. The development of computer-adaptive testing has reflected the carrying over of this principle to the computer; the selection and sequence of items depend on the pattern of success and failure experienced by the respondent. Most commonly, if the respondent succeeds on a given item, one of greater difficulty is presented, and if the respondent experiences failure, then an easier item is presented. The testing continues until sufficient information has been gathered to assess the particular respondent's ability. At present, most such tests are limited to the multiple-choice format, and in this respect computer-adaptive testing is known to be more efficient and more accurate than conventional fixed-length tests employing multiple-choice items (Tung, 1986).

Stevenson and Gross (1991) designed a test to obtain English proficiency information for placement in ESOL/Bilingual sixth-to-eighth-grade classes and exit from these classes. The reading component of the test included, among other things, forty-eight "functional reading" items to assess main idea, inference, and detail skills (e.g., reading want ads, or using tables and forms). Kaya-Carton, Carton, and Dandonoli (1991) report successful efforts to construct an ACTFL-based computer-adaptive test of French reading proficiency that uses both multiple-choice and multiple-choice cloze items.

Madsen (1991) relates the problems encountered when attempting to use longer prose passages in computer-adaptive testing. The problem was that missing an item would result in the respondent having to read a new lengthy text, which respondents found objectionable. The problem with providing them other items on the same text was the possibility that these alternative items would overlap with the previous item, making them easier to answer or tapping trivial details. The solution was to restrict the text to one to three sentences of prose, followed by four-option, multiple-choice paraphrases or comprehension questions.

Perhaps a major challenge for the computer-adaptive movement, and for computer-based assessment in general, is to produce assessment instruments that are consistent with theories of reading comprehension and that encompass multiple dimensions, such as world knowledge, language and cultural background, type of text, and reading styles (Canale, 1986). The line of development that Canale proposed for computer-based assessment was that it move from simply mechanizing existing product-oriented reading comprehension item types to the inclusion of more process-oriented, interactive tasks that could be integrated into broad and thematically coherent language use/learning activities, such as "intelligent tutoring systems."[13] It is fair to say that systems such as LUCAS are moving more in the direction that Canale had envisioned, since its authors are concerned about adding a test-processing component whereby respondents would supply information regarding their test-taking strategies and their reactions to items as they proceed through the test (Alderson & Windeatt, 1992).

Principles for Assessing
L2/FL Reading Comprehension

In this chapter we have presented and discussed a number of testing methods for assessing reading comprehension. Ideally, any assessment would include more than one of these methods. There are also various principles that we might wish to apply to whatever methods we choose in order to ensure that the methods are being used in a manner that works well for the respondents. Let us highlight some of these principles (based largely on Swaffar, Arens, & Byrnes, 1991):

1. Choose a text with a familiar topic, that is interesting, has an unambiguous intent, and is of an appropriate length. Sometimes "doctoring" the text can help to clarify a confused message, while at other times lexical simplification can produce ambiguity in the text.
2. Where appropriate, allow students to do some or extensive conceptualizing in their L1.
3. Determine the reasoning behind the students' conclusions.
4. Design the assessment tasks so that students can demonstrate the schemata that they have for the content, textual organization, and language of the given text(s).
5. Be flexible about acknowledging individual interpretations that students may have for texts.

Conclusion

This chapter has looked at types of reading, the types of meaning that are involved in reading comprehension, the comprehension skills involved, and testing methods. We first looked at a communicative test of reading comprehension, the storyline method. Then we discussed fixed-response formats such as multiple-choice and various alternatives to it. Next we discussed structured-response formats such as cloze and C-test with respect to what they measure, and we questioned their value in assessing reading comprehension at the macro-level. We considered recall protocols as yet another structured-response format, one that is believed by its proponents to be highly effective. We illustrated several formats for testing vocabulary knowledge, with the understanding that measures of vocabulary knowledge are most likely bound to fall short of measuring depth of vocabulary control. We discussed computer-based tests as an avenue for reading comprehension testing that will expand in the years to come. Finally, we offered some principles for assessing L2/FL reading comprehension.

As we have noted repeatedly in the book, assessment of reading may prove to be fairer if it involves multiple measures of the same skills, since different types of measures could yield results that differ slightly or even greatly.

Discussion Questions and Activities

1. Here is a test-analysis activity to help you get beyond the labels that adorn reading comprehension tests and the often cursory descriptions that accompany such measures. Take a reading-assessment instrument that you have available—a standardized, commercially available test, an instrument that your department developed, or whatever. You could do this on your own or, if possible, have every student in a language-testing class do this exercise individually with the same instrument and then have them compare their results, paying attention both to areas of agreement and to discrepancies about what items seem to measure. Try to determine which comprehension skills are meant to be tested by each item on the test. Also determine how useful the Alderson and Lukmani taxonomy is in your efforts to label the comprehension skills being tested.

2. As a test development activity, devise your own storyline test. An effective way to do this is as a workshop activity. The teachers in your department form small groups, each group being responsible for one task on the test. If possible, try out your storyline test (or parts of it) on language students at the intermediate or advanced levels. When the results are in and have been analyzed, determine the strengths and weaknesses of the test you designed. Then return to the guidelines offered in this chapter as a means of assessing your experience with the method.

3. According to this chapter, what alternative multiple-choice formats are there instead of the traditional one? Try out one of these by designing and piloting several items using that format. Then compare it with the traditional approach, and discuss your findings with your peers.

4. You have been asked to update your ESL colleagues on cloze tests and C-tests. Your colleagues have asked you to comment on the special features that the C-test provides beyond those provided by the cloze test. They are particularly interested in finding out just what each test measures. You decide to demonstrate to them what these measures typically assess, and in order to do so you prepare for them several short measures as samples. Conduct such an exercise.

5. This chapter suggests that the importance of syntax in L2 reading comprehension has been overstated. However, under what circumstances might syntax play an important role in comprehension?

6. Do you accept the view that vocabulary items usually just "scratch the surface" of knowledge that respondents have or do not have? Can you think of vocabulary items that would go further in tapping breadth and depth of knowledge? Design several such items, and try them out in class.

Notes

1 *Sampling* is used here to imply that the reader does not read every feature of every letter of every word, but rather focuses on certain features, certain words, perhaps certain phrases in order to get a sense of the text's meaning.

2 According to Just and Carpenter (1987:26), eye fixations occupy 90 to 95 percent of the time spent in reading and the average fixation in native-language reading lasts about 250 milliseconds. The average duration increases with the difficulty of the text.

3 On the basis of a series of studies with university-level readers of a target language, Ulijn (1981) concluded that whereas thorough conceptual analysis was needed in order to extract

meaning from text, thorough syntactic analysis was not. However, he conceded that complex syntax could cause reading difficulties.

4 It should be pointed out that the reader was a native Hebrew speaker. The fact that Hebrew is read without vowels might have contributed to the substitutions.

5 Grellet (1981) devotes a full volume just to the issue of designing instructional tasks (not tests) that reflect different types of reading.

6 Rickard (1979) also found that the reader's first language (Chinese, Japanese, Persian, and Spanish, respectively) influenced perceptual strategies in reading English—specifically, in determining which sentence of a pair was a correct paraphrase or expansion of another sentence.

7 That is, a comparison of forms in the native language and in the target language; see Stockwell, Bowen, and Martin (1965) for an example of a contrastive analysis of English and Spanish grammatical structures.

8 This position is an endorsement of the need to take into account "perceived validity" (Low, 1985), as discussed above.

9 The point here is that such cases of bias can be viewed as a good thing—as intentional bias. The aim would be to set up tasks that test takers will be motivated to participate in, such as those that approximate real-life situations (Spolsky, 1985).

10 In other words, if there really is a lack of fit between respondents' productive and receptive skills, respondents may be able to identify the correct response in a multiple-choice item but not be able to produce the form when speaking or writing.

11 We should note that both Meyer's and Johnson's systems of analysis were based on L1 protocols of L1 texts. Thus, if the text is in the L2, the propositional analysis into four categories is also conducted in the L2, but the recall protocol is in L1, which means that the teacher/test scorer has an extra step of cross-language propositional analysis.

12 Actually, a recent study found that for advanced Japanese ESL students, whether the recall of ESL texts was in the native language (Japanese) or in the second language (English) did not make a significant difference (Upton, 1993).

13 In intelligent tutoring systems, the computer diagnoses the students' strategies and their relationship to expert strategies, and then generates instruction based on this comparison.

Chapter 8:
Assessing
Listening and
Speaking

In the previous edition of this book, we noted that the pendulum swings back and forth with regard to the aspects of language that are assessed. At that time, the assessment of functional language ability had just come into vogue. Fifteen years later, we seem to have reached a compromise between the assessment of functional language ability in an integrative way and the assessment of linguistic knowledge through the testing of more or less discrete linguistic items. It is fair to say that the pendulum has not swung all the way back toward discrete items in that the emphasis is still very much on communicative competence, but there is also a concern that the need to assess the building blocks of such competence is not forgotten. Of course, in some classrooms in various parts of the world, the pendulum never swung toward the assessment of functional language ability in the first place—some classrooms meet trends with resistance, either because of traditional attitudes or because of lack of contact with the trends.

This chapter begins with a brief introduction to the assessment of listening comprehension, from the most discrete-point items to the most integrative and most communicative items and procedures. This introduction is intended to deal with the assessment of listening comprehension almost in passing and simply to be suggestive of issues and means for assessing this area.[1]

The bulk of this chapter will take an in-depth look at certain aspects of the assessment of speaking, namely, the use of direct and semi-direct interviews and rating scales for assessing communicative ability. The chapter ends with a practical exercise in the rating of more advanced speaking ability—three speakers' efforts at producing speech acts (apologies) in English as a foreign language. The focus will be on more advanced speaking, since other textbooks have tended to emphasize the assessment of basic speaking abilities (e.g., pronunciation, reading aloud, retelling stories, telling stories from pictures, and so forth; see Heaton [1990], Chapter 4, for an example).

Assessing Listening Skills

From Discrete-Point to Integrative Listening Tasks

The following are examples of listening comprehension items and procedures, ranging from the most discrete-point items, with a traditional focus on isolated language forms, to more integrative assessment tasks. The teacher must decide when it is appropriate to use any of these approaches for assessing listening in the classroom. In going through this section, it may be useful for the reader to consider the extent to which given items and procedures are more discrete-point or more integrative in nature.

Discrimination of Sounds

Sound-discrimination items have been popular for some time and are of particular benefit in assessing points of contrast between two given languages. Ideally, the respondents are required to listen for and identify sound distinctions that do not exist in their native language. For example,

a. The respondents indicate which sound of three is different from the other two.
    (Taped stimulus): (1) sun, (2) put, (3) dug
    (Response choices): (a) 1 (b) 2 (c) 3
b. These sounds could be in sentence context.
    (Taped stimulus):
    (1) It's a sheep. (2) It's a sheep. (3) It's a ship.
    (Response choices): (a) 1 (b) 2 (c) 3
c. The respondents are to indicate whether two phrases have the same intonation.
    (Taped stimulus): You're coming?/You're coming.
    (Response choices): (1) same (2) different
d. The respondents must determine the meaning of the phrase from the intonation.
    (Taped stimulus): Good morning!
    (Response choices):
    (1) happy to see employee
    (2) annoyed that the employee is late to work

Listening for Grammatical Distinctions

When listening for grammatical distinctions, the respondents could listen carefully for inflectional markers. For example, the respondents must determine whether the subject and verb are in the singular or the plural:

(Taped stimulus): The boys sing well.
(Response choices):
(1) singular (2) plural (3) same form for singular and plural

Listening for Vocabulary

The respondents perform an action in response to a command (e.g., getting up, walking to the window) or draw a picture according to oral instructions (e.g., coloring a picture a certain way, sorting a set of objects according to instructions).

Auditory Comprehension

a. The respondents indicate whether a response to a question is appropriate. For example,

(Taped stimulus): How're you gonna get home? At about 3:30 p.m.

(Response choices): (1) appropriate (2) inappropriate

b. The respondents hear a statement and must indicate the appropriate paraphrase for the statement.

(Taped stimulus): What'd you get yourself into this time?

(Response choices): (1) What are you wearing this time?

(2) What did you buy this time?

(3) What's your problem this time?

c. The respondents listen in on a telephone conversation and at appropriate times must indicate what they would say if they were one of the speakers in the conversation.

(Taped stimulus):

Mother: Well, Mary, you know you were supposed to call me last week.

Mary: I know, Mom, but I got tied up.

Mother: That's really no excuse.

Mary: (Response choices):

(1) Yes, I'll call him.

(2) You're right. I'm sorry.

(3) I've really had nothing to do.

Communicative Assessment of Listening Comprehension

There has been a general effort in recent years to make communicative types of listening comprehension tests more authentic. For example, it has been suggested that increased attention be paid to where the content of the assessment instrument falls along the oral/literate continuum—for instance, from a news broadcast (most literate), to a lecturette (perhaps a mix of literate and oral), to a consultative dialogue (most oral)—and to take these differences into account in the assessment of aural comprehension. Research has indicated that we can expect better performance on aural comprehension of more orally oriented texts (Inbar, 1988). The same work has also shown that higher-level students are more likely to use top-down processing, while lower-level students tend to use bottom-up or data-driven processing. There is also a need to avoid assessing facts that are trivial in a given situation, for this requires respondents to engage in a specialized form of listening with an emphasis on rote memory, and authentic listening tasks do not usually make such demands on the listener.

Lecture task. The respondents hear a lecture, with all the false starts, filled pauses, and other features that make it different from oral recitation of a written text. After the lecture, tape-recorded multiple-choice, structured, or open-ended questions are presented, with responses to be written on the answer sheet. The lecturer could use a series of key discourse markers to assess how well the listeners pick up on these organizational cues to meaning. At the macro-level, such markers could involve meta-statements about major points in the lecture. At the micro-level, such markers could signal ties between sentences, the framing of ideas, or pauses between segments. A study by Chaudron and Richards (1986) found that the perception by ESL respondents of macro-level markers in a lecture made a significant difference in their ability to fill in a cloze test after the lecture.

Dictation as a communicative test. Dictation can serve as a measure of auditory comprehension if it is given at a fast enough pace so that it is not simply a spelling test (Oller, 1979; Stansfield, 1985). The pace is determined by the size of the phrase groups between pauses, the length of the pauses, and the speed at which the phrase groups are read. Nonnative respondents must segment the sounds into words, phrases, and sentences. It has been found that they make the following types of errors on this form of dictation (Oller, 1972):

1. Inversion
2. Incorrect word choice (through misunderstanding of grammar or lack of vocabulary)
3. Insertion of extra words
4. Omission of dictated words

A variation on the use of dictation as a measure of general listening ability involves scoring by chunks or meaningful segments, not by words (Savignon, 1982; Cziko & Nien-Hsuan, 1984). Another approach cited in the literature is that of multiple-choice dictation, whereby the respondents are required to retain a stimulus statement while locating the correct printed version of the statement in the test booklet. The printed options assess the relationship between elements within the sentence(s), rather than spelling or discrimination of minimal sound differences (Stansfield, 1985).

Interview topic recovery. It has been suggested that assessment move beyond the use of listening comprehension scales that are concerned with surface features of language and thus may be inadequate predictors of the ability to comprehend in oral interaction. The basis of the contention is that traditional measures of listening are rarefied examples of "canned" language, rather than reflecting real-world listening needs, such as in a genuine conversation with an interlocutor. An example of a more interactive task would be that of *interview topic recovery*—wherein respondents are assessed on the basis of their success at extracting information from an interlocutor on a given topic. For instance, they could be asked to interview an interlocutor as if preparing a report for a governmental agency on the situation of migrant workers (Schrafnagl & Cameron, 1988).

Verbal report data on listening comprehension tasks. Verbal report methods have helped us get beyond the abstract labels on assessment measures and beyond our preconceived notions about what listening comprehension measures are actually measuring. It appears that, as could be the case with reading comprehension items, the same listening comprehension item could be assessing different skills among different respondents—anything from vocabulary to inference to memory. And within a skill area, such as lexical ability, different respondents can have different sets of knowledge depending on their needs and interests, and this will differentially influence their performance.

Research Notes

In a study of two native Spanish speakers and two native English speakers interacting in English-speaking situations, Hawkins (1985) found that the nonnatives' "appropriate responses" were not completely reliable. The situations involved one speaker having information that the other needed to complete a task (e.g., the contents of a grab bag or a matching pictures task). Nonnatives gave appropriate responses even though they did not comprehend the utterance directed at them. Hawkins' check on comprehension involved having the nonnatives provide verbal reports on what they were thinking at the point in the interaction where they responded. Her recommendation was to make sure that a listening comprehension response clearly indicates whether the respondent has understood the utterance.

Questions that seemed to be assessing one particular skill turned out through introspection to be assessing a number of different skills. A given student would use different skills to answer items that were ostensibly similar, and different students answered the same test item in different ways—a vocabulary item for one student, a test of inference for another, and a test of memory for a third.

Following a similar line of investigation, Buck (1990) collected verbal report data from Japanese college students who were thinking aloud as they performed EFL listening tasks on a narrative text. He found that each test response was a unique event, an interaction between a number of variables, many of them personal and particular to that listener on that occasion. His conclusion was that "language comprehension is, by its very nature, multidimensional, and testing it only increases the number of dimensions involved in the process. In such a case it is obviously not possible to say what each item measures" (1990:424-425).

Buck went on to note that each factor in listening comprehension appears to be multifaceted. For example, lexical knowledge is not on a linear progression from "none" to "high level." Different learners have knowledge of different discourse domains and different lexical sets, depending on their needs and interests. He concluded that listening comprehension could not be a unidimensional trait.

In this section we have moved from the more discrete types of listening comprehension assessment tasks to the more integrative and have seen that the more integrative the tasks, the greater the confusion there may be about just what aspects of listening comprehension are in fact being assessed from item to item and procedure to procedure.

Assessing Speaking Skills

The assessment of spoken language has evolved dramatically over the last several decades from tests of oral grammar and pronunciation to interviews and, more recently, to multiple tasks, often collected over time. We will start by considering standard interviews, proceed to modified interview tasks, consider semi-direct tests (i.e., talking to tape recorders rather than to live interlocutors), and finally refer to other multiple measures, with our focus on role play aimed at assessing the ability to perform speech acts and other language functions.

The Interview

There are by now numerous structured interview measures available, all intended for assessing second-language speaking among adults (see Alderson, Krahnke, & Stansfield, 1987), yet only recently have these instruments begun to be rigorously scrutinized as to the nature of their tasks, the data produced, and the quality of the ratings. For example, Perrett (1990) argues that despite the oral interview's high face validity as an elicitation device for communicative language assessment, the range of linguistic phenomena that the interview can elicit is limited. She contends that whereas the oral interview can assess phonological aspects, lexicogrammatical aspects, and certain discourse aspects, it does not assess well (or at all) control over topic or text type, interactive aspects of discourse such as speech functions or exchange structure, or use of language in other situations.

Perrett illustrated these limitations by using six from a stratified random sample of forty-eight interviews collected in 1985 by the Australian Adult Migrant Education Service (AMES). The sample included three Polish women and three Vietnamese men. Ninety percent of the questions asked were, in fact, asked by the **interviewer** of the **interviewee**, and these questions and answers constituted the bulk of the interview. Furthermore, limitations in the range of discourse used by the interviewees were not due to limited language proficiency, since there was very little distinction in discourse between the beginning and the intermediate-level speakers. As Perrett put it,

> the covert, but real, purpose of the language testing interview is to display the language proficiency of one participant. This orientation results in a one-way flow of personal information in order to exhibit language fluency. The question of what information is exchanged is secondary. (1990:234-235)

Perrett went on to note other limitations in the interview as a method of assessment. For example, the interviewer's role is not to talk at length, but instead to encourage the interviewee to speak. Furthermore, not only is the interviewer often a stranger to the respondent, meaning that the social distance between the two is great, but the interviewer is also in a role of considerable power, depending on the importance of the ratings that the interviewee receives. Perrett noted that it could be advisable to change the discourse patterns of the interview, such as by having the interviewer mumble and ask ambiguous reference questions in order to prompt the interviewee to ask questions of clarification. Nonetheless, it is still not possible through an interview format to assess the subject's ability to control conversation, produce topic initiations, or to assume responsibility for the continuance of the discourse. Perrett concluded that there are situations in which the interview should be abandoned in favor of other types of oral elicitation techniques.

Another study found empirical evidence to support the notion that the typical interview is asymmetrical in nature, with the interviewer being clearly in control. A study of native-nonnative discourse in thirty oral interviews on the Cambridge First Certificate in English Examination found that the native-speaking examiners controlled what was discussed, even though the nonnatives spoke twice as much (Young & Milanovic, 1992). Likewise, the nonnatives' utterances were far more likely to be contingent upon a previous utterance by the examiner than vice versa.

It is becoming increasingly clear that the rating of such interviews requires careful scrutiny beyond the traditional interrater reliability checks. For example, research evidence suggests that raters coming from different work-related backgrounds may differ in what they look for in the English of nonnatives. For example, employee raters were found to use different criteria for rating a job interview at an electronics company than those used by medical personnel for rating a medical interview (Meldman, 1991).

Meldman had four supervisors at an electronics company rate a job interview, along with eight EFL teachers and an expert rater, and had two nurses rate a medical interview, along with the expert and the teachers. She found that those who dealt with limited English speakers in the work place rated "ability to ask questions" most highly, while medical personnel were most concerned with "ability to give accurate information." Her study implied that the incorporation of ratings of native speaker judges familiar with the demands of communication in a specific occupational or everyday setting could improve the validity of the assessment procedure.

The Meldman study also points up the need to consider just which communicative functions are to be elicited in given tasks and whether they are the ones that should be assessed for the given respondents. Likewise, the instructions to raters on the communicative functions that are to be assessed (such as asking questions or giving information accurately) and the weight that the correct use of each function is to receive should be clear. A more componential or multitrait approach to the rating of speaking may also be possible, and this will be discussed in the next chapter with respect to the assessment of written essays. In such an approach, the traits to be used for ratings would vary according to the local context and relevant domain(s) of language behavior. For example, there may be different rating scales according to whether the respondents were asking questions in the work place or providing information about a patient at a hospital.

Now let us look at one of the more prominent sets of scales being used to assess oral proficiency in an interview format, and then we will consider a modification of these procedures, namely, the semi-direct test, which was developed to meet the needs of large-scale assessment, especially in parts of the world where there are no native-speaking interviewers available.

The ACTFL Proficiency Scale
for Use with Interviews

The ACTFL proficiency scale is actually a composite of three sets of guidelines from ACTFL, from the Educational Testing Service (ETS), and from the Interagency Language Roundtable (ILR). According to Lowe (1988), these proficiency scales assess achievement (i.e., mastery of functions, content, and accuracy) and functional ability with the language (i.e., ability to use the knowledge) in single global ratings. These guidelines grew out of earlier sets of scales that had sometimes divergent purposes. Until the late 1970s, universities had favored testing knowledge of literature, but at this point government agencies and academic institutions began to collaborate in the assessment of functional language ability.

Although the ACTFL scales were first developed for assessment of speaking, they have been extended to assess all four language skills (Lowe, 1988). In their traditional form there is a warm-up, a level check to determine the respondent's level of proficiency, a probe through questions or discussion of a topic to show the limits of the student's skills, and a wind-down to get the student back to a comfortable conversational level. The topics of the interviews include school-related and work-related questions, questions about leisure activities, and questions about daily schedules and future plans. More recently, the interviews have also included role-play situations for respondents who have adequate language skills. Such role plays probe for the ability to handle social functions such as greetings, invitations, and other speech acts.

The levels for the ACTFL scales are superior; advanced-plus; advanced; intermediate-high, mid, low; and novice-high, mid, low (see Byrnes, Thompson, & Buck [1989]; and Hadley [1993:13-21]). In rough terms, those speakers rated *superior* can support an opinion, hypothesize, discuss abstract topics, and handle a linguistically unfamiliar situation; errors virtually never interfere with communication. Those rated *advanced* can narrate and describe in the different tenses/aspects and can handle a complicated situation or transaction; they can be understood without difficulty. *Intermediates* can maintain simple face-to-face conversations by asking and responding to simple questions on familiar topics and can handle a simple situation or transaction; they can be understood, with some repetition. *Novices* have little or no functional ability, and can communicate only minimally with formulaic and rote utterances in highly predictable common daily settings; they may be difficult to understand.

Within the superior, advanced, intermediate, and novice levels, speakers are assessed for their speaking proficiency within different contexts (formal versus informal), with different content (general interest topics versus special fields), by text type (extended versus more limited discourse), and according to areas of accuracy. These areas of accuracy include

1. *Fluency*—smooth flow of speech with the use of rhetorical devices to mark discourse patterns
2. *Grammar*—control of complex and simple constructions
3. *Pragmatic competence*—use of conversation-management devices to get the message across and to compensate for gaps
4. *Pronunciation*—degree of influence of native-language phonological features
5. *Sociolinguistic competence*—use of appropriate social registers, cultural references, and idioms
6. *Vocabulary*—breadth of vocabulary and knowledge of vocabulary in field of interest or expertise

In order to become certified as an ACTFL examiner, it is necessary to participate in a week-long training session. This training deals only with oral language proficiency. The certification requires that the participants accurately rate several sets of tapes of oral interviews. In order to maintain their certification, examiners must become recertified every two years by rating a new set of tapes. Given the time and expense involved in ACTFL certification, local institutions may choose to offer a modified form of ACTFL assessment, possibly even replacing the one-on-one interview format with a group format (Rebecca Oxford, personal communication). At the University of Minnesota, for example, foreign-language teaching assistants are trained to give a "Limited Oral Proficiency Interview" in which they just need to distinguish an *intermediate-mid* from an *intermediate-low* and anything lower, since intermediate-mid is considered the minimum level in order to pass the speaking proficiency subtest of the Graduation Proficiency Test. When questionable cases arise, the tapes of the interviews are rated by a faculty member with extensive ACTFL training and/or by other teaching assistants as well.

While there are those who think that assessing proficiency can be viewed as a matter of which scales to use and how to improve them (see Lowe & Stansfield, 1988), there are also those who believe that it is inappropriate to conduct assessment through the use of such proficiency scales. First, single scales—especially in academia—may weaken the validity of the measure in that they lump together a variety of different behaviors in a presumed unidimensional scale (see Bachman [1988], Lantolf & Frawley [1988], and Shohamy [1990b]). The use of such scales also depends upon certain assumptions about what is taught in class and what can therefore be achieved by students. Some contend that such measures are intended to assess language ability beyond achievement in a given course or set of courses, since learners would be expected to have other exposures to the language that would enhance their general proficiency. In reality, however, students of certain languages may not have any out-of-class contact with the language. For this reason, obtaining background information of this nature from students during ACTFL assessment, or during any other assessment for that matter, would be useful.

Regarding the administration of the ACTFL Oral Interview, there are various problem areas. While the aim is to assess oral proficiency, students who have had limited out-of-class exposure to the commonly taught languages and students studying lesser taught languages may have difficulty developing their proficiency beyond the vocabulary and structures that they are given in class. For these students, the knowledge that can be assessed may be closely tied to the specific curricular items, so the measure is likely to be assessing achievement more than general proficiency.

Second, there is the danger that the generic scale may simply be translated in order to implement it with languages for which such a scale would actually need to be modified. Additionally, the situations used as prompts may not translate across cultures. For example, problems arose with the design of a test of oral Japanese at the University of Minnesota. The use of a situation that worked for other languages and cultures, namely, that of calling a babysitter to ask her to come over that evening, was found to be inappropriate for use on the Japanese test. Apparently, calling a babysitter is uncommon in Japan since members of the extended family would be expected to help out. In another situation, where students had to respond as if they were in a metro station in Tokyo, the problem was that the students had never been to Japan and had not studied about the Japanese metro. Hence, they were at a loss as to how to react (Y. Johnson, 1991).

Third, Ross and Berwick (1992) call attention to what they see as a little explored phenomenon associated with interviews, namely, that of interviewer efforts at accommodation. They found that or-questions, slowdowns, and display questions were used most frequently to accommodate the lowest-proficiency interlocutors. They suggest that overaccommodation may diminish the power of the probe, which is intended to push an interviewee's performance of oral proficiency to its limits. They warn that interviewers should be aware of the consequences of their inclination to accommodate to nonnatives at the different levels of proficiency, regardless of the interviewees' need for it.

Fourth, there is the danger that such rating scales might be used as a curriculum. In other words, while the ACTFL guidelines focus on specific aspects of the respondents' language, the scales do not in and of themselves provide guidelines on how teachers should conduct their instruction in order to bring students closer to mastery. Thus, the scales are not meant to be the basis for teaching.

Fifth, another worrisome problem about such scales is that on a superficial level it may be possible to teach to the test. In fact, Loughrin-Sacco (1990) found that enhanced performance on the Oral Proficiency Interview (OPI) was trainable. He discovered that if respondents on the Spanish OPI made more use of cohesion markers such as *primero*, *entonces*, and *pues*, their oral production was more likely to receive a "paragraph-level discourse" rating rather than the lower "sentence-level discourse" rating. Thus, in order to have their students do better on such measures, teachers might have them practice speaking in paragraphs and using markers of cohesion in order to get higher scores. This could create an illusion that the students' general proficiency was higher than it really is.

Sixth, as more research is conducted on the rating processes, it is becoming clearer that the scales are not necessarily rater friendly at all levels. For example, Ross and Berwick (1992) found that interviewers may have difficulty applying ACTFL/ETS guidelines with enough precision to support a rating task of, say, distinguishing a 2 from a 2+. They did a detailed analysis of fifteen tapes of oral proficiency interviews in Japanese, each rated at one of four levels (1+, 2, 2+, or 3). Their finding calls attention to what may be uncertainty among interviewers in certain assessment situations about what interviewees are supposed to be able to do with the language. There may not have been enough probes for raters to accurately determine the proficiency of the given respondent. Additionally, the guidelines may be inadequately learned or may themselves be so arbitrary or incomplete as to render them impractical for interacting with learners at certain levels, whatever their ultimate value in assisting a choice of rating.

A final criticism that has been raised is that for such scales to be properly assessed by the test users, they should appear in the professional literature with complete research documentation—that is, with a full description of the empirical research undertaken to produce them. Otherwise, it is difficult to determine whether such scales are truly based on some theoretically and empirically validated progression in second- or foreign-language skill development.

Semi-Direct Interviews

As Underhill (1987), Shohamy (1988), and others have suggested, in order to obtain a valid overall picture of oral proficiency, it is necessary to use a combination of assessment methods. Oral interviews are making increasing strides in this direction, especially some of the semi-direct tests of speaking, which comprise different types of tasks. The fact that they constitute multi-task assessment instruments without the need for an interviewer gives them particular appeal.

The following is a description of just such a semi-direct test, the Simulated Oral Proficiency Interview (SOPI) in its preliminary Portuguese version (Stansfield, Kenyon, Doyle, Paiva, Ulsh, & Cowles, 1988). (I discuss this oral language measure here because I was asked to review the test and had an opportunity to "take it" in the process [Cohen, 1989].)[2] Although some respondents on the SOPI have expressed a preference for live interviews, citing the unnaturalness of speaking to a machine in the field testing of the instrument, this semi-direct test has been found to correlate highly with a direct measure of oral proficiency—the Oral Proficiency Interview (r = .93)—and interrater reliability on the test was found to be uniformly high (r = .95) (Stansfield et al., 1990). Thus, the following discussion reflects a personal appraisal of the instrument and need not reflect that of others. The intention is to raise several issues regarding the validity of the measure, rather than its reliability. Let us look at the instrument subtest by subtest.

Personal Conversation. The respondent is asked in Portuguese approximately ten questions about family, education, and hobbies, and is to respond to each one in order. This section is intended to serve as a warm-up—to help respondents begin thinking in the target language, while being asked questions about their personal life that might well come up in a normal conversation. Yet some of the questions asked by the interlocutor are not necessarily the usual questions that would come up in a conversation. Instead, they seem to reflect the sorts of traditional questions that have been asked in oral interviews for many years—questions for which respondents have notoriously memorized their answers in advance. It is true that this portion is intended as a warm-up, but in fact, some of the questions seem somewhat peculiar, at times containing linguistic curiosities in their structure in order to test certain verb tenses (e.g., conditionals).

Giving Directions. The respondent is shown a pictorial map in the test booklet and is instructed to give directions between two points on the map. In this and in all subsequent sections, instructions are provided in English. Actually, in real-life situations nonnatives are more likely to have to understand such directions than to give them, but the task was still tricky, because the map was unconventional—it did not have the usual array of streets at right angles to each other. I had conceptual problems in preparing my directions, only partly due to possible language deficiency and partly due to my difficulty in relating to the map. This also brings up the issue of equivalence across different versions of the same test. Differences in a picture, map, or other stimulus may produce different types of data in respondents but may nonetheless call for differing cognitive tasks, which can have a subtle or not so subtle effect on the results.

Detailed Description. The respondent is shown a drawing representing a variety of objects and actions and is instructed to describe the picture in detail. I found this section to be traditional and not "communicative" in the modern sense of the term. As an assessment format, it has existed for many years, though usually with an examiner prompting an oral response, especially in cases where the respondent says little or nothing. This task seems to test extensively for specialized vocabulary.

Picture Sequence. The respondent is instructed to speak in a narrative fashion about two sets of four or five pictures in sequence, each time being called upon to use different tenses in the narration. This section also seems somewhat traditional. Like the preceding one, this task assesses specialized vocabulary—with somewhat more emphasis on verb tense—but it seems possible for a respondent to describe the sequence entirely in one tense, either the past or the present.

Topical Discourse. The respondent is instructed to talk about five topics, each involving specialized content. The topics are read aloud on the tape and are also written in English in the text booklet. In my opinion, this section is the most problematic. Each of the five topic areas calls for far more preparation time than the fifteen seconds allowed, in order to make a truly cohesive and coherent response. Of course, it could be argued that the items are only partially scored for their cohesive and coherent nature and that the scoring is for holistic or integrative proficiency. But the sense of control that the respondent experiences undoubtedly plays more than a minor role—especially in an interviewer-absent situation such as this.

Part of the difficulty lies in the fact that the several sentences describing the topic are presented in English with the response to be in Portuguese. For me, this usually means that there is a need to translate the instructions into Portuguese before commencing. The provision of bilingual instructions would have eliminated this need for translation, although it would also provide some of the vocabulary for which the items were undoubtedly testing. In a truly communicative context, a native would, in fact, give clues to vocabulary in the very asking of the question, so the provision of a Portuguese version of the questions would actually be consistent with typical conversational contexts.

Situations. The respondent hears and reads, in English, five descriptions of situations in which a specified audience and communicative task are identified. The situations assess the ability to handle interactive situations through simulated role-playing tasks—tasks involving, for example, the use of appropriate speech acts such as requesting, complaining, apologizing, and giving a formal toast. This section forces the respondent to be creative in the use of responses that are socioculturally and sociolinguistically appropriate in order to carry out a specified task as "natively" as possible. In this instance, bilingual instructions would have been invaluable, since most of the situations involved some defective item for which a complaint was being lodged, but the item itself reflected low-frequency vocabulary. How do you complain about a thing you cannot name? Personally, I found several of the situations rather uninteresting or even unrealistic, but I realize that this could well be a matter of personal taste.

In summary, the aim of the SOPI is to shorten test time while obtaining a broader sampling of the speaker's interlanguage than an oral interview would generally do, in a reliable, valid, and efficient manner. The test would appear to be succeeding. Nevertheless, perhaps future revisions of this test could address certain issues:

1. The authenticity of conversational questions
2. The lack of enough time to prepare a response
3. Problems of cognitive ability in map reading
4. The language of the instructions
5. The human-interest value of the situations

Although performances on the Hebrew version of the SOPI and the Oral Interview have correlated highly with each other (Shohamy & Stansfield, 1990), the SOPI was found to have more of the features of a literary genre and the Oral Interview more of the features of an oral text (Shohamy, 1991). For example, there were more paraphrasing and self-correction on the SOPI than on the Oral Interview, and more switches to native language on the Oral Interview.

In addition, the SOPI's holistic scoring is problematic. Whereas this instrument provides an array of speaking samples, for content vocabulary, function, and contextualized use of structure it uses a single rating instead of multiple ratings. The same criticism leveled against the Oral Proficiency Interview—that the single scale is too limiting (Bachman, 1988; Lantolf & Frawley, 1988)—can be leveled against the SOPI scales. The single-rating scale lumps together different behaviors in a presumed unidimensional scale of speaking that often does not reflect reality. Hence, the test constructors deserve praise for producing this test, but the potential limitations both in this test and in others like it should be addressed as the semi-direct testing effort progresses.

The Speaking Proficiency English Assessment Kit (SPEAK; Educational Testing Service, 1985) is another example of a semi-direct test that attempts to break away from the traditional interview format. The version of the test which first appeared in 1980 requires respondents to respond to seven prerecorded subtests and to record their responses onto another audio channel or onto a separate tape recorder, depending on the equipment available.

The sections included
1. Answering questions about self as an unscored warm-up exercise
2. Reading a printed paragraph aloud
3. Oral completion of partial sentences as written prompts (e.g., "Whenever John comes home . . .")
4. Telling a continuous story about a series of drawings after receiving a prompt such as "One day last week . . ."
5. Responding to a series of question about a drawing depicting an event—e.g., an accident between a car and a bike
6. Giving opinions on topics of international concern (e.g., automobile pollution) or describing certain objects (e.g., a telephone)
7. Explaining a schedule or notice describing activities of a class, club, or conference

Respondents are rated for overall comprehensibility and for pronunciation, grammar, and fluency. Currently, this test is under revision in line with developments in the field.

Because the international teaching assistants at Penn State University complained about the format of sitting in a cubicle and interacting with a tape recorder, a direct rather than a semi-direct version of the SPEAK test was developed, calling for the presence of two trained evaluators rather than using taped elicitations (K. Johnson, 1991). The test still begins with a short informal interview (warm-up phase). The oral recitation and the oral completion of partial sentences were eliminated, so the test comprises four sections:

1. A picture sequence—telling a story
2. A picture description

3. Free response—the respondent's opinion on topics of international concern
4. Describing a schedule—presenting the contents of a syllabus or an announcement to a group of students

Evaluators are allowed to explain unfamiliar vocabulary words appearing in the directions. The interviews take fifteen minutes and are tape-recorded. If there is a large (more than fifty-point) discrepancy between evaluators, then a third evaluator is called in. Evaluators get eight to ten hours of training on rating pronunciation, fluency, and comprehensibility.

Other feedback regarding the SPEAK test includes the finding that the test has a ceiling effect—that is, it does not discriminate higher-level language proficiency abilities necessary for, say, becoming a language teacher from somewhat lower-level proficiency adequate for being just a language user (Herb Seliger, personal communication). Partly because of this ceiling effect, institutions such as Iowa State University have added a field-specific teaching performance test, called TEACH (Dan Douglas, personal communication). This test calls for respondents to present a five-minute lesson on an assigned topic in their field (twenty-four-hour preparation time) and three minutes of question-answer interaction with a small audience of undergraduates. The presentation is videotaped and scored by trained SPEAK raters for the following:

1. Language comprehensibility (according to SPEAK)
2. Cultural ability (U.S. academic code, nonverbal behavior, "rapport")
3. Communication skills (organization, expression, use of evidence, eye contact, blackboard use, "presence")
4. Interaction (listening, question handling/responding)

Tests such as the one just described have been constructed primarily to assess the spoken English of international teaching assistants. Not only is there a concern for assessing whether these individuals have the general speaking proficiency necessary for teaching, but also an interest in assessing their oral language skills in the specific domain in which they will be teaching. Thus, a series of tests have been developed for assessing speaking proficiency in domains such as chemistry (CHEMSPEAK), mathematics

(MATHSPEAK), physics, and agribusiness (Smith, 1989, 1992; Douglas & Selinker, 1991, 1993; Douglas & Simonova, 1993). The format for the MATHSPEAK assessment instrument (Douglas & Selinker, 1993) is as follows:

Section One: Talking about math as if talking to another student.

Section Two: Reading a printed paragraph aloud as if in the role of a math teacher reading a textbook to students.

Section Three: Sentence completion—imagining that a math instructor has spoken to the respondent and only the first part was heard; the respondent has to guess the rest.

Section Four: Referring to three diagrams in explaining three cases of the roots of a quadratic equation as if in the role of teacher.

Section Five: Answering questions about a theorem as if the questions had been from students.

Section Six: Giving an opinion on topics of interest to mathematicians.

Research Notes

Douglas and Selinker (1993) report on a small-scale study in which international grad students who had taken SPEAK also took MATHSPEAK. They found that the reliability for MATHSPEAK was not high and that the raters sometimes had difficulty separating content from language ability. Of the twelve math students who took it, seven did better on MATHSPEAK while four did better on the more general SPEAK test. This finding would lend support to the notion that oral language needs to be assessed through multiple measures.

Warm up/Rehearsal/Practice

Regardless of the speaking abilities being assessed, allowing time for a genuine warm-up exercise will probably enhance results. For language learners who have not achieved speaking fluency, a test of speaking may be traumatic and problematic if the respondents feel out of contact with the language, at least at the outset. Therefore, it is important to activate what has been referred to as the "din in the head." According to Krashen (1985), we need at least one to two hours of good quality input in a foreign language that we are not "advanced" speakers of in order to activate the din in the head. This "din" is actually a result of the stimulation of our *language acquisition device*.[3] Again according to Krashen, the din will wear off after several days.

We need to be wary of possible "pseudo warm-ups," such as found in "Personal Conversation," the first subtest of the SOPI described above (Stansfield et al., 1988). Subtests that function more as probes for certain vocabulary and syntactic structures, rather than as true warm-ups, may not serve to activate the din in the head.

One activity that could perhaps serve as a genuine warm-up would be the "4-3-2 Technique for Information Transfer and Retelling" (Arevart & Nation, 1993). The task calls for speakers to convey certain meaningful information to listeners in a long turn of spoken language that the speakers construct for themselves. The first turn is for four minutes. Then the speakers go over the same material, this time in three minutes, and finally repeat the same message in two minutes. The speakers learn through this exercise that more can be said, more effectively, and in less time when the mind has a chance to rehearse the target-language material. As a warm-up exercise in a speaking test, this activity can help build the respondents' confidence in their ability to say things effectively.

Multiple Measures of Speaking Ability

In recent years there has been a marked shift from the assessment of speaking skills in an isolated fashion to that of assessing them more integratively. Also, experts are aware of the importance of using more than one measure of speaking, such that more than one type of speech interaction is tapped for each learner. The following are some of the possibilities:

1. Giving a verbal essay (speaking for three minutes on a specified topic)
2. Giving an oral presentation or lecture (differing from the verbal essay in that the respondent is allowed to prepare) (Weir, 1990)

3. Reporting the contents of an article read in the native language
4. Participating in group discussion on a common and possibly controversial theme
5. Taking part in role play

We note that the last of the assessment activities on the list, *role play*, actually encompasses a number of activities—from the role-play interview, in which respondents supply a single utterance after receiving a prompt, to the open-ended role play, which is acted out to its logical completion. One type of acting out encompasses both *socio-drama* (Scarcella, 1983) and *scenarios* or *strategic interaction* (DiPietro, 1987). In these special forms of role play, an open-ended story with a conflict is presented and the students in the class are given the task of arriving at various solutions. The students are encouraged to make multiple passes through the role play until they are satisfied with the outcome. Furthermore, students assign themselves to roles according to how well they relate to those roles, and usually they are coached by their peers. In the scenario approach, the students are split into two groups or factions, each one representing one side in the conflict. Members of each group coach their representative whenever necessary.

Besides the concern for including multiple tasks, it has also become more common to establish which speech functions are to be assessed in each type of interaction:

Task	Function
Reporting	stating the main ideas and expressing an opinion about them
Discussion	arguing
Role play	producing a given speech act (e.g., requesting, complaining, apologizing, or complimenting)
Lecturing	defining terms

Likewise, it may be advisable or even crucial to establish the following dimensions for any given task:

- The topic of the interaction
- The level of formality (informal, consultative, formal)

- The number of participants
- The relative status of the participants (high/low, low/high, equal)
- The familiarity of the participants with each other (stranger, acquaintance, friend)
- The gender of the participants

Each interaction is then rated on a series of scales, including more traditional measures of grammatical accuracy, but also including and perhaps emphasizing the control of sociolinguistic appropriateness and of discourse functions (Shohamy, 1988, 1990a).

Brown and Yule (1983) point out that spoken language has incomplete sentences, has nonspecific words, and may contain relatively little information in any given chunk. Typical classroom interactions involve teacher utterances and short learner responses. If the assessment of speaking depends on full learner responses and presumes that the respondents' sentences will be complete, word choice will be precise, and utterances will be replete with information, then the language assessor needs to be aware that such a situation is probably a radical departure from what typically goes on in the classroom.

Brown and Yule were perhaps among the first to recommend that teachers collect *oral portfolios* of student speaking ability as a means of assessment, although they did not refer to the data gathering in terms of oral portfolios. They stressed the importance of keeping taped records of learners' speaking ability in different modes over time, with each student asked to do the same thing— for example,

- Describe objects
- Give instructions for assembling equipment or draw a diagram
- Read a map
- Tell stories
- Give eyewitness accounts
- Express opinions

The drawing or map-reading tasks would involve an information gap, in which only the speaker has the drawing and has to convey to the listener what to draw.

Yule and Tarone (1990) conducted an exploratory investigation in which twenty-seven ESL students and nine native English speakers were paired off in what was intended to be a reasonable facsimile of communicative behavior. One member of the pair needed to obtain information being communicated by the other member, with nonnatives in separate pairs from natives. The tasks were conducted at a table with a low barrier. The speaker looked at visual stimuli on a video screen and was tape-recorded while performing three tasks:

1. Describing objects (e.g., equipment for horse care)
2. Giving instructions (e.g., making coffee with a coffee maker)
3. Narrating what was shown on the screen (e.g., a classroom event involving a teacher and two students)

The listeners were instructed not to ask for clarification or provide any verbal feedback at all so that the speakers would not end up simply answering the listeners' questions. In the description task, the listeners had a photo of the horse brush that appeared on the screen for the speakers but also had photos of two other types of brushes, and had to select the right one. In the instruction and narrative tasks, the listeners had three sets of three photos for each task. Only one of these sets had the photos arranged in the right order. The listeners had to choose the set which best reflected the order of instructions/events that they heard. The speakers and listeners switched roles for a second round. Yule and Tarone found the tasks provided the nonnative speakers with opportunities to produce extended spoken discourse in the second language.

In more recent work, Yule introduced the element of conflicting information. In a task where a speaker had to give directions to a listener, with both referring to a map, the listener's version of the map contained items that were different from the speaker's map. For example, in the sender's map there was a building labeled "Shoes" that in the receiver's map was labeled "Bookstore," and the sender had only one "Bank" whereas the receiver had that bank plus two other bank buildings. The interlocutors had to sort out the discrepancies in order for the listener to follow the speaker's directions correctly (Yule, Powers, & Macdonald, 1992).

Brown and Yule (1983) also provided guidelines for teachers on the types of speaking data they should be collecting from their students when they are engaged in interactive communicative tasks:

1. Speech that has a purpose
2. Extended chunks of speech
3. Speech that is structured or organized—enough so that the listener does not have to work at understanding what is being talked about
4. Tasks where the amount of speech is controlled
5. Tasks for which *communicative effectiveness* is quantified—that is, there is a specific number of points of required information to be conveyed

Rating Scales for Assessing Communicative Ability

In her pioneering effort on communicative ability in a second language, Savignon (1972) provided four communicative settings for the purposes of assessing functional speaking ability: discussing a topic with a native speaker of the second language, interviewing a native speaker as if for a newspaper article, reporting facts about oneself or one's recent activities, and describing what someone is doing.

It is important to consider the way in which such data are elicited—i.e., the item-elicitation format. Some elicitation formats are more open-ended than others. The degree of structure in the situations may influence student output. Also, certain tasks may call for more role-playing ability than other tasks, especially if they put the respondents in situations that they have not previously experienced (perhaps not even in their native language). At times, respondents may point out that a given role-play situation happens to them all the time. They may indicate that they had performed that speech act in that very same situation on the previous day (e.g., "requesting that a neighbor turn down loud music late at night"). At other times, respondents may make it clear that they have never had to perform the speech act in that situation.

In instances where the respondent has never had to react in such a situation (e.g., "apologizing for keeping a classmate's book two weeks beyond the agreed date"), it could be argued that the instrument is forcing unnatural behavior and that if the respondent is not a good actor, the results might be problematic. In cases where the respondents are asked to play a role that is out of character for them, the challenge for the researcher would be to distinguish the respondents' sociolinguistic proficiency from their situational adeptness or acting ability.

One way to void such a situation would be to allow respondents to opt out of the speech act (Bonikowska, 1988) as we do in real life. If they deflect the stimulus, the interlocutor would not pursue the issue. This is often the case in the real world, where a person may opt **not** to apologize, complain, or request something. However, allowing for opting out leaves gaps in the data, so researchers and evaluators tend to request that respondents produce an answer for each situation—even in face-threatening situations (Brown & Levinson, 1987). As mentioned above, the socio-drama format allows for students to participate only when they relate to a role and feel comfortable playing it (Scarcella, 1983). Perhaps the measurement instrument could be designed so that the respondents choose the role(s) that they want to play. Regardless of how the data are elicited, the issue still remains of how the data are rated.

As indicated in Chapter 2, efforts by Olshtain and myself to use the Canale and Swain (1980) framework led us to modify the scales so that they would be more functional for assessing oral communicative ability. First, raters in a study by Cohen and Olshtain (1993) had difficulty identifying clear examples of utterances that would be rated for discourse competence (e.g., ambiguous uses of cohesion such as "We didn't see you!" after hitting a car). Hence, the discourse competence scale was dropped. Second, given the problems in rating discourse, instead of breaking the sociolinguistic competence scale out into sociocultural rules and discourse rules, we created two separate scales: sociocultural ability and sociolinguistic ability. This distinction was found to work in producing ratings that were relatively consistent over various groups of raters.

For the purposes of this volume, we will be using a modified set of rating scales of *oral language communicative ability* that are meant to reflect assessment trends in the 1990s and that are intended to be used by the classroom teacher primarily for students at the intermediate or advanced levels of language proficiency. These ratings are based on the theoretical frameworks of Canale and Swain (1980) and Bachman (1990) and on the research by Raffaldini (1988) and by Cohen and Olshtain (1993). For the purpose of ease in rating, communicative language ability is rated by three scales: 1) sociocultural ability, 2) sociolinguistic ability, and 3) grammatical ability. Therefore, the scales are not comprehensive of all aspects of communicative ability but are intended to assess the major aspects.

The Cohen and Olshtain Communicative Ability Scales

Sociocultural ability. This scale assesses the **appropriateness** of the sociocultural strategies selected for realizing speech acts in a given context, taking into account (1) the culture involved, (2) the age and sex of the speakers, (3) their social class and occupations, and (4) their roles and status in the interaction. For example, while in some cultures (such as the U.S.) it may be appropriate for speakers to suggest to a boss when to make up a meeting that they have missed through negligence, in other cultures (in Israel, for example) such a repair strategy might be considered out of place in that it would most likely be the boss who makes the decision.

This scale also evaluates what is said in terms of the **amount** of information required in the given situation, and the **relevance** and **clarity** of the information actually supplied. The amount of information related can be a major concern—whether the learner supplies the appropriate amount of information in reporting or describing some idea, statement, or action (i.e., not too much or too little; Grice [1975]). For example, let us take the following situation used in a study by Levenston (1975):

> You buy some milk, but when you get home you find that it is sour. You take it back to the store and speak to the manager.

Given this situation, native speakers said such things as "I bought this milk here this afternoon, and it's sour." The natives were leaving it up to the manager to suggest an exchange. On the other hand, the foreign learners unnecessarily added such utterances as "And so, I would like you to change this milk for another one" (Levenston, 1975). Blum-Kulka and Olshtain (1986) also found that the responses of nonnatives, especially intermediate and advanced speakers, were excessively verbose. Learners with limited language actually responded more like natives. Edmondson and House (1991) refer to this phenomenon as *waffling*—that is, talking too much as a compensation strategy in communicative tasks. One explanation that they give for this behavior is that the speaker is lacking confidence and eager to ensure that the message gets across.

The relevance or contextual accuracy may also be of concern. Sometimes, as an artifact of a testing situation in which both the respondent and the examiner "know" that what is said is less important than how it is said, respondents may say what they are most capable of saying rather than what they want to say. Evidence to this effect emerged from a study of speech-act production (Cohen & Olshtain, 1993). In a role-play situation where the respondent was late for a study date with a friend, one respondent wanted to indicate that the bus did not come, but during retrospective self-observation she reported that she could not find the words in English, so instead she said, "I missed the bus." In a situation of asking the teacher for a lift home, another respondent said, "My bus is very late," which she saw right away to be incorrect. As she explained it through verbal report, "I meant that it wouldn't be leaving until later in the evening, but grammatically the sentence was OK, so I left it. I let it go because it wasn't so bad—she would understand what I meant." At times the utterances may pass without notice, while at other times they stick out in the interaction as being somewhat incoherent.

So the sociocultural ability scale actually assesses three distinct dimensions at the same time: (1) sociocultural appropriateness, (2) situational relevance and accuracy, and (3) proper amount of information. This is why *and/or* is used repeatedly in the descriptions at the different scale levels.

The *sociocultural ability scale* is as follows:

5— The message is socioculturally appropriate, reflects the situation clearly, and contains the proper amount of information.

4— The message is for the most part socioculturally appropriate, reflects the situation relatively clearly, and/or generally contains the proper amount of information.

3— The message is somewhat lacking in sociocultural appropriateness, calls for some interpretation to be understand, and/or contains too much or too little information.

2— The message is mostly lacking in sociocultural appropriateness, calls for much interpretation to be understand, and/or contains too much or too little information.

1— The message is completely lacking sociocultural appropriateness, is not clear, and/or contains far too much or too little information.

Sociolinguistic ability. The scale for sociolinguistic ability is intended to assess **the use of linguistic forms to express the intent of the speech act** (e.g., regret in an apology, the grievance in a complaint, the objective of a request, or the refusal of an invitation). For example, when students are asked to dinner by their professor and they cannot make it, "no way!" would probably constitute an inappropriate refusal, unless the students had an especially close relationship with their professor and the utterance were made in jest. This category assesses the speakers' control over the actual language forms used to realize the speech act (e.g., "sorry" versus "excuse me," "really sorry" versus "very sorry"), as well as their control over the register of the utterance, from most intimate to most formal language.

The *sociolinguistic ability scale* is as follows:

5— the speaker uses linguistic forms that are fully appropriate for expressing the intended speech act.

4— the speaker uses linguistic forms that are mostly appropriate for expressing the intended speech act.

3— there is some use of inappropriate linguistic forms for expressing the speech act.

2— there is much use of inappropriate linguistic forms for expressing the speech act.

1— there is continuous use of inappropriate linguistic forms for expressing the speech act.

Grammatical ability. This scale deals with **how acceptably** words, phrases, and sentences are formed and pronounced in the respondents' utterances. The focus is on clear cases of errors in form, such as the use of the present perfect for an action completed in the past (e.g., "We have seen a great film last night"), as well as on matters of style (e.g., the learner uses a passive verb form in a context where a native would use the active form: "I lost your book" versus "The book was lost"). Major errors might be considered those that either interfere with intelligibility or stigmatize the speaker. Minor errors would be those that do not get in the way of the listener's comprehension or annoy the listener to any extent. Thus, getting the tense wrong in "We have seen a great film last night" could be viewed as a minor error, whereas producing "I don't have what to say" by translating directly from the appropriate Hebrew language ("I really have no excuse") could be considered a major error since it is not only ungrammatical but also could stigmatize the speaker as rude and unconcerned, rather than apologetic.

The *grammatical ability scale* is as follows:

5— no major or minor errors in structure or vocabulary

4— no major errors and only several minor ones

3— several major errors and a fair number of minor ones

2— a somewhat frequent number of major and minor errors

1— frequent major and minor errors

We see that the sociocultural scale focuses on the appropriateness of **what** the respondents say in the given situation, while the sociolinguistic and grammatical scales focus on the appropriateness and grammaticality of **how** they say it. However, note that the sociolinguistic scale takes the how to a new level of analysis. Traditionally, assessment of oral language stopped at evaluation of grammar, vocabulary, and pronunciation. But now we are suggesting that there is a need to go beyond the level of grammatical acceptability to that of sociocultural and sociolinguistic appropriateness.

However, the scales for grammar, vocabulary, and pronunciation would still be of prime importance for beginning learners, since these speakers would be in the process of sorting out basic features of the language and would not yet be tackling more complex aspects. For example, a study of requests by beginning college learners of Spanish found that only 26% of learners used politeness strategies in Spanish, while 95% of an English-speaking sample did so in English (Koike, 1989).

Factors Beyond the Scales

Strategic ability. As noted in Chapter 2, an earlier version of the above scales included a scale for strategic ability as well. This scale was initially intended to assess how effectively the respondents execute the utterances, especially when ability in one of the other categories is lacking. In other words, this scale put the emphasis on *compensatory strategies*—that is, strategies used to compensate or remediate for a lack in some language area (Canale & Swain, 1980). Piloting of the scale demonstrated that raters had difficulty obtaining empirical observational data for the following scale:

3— the respondent effectively compensates for any deficiencies in language proficiency through the use of communication strategies.
2— the respondent sometimes makes use of communication strategies.
1— there is little or no sign that the respondent makes use of strategies to help in planning or executing utterances.

The problem was that the raters often could not tell from listening to the utterances whether the respondents had used any communication strategies and, if so, which ones. In such cases, would they award a 3 or a 1? So it was not surprising that the interrater reliability for five raters rating the fifteen speakers on six speech act situations in the Cohen and Olshtain (1993) study was lowest on the strategic ability scale. Having the respondents provide verbal report data while taking an oral assessment measure would probably be necessary for us to know whether a particular part of a response was a product of a successful use of strategic ability. And even this research methodology may not be completely successful at obtaining information about compensatory strategies.

As noted in previous chapters, Bachman (1990) provided a theoretical model for broadening strategic ability beyond the compensatory level by including an *assessment component* whereby the respondent (in the case of language testing) sets communicative goals, a *planning component* whereby the respondent retrieves the relevant items from language ability and plans their use, and an *execution component* whereby the respondent implements the plan. In theory, when respondents are given a situation in which to perform an oral role play, for instance, they may do as follows:

1. Assess the situation and identify the information that is needed in that context.
2. Plan out their response and go about retrieving from their language ability the grammatical, discourse, and sociocultural features needed for the role play.
3. Execute the role play.

After they finish, they may again perform an assessment to evaluate the extent to which the communicative goal was achieved.

As is the case with any theoretical model, test takers may make differential use of the components of this model when performing specific assessment tasks. For example, there are respondents who might not assess the situation before starting the role play and, because of this, may violate certain sociocultural conventions. Likewise, some respondents plan out their utterances before producing them while others just start talking on an "on-line" basis. Recent research involving the use of verbal report directly after the performance of oral role-play interaction is beginning to obtain data regarding the extent of assessment and planning actually taking place before the execution of apologies, complaints, and requests (Cohen & Olshtain, 1993).

However, a fair number of test-taking strategies associated with strategic ability may still be compensatory. Respondents often omit material because they do not know it when put on the spot. They come across as terse, not because they know that this is appropriate but because they are lacking enough language to be more verbal. In addition, they may engage in avoidance and produce different material from what they would like to, with the hope that it will be acceptable in the given context. They may also paraphrase, simplify, or approximate when the exact word escapes them under the pressure of assessment or possibly because they simply do not know the word that well or at all. So when respondents cannot think of the exact word, they might use a paraphrase instead (e.g., *a body with water all around it* for *island*). In this fashion, clever respondents may avoid using language forms that they are unsure of and thus leave an impression that they are more skillful in terms of their grammatical or sociolinguistic ability than they actually are.

Bachman (personal communication) suggests that while strategic ability would probably not be used in a set of rating scales for assessing communicative ability, the test constructor should be concerned with considering the types and extent of strategic ability that might be called upon in an effort to answer given test questions (see also Bachman, Purpura, & Cushing, 1993). In addition, there is a need to expand the typical use of the concept of strategic competence to encompass compensatory and non-compensatory behaviors not just in speaking, but in reading, listening, and writing as well (Oxford & Cohen, 1992).

For example, a study of test-taking strategies among nonnatives on a reading comprehension test revealed that respondents used certain strategies differently, depending on the type of question that they were asked. The strategies of "trying to match the stem with the text" and "guessing" were reported more frequently for inference-type questions than for the other question types, such as direct statement or main idea. The strategy of "paraphrasing" was reported to occur more in responding to direct statement items than with inference and main-idea question types (Anderson, Bachman, Perkins, & Cohen, 1991). Such strategic ability data are apparently still lacking with regard to speaking tests.

Fluency. We note that the traditional scale for *fluency* is not included in the above set of communicative ability scales, but while it used to be conspicuous in such scales. This is because it is not easy to assess fluency, even impressionistically. For example, there are problems associated with criteria such as *speed* or *ease of speech*. For one thing, people differ in terms of speech rate even in their native language, and speaking "easily" does not necessarily mean speaking "appropriately." In going back over transcripts of oral exams, Kato (1977) found that certain nonnative students that he and others had marked as more fluent than other students were actually not as good at selecting appropriate vocabulary or at grammatical control. In fact, the very hesitation phenomena (e.g., pauses filled with *er* or *uh*) that make a foreign speaker's speech seem broken may really be signs that the speaker is searching for the appropriate lexical item or grammatical structure.

Researchers have in fact suggested that any simplified rating scales of fluency are of dubious value, since natives may perform more poorly than nonnatives in that nonnatives are making a conscientious effort to speak without obvious hesitation, to use longer sentences, and to use an accelerated tempo (Sajavaara & Lehtonen, 1978). It has even been suggested that it may be valuable to teach students how to be *disfluent* so that they can sound more native-like. Lehtonen put it as follows:

> To be fluent in the right way, one has to know how to hesitate, how to be silent, how to self-correct, how to interrupt and how to complete one's expression. According to this definition of fluency, one must speak in a way that is expected by the linguistic community and that represents normal, acceptable and relaxed linguistic behavior. Testing of this quality of speech is not possible by means of any instrumental method. (1978:12)

The Reliability and Validity of Speaking Scales

Given the three-scale rating scheme presented above, the classroom teacher will have to make reliable use of the scales across students and with the same student over time, and this task of establishing *reliability* (getting an accurate and consistent assessment) will probably call for some practice on the teacher's part. Although experts agree that a rigorous, reliable rating of speaking ability requires the use of at least two or more judges, classroom teachers do not usually have the luxury of calling in another judge, unless they have access to, for example, practice teachers. In some settings, other students could act as judges, or it could simply be clear from the outset that the ratings are impressionistic and intended as suggestive of the relative strengths and weaknesses of each learner.

There is also a problem of *validity*. Students may not speak in class the way they actually would if performing in the real world. They may be using inappropriate constructions precisely because they feel these are expected in the classroom. In fact, the students should be aware of just what each rating scale is rating and should try their best to perform the task as naturally as possible—for example, to throw themselves into the role that they are playing in a dialogue. This extra motivation on the part of the student to perform in as native-like a way as possible may result in integrative test-response data that are more natural. Situations that reflect common real-world events and situations that encourage the respondents to focus away from *form* and onto the *content* of the situation can also be helpful.

Classroom Procedures for Rating Communicative Ability

It is possible to set up classroom tasks so that students can engage in peer ratings of speaking. Rating activities could include pairs of students taking turns engaging their partners in short (ten- to fifteen-minute) conversations while a third student serves as a rater. In order to simulate a typical non-classroom situation (in environments where learners come in regular contact with native speakers), students should converse with a native speaker aside from the teacher. Learner-to-learner dialogues (referred to as "interlanguage talk"; see Krashen [1982]) are probably different from learner-to-native speaker dialogs in specific ways. Learners may sound more native-like when addressing a native speaker expressly because the demands are greater and their motivation is therefore enhanced. Clearly, learners will differ in this respect.

The teacher may wish to make an audiotape or even a videotape (if equipment is available) simply to verify one or more aspects of the ratings after the conversation is over, but the conversation need not be taped. Ratings are better conducted while the students are speaking. Obviously, this means that the teacher will have to practice using the ratings and having students use them with their peers. Such a classroom exercise and rating scale could be used occasionally even at the beginning levels of language learning. Scores might be expected to be higher for students taking a course that stresses conversation and especially the teaching of functional language use—including, for example, appropriate speech acts for given discourse situations.

The exercise that appears below is intended to clarify the procedures for rating communicative language ability. The data are taken from the Cohen and Olshtain study of speech act production (1993). In all cases the respondents were Hebrew native-speaking undergraduates. Their interlocutor was a native English speaker from Australia, and the data were collected in a videotaped role-play situation at the Hebrew University of Jerusalem. Along with these two apology situations, the three EFL students whose responses appear below had two complaint and two request situations to respond to as well (as did twelve other respondents in the study).

Exercise in Rating Communicative Language Ability

The two apology situations that the respondents had to role play were as follows:

1. You arranged to meet a friend in order to study together for an exam. You arrive half an hour late for the meeting.
2. You promised to return a textbook to your classmate within a day or two, after xeroxing a chapter. You held onto it for almost two weeks.

For the sake of this rating exercise, we will take the responses to both apology situations together as one speech sample. In fact, there may be some differences in speech-act behavior when addressing friends as opposed to acquaintances, but these are probably not substantial. According to Wolfson's findings with regard to compliments (1989), we might expect greater differences in speech-act behavior between friends or acquaintances than between intimates or strangers. The degree of familiarity at the two extremes of social distance might result in shorter utterances than with friends or acquaintances.

Instructions: Rate each of the three speakers on each of the four following scales, giving them a score from 5 (the highest rating) to 1 (the lowest rating) on each scale.

A. Sociocultural Ability

5— the message is socioculturally appropriate, reflects the situation clearly, and contains the proper amount of information.

4— the message is for the most part socioculturally appropriate, reflects the situation relatively clearly, and/or contains the proper amount of information.

3— the message is somewhat lacking in sociocultural appropriateness, calls for some interpretation to be understand, and/or contains too much or too little information.

2— the message is mostly lacking in sociocultural appropriateness, calls for much interpretation to be understand, and/or contains too much or too little information.

1— the message is completely lacking in sociocultural appropriateness, is not clear, and/or contains far too much or too little information.

Rating for Respondent
#1 __ #2 __ #3 __

B. Sociolinguistic Ability

5— the speaker uses linguistic forms that are fully appropriate for expressing the intended speech act.

4— the speaker uses linguistic forms that are mostly appropriate for expressing the intended speech act.

3— there is some use of inappropriate linguistic forms for expressing the speech act.

2— there is substantial use of inappropriate linguistic forms for expressing the speech act.

1— there is continuous use of inappropriate linguistic forms for expressing the speech act.

Rating for Respondent #1 __ #2 __ #3 __

C. Grammatical Ability

5— no major or minor errors in structure or vocabulary
4— no major errors and only several minor ones
3— several major errors and a fair number of minor ones
2— a somewhat frequent number of major and minor errors
1— frequent major and minor errors
Rating for Respondent #1 __ #2 __ #3 __

The responses will be presented by respondent with a suggested set of ratings for that respondent. These ratings are merely suggestive in that the teacher will need to finalize local criteria for assigning rating scores, given the proficiency level of the students, the conditions under which the task was conducted, and so forth.

Respondent #1: Shalom

The Meeting

Friend: I've been waiting for you at least half an hour.

Shalom: I'm sorry—I—I'm sorry. Don't be angry with me. I just— my calculation was wrong. I thought—it usually takes me half an hour in the bus, and it took me an hour now because I usually travel in the morning and it's much easier. Now it's lots of traffic problems.

F: Well, I thought—you know—people know when there's traffic and when there isn't, so you should've allowed more time.

Shalom: Yeah, OK. Don't make a big thing about it. It's only half an hour.

F: OK, so let's not waste more time. We'll study.

The Book

Classmate: I'm really upset about the book because I needed it to prepare for last week's class.

Shalom: Yeah, I'm sorry. I—I completely forgot about it. Sorry. I have nothing to say.

C: You have nothing to say! Well, it's not good enough. You should have something to say.

Shalom: Yeah. No. If there anything I can do to—to—com- something you.

C: Compensate.

Shalom: Compensate you, just say it. I'm sorry, really sorry.

C: Well, there's not really anything. It's too late now, but you know, next time could you please give it on time?

Shalom would get a **3** in *sociocultural ability*. His comment "Don't make a big thing about it" in the Meeting situation and "I have nothing to say" (meaning "What can I say?" or "I have no excuses") in the Book situation both come across as unapologetic and even rude. Hence, on the basis of these utterances he would be rated as mostly lacking in sociocultural appropriateness (2), but other things he says are for the most part socioculturally appropriate (4). Hence, the averaged rating would be a **3**. In *sociolinguistic ability*, he would get a **4** because the linguistic forms are mostly appropriate—those for acknowledging responsibility and for giving explanations. He neglected to intensify his expression of apology until the end of the Book situation, when he finally said, "I'm sorry, really sorry." Otherwise he just said, "I'm sorry," which does not sound so regretful. Also, he was unable to complete his offer of repair, since he did not fully know the word *compensate*. With respect to *grammatical ability*, he would get a **3** in that he had a fair number of minor errors of vocabulary and grammar ("my calculation was wrong" instead of "my calculations were off"; "to—com-": vocabulary retrieval problem; "in the bus" instead of "by bus"; "it's lots of traffic problems"; "If there anything I can do").

Respondent #2: Nogah

The Meeting
Friend: I've been waiting at least half an hour for you!
Nogah: So what! It's only an—a meeting for—to study.
F: Well. I mean—I was standing here waiting. I could've been sitting in the library studying.
Nogah: But you're in your house. You can—you can study if you wish. You can do whatever you want.
F: Still pretty annoying—I mean—try and come on time next time.
Nogah: OK, but don't make such a big deal of it.
F: OK.

The Book

Classmate: I'm really upset about the book, because I needed it to prepare for last week's class.

Nogah: I really feel sorry. It's too bad that you haven't told me before. I forgot. I don't know what's to—what—I don't have what to say—you're right in whatever you—you say.

C: Well, you know—I'll have to really think about it next time if I lend you a book again because—you know, I needed it and. . . .

Nogah: You're right. You're totally right.

C: OK.

Nogah gets a 3 on *sociocultural ability*. Her performance in the first situation would probably warrant a 1 since she rejected the need to apologize and put the responsibility on the shoulders of the offended party. This message would be an example of one that is completely lacking in sociocultural appropriateness. However, her response in the Book situation would be rated a 5, so her average response would be a 3. With regard to *sociolinguistic ability*, Nogah apologized only in the Book situation. Her utterance "I really feel sorry" instead of "I'm really sorry" is a bit awkward, but otherwise the forms are fine, such as her acknowledgment of responsibility ("I forgot"). Thus, her linguistic forms would be rated 4, mostly appropriate, for expressing the intended speech act. As for *grammatical ability*, she had a fair number of major and minor errors ("only a meeting to study," "too bad you haven't told me before," "I don't have what to say"), and so would receive a 2.

Respondent #3: Riki

The Meeting

Friend: I've been waiting at least half an hour for you!

Riki: I'm very sorry, but I—I met some friends and they stopped me and I couldn't go on. I'm—I'm really sorry.

F: Well, I mean, couldn't you have told them that you'd see them later, because I was here waiting for you and you know it's not. . . .

Riki: It's people that I didn't see for a long time—I haven't seen for a long time, and I—I just needed to talk to them, but—I'm sorry, and I figured you'll understand it.

F: OK, so, let's go and study.

The Book

Classmate: I'm really upset about the book because I needed it to prepare for last week's class.

Riki: I'm sorry to tell you, but I kind of lost your book—and I just felt very—unkind to go—to come and t-tell you what—what happened so I waited for a time but—now I know I should have—should have been doing this—before.

C: Well, I mean, you could've—should've told me straight away because I could've gone and bought another book, and now I don't have a book and I don't have my homework, and it's bad news!

Riki: But—but there is good news in this because I—I bought a book for you and second thing that I made the homework. So you can take from me for this time.

C: Oh—that's good. OK. In that case I'm not angry.

Riki would get a **4** for *sociocultural ability* since although her message is socioculturally appropriate (with the expression of apology, acknowledgment of responsibility, explanation, and even an offer of repair in the Book situation), her responses contain a bit too much information. With respect to *sociolinguistic ability*, she would get a **5** since her linguistic forms are fully appropriate for the intended speech act. Her *grammatical ability*, on the other hand, would be rated only a **1** because there are frequent major and minor errors in structure ("I couldn't go on," "It's people that," "I figured you'll understand it," "I just felt very—unkind to go—to come and t-tell you," "and second thing that I made the home-work," "So you can take from me for this time.").

If we were totaling scores just on these two situations (usually there would be more), then we would have the following results:

Ability	Shalom	Nogah	Riki
sociocultural	3	3	4
sociolinguistic	4	4	5
grammatical	3	2	1
Total	10	9	10

Shalom and Riki both received 10 points and Nogah 9. However, we can see how totaling the respondents' scores masks the differences across respondents in terms of their areas of strength and weakness. For example, although the total scores were 9 and 10, there was fluctuation across situations (in the case of Nogah) and fluctuations across speakers on the sociocultural ability scale. On the sociolinguistic ability scale, Riki received a 5, with the other two receiving 4. Performance on this scale would suggest that when the respondents used the appropriate sociocultural semantic formulas or strategies, they tended to use the appropriate linguistic forms.

The real fluctuation was on the grammatical ability scale, where scores ranged from 3 in the case of Shalom to 1 in the case of Riki. Note that performance on the grammatical ability scale was not necessarily related to performance on the other scales. Such a finding underscores the importance of separating sociolinguistic abilities from grammatical performance. Thus, maintaining the use of all three of these scales for this diagnostic purpose would probably be important.

Discussion of the Exercise

There is no doubt that an exercise like this raises more questions than it answers. First, we have to remember that we are assessing spoken dialogue from a written text. In actual dialogues, inappropriate phonological features (segmental and suprasegmental) often interfere with comprehension at a basic, encoding level. Not only might the execution of certain vowels or consonants produce an utterance that is incomprehensible, grating, or even offensive to natives, but intonation and stress can also produce such results.

Moreover, if raters rate from a videotape, *paralinguistic* features, or non-vocal phenomena, can play a role in the ratings as well—either intentionally or inadvertently. In other words, a rater may be influenced by the sincerity of the look on the apologizer's face. It would be up to the test constructor to determine whether such paralinguistic features are to be included in the assessment instrument.

Second, native speakers vary in their tolerance for nonnative features. Note that in the above examples, all the nonnative data were produced by native Hebrew-speaking Israelis. Some readers may have had difficulty relating to the examples from this specific language and cultural background. However, raters who are unfamiliar with the particular speech community may actually give more unbiased, impartial ratings. On the other hand, as a result of training and/or experience with respondents from the given sociocultural group, teachers/raters become overly sympathetic listeners and fully reconstruct in their own minds what students meant to say when they produced an unclear utterance. In such cases, it may be difficult for the raters to find genuinely unclear utterances that would affect the student's sociocultural ability rating.

Furthermore, is it fair to compare nonnatives with some sort of native model? If we use a native model, which native model should we use—that of a peer, with the same educational background, assuming the same role? Would it be more appropriate to use a highly educated nonnative model?

While the language-assessment literature has raised the issue of communicative ability speaking as a **measurable** phenomenon, the preceding examples indicate some of the difficulties in actual measurement. Let us take the sociocultural ability issue. In the case where Nogah answered with an attack rather than an apology, the response was rated as inappropriate for the given English-speaking context, but such responses are often heard in Hebrew within the Israel cultural context. One way for an Israeli to respond in Hebrew when caught in an apology situation is to blame the other person or to belittle the infraction (e.g., "Don't make a big deal about it."). A case could be made that downplaying the importance of an apology is also a sign of sociocultural ability and is deserving of a high rating. In this role-play situation, the respondent was not instructed about how important it was to keep the relationship intact by using, say, a profuse apology. In fact, respondents could have been instructed on how they were to respond in each speech-act situation—e.g., obstinately, obsequiously, or penitently.

The reader will also notice that the number of points to be awarded within a given category is not a matter of certainty. There are as yet few clear-cut guidelines on what constitutes, for example, a 2 or 3 in sociocultural ability. A five-point scale is suggested—in keeping with other common scales, such as those used with the ACTFL guidelines. When there are more scale points, raters sometimes are reluctant to use the extremes or the middle. But at what point has the respondent made a sufficient number of grammatical errors for the rating to drop from a 4 to a 3, for example? Furthermore, it is difficult to distinguish major from minor errors and to determine how many of each warrant a shift from one scale level to another. It may also be that respondents avoid displaying more than one such error in a testing situation (say, through the use of strategic ability) while such errors are actually widespread in the respondent's oral language under non-testing conditions. For example, perhaps Shalom has a real problem in copula (*to be*) omission because there is no present tense copula in Hebrew ("If there anything I can do to . . ."), but in this sample he only displays one such instance of copula omission.

We can see that this type of three-scale rating is broader than traditional scales, which have tended to focus on those behaviors that all appear here under the heading of "grammatical ability"—wherein each of the components is fleshed out (e.g., vocabulary, morphology and syntax, and phonology). Rating scales like the one presented in this chapter should help students to get a better idea of what it means to gain communicative control of the language.

Finally, note that the sociocultural, sociolinguistic, and grammatical scales we have presented are in many ways intended to be suggestive of alternatives for breaking away from traditional approaches to the rating of speaking.

Conclusion

In the first portion of this chapter, we presented examples of listening comprehension items and procedures, ranging from the most discrete-point items, with a traditional focus on isolated language forms, to more integrative assessment tasks. The second portion started by considering traditional and modified interviews, and semi-direct tests. We raised issues regarding the use of the interview as a method for assessing speaking, and we proposed alternatives. We then focused on role play aimed at assessing ability to perform speech acts and other language functions. The chapter ended with a practical exercise in the rating of three speakers' efforts at producing speech acts (apologies) in English as a foreign language.

Regardless of whether teachers and test constructors use more traditional or more innovative means of assessing listening and speaking in the classroom and beyond it, it is beneficial for them to be aware of the available options. It may just be that a particularly difficult group to teach comes alive when the teacher chooses test-unlike activities (Davies, 1990) such as role-playing, for example, instead of or in combination with a more traditional speaking task that emphasizes grammatical accuracy.

Discussion Questions and Activities

1. It can be inferred from this chapter that listening comprehension tests may use input that is at the wrong place on the oral/literate continuum for what is intended to be assessed. Prepare a mini-presentation to your fellow teachers in which you explain this point, demonstrate to them how they have neglected this issue in the past, and give them examples of how to use the oral/literature continuum more effectively.

2. You are called in as a consultant in language testing for a community college whose foreign-language programs have for many years been using a relatively traditional oral interview as a means of assessing speaking ability. Identify at least three potential problems that are brought up in this chapter's general discussion of the interview format for assessing speaking ability (for example,

limitations on the discourse produced by such an elicitation method), and prepare a case to present to the community college staff regarding some ways of avoiding these potential problems.

3. The ACTFL guidelines provide a set of speaking tasks in an interview format. What are some of the potential pitfalls of such tasks, and what steps could be taken to increase the validity of the measure?

4. What is the special contribution of semi-direct tests? In what ways are such tasks similar to and different from direct oral tests? Under what conditions might you recommend use of a semi-direct test?

5. You have found in the high school French classes that you teach that students do not always seem adequately warmed up when they take speaking tests. Prepare a procedure for giving a proper warm-up, write down its details, and try it out. Ask the students afterwards whether this procedure has in any way changed their experience when taking this speaking measure.

6. Devise your own speech-act situations, and, along with some of your peers, rate the performance of nonnatives by using the sociocultural, sociolinguistic, and grammatical ability scales presented in this chapter. What are some benefits of using this approach to rating speaking data? Do you see any deficiencies in these scales? If so, what are they?

Notes

1   For far more comprehensive coverage, see Buck's (1990) doctoral dissertation, which won the Educational Testing Service's 1993 TOEFL Research Award for the best dissertation on language testing.

2   The Portuguese SOPI has now been revised, and a report of the Hebrew SOPI has also appeared in the literature—a test with a U.S. version written for respondents not familiar with Israeli culture and an Israeli version intended for respondents who have been to Israel and are familiar with its culture (Shohamy & Stansfield, 1990).

3   I.e., the black box or mechanism in the brain that is responsible for language acquisition.

Chapter 9: Assessing Written Expression

In this chapter we will first examine current practices in writing instruction and link these up with the assessment of writing. We will then consider the construction of writing instruments, the taking of them, and the rating of the results. This will be followed by a practical exercise in rating three essays by using different scales—holistic, analytic, primary trait, and multitrait. Next, we will consider the use of portfolios as an alternative to traditional assessment of writing. Finally, we will consider the assessment of summarizing ability, which actually calls for measuring performance at the intersection of reading and writing.

The Teaching and Learning of Writing

Since a major concern in writing assessment has been that of closing the gap between teaching and assessing (White, 1985), we will begin by considering the teaching and learning contexts of writing. Teachers assign writing tasks for different instructional purposes (Raimes, 1987):

1. To have learners imitate some model of writing
2. To train learners in the use and manipulation of linguistic and rhetorical forms
3. To reinforce material that students have already learned
4. To improve learners' writing fluency
5. To encourage authentic communication whereby the writer really wants to impart the information and the reader is genuinely interested in receiving it
6. To learn how to integrate all the purposes above, with the emphasis on improving the whole performance, not just one of its aspects

These purposes are stated more in terms of what **teachers** may wish to use writing for—that is, for drill or for communication—than in terms of what **students** may wish to get out of a given writing task. Cumming (1990b) describes three specific kinds of learning that students may wish to derive from their writing:

1. Assessing and seeking out improved uses of language—for example, engaging in word searches in order to produce the best phrasing
2. Testing functional hypotheses about appropriate language usage while writing—attempting to match their expressions to target-language norms for producing grammatical structures in writing
3. Comparing cross-linguistic equivalents—using writing as a way to try out hunches about ways that native-language words and phrases are represented in the target language

Not only can we write for different instructional purposes and personal learning goals, but we can also select different types of writing that are consistent with our purposes. Types of writing include *expository writing*—to explain or inform; *persuasive/expressive writing*—to convince; *narrative writing*—to relate a series of events; *descriptive writing*—to offer a sensory impression of an object or feeling; and *literary writing* —to create exemplary text (in the form of a novel, poem, ballad, and so forth). Usually, writing for a given purpose may involve the use of several different types. For example, a lesson intended to train learners in the use of past tense may require that the students write a narrative in the present tense and then change it to the past tense. Likewise, a lesson meant to emphasize communication could ask students to write a letter to convince a company that its hiring policies are inequitable.

In recent years, the process approach to writing has begun to replace the more traditional product-oriented approach in numerous second-language writing programs. The process approach emphasizes the notion that writing is a process wherein the finished product emerges after a series of drafts. The process approach puts emphasis on an incubation period, in which the written piece takes shape. The writer's awareness of writing processes is heightened, and, ideally, the work comes to a teacher for appraisal only at the point when the writer is satisfied with the result. The composition has usually gone through several rounds of peer evaluation and self-assessment **before** it reaches the teacher for his or her assessment.

Along with the focus on process, there has been a commensurate de-emphasis of grammar and mechanics. While grammar and mechanics may have importance for certain types of writing, they are now being de-emphasized, since evaluators of nonnatives' written work are using a broader communicative perspective. A learner's motivation to write can be negatively affected by a teacher's untimely or exclusive focus on surface issues of form (e.g., grammatical concerns, spelling, and punctuation). Hence, there is a growing concern to enhance the nonnative writers' awareness of writing errors that impede written communication and to distinguish those errors from ones that **do not** impede communication. This aim has led to involving students more in the assessment process, including involving them increasingly in self-assessment of their own writing.

Furthermore, popular models of writing are now emphasizing that writing is not properly characterized when it is seen as a linear set of stages, starting with prewriting, then writing, and then review. Instead, writing is seen as one continuous process that is *recursive* in nature (Flower & Hayes, 1984). In other words, writers go back to go forward. Writers are also seen to differ in the manner in which they return to previous stages or issues in their efforts to plan, generate, and evaluate written text.

If we focus just on the initial phase of writing, for example, we will note considerable differences across writers. According to Arndt (1987), there are at one extreme *outliners*, who need a whole session just to plan out what they will write, and there are at the other extreme *listers*, who write quantities of text without concern for how it fits together. The basic distinction here concerns the extent to which writers generate their texts on an "on-line" basis, as opposed to planning or prewriting before they write for most or all types of writing. Furthermore, writers differ in terms of how they review their writing, if at all. Review, resulting in major revisions and/or minor edits, may take place frequently in little spurts, at the end of a large chunk of text, at the completion of the draft, or according to some combination of the three.

One of the noteworthy features of the current process model of writing is that it is in part derived from writers' verbal report protocols, often in the form of think-aloud, stream-of-consciousness data. In other words, the model reflects writers' ongoing accounts of what they are doing while they are in the process of writing: a description of the writing act based on writers' notes, the writing itself, the way in which writers read and reread what they have written, and meta-comments that they make about their writing. Such descriptions are more authentic than intuitively based ones. As with the reading act, it is possible to obtain insights on what effective writing strategies may entail by examining descriptions of how writers write. These descriptions can provide less successful writers with strategies that may prove beneficial for them, depending on their language proficiency and learning style.

Such studies have helped researchers get a preliminary picture of ways in which L1 and L2 writing are similar and different (Krappels, 1990). A lack of L2 writing competence has been found to result more from the lack of composing competence than from the lack of linguistic competence, and skill or lack of skill in L1 composing carries over to composing in the L2. Furthermore, although certain L2 writing tasks are likely to elicit more L1 use, L2 writers vary in the ways in which they call up their L1 while writing in the L2.

The Assessment of Writing

Once a piece of writing has—if possible—undergone a series of drafts and is ready for assessment, the issue is one of what to assess. Evaluation can be a real challenge in that there are numerous things that could logically be evaluated, such as

- *Content*—depth and breadth of coverage
- *Rhetorical structure*—clarity and unity of the thesis
- *Organization*—sense of pattern for the development of ideas
- *Register*—appropriateness of level of formality
- *Style*—sense of control and grace
- *Economy*—efficiency of language use
- *Accuracy of meaning*—selection and use of vocabulary
- *Appropriateness of language conventions*—grammar, spelling, punctuation
- *Reader's understanding*—inclusion of sufficient information to allow meaning to be conveyed
- *Reader's acceptance*—efforts made in the text to solicit the reader's agreement, if so desired[1]

The reality is that only some of these dimensions are evaluated in any given assessment of writing ability, due to a host of factors, such as time available for assessment, cost of assessment, relevance of the dimension for the given task, and the ease of assessing that dimension.

The assessment of written expression has been described as a complex interaction among three sets of factors: the knowledge that the test maker has about how to construct the task, the knowledge that the test takers have about how to do the task, and the knowledge that the test raters have about how to assess the task (Ruth & Murphy, 1984). In the test-construction stage, the important issues are

1. The test makers' understanding of the purpose of the given assessment
2. Their knowledge about notions of language and the act of writing, about theories of rhetoric, and about discourse structure
3. Their assumptions about the students' world knowledge
4. Their beliefs about the contexts in which tests are taken

Ruth and Murphy also note that the outcome—the test item/topic—is a highly specialized form of discourse.

In the test-taking stage, test takers read the text of the topic and try to understand the expectations and assumptions of the test maker, possibly encountering ambiguities and mixed messages. The congruency between the intended and the understood meaning will depend on the characteristics of the text and of the readers. In the rating stage, the test raters' assumptions, expectations, preferred rhetorical models, world knowledge, biases, and notions of correctness come into play.

In the remainder of this chapter, we will look at the issues of constructing, taking, and rating tests of written expression. Then we will examine the assessment of writing through the use of portfolios and the interaction of reading and writing through the task of summarization.

Constructing Measures of Written Expression

Perhaps the main thing to be said about designing tests of written expression is that they are a poor substitute for repeated samplings of a learner's writing ability while not under the pressure of an exam situation. The process-oriented approach would suggest that it is unnatural for a learner to write a single draft of a composition and submit it for a grade. Instead, learners prepare multiple drafts that are reviewed both by peers (in small groups) and by the teacher at the appropriate time. For this reason, the notion of *writing portfolios* has become popular, especially in native-language writing, and we will consider portfolios later in this chapter. At present let us focus on the construction of the more traditional form of assessment, the written essay test or subtest.

Aside from the issue of rating scales (which will be considered below), the main concern in the construction of an essay test is that of the *prompts* for writing. The assessment of students' writing depends on the adequacy of their written responses to one or more prompts on a test. Hence, those prompts must be written in the most writer-friendly way possible. Within the last decade, special attention has been paid to writing topics and prompts. It has been noted that in an essay test where the topic is not clear to the writer, a misinterpretation may result that possibly has serious consequences (Ruth & Murphy, 1984). In such cases the rater may not be able to tell whether ambiguity in the composition is the result of lack of knowledge on the part of the student or the result of poorly written items on the part of the test constructor.

Ruth and Murphy (1984) subdivide response errors into three distinct categories:

1. *Instrument errors:* These are instances where certain linguistic features of the writing topic seem to cause misinterpretations among the respondents. For example, the respondent interprets the word *profit* in the essay prompt as *prophet*, and then writes an essay about the wrong topic altogether. The misinterpretation could involve just one part of the topic and not its entirety. In any event, the source of the confusion would be said to lie with the instrument itself.

2. *Respondent errors:* These are errors that result from a misreading of the topic by the respondents or by the rater. In other words, the topic is unambiguous, but due to (a) anxiety, (b) haste,

(c) judgments based on prior knowledge, (d) not enough language proficiency to understand the prompt, or some combination of these, respondents misinterpret what is requested of them.[2] Also, raters may misinterpret the topic and thus may introduce systematic errors and hence unreliability into their ratings of the essays. (More will be said later about the process of rating.)

3. *Contextual errors:* These are procedural errors that arise when students fail to understand how rules of normal discourse may be suspended in a writing test. For example, the students are asked to write a letter to a **friend**, but in reality this testing task is demanding a higher, more formal level of performance than would be expected in a genuine letter to a friend. Whereas friends do not take off points for misspellings, poor punctuation, and lack of clarity, teachers/test constructors may well do so.

In a more recent publication, Ruth and Murphy (1988) give a list of "shoulds" for appropriate writing topics, based on their research and experience in the field. They would suggest the following:

1. Topics should not have too much information in them because this could lead to a simple rehashing of the information in the prompt.
2. The prompt should indicate the audience to be addressed—for example, self, teacher (pupil to teacher, pupil to examiner, pupil to trusted adult), wider audience, unknown audience.
3. The writing assignment should not be
   a. too large
   b. too insignificant
   c. too abstract.
4. The topic should be of potential interest to the writer and to the rater.
5. Topics to be avoided:
   a. those with hidden biases
   b. those which are controversial
   c. those which will be difficult to assess.

6. The essays should be based on data that are provided.
7. The essays should be meaningful, given the writer's experience.
8. It should not be too difficult or too easy to write the essay.
9. The essays should allow for assessment of all students according to their abilities.
10. Writing tasks should have limits on content, form, or both.
11. Care must be taken in the wording of the topic—for example, the use of the generic "tennis shoes" instead of the more specialized and perhaps culturally specific Adidas or sneakers (Ruth & Murphy, 1988:59-63).

Ruth and Murphy note that developing appropriate topics continues to be an art rather than a science. Thus, the challenge for the test maker is to provide the respondents with specific and supportive guidelines on the nature of the task. The following might be an example of a specific and supportive prompt:

> Your boss has asked you to rough out an argument for why the factory employees should not get longer coffee breaks. Try to present your arguments in the most logical and persuasive way. Do not worry about grammar and punctuation at this point. There is no time for that now. Just concern yourself with the content of your ideas, their organization, and the choice of appropriate vocabulary to state your case, in about 300 words.

Although teachers may have certain preconceived notions about which prompts will be more demanding of essay writers than others, the reality may be different. In fact, some research shows that providing prompts of a personal versus an impersonal nature may either have no effect (Spaan, 1993) or the opposite effect from that expected—the personal prompts did not produce higher scores (Hamp-Lyons & Prochnow, 1990).

Research Notes

In the Spaan (1993) study, eighty-eight ESL students each wrote two essays as part of the Michigan English Language Assessment Battery (MELAB). Thirty-six of these respondents wrote essays using a personal, autobiographical prompt about "time" and an impersonal, argumentative prompt about "energy," while fifty-two wrote on a personal prompt about "talk" and an impersonal prompt about "soldiers," with the order of the two prompts rotated. The essays were assessed holistically. The researcher found that giving respondents a choice of prompts did not have a significant effect on the results.

A study by Hamp-Lyons and Prochnow (1990) investigated "expert" judgments of prompt difficulty in order to discover whether such judgments could be used as a source of information at the item-writing stage of test development. Four judges were asked to assign difficulty ratings to sixty-four prompts that had been used on various versions of the MELAB. Expert judges (two trained MELAB composition readers and two ESL writing experts) were found to share considerable agreement about prompt difficulty, prompt task type, and difficulty of prompt task type, but essay scores were the reverse of what was predicted: *public* prompts (i.e., prompts calling for the writer to take a public orientation toward the subject matter) led to higher scores than *personal* prompts (prompts with a more private orientation).

Based on the literature, the authors had hypothesized that the public prompts would be more difficult than the personal ones. One explanation was that the experts were compensating for the difficulty of the prompts in their ratings (i.e., that the public prompts were more difficult than the personal ones). Another explanation was that the difficulty of the public prompt could have made the writers work harder at it and hence make higher scores. Another possibility was that writers chose prompts that matched their self-evaluated ability level— that is, if they evaluated themselves as weaker writers, they would select the easier prompts (in this case, the personal one) and would consequently perform better than if they had selected the more difficult prompt. For example, if students evaluated themselves as stronger writers, they would be more likely to choose to write an L2 essay on ecology with a difficult public prompt, but a self-evaluated weak student would go for the essay about a momentous family experience—the personal prompt—because they might feel that writing about family puts them on safer ground.

The Taking of Measures of Written Expression

It has become clear over the years that tests of writing have at times produced unnatural language samples from respondents. For example, a study by Ruth and Murphy had eleven high school students provide verbal report concerning their interpretation of the topic and plans for L1 writing beforehand, and then looked retrospectively at the differences between what was planned and what was actually written (1988:155ff). Among other things, some respondents indicated that the testing context appeared to provoke a "search" for the single "correct" answer. For others, the testing context appeared to trigger a preprogrammed performance. There is also something quite rarefied about expecting respondents to "display" what they know about writing in one canned session.

Ruth and Murphy came to the following conclusions:

1. Writers will differ in their notions about the significance of particular features of the topic.
2. Students and their teachers (raters) differ in their recognition and interpretation of salient points in a writing topic (with teachers having a wealth of professional experience in the evaluation of writing while students have only their own experience as test takers).
3. Student writers may construct different writing tasks for themselves at different stages in their development.

It would be necessary for the teacher/rater to have rating scales sensitive enough to pick up these sometimes subtle differences in the developmental level of writers.

Given the huge demands placed on the respondent, especially when asked to compose text in a second or foreign language, obtaining a more rehearsed sample of writing behavior in keeping with the process approach would be beneficial. For example, respondents could perform a Loop Writing Exercise (Hughey, Wormuth, Hartfiel, & Jacobs, 1983) as a means of warming up to the writing process and in lieu of a genuine multiple-draft approach. In this kind of test or subtest, the respondents write the first loop on a given subject for ten minutes without stopping, changing, or correcting. Then they read what they have written, sum up what they wrote in that loop, and take the kernel idea from this ten-minute loop as the starting point for the next ten-minute loop. This procedure is repeated a third time, with the main idea of the second loop as a starting point for the third loop. The task may function best if the respondents are discouraged from simply copying over their previous version with minor changes. Instead, they should be encouraged to set aside the previous version and to start anew. By being asked to write without editing, respondents are freed to discover and explore their thoughts, feelings, and perceptions.

The Rating of Measures of Written Expression

We will now look at four principal types of scoring scales for rating essays—holistic, analytic, primary trait, and multitrait. Then we will engage in an activity intended to illustrate the ways in which these scales are similar and different from one another.

Holistic Scoring

A holistic-assessment scale is one that is based on a single, integrated score of writing behavior. Since holistic scoring requires a response to the writing as a **whole**, respondents are unlikely to be penalized for poor performance on one lesser aspect (e.g., grammatical ability). In fact, the approach generally puts the emphasis on what is done well and not on deficiencies (White, 1985). The approach allows teachers to explicitly assign extra or exclusive weight to certain assessment criteria deemed important for the given task (see Figure 9.1).

Figure 9.1

Holistic Scoring

Advantages
1. Since holistic scoring requires a response to the writing as a **whole**, respondents do not run the risk of being assessed solely on the basis of one lesser aspect (e.g., grammatical ability).
2. The approach generally puts the emphasis on what is done well and not on deficiencies. The approach allows teachers to explicitly assign extra or exclusive weight to certain assessment criteria.

Disadvantages
1. One score does not provide diagnostic information.
2. It is difficult to interpret the meaning of a composite score to the raters and to the score users.
3. The approach lumps together in one score what for a given respondent may constitute uneven abilities across subskills.
4. Raters may overlook one or two aspects of writing performance.
5. Any differential weighting of aspects of writing may produce unfair results.
6. The approach penalizes efforts at development, since writers may display only **novice** ability with **more complex** forms, while those using simpler forms get higher ratings.
7. Longer essays may receive higher ratings.
8. Reducing a score to one figure reduces reliability.
9. Efforts at ensuring reliability of ratings may be at the expense of validity.
10. In L2 writing, the rating scale may confound writing ability with language proficiency.

However, there are a number of problems associated with holistic scales (Hughes, 1989; Huot, 1990b; Hamp-Lyons, 1991b). First of all, the focus on producing one single score is unsuitable for informed decisions about the writers' strengths and weaknesses. Second, it is difficult to interpret and explain the meaning of such scores to the raters and the score users (writers, parents, teachers, and counselors). A number of sample papers would be needed to make each level clear to both groups. Third, the approach lumps together in one score what for a given respondent may constitute the uneven development of abilities in individuals across subskills. (For example, a given individual may be strong in content and organization but weak in grammar, and the score will reflect a collapsing of the three.) Fourth, since raters are not compelled to consider a series of different aspects of writing performance, they may overlook one or two aspects to the detriment of some or many of the writers. Fifth, while any differential weighting of aspects of writing may produce unfair results, it is difficult for raters to give equal weighting to all aspects as they go from paper to paper. Certain essays naturally evoke certain elements within the holistic scale, while other essays evoke other elements. Sixth, a decrease in score may actually represent a progression—an increase in the student's repertoire of rhetorical abilities but a more limited ability in using complex forms. In addition, essays that are lengthier may receive higher ratings, since length suggests greater effort. In actuality, the greater length may simply mean that the writer is padding the essay unnecessarily.

Reducing the results of essay writing to a single score makes the outcome less reliable than with ratings including a series of scores. In addition, efforts at ensuring reliability of ratings may decrease validity. This is because in order to ensure reliability, the raters are trained in holistic procedures, which in turn alters the process of reading the essays and of scoring them. Instead of making meaning from text, the raters-as-readers are reduced to a set of negotiated principles, and their ability to make sound choices is distorted (Huot, 1990b). Finally, in L2 writing, the rating scale may confound writing ability and language proficiency. In other words, the respondents may be good writers but weak in L2 proficiency or vice versa, and the holistic score simply lumps these abilities together.

Analytic Scoring

Analytic scoring calls for the use of separate scales, each assessing a different aspect of writing—for example, content, organization, vocabulary, grammar, and mechanics. Often a scale for *cohesion* (i.e., the signaling of grammatical and lexical ties within a text) is subsumed within *organization*, but sometimes it stands as a separate scale, as in the TEEP Attribute Writing Scales (Weir, 1990:69). For one thing, the use of separately delineated scales may guard against the possibility that raters will collapse categories during the rating process, since they must produce a separate rating for each scale. Also, an analytic marking scheme is a more useful tool for the training of raters and the standardization of their ratings than is a holistic one (Weir, 1990) (see Figure 9.2).

Figure 9.2

Analytic Scoring
Advantages 1. Analytic scales guard against the collapsing of categories. 2. Training of raters is easier when there is an explicit set of analytic scales. **Disadvantages** 1. There is no assurance that analytic scales will be used according to the given criteria; rating on one scale may influence rating on another. 2. Writing is more than the sum of its parts. 3. Individual scales may call for qualitative judgments that are difficult to make. 4. Use of analytic scales may favor essays where scalable information can be extracted quickly. 5. The scales may not be informative for respondents, especially if scales of concern to them are somewhat neglected by the raters.

On the minus side, there is no assurance that each analytic scale will be used properly, according to its own criteria. Rather, the results in rating one scale may influence the rating of another (the *halo effect*). The work of Hamp-Lyons (1989) and others is revealing that raters of writing face a number of difficult and sometimes insurmountable challenges in attempting to operationalize rating scales. They often need to make qualitative judgments that even the best "model answers" cannot help them to resolve. Some scales included in Hamp-Lyons' (1989) analytical scoring had to be eliminated or collapsed for lack of clear and detailed indicators—for example, *register*.

In addition, White (1985) finds little evidence that writing quality is the result of the accumulation of a series of subskills. Thus, for him and others, a lack of agreement on subskills suggests that writing is more than the sum of its parts. Furthermore, individual scales may call for qualitative judgments that are difficult to make (e.g., regarding the level of coherence in an essay or the acceptability of the style). Also, the use of analytic scales can favor those written responses whose format makes it possible to extract information rapidly (Hamp-Lyons, 1989). This is one reason why comments about grammar abound on essays—grammatical errors are some of the most external and easily accessible features of an essay. Finally, the scales may not be helpful to respondents, especially if the scales they are concerned about are somewhat neglected by the raters. For example, the writers may wish to receive feedback on their ideas and organization, but actually find their grammar and mechanics receive more attention by the teacher/rater.

Research Notes

Cumming (1990a) studied the way in which seven teacher trainees and six experienced ESL teachers assessed twelve compositions written by adult students at intermediate and advanced proficiency levels. The respondents represented both average and professionally experienced writers in their native language. The ESL teachers were asked to assess the compositions on three undefined dimensions—language use, rhetorical organization, and substantive content. The results showed that although the expert and novice raters differed somewhat in their use of different rating behaviors, both sets of teachers rated L2 proficiency and writing skills as **separate**, non-interacting factors.

In another study, Hamp-Lyons and Prochnow (1989) had six highly experienced raters of MELAB compositions score and apply analytic rating scales to 200 essays. They found little agreement among raters as to the scores that they assigned to these rating scales. Next, sixty university ESL essays were rated holistically and then analytically by ten raters. In this instance they found higher agreement, but raters still differed in the analytic scales that received more importance. For one rater the differences were on the ratings for *structure*, for another *structure* and *vocabulary*. Also, the nine points on the scale were not seen as equidistant. Points 5 and 6 were seen as the same on the scale for *organization*. Analytic ratings were not found to benefit the weaker writers, but simply worsened their scores.

Primary Trait Scoring

In an effort to obtain more information than a single holistic score and to clearly define the features of writing being judged, the *primary trait* scoring method was developed by the National Assessment of Educational Progress (NAEP) in the mid 1970s (Lloyd-Jones, 1977). Freedman (1991) notes that while the actual criteria used to judge writing holistically emerge from the writing that the students do, the goal of primary trait scoring is to predetermine criteria for successful writing on a particular topic. The primary trait is identified and defined by the test constructor, who decides what will constitute successful writing on each topic on the test. Thus, the traits will vary depending on the topics.

The primary trait approach represents a sharpening and narrowing of criteria to make the rating scale fit the specific task at hand (White, 1985). The detailed attention to specific aspects of writing also allows for an entire assignment to focus on one issue

Figure 9.3

Primary Trait Scoring

Advantages
1. The primary trait approach represents a sharpening and narrowing of criteria intended for holistic scoring.
2. Detailed attention to just certain aspects of writing allows for attention to one issue at a time.
3. The approach supports teachers' knowledge that it is difficult to do everything at once.

Disadvantages
1. Respondents may have trouble focusing exclusively on the one specified trait while writing and may inadvertently include other traits.
2. By measuring only one aspect of writing, such scales may not be integrative enough, given the task at hand.
3. A specific aspect of writing may not deserve to be considered *primary*.
4. Complex primary trait rating schemes may give fewer points to an excellent partial response than to a weaker answer that touches more bases.

---

at a time. The primary trait approach supports teachers' knowledge that it is difficult to do everything at once (see Figure 9.3).

On the minus side, raters may have difficulty focusing exclusively on the one specified trait while rating. They may inadvertently include other traits. Hamp-Lyons contends that this may be a serious threat to the reliability of such primary trait ratings. Her claim is based on data from verbal report studies that she conducted in which the raters' judgments of one trait were found to be influenced by the quality of others (Hamp-Lyons, 1991b:247). She concluded that primary trait scoring may be little different from *focused* holistic scoring, where raters try to focus on certain key traits of textuality while they read the essays. Second, by measuring only one aspect of writing, such scales may not be integrative enough, given the task at hand. In addition, who is to say that an aspect of writing that is singled out for assessment purposes deserves to be labeled as *primary*? This can be another source of contention with regard to primary trait scoring.

Finally, complex primary trait rating schemes may give fewer points to an excellent partial response than to a weaker answer that touches more bases. Freedman (1991) gives an example of this problem, based on the following prompt:

> Some people believe that a woman's place is in the home. Others do not. Take ONE side of the issue. Write an essay in which you state your position and defend it. (Lloyd-Jones, 1977:60)

The primary trait rating scale was as follows:

0—the writer gives no response or a fragmented response.
1—the writer does not take a clear position, takes a position but gives no reason, restates the stem, gives and then abandons a position, presents a confused or undefined position, or gives a position without reasons.
2—the writer takes a position and gives one unelaborated reason.
3—the writer takes a position and gives one elaborated reason, one elaborated reason plus one unelaborated reason, or two or three unelaborated reasons.
4—the writer takes a position and gives two or more elaborated reasons, one elaborated reason plus two or more unelaborated reasons, or four or more unelaborated reasons.

According to Freedman (1991), the NAEP scoring rubrics have apparently gotten less specific over the years, but still there is a problem if the respondents choose simply to point out the complexity of the issue of a woman's place rather than taking sides. These students would receive a 1 score but might write a better essay than students who take a side and provide one or more reasons. And students who give one elaborated reason and therefore receive a 3 score could be writing a far better essay than students who give four or more unelaborated reasons and receive a score of 4.

Multitrait Scoring

In multitrait scoring the essay is scored for more than one facet or trait, but not in the fashion of the analytic scoring of the 1960s and 1970s. The multiple traits (usually three or four) are developed by a local group of teachers so that the prompts are consistent with those traits. Two examples of traits might be "the ability to read a text and summarize it" and "considering both sides of an issue and arguing on behalf of one position." These skills are usually not included in test scales for writing. Although multitrait scoring methods might still look somewhat like the traditional analytic scoring method, the test constructors actually spend more time on the constructs for the scales and the validation processes.[3] They attend to contextual needs and constraints, and make adaptations accordingly. They also need to be aware of the roles of the raters as well as those of the writers. With analytic scales, little or no focus is generally given to the processes that raters go through to produce their ratings.

In addition, the multitrait approach allows for flexibility in scoring in cases where raters have different personal reactions to a piece of writing. Discrepancies can be negotiated and compromises reached more easily than with more abstract and fixed holistic scoring (Hamp-Lyons, 1991a:250-251). Validity is improved because the test is based on expectations in a particular setting—for example, academic writing or writing at the work place. Because the ratings are more task specific, they can provide more diagnostic information than do generalized rating scales. If the rating scales are genuinely aligned with the instructional objectives, then there is a possibility of a positive backwash effect on teaching and learning from using the multitrait approach (see Figure 9.4).

Figure 9.4

Multitrait Scoring

Advantages
1. The traits need not be those appearing in generalized writing scales, but rather can reflect specific aspects of writing of local importance.
2. This approach allows for flexibility in scoring in cases where the writer does something different.
3. Validity is improved because the test is based on expectations in a particular setting—for example, a college or work place.
4. The ratings may provide more diagnostic information than do generalized rating scales.
5. There is a positive backwash effect on teaching and learning.

Disadvantages
1. It may be difficult to identify and empirically validate traits that are especially appropriate for the given context.
2. If the traits are specific to a local context, the raters may fall back on traditional generalized concepts in their actual ratings.

On the minus side, it may be difficult to identify and empirically validate traits that are especially appropriate for the given context. And even if the traits are specific to a local context, the raters may still fall back on traditional generalized concepts in their actual ratings.

An Exercise in Rating

The following exercise is intended to provide a sense of how the four types of rating scales function and how they relate to one another. The exercise does not illustrate samples of writing at all proficiency levels across the four types of scales, as such samples are provided elsewhere. For example, Jacobs, Zinkgraff, Wormuth,

Hartfiel, and Hughey (1981) offer samples of writing at all proficiency levels for their English Composition Profile, which is intended as a holistic measure that integrates the ratings from five subscales (content, organization, vocabulary, grammar, and mechanics). Likewise, Educational Testing Service provides samples of writing at the six different levels of proficiency for its Test of Written English (TWE), from *incompetence* to *clear competence* (Educational Testing Service, 1992).

In this exercise you will be rating three essays that were written by advanced-intermediate ESL students in response to a prompt that was part of a study by Cohen and Tarone (forthcoming):

> Below you will find two brief articles with conflicting views on the same theme treated academically ("Brain structure explains male/female differences," "Brain structure does not explain male/female differences"). You are requested to role-play a professor who had taken a public stand in favor of the views expressed in one of the articles (whichever you wish), but who has now found irrefutable evidence to favor the views expressed in the second article. So, your task is to summarize both articles, indicate the position you now take, and admit your error in having previously taken a counter position.

(Note: The two articles can be found in the Appendix at the end of this chapter.) Here are the three essays:

Essay 1

Written by a female Thai-speaking advanced-intermediate ESL graduate student:

> Artical of Daniel Goleman said that differences anatomical structure between men's and women's brains. Women on average have superior verbal abilities to men. Men on average tend to be better than women on certain spatial relationship. According to, this artical was supported by Dr. Witelson. He found the part of the brain of women. The larger isthmus in women is thought to be

related to women's superiority on some tests of verbal intelligence and the isthmus might have to do with the advantage of men on test of spatial relations.

Artical of Anne Fausto-Sterling said that human have two brains, the left hemisphere of the brain appears specialized to carry out analysis, computation and sequential tasks, in the right half resides artistic, abilities and emotional. The idea of brain hemisphere specialization said nothing about sex differences. But not long after scientists to suggest that left-right brain hemisphere could explain supposed male or female difference in verbal, spatial and mathematical ability.

My opinion: I'm agree with "Brain Structure Explains Male/Female Differences" because Part of the brain of female is excellence in verbal task. It is developing more than this part of male and Brain of male is skill in spatial visualization. It is developing more than this brain of female, However, experience and learning are riscue speacial skill for male and female.

Essay 2

Written by a female Korean-speaking advanced-intermediate ESL graduate student:

Researchers who believe difference in men and women had a question about recovery rate of brain damage. They found sex difference in brain structure. They discovered that women dominated verbal ability and men dominated geometric imaginary ability. They insisted that this ability difference is dued to anatomical differences. But it doesn't mean brain size difference. One study involed that blood supply to brain. This sex difference discovery will help that doctor and other health team provide a difference therapy to women and men.

Researchers who believe no difference between men and women insisted that any reports can't prove difference in women and men. Any reports can't support their opinion. Although some different patterns of brain existed, it is weak evidence to support difference brain structure in men and women.

I believed that no difference existed between men and women. Because I am women and I taught that any ability difference doesn't exist between men and women.

But now I think that some difference really exists in men and women's brain. Although human's brain structure veil mystery, I believe anatomical difference. And I consider to environmental influences, too. Because I think that any difference can't find in neonate. Brain structure is shaped one's growth. Girls like to play in indoor. For example, she plays with doll and cheats with other girlfriend. But boys like to play in outdoor. He likes to run around their town and forest.

I believe that anatomical difference exists in human's brain. But I don't think that sex germ doesn't have any difference.

Essay 3

Written by a male German-speaking advanced ESL graduate student:

Obviously there are male/female differences in verbal, spatial and mathematical ability. What are the reasons for these differences? There are different points of view. One part of the researchers which I belonged to for a long time supposes that these differences can be explained by anatomical differences in the brains of men and women. Others argue that these differences are due to social bias and environmental influences.

The theory of anatomical differences is supposed by some preliminary small-scale studies (for a summary see Goleman 1989). It was reported that parts of the corpus callosum connecting the left and the right hemispheres of the brain and isthmus connecting the verbal and spatial centers on the right and left hemispheres are larger in women than in men. That is thought to be related to women's superiority on some tests of verbal intelligence. The studies did not provide satisfactory explanations for men's superiority in tests of spatial relations until now.

It is a fact that women have better results in tests of verbal intelligence and men have better results in tests of spatial relations. But there is no reason to suppose that this is related to the differences in the division of labour between left and right hemisphere in women and men.

There are great differences in the mental abilities of different person of the equal sex, too.

It think there much further research required. I tend to an explanation based on social bias and environmental influences.

Now you are to assess each essay by using the four rating scales that appear below—holistic, analytic, primary trait, and multitrait. You will note that the holistic scale reflects a **focused** holistic approach since the aspect of content deals directly with the main ideas of the texts and with the indication of change of opinion. You should also assume that you and colleagues drew up the multitrait rating scales based on the constructs that you wanted to assess—namely, the academic skill of presenting two conflicting views in the literature and the written speech act of indicating a shift of view from support of one of the views to support for the other.[4] Be sure to complete your own ratings on the four scales before you check the suggested ratings provided.

Holistic Scoring

5—the main idea in each of the two articles is stated very clearly, and there is a clear statement of change of opinion. The essay is well organized and coherent. The choice of vocabulary is excellent. There are no major or minor grammatical errors. Spelling and punctuation are fine.

4 —the main idea in each article is fairly clear, and change of opinion is evident. The essay is moderately well organized and is relatively coherent. The vocabulary is good, and there are only minor grammatical errors. There are a few spelling and punctuation errors.

3—the main idea in each of the articles and a change of opinion are indicated but not so clearly. The essay is not so well organized and is somewhat lacking in coherence. The vocabulary is fair, and there are some major and minor grammatical errors. There are a fair number of spelling and punctuation errors.

2—the main idea in each article and change of opinion are hard to identify in the essay. The essay is poorly organized and relatively incoherent. The use of vocabulary is weak, and grammatical errors appear frequently. Spelling and punctuation errors are frequent.

1—the main idea of each article and change of opinion are absent in the essay. The essay is very poorly organized and generally incoherent. The use of vocabulary is very weak, and grammatical errors appear very frequently. Spelling and punctuation errors are very frequent.

Essay 1 _____   Essay 2 _____   Essay 3 _____

Analytic Scoring

Content: Essay 1 _____   Essay 2 _____   Essay 3 _____
5—excellent: main ideas stated clearly and accurately, change of opinion very clear
4—good: main ideas stated fairly clearly and accurately, change of opinion relatively clear
3—average: main ideas somewhat unclear or inaccurate, change of opinion statement somewhat weak
2—poor: main ideas not clear or accurate, change of opinion statement weak
1—very poor: main ideas not at all clear or accurate, change of opinion statement very weak

Organization: Essay 1 _____   Essay 2 _____   Essay 3 _____
5—excellent: well organized and perfectly coherent
4—good: fairly well organized and generally coherent
3—average: loosely organized but main ideas clear, logical but incomplete sequencing
2—poor: ideas disconnected, lacks logical sequencing
1—very poor: no organization, incoherent

Vocabulary: Essay 1 _____   Essay 2 _____   Essay 3 _____
5—excellent: very effective choice of words and use of idioms and word forms
4—good: effective choice of words and use of idioms and word forms
3—average: adequate choice of words but some misuse of vocabulary, idioms, and word forms
2—poor: limited range, confused use of words, idioms, and word forms
1—very poor: very limited range, very poor knowledge of words, idioms, and word forms

Grammar: Essay 1 _____   Essay 2 _____   Essay 3 _____
5—excellent: no errors, full control of complex structure
4—good: almost no errors, good control of structure
3—average: some errors, fair control of structure
2—poor: many errors, poor control of structure
1—very poor: dominated by errors, no control of structure

Mechanics: Essay 1 _____   Essay 2 _____   Essay 3 _____
5—excellent: mastery of spelling and punctuation
4—good: few errors in spelling and punctuation
3—average: fair number of spelling and punctuation errors
2—poor: frequent errors in spelling and punctuation
1—very poor: no control over spelling and punctuation

Primary Trait Scoring

(Rating just for Change of Opinion)
5—the writer makes very clear what the former position was, what the current position is, and why a change of position occurred.
4—the writer makes generally clear what the former position was, what the current position is, and why a change of position occurred.
3—the writer makes fairly clear what the former position was, what the current position is, and why a change of position occurred.
2—the writer does not make clear what the former position was, or does not state a current position explicitly, and there is no clear indication of a change of opinion.

1—the writer produces a fragmented response in which it is difficult to determine any position.

Essay 1 _____   Essay 2 _____   Essay 3 _____

Multitrait Scoring

Main Idea/Opinion	*Rhetorical Features*	*Language Control*
5—The main idea in each of the two articles is stated very clearly, and there is a clear statement of change of opinion.	A well-balanced and unified essay, with excellent use of transitions	Excellent language control, grammatical structures and vocabulary are well chosen.
4—The main idea in each article is fairly clear, and change of opinion is evident.	Moderately well-balanced and unified essay, relatively good use of transitions	Good language control and reads relatively well, structures and vocabulary generally well chosen.
3—The main idea in each of the articles and a change of opinion are indicated but not so clearly.	Not so well-balanced or unified essay, somewhat inadequate use of transitions	Acceptable language control but lacks fluidity, structures and vocabulary express ideas but are limited
2—The main idea in each article and/ or change of opinion is hard to identify in the essay or is lacking.	Lack of balance and unity in essay, poor use of transitions	Rather weak language control, readers aware of limited choice of language structures and vocabulary.

1—The main idea of each article and change of opinion are lacking from the essay.	Total lack of balance and unity in essay, very poor use of transitions	Little language control, readers are seriously distracted by language errors and restricted choice of forms.
Essay 1 ____	Essay 1 ____	Essay 1 ____
Essay 2 ____	Essay 2 ____	Essay 2 ____
Essay 3 ____	Essay 3 ____	Essay 3 ____

Now let us compare the ratings that you came up with to those that I arrived at. Pay particular attention to differences in our ratings because these may be symptomatic of precisely those weaknesses inherent in each of the sets of scales. Some of these weaknesses are not necessarily eradicated by using more than one rater since this may merely compound the error variance. Instead, we may need to revise the rating categories or use another scale for that particular essay task.

On the *holistic scale*, writer 1 would get a 2, writer 2 would get a 3, and writer 3 would get a 3 or possibly a 2, depending on the weight given to the first aspect: "clear indication of the main ideas and change of opinion." While writer 2 did not express a **change** of opinion, writer 3's change of opinion is hard to identify. Here we encounter a weakness in the holistic approach—the possibility that an essay corresponds to one level for most of the description but to another level for one or more crucial aspects. A compromise would be to give half scores (e.g., 2.5), but this does not solve the problem of dealing with integrated descriptions such as these.

With respect to the *analytic scales*, my ratings would be as follows:

	Writer 1	Writer 2	Writer 3
Content	2	3	2
Organization	2	3	3
Vocabulary	2	2	4
Grammar	2	2	4
Mechanics	2	3	5

We can see that it is easier to rate analytically than holistically in this case. Each individual dimension gets rated separately, and there is little need to compromise or downplay one aspect because of another. All the same, there are some problems, especially in rating the first essay. Writer 1 received a 2 for Content but actually could have been rated 1 or 1.5 since there was no change of opinion statement. With regard to Vocabulary, writer 1 could receive a 2, but there could still be doubt as to her actual control of vocabulary since most of the more difficult words could simply have been copied from the articles without being understood.

The *primary trait scale* produces a 3 for writer 2 and a 2 for writers 1 and 3. We can see how this scale then would be to the disadvantage of the third writer, who is superior to the second writer and far superior to the first in a number of aspects, as can be seen from the ratings on the analytic scales.

With regard to the *multitrait scale*, we have the following results:

	Main Idea/ Opinion	Rhetorical Features	Language Control
Writer 1	2	2	2
Writer 2	3	3	2
Writer 3	2	4	4

If these scales are an outgrowth of collaborative work among colleagues and reflect the dimensions that are to be measured, then they may be a more valid measure of this specific writing task than some other more general measure.

Hopefully, this exercise has demonstrated how the same written text can be assessed according to a host of different scales and how for a given writing task some scales may produce more unequivocable results than do others. Although it may be easier to use generalized scales, we can see how more specialized ones can assist raters in making their ratings fit the given task as closely as possible.

Rating Behaviors

Now that we have had an exercise in rating, let us ask the question "What do raters pay attention to?" The literature both in L1 and L2 writing has suggested that raters tend to focus too much on grammar and mechanics, even though the raters themselves may not recognize this. Even if they focus on content, different raters tend to use different criteria for rating and are sometimes impervious to the criteria that are included in the guidelines. Furthermore, efforts at training raters do not seem to influence novice raters' performance that much, and this group seems to indulge in editing the essays more than do the expert raters—even when the papers are not going to be returned to the respondents. Finally, it appears that in L2 ratings, familiarity with the language and cultural background of the respondent may result in biased ratings in favor of the writer.

Research Notes

In a study of L1 writing, Rafoth and Rubin (1984) conducted an experiment in which four versions of essays were prepared—with high (i.e., extensive) versus low content and with fourteen mechanical errors versus none (mechanical errors that did not interfere with comprehension but just violated editorial conventions). The raters were asked to rate for ideas, organization, style, wording, grammar, punctuation, and spelling. The raters were also asked to rate in one of three ways—for content, for mechanics, or "as you normally would." They found that regardless of the writing content (high/low) or evaluational criteria, college instructors' perceptions of composition quality were most influenced by *mechanics*, which colored judgments of ideas, punctuation, organization, and overall mechanical corrections. Amount of content did not affect rating of quality of ideas. Poorer ideas were reported when there were violations of mechanical conventions. The conclusion was that raters do not distinguish content from mechanics.

In a study of ESL writers responding to the writing subtest of the Australian Occupational English Test, *grammar* was found to be the best predictor of performance (McNamara, 1990). The researcher felt that there was a tacit agreement among the raters to give considerable weight to the control of linguistic features, even though this was not stressed in the criteria for assessment. In this study there was no direct confirmation of the criteria used in rating.

In other studies, verbal-report techniques have been used to investigate more directly the criteria that the raters are actually drawing on when making their ratings. For example, Huot (1990a) reports on a study by Vaughn and then one by himself in which raters provided such verbal report while rating. In the Vaughn study, nine raters scored six L1 compositions by using a six-point scoring rubric that produced 100 points in fourteen categories. While teachers commented most on *content*, which could be viewed as a positive finding, they were found to differ in their rating strategies, and some raters' major reason for passing an essay was **not** included as a possible reason within the scoring guide, but rather was based on individual judgment. The Huot study, which used verbal report with eight raters of forty-two L1 essays, found experienced raters to have both more efficient rating strategies and a greater range of responses to the writers. Yet there were no differences in rating criteria between trained and untrained raters, and *content* and *organization* received the most attention, which again could be viewed as a good sign.

With regard to raters' attention to the guidelines for rating, Connor and Carrell (1993) found that the five TOEFL-trained raters that they studied did not pay attention to how well the writers addressed the specific rhetorical requirements in the prompt, although they were trained to do so. Connor and Carrell investigated how raters interpreted the prompt, read the essays of five ESL graduate-student writers, and rated them, using the Test of Written English (TWE) scoring guide (Educational Testing Service, 1992). Even in the case of an essay that clearly slighted the task as specified in the prompt, the raters did not comment. The study also looked at the writers' own perceptions of the task. Not only did a content analysis of the essays reveal writers' lack of attention to parts of the prompt, but the verbal report data from the writers while writing also lacked any mention of the prompt's specific demands.

When three groups of raters' verbal reports were compared—those of students, novice teachers, and expert teachers—it was found that the three groups had three **different** sets of criteria for judging student writing (Ruth & Murphy, 1988: Chapter 10). The students' frame of reference was based on their familiarity with the teacher's expectations and on standards set forth in the classroom, along with criteria established by the scoring categories. The novice teachers' evaluations were based on limited experience, with the training process having little effect. Rather, they drew on their own idiosyncratic definitions of what constitutes good writing. Expert teachers, on the other hand, drew on years of experience and on preexisting notions of what constitutes good writing within a given scoring category.

In the Cumming (1990a) study mentioned above, verbal report revealed twenty-eight decision-making behaviors that both the seven novice raters and six expert raters used, with a variation in use between the novices and experts. Seven of these behaviors involved *interpretation* strategies used to read the texts (e.g., skim the whole text to obtain an initial impression, classify errors, edit phrases) and twenty-one *judgment* strategies used to evaluate qualities of the texts (count propositions to assess total output, assess interest, and so forth). *Editing phrases* and *classifying errors* accounted for more than 90% of the total number of behaviors reported. Thirty percent of novice behavior involved editing phrases. Experts more frequently directed their decision making toward an integration of a situational and text-based model.

While the expert teachers in Cumming's (1990a) study were found to have a fuller mental representation of the task of evaluating the compositions and used a large number of diverse criteria to read and judge students' texts, the novice teachers used only a few of these component skills and criteria, instead calling on their general reading abilities. They edited the texts extensively, even though these edits were not going to reach the students. Thus, their decision making involved a text-based editing strategy, with rapid judgments of quality often based on unexplicit criteria.

Finally, in a study on the training of raters to become better raters of English-for-Academic-Purposes (EAP) prose, Hamp-Lyons (1989) illustrated how a rater with Japanese language cultural knowledge rated the EAP essays written by Japanese ESL students differently from raters without such knowledge. In fact, this rater interpreted the Japanese ESL students' EAP texts without difficulty. As the rater said in a later discussion, "Is it a Japanese? Yes, I could've told you. I'm used to . . . knowing the Japanese . . . certain cohesive gaps" (Hamp-Lyons, 1989:233). Hamp-Lyons raised the issue of how the "true" writing proficiency of a writer can be established through ratings when part of the response is based on the individual characteristics of the rater (qualifications, years of teaching, places taught in) and part is common (i.e., experience as an English L1 or ESL teacher). She concluded that raters' familiarity with the writers' language and culture could produce rhetorical transfer that would affect the ratings.

Given the findings on how raters tend to perform, the following is a list of goals that a training program for raters of writing may want to incorporate:

1. Make sure that the raters gain the ability to give each assessment category the designated focus, whether or not it be equal focus.
2. Make sure that the raters use the **same** criteria for rating and that they all have the **same** understanding of what these criteria mean.
3. Strive to have novice raters approximate expert raters in terms of their rating behaviors.
4. If possible and if appropriate, provide for all raters training that will help them be sensitive to the rhetorical strategies of writers from other language and cultural backgrounds.[5]

Assessment of Writing Through Portfolios

What Writing Portfolios Entail

Writing through portfolios was devised as a means of providing a viable and potentially preferable alternative to a test of written composition. Portfolio evaluation is a system of assessment intended to help teachers get a more natural and prolonged assessment of students than through traditional means of assessment. The way the system works is that the students prepare for their portfolio a series of compositions, where each may represent a different type of writing—for instance, one a narrative, descriptive, or expressive piece, the second a formal essay, and the third an analysis of a prose text (Belanoff & Elbow, 1986). Hence, the portfolio represents multiple measures of the students' writing ability. Among the writing samples offered may be one or more pieces of in-class writing that have not received feedback and have not been revised. Murphy and Smith (1991) suggest that the portfolio be long enough to be representative but not too long. They refer to a *process-folio* as being a portfolio that includes multiple drafts.

According to Belanoff and Elbow (1986), teachers should form groups of four to six (without the writer's teacher) to screen the portfolio pieces and to determine whether they are acceptable. Murphy and Smith (1991) indicate that whether teachers participate in the choice of writings for the portfolio is a debated issue, and they suggest that it is perhaps best if students are the sole determiners so that they really **own** their portfolio. The goal is to produce portfolios that feature the students' best work—showing what they know and how they progress over time.

The Advantages of Portfolios

Belanoff and Elbow (1986) view the portfolio approach as a better reflection of the complexities of the writing process than conventional tests. In contrasting portfolios with traditional testing, Murphy and Smith (1991) note that in the portfolio approach students are encouraged to use their teachers and classmates as resources, while students taking tests are usually not allowed to talk or ask for help. In addition, portfolios are intended to encourage work in which the motivating factor is not that of getting a grade but of becoming more precise writers. Hence, students are encouraged to review and revise their drafts.

Murphy and Brown also mention portfolio **audits** by the learner as a good way to stimulate reflective thinking. By means of these audits, students are asked to take stock of what is in their portfolios, what they are still working on, and what they would like to write for the portfolio. With regard to evaluation of the writing, it is noted that the students can set their own criteria. Criteria that have been set by high school students include categories such as versatility and adaptability, completeness, carefulness, beauty and power, and responsibility. Whether to assign a grade is also a debated issue. In some cases it has been determined that it is better not to assign a grade, whereas in other cases students expect it. In those cases, the grade is assigned at the end of the writing period and not for every entry into the portfolio. This grade is a joint teacher-student effort.

The emphasis with portfolio work is on the sense of community—peers sharing drafts, assistance from teachers and tutors—while the traditional testing of writing requires solitary work. With portfolios, students and teachers are in a partnership to help students become better writers. Thus, the message is delivered clearly to the students that thinking and writing are enhanced by conversations with peers and teachers, and teachers are put in the role of the students' allies. In addition, the teacher groups are a community as well and begin to have more common criteria for judging student work. So the approach in some ways conditions students to draw more on community resources in their writing, just as skilled writers often draw on their community of colleagues to get feedback in order to improve their work.

Research Notes

Simmons (1990) reports on a study of twenty-seven fifth graders in Durham, New Hampshire, who were assessed according to holistic scoring of a timed essay test and three essays that the students selected from their portfolios as representative of their work. It was found that those students who chose more types of writing (narrative, poetry, description, exposition, argument) tended to score higher. The longest papers also rated the best (440 words), but some of the lowest performers had papers that were nearly as lengthy (410 words). Simmons also compared teacher and student criteria for evaluating the writing. He found that the teachers favored ideas and organization, while students listed flavor and experience (i.e., the experience of writing or sharing the work). However, students with average scores and the raters of these students both left "flavor" off their lists. The four top writers (girls) agreed with their raters (women teachers) while the other highest scorers tended to disagree most with teacher judgments.

In another report on the use of portfolios with eleventh-grade L1 writers, students were trusted to generate their own topics and were allowed to generate different types of texts: responses to literature, letters to guests in class, and critiques on the work of a visiting poet (Herter, 1991). Students apparently learned to become accountable, given the semipublic nature of portfolios. One student discovered that she enjoyed writing entertaining stories. The students' authority as writers, editors, and audience was validated by their experience with one another's texts. They developed lists of criteria by which they chose to measure their own writings—for example, a story was to hold their interest, to include details, and to have a dramatic ending. By the end of the year, the students were able to select their most meaningful pieces of writing in a variety of forms, and to justify their selections based on their own criteria. However, these criteria were found to differ from those of the teacher. The students came to see assessment as a recursive practice—checking back to reevaluate contents and reexamine contexts. Students began to appreciate the incubation period that some forms of writing need. The author found that it took time for her students to acquire and employ these assessment techniques.

Freedman (1991) reported on the development of the Primary Language Record (piloted in fifty schools in Great Britain), which consisted of protocols at the elementary level. She also mentioned the British General Certificate of Secondary Education (GCSE), taken at the end of the tenth grade, which permitted the use of a folder of coursework (portfolios) as part or all of the English language examination. This folder apparently must have a variety of functions for a variety of purposes and audiences—report, description, argument, persuasion, narrative fiction, poems, response to texts—assembled over a two-year period. For each exam the student and teacher choose the five best pieces that cover the assessment objectives.

Problems with Writing Portfolios

Elbow and Belanoff (1986) reported on some of the problems in using portfolios, based on their work with L1 college composition at SUNY-Stony Brook. One problem that arises is that teachers have a lot of work to do in this approach to assessment, even though they only have to provide a "yes" (include in the portfolio) or "no" (do not include it) judgment on portfolios (except for failing papers, where comments are necessary). Hence, there is the issue of how much time the teachers are willing to devote to this endeavor.

Another problem is that the approach may make teachers anxious since any failures will reflect on them. Also, as with any form of assessment, there may be a tendency to teach the course to the portfolio. In addition, the reliance on group decisions by teachers puts strain on relations when teachers disagree over verdicts. Finally, the emphasis on revising (even in the case of certain "failed" portfolios) has been viewed as pampering students too much and letting lazy students get by.

Hamp-Lyons and Condon (1993) report a study at the University of Michigan where 12% of the entering students participated in a half-term practicum in academic writing, in which they prepared portfolios of two revised essays and two essays written in class, one an impromptu essay and the other a reflective piece. The readers were requested to keep a log of the criteria that they used in assessing the portfolios and of the processes involved. The authors saw the need for standardizing sessions to determine how to do portfolio assessment.

An important thrust of the study was to question basic assumptions about portfolios. The first such assumption was that the presence of a large number of texts means that evaluation takes into account the *variation in quality* within each portfolio. However, they found that readers do not read the whole portfolio before making their assessment. Rather, they usually base their assessment on the first half of the first essay. The second assumption was that there would be multiple genres represented in the portfolio. In fact, many of the students' portfolios contained only one genre, *argumentation*. The students' reading logs did not indicate any awareness of different genres—just of the essay being either revised or impromptu. Furthermore, it was found that some readers took a preference to one or another genre when making their assessments. Some gave greatest value to impromptu writing while others let revised papers carry the most weight.

The third assumption was that the portfolios would make process easier to see in a student's writing—but only if the portfolios contained drafts as evidence of the writing processes undergone prior to the product.[6] Without seeing the multiple drafts, readers were unable to determine whether to reward the effort at improving the writing in subsequent drafts. Some readers simply undervalued the impromptu writing, assuming that the revised essays had to be more competent.

The fourth assumption was that the portfolio assessment would allow pedagogical values to be taken into account, but it became clear that there was little consensus on what these values were. Also, there was an assumption that portfolios would help build this consensus, but faculty members had large differences as to pedagogical goals. Imposing strict criteria for writing whereby writers would specify their genre was difficult. Furthermore, readers would have to answer specific questions about how they arrived at their holistic rating for each essay they read and/or about the portfolio as a whole. Another approach would be that of using fewer texts (say, two) and more stages or drafts. Hamp-Lyons and Condon (1993) noted that the portfolio assessment effort would ideally move towards creating a clear community of attitudes about writing pedagogy. For example, teachers would need to agree on the importance of academic writing and more specific issues, such as whether grammar errors in the final drafts would be deemed important.

Yet other problems with portfolios have been emerging (Hamp-Lyons, 1993). One problem is that when portfolios are graded, the grades have tended to cluster close together (e.g., from A- to B+). This lack of discrimination across portfolios has served to obscure actual differences between the better and poorer writers. Another problem results from the students' teacher doing the grading. The teacher needs to switch from a nurturing role of mentor and guide to that of an evaluator and grade giver. While this type of switch takes place in a variety of assessment situations in the classroom, the switch is especially acute in the area of writing, since the portfolio model puts so much emphasis on teacher mentoring.

Given the various potential problems with portfolios and native writers, Hamp-Lyons (1993) provides a set of steps that should be taken in order to ensure an equitable portfolio assessment for L2 learners:

1. Make sure that each writing task is adequately specified so that the nonnatives know what to write and how to write it.
2. Train learners in strategies they might want to use while preparing their portfolios.
3. Determine scoring criteria for every task separately.
4. Determine the criteria for selecting the writings to appear in the portfolio.
5. Provide training for the raters on the various sets of selection criteria.

Assessing the Interaction of Reading and Writing: Summarization

Whereas activities such as summarizing a text or integrating information from a group of texts have existed as testing activities for many years, only recently have researchers made a concerted effort to describe such activities in terms of the interaction of reading and writing, and to look closely at what is involved.

Tests of summarization are complex. The reading portion entails identifying topical information, distinguishing superordinate from subordinate material, and identifying redundant and trivial information. The writing of the summary involves the selection of topical information (or generating it if it is not provided), deleting trivial and redundant information, substituting superordinate material, and restating the text so that it is coherent and polished (Kintsch & van Dijk, 1978; Brown & Day, 1983).

In order to summarize successfully, respondents need both reading and writing skills. First, they must select and use those reading strategies appropriate for summarizing the source text—namely, identifying topical information, distinguishing superordinate from subordinate material, and identifying redundant or trivial information. Then they must perform the appropriate writing tasks to produce a coherent text summary; selecting topical information or generating it if none appears explicitly in the text, deleting trivial or redundant material, substituting superordinate terms for lists of terms or sequences of events, restating the text so that it sounds coherent, and polishing it so that it reads smoothly (Kintsch & van Dijk, 1978; van Dijk, 1980; Brown, Campione, & Day, 1981; Brown & Day, 1983; Chou Hare & Borchardt, 1984; Basham & Rounds, 1986; Davies & Whitney, 1984).

Summarizing tasks on reading comprehension tests have a natural appeal as "authentic" tests in this era of communicative language testing, given the fact that they attempt to simulate real-world tasks in which nonnative readers are called upon to read and write a summary of the main ideas of a text. The results are intended to reflect how the respondents might actually perform on such a task. In fact, a real-world summary is often quite different from a test summary. Real summaries are usually prepared for others who have not read the text and simply want to know what it is about. Such readers would probably not be fussy about the form in which the summary appears. On the other hand, test summaries usually have restrictions on length, format, and style, and are prepared for an assessor who has already decided what the text is about and wants to see how well the respondents can approximate this perception.

Thus, the test summary may result in a mismatch whereby respondents use one set of criteria in preparing their summaries, while the raters use another in assessing them. For example, there are undoubtedly differences of perception regarding what a *main idea* consists of and the appropriate way to write about it (e.g., precisely how telegraphically). There may also be differing views about the acceptability of introducing commentary into the summary. Research by Basham (1987) with Alaska Native American students showed that these respondents used their own world view as a filter in the summaries that they wrote, personalizing them. If such differences are not eliminated through prior training and/or through careful instructions on the test, there could be a gap between the way the summary task is executed and the criteria used by the raters to evaluate it.

Along with possible cultural differences, there are other potential causes of discrepancy between the way respondents are "supposed" to prepare summaries and the way they actually do it. The following Research Notes detail some studies that looked at how summaries are actually written.

Research Notes

A study of forty Hebrew-speaking university students writing EFL summaries found that while the notes they took on the text were of a word-level, bottom-up nature, their summaries were conducted on a top-down basis that drew more on their general knowledge. The conclusion reached by the researchers was that the reading was fragmented, rather than indicating ongoing interaction with the text that would combine top-down and bottom-up analysis (Kozminsky & Graetz, 1986). Likewise, a survey of Brazilian studies of reading processes (Cohen, 1987a) indicated that the respondents were often not executing summarizing tasks in a way consistent with the model of what summarizing should involve. A study of six EFL graduate students by Holmes (1986) found that the students did little monitoring of the summaries that they were asked to write. Also, they read in a linear and compartmentalized manner, rather than globally to extract the main ideas.

Consistent with Holmes's study, a study by Gimenez (1984) of five EFL graduate students revealed their major summarizing strategy to be that of word-level processing as opposed to syntactic analysis or text-level analysis. Often the summaries reflected a focus on only part of the text, with the interpretation of the text based on the words that the subject had learned (however effectively) during the reading of the text, along with previous knowledge.

In a study comparing a group of high-proficiency college-level EFL students with a low-proficiency group, Johns and Mayes (1990) found neither group to be using macro-propositions[7] in their summaries. Furthermore, the low-proficiency students were found to be doing a considerable amount of direct copying of material from the source text into their summaries, since it was required that the summaries be written in the second language as well. In an earlier study, Johns (1985) had found that underprepared natives were likewise more prone to use reproductions (copying and paraphrase) in their summaries than to use macro-propositions. In a case study, Sarig (1993) helped explain the propensity to lift material directly out of the text for use in summaries. She found conceptual transformation or reconceptualization at the macro-level to be a skill that did not come naturally either in native or foreign-language summarizing for a competent college student. She concluded that it had to be taught explicitly. Nonetheless, the explicit teaching of such reconceptualization may not yield such positive results. For example, Bensoussan and Kreindler (1990) found that whereas EFL students with a semester's training in summary writing now saw summaries as an important tool for grasping the gist of a text, they still expressed frustration at their inability to distinguish macro- from micro-propositions.

I also conducted a study that had as its main purpose the investigation of ways in which respondents at different proficiency levels carry out summarizing tasks on a reading comprehension test (Cohen, in press). The respondents for that study were five native Portuguese speakers who had all recently completed a course in English for Academic Purposes (at the Pontifícia Universidade Católica de São Paulo, Brazil) with an emphasis on reading strategies, including summarizing. They represented three proficiency levels.

The findings showed that the respondents in that study had little difficulty identifying topical information, yet they had trouble distinguishing superordinate, non-redundant material from the rest, due in large part to their insufficient grasp of foreign-language vocabulary. For their written summaries, they did not need to generate topic information; all the texts provided it. However, they did not have a good sense of balance with respect to how much to delete. They were either too vague and general or too detailed. While there was some concern for coherence, there appeared to be relatively little attention paid to producing thoroughly organized and polished summaries. In essence, the respondents in the study appeared to be more concerned about their interpretation of the source text than they were about their production of written summaries.

Aside from problems that test respondents have in preparing summaries of texts, there is the further problem of the reliability of the ratings of these summaries. For instance, it has been found that the statistical results from summarizing tasks are not always consistent with results from other types of tests (e.g., multiple-choice, short-answer, and cloze). Shohamy set out to compare tests of summarizing EFL texts to tests with a multiple-choice and an open-ended response format—with responses either in the native language or the foreign language, depending on the test version. She found the results from the summarizing data so inconsistent with the results on the other subtests that she eliminated the findings from the published study (Shohamy, 1984).[8]

Research Notes

The author's recent study (Cohen, in press) also investigated how **raters** dealt with the responses of the five participating students. (See Research Notes, page 345.) Two EAP course instructors who typically rated the EAP exams of summarizing skill at that institution also participated in the study as raters. The study found that there were some inconsistencies in the raters' behaviors, underscoring the importance of developing rigorous rating keys with main ideas and connecting schemata for each text.

The main purpose of the author's latest study on summarizing (Cohen 1990b, 1993) was to determine the effects of specific guidelines in the taking and the rating of tests of summarizing ability—tests in which respondents read source texts and provide written summaries as a measure of their reading comprehension level as well as of their writing ability. The study also looked at interrater agreement regarding the rating of specific ideas within the summaries.

The subjects for this study were sixty-three native-Hebrew-speaking students from the Seminar Hakibbutzim Teacher Training College in Tel Aviv. Twenty-six were from two high-proficiency EFL classes, and thirty-seven were from two intermediate EFL classes. Four raters assessed the students' summaries in the study. The two who rated the Hebrew summaries of the Hebrew texts were both native speakers. Of the two rating the Hebrew summaries of the EFL texts, one was a native speaker and the other an English speaker. Five texts were selected for the study, two in Hebrew and three in English (each intermediate and advanced EFL student being asked to summarize two). Two sets of instructions were developed. One version was **guided with specific instructions** on how to read the texts and how to write the summaries. The other version had the typically **minimal instructions**. The scoring keys for the texts were based on the summaries of nine Hebrew-speaking and nine English-speaking experts, respectively. All sixty-three respondents summarized the first Hebrew text, fifty-three summarized the second Hebrew text, and on the average, slightly more than a third of the students wrote summaries for the EFL texts.

The study demonstrated that while the guided instructions had a mixed effect on the summarizing of native-language texts, they had a somewhat positive effect on the summarizing of foreign-language texts. An analysis of the summaries on an idea-by-idea basis revealed that the guided instructions actually seemed both helpful and detrimental in the summarizing of texts. In some cases the guided instructions assisted respondents in finding the key elements to summarize, and in other cases they probably dissuaded the respondent from including details that were in fact essential in the eyes of the experts upon whom the rating key was based. A close-order investigation of consistency across raters on an idea-by-idea basis revealed that certain ideas (e.g., some global ideas, as well as matters of detail) seemed to be susceptible to disagreement more than others.

Given the lack of clarity that often accompanies summarization, it may be useful to give specific instructions on how to go about this task. The following is an example:

Instructions on how to read:
- Read to extract the most important points—for example, those constituting topic sentences signaled as crucial by the paragraph structure, points that the reader of the summary would want to read.
- Reduce information to superordinate points.
- Avoid redundant information—otherwise, points are taken off.

Instructions on how to write:
- Prepare in draft form and then rewrite.
- Link points smoothly.
- Stick to the specified length for the summary (e.g., 10% of original text, so 75 words for a 750-word text).

- Write the summary in your own words.
- Be brief.
- Write legibly.

Raters can also be helped by specific instructions on how to assess the summaries:

- Check to see whether each important point is included (points that were agreed upon in advance by a group of experts).
- Check to make sure that these points are linked together by the key linking/integrating elements on the master list.
- Take point(s) off for each irrelevant point.
- Take points off for illegibility.

Thus future testing could provide more guidance in the instructions so that the respondents receive what amounts to a "mini-training" in how to perform the tasks at hand. Especially under the pressures of a testing situation, anxiety-prone students may lose sight of effective means for responding to the tasks. Instructions that give a certain amount of guidance may be more beneficial than the traditional instructions that are perfunctory and to which respondents do not tend to pay much attention anyway.

Conclusion

In this chapter we looked at the fit between the teaching and the assessment of writing, the construction of measures of written expression, the taking of such measures, and the rating of them. We looked at the nature of the prompts used in assessing essay writing ability and the process of rating the output. Then we addressed the advantages and disadvantages of four sets of rating scales for assessing compositions: holistic, analytic, primary trait, and multitrait. An exercise in rating compositions using all four types of scales was then provided, followed by a discussion, in order to give the reader a better sense of what each of these scales actually measures.

Next, we discussed an alternative to traditional essay tests in the form of portfolios. We then considered the assessment of the interaction between reading and writing and explored tasks that combine the two, such as summary writing. We noted that for summaries, as for other complex test tasks, more explicit instructions may be of benefit to the respondents as a form of mini-training.

Discussion Questions and Activities

1. This chapter offers a host of cautions about prompts for essay questions. In an effort to determine whether your foreign-language department staff is aware of possible pitfalls in the use of prompts, collect a set of essay prompts used by your colleagues to assess essay writing, and check to see how many of these cautions they have paid heed to. Report back to your colleagues regarding your findings.

2. Identify a specific context in which you would need to assess essay-writing ability. Which of the concerns articulated by Ruth and Murphy with regard to the knowledge of the test maker, the test taker, and the test rater would you consider as "high priority" for the assessment needs that you have? Plan three workshops—one for each target group—in which you would provide training to assist the group in performing its role more effectively.

3. As an activity to conduct along with your colleagues, generate your own set of scales for rating compositions—holistic, analytic, primary trait, and multitrait—based on your local needs. In what ways are these four sets of scales measuring the same thing? What are the differences?

4. There is a positive aura associated with writing portfolios. Portfolios are seen as a solution to the problem of assessing students' writing based on one-shot assessment. What are some of the potential advantages that the portfolio approach provides those interested in assessing written work? Also, what are the aspects of portfolio assessment that need to be carefully monitored? What other items, if any, would you add to Hamp-Lyons' checklist?

5. Why does this chapter make a point about the instructions on summarization tasks? As an activity, take a summary task or some other complex testing task, and write out explicit instructions that constitute a mini-training. Give this version to one group of students and the traditional brief instructions to another group. Then compare the results.

Appendix

Articles with Conflicting Views
for the Writing Exercise
(pages 350-354)

Daniel Goleman,
"Brain structure explains male/female differences"

Anne Fausto-Sterling,
"Brain structure does not explain male/female differences"

Brain Structure Explains
Male/Female Differences

Daniel Goleman

(excerpted from "Subtle but intriguing differences found in the brain anatomy of men and women," *New York Times*, April 11, 1989)

Researchers who study the brain have discovered that it differs anatomically in men and women in ways that may underlie differences in mental abilities.

The findings, although based on small-scale studies and still very preliminary, are potentially of great significance. If there are subtle differences in anatomical structure between men's and women's brains, it would help explain why women recover more quickly and more often from certain kinds of brain damage than do men, and perhaps help guide treatment.

The findings could also aid scientists in understanding why more boys than girls have problems like dyslexia, and why women on average have superior verbal abilities to men. Researchers have not yet found anything to explain the tendency of men to do better on tasks involving spatial relationships.

The new findings are emerging from the growing field of the neuropsychology of sex differences. Specialists in the discipline met at the New York Academy of Sciences to present their latest data.

Researches on sex differences in the brain has been a controversial topic, almost taboo for a time. Some feminists fear that any differences in brain structure found might be used against women by those who would cite the difference to explain "deficiencies" that are actually due to social bias. And some researchers argue that differences in the brain are simply due to environmental influences, such as girls being discouraged from taking math seriously.

The new research is producing a complex picture of the brain in which differences in anatomical structure seem to lead to advantages in performance on certain mental tasks. The researchers emphasize, however, that it is not all that clear that education or experience do not override what differences in brain structure contribute to the normal variation in abilities. Moreover, they note that the brains of men and women are far more similar than different.

Still, in the most significant new findings, researchers are reporting that parts of the corpus callosum, the fibers that connect the left and right hemispheres of the brain, are larger in women than men. The finding is surprising because, over all, male brains—including the corpus callosum as a whole—are larger than those of females, presumably because men tend to be bigger on average than women. . . .

"This anatomical difference is probably just the tip of the iceberg," said Sandra Witelson, a neuropsychologist at McMaster University medical school in Hamilton, Ontario, who did the study.

The part of the brain which Dr. Witelson discovered is larger in women is in the isthmus, a narrow part of the callosum toward the back. . . .

Dr. Witelson's findings on the isthmus are based on studies of 50 brains, 15 male and 35 female. The brains examined were of patients who had been given routine neuropsychological tests before they died.

"The isthmus connects the verbal and spatial centers on the right and left hemispheres, sending information both ways—it's a two-way highway," Dr. Witelson said. The larger isthmus in women is thought to be related to women's superiority on some tests of verbal intelligence. It is unclear what, if anything, the isthmus might have to do with the advantage of men on tests of spatial relations.

The small differences in abilities between the sexes have long puzzled researchers.

On examinations like the Scholastic Aptitude Test, which measures overall verbal and mathematical abilities, sex differences in scores have been declining. But for certain specific abilities, the sex differences are still notable, researchers say.

While these differences are still the subject of intense controversy, most researchers agree that women generally show advantages over men in certain verbal abilities. For instance, on average, girls begin to speak earlier than boys and women are more fluent with words than men, and make fewer mistakes in grammar and pronunciation.

On the other hand, men, on average, tend to be better than women on certain spatial tasks, such as drawing maps of places they have been and rotating imagined geometric images in their minds' eye—a skill useful in mathematics, engineering and architecture.

Of course, the advantages for each sex are only on average. There are individual men who do as well as the best women on verbal tests, and women who do as well as the best men on spatial tasks.

One of the first studies that directly links the relatively larger parts of women's corpus callosums to superior verbal abilities was reported at the meeting of the New York Academy of Sciences by Melissa Hines, a neuropsychologist at the University of California at Los Angeles medical school.

Dr. Hines and her associates used magnetic resonance imaging, a method that uses electrical fields generated by the brain, to measure the brain anatomy of 29 women. They found that the larger the splenium in the women, the better they were on tests of verbal fluency.

There was no relationship, however, between the size of their splenium and their scores on tests of spatial abilities, suggesting that differences in those abilities are related to anatomical structures in some other part of the brain or have nothing to do with anatomy. . . .

One study involved cerebral blood flow, which was measured while men and women listened to words that earphones directed to one ear or the other. The research, conducted by Cecile Naylor, a neuropsychologist at Bowman Gray School of Medicine in Winston-Salem, N.C., showed that the speech centers in women's brains were connected to more areas both within and between each hemisphere.

This puts men at a relative disadvantage in recovering from certain kinds of brain damage, such as strokes, when they cause lesions in the speech centers on the left side of the brain. Women with similar lesions, by contrast, are better able to recover speech abilities, perhaps because stronger connections between the hemispheres allow them to compensate more readily for damage on the left side of the brain by relying on similar speech centers on the right.

Brain Structure Does Not Explain Male/Female Differences
Anne Fausto-Sterling
(from *Myths of Gender: Biological theories about women and men*, Basic Books, 1985)

Functionally, humans have two brains. The idea has become sufficiently commonplace to appear even in the daily newspaper cartoons. While the left hemisphere of the brain appears specialized to carry out analysis, computation, and sequential tasks, in the right half resides artistic abilities and an emotional, nonanalytic approach to the world. As originally developed, the idea of brain hemisphere differentiation said nothing about sex differences. But it didn't take long for some scientists to suggest that left-brain hemisphere specialization could "explain" supposed male/female differences in verbal, spatial, and mathematical ability. The development, dissemination, and widespread acceptance of such ideas provides a second and still very active example of science as social policy.

Not long after the discovery of hemispheric specialization, some scientists began using it to explain both the supposed female excellence in verbal tasks and the male skill in spatial visualization. Dr. Jerry Levy—who during and after her time as Dr. Roger Sperry's student, played an important role in defining the modern concept of hemispheric specialization—hypothesizes that the most efficiently functioning brains have the most complete hemispheric division of labor. Women, she suggests, retain a capacity for verbal tasks in both hemispheres. In other words, they are less lateralized for speech than are men. When verbal tasks in women "spill over" to the right side of the brain, they interfere with the right hemisphere's ability to perform spatial tasks. Men, in contrast, have highly specialized brain halves—the left side confining its activities solely to verbal problems, the right side solely to spatial ones.

Let's suppose for a moment that male and female brains do lateralize differently and ask what evidence exists to suggest that such differences might lead to variations in performance of spatial and verbal tasks. The answer is, quite simply, none whatsoever. Levy derives the idea not from any experimental data but from a logical supposition. In her later work she takes that supposition and "reasons" that "a bilaterally symmetric brain would be limited to verbal or spatial processing. . . ." Psychologist Meredith Kimball reviewed the small number of studies that might act as tests of Levy's logical supposition and came up empty-handed, concluding that there is no evidence to support the key assumption on which Levy builds her hypothesis.

Nevertheless, the proposal that men and women have different patterns of brain lateralization has provoked enormous interest. Scientists have published hundreds of studies, some done on normal subjects and others derived from subjects with brain damage due to stroke, surgery, or accident. The idea that verbal function might operate differently in male and female brains came in part from a long-standing observation: among stroke victims there appear to be more men than women with speech defects serious enough to warrant therapy. There may be a number of explanations for why men seek speech therapy more frequently than do women. To begin with, more males *have* strokes. Also, it is possible that males seek remedial therapy after a stroke more frequently than do females. And strokes may affect speech less severely in females because females have better verbal abilities before the illness.

Some researchers have attempted to sort out these possibilities, but a controlled study of stroke victims is extremely difficult. One reason is that there is no way of knowing for sure whether male and female victims under comparison experienced exactly the same type of brain damage. Even comparisons of individuals who had surgery performed on similar parts of their brains are probably quite misleading because of variation in brain morphology from individual to individual. It would be possible to ascertain the exact regions of the brain affected only by looking at microscopic sections of it, a practice that is routine in animal experiments but would of course be impossible with live human beings. Extensive reviews of clinical studies reveal a great deal of controversy about their meaning, but little in the way of strong evidence to support the idea that women have bilateralized verbal functions. Consider the statement of Jeanette McGlone, a scientist who believes her work to *support* the differential lateralization hypothesis:

> Neither do the data overwhelmingly confirm that male brains show greater functional asymmetry than female brains. . . . One must not overlook perhaps the most obvious conclusion, which is that basic patterns of male and female brain asymmetry seem to be more similar than they are different.

If this is the kind of support the proponents of sex differences in laterality put forward, then it is amazing indeed that the search for sex-related differences in brain lateralization remains such a central focus of current research in sex-related cognitive differences.

In addition to looking at patients with brain damage, researchers have tested Levy's hypothesis using normal individuals. The most common way of measuring hemispheric specialization in healthy people is by the dichotic listening test. To look for language dominance, experimenters ask the subject to don a set of headphones. In one ear the subject hears a list of numbers, while in the other he or she simultaneously hears a second, differential list. After hearing the two lists, the subject (if not driven nuts) must remember as many of the numbers as possible. Usually subjects can recall the numbers heard on one side better than those heard on the other. Some experimenters believe that right-ear excellence suggests left-hemisphere dominance for verbal abilities and vice versa, but this conclusion ignores other possibilities. Individuals who take the tests may develop different strategies, for instance, deciding to try to listen to both sets of numbers or to ignore one side in order to listen more closely to the other.

Some scientists have reported sex differences in performance on dichotic listening tests, but three reviews of the research literature indicate a lack of solid information. Many studies show no sex differences and, in order to show any differences at all, large samples must be used, all of which suggests that same-sex disparities may be larger than those between the sexes. One reviewer, M.P. Bryden, ends her article with the following comments:

Any conclusions rest on one's choice of which studies to emphasize and which to ignore. It is very tempting to . . . argue that there are no convincing data for sex-related differences in cognition or cerebral lateralization. . . . In fact, what is required is better research.

Analogous methods exist for studying visual lateralization. Tests utilize a gadget called a tachistoscope, through which a subject looks into a machine with an illuminated field. The machine flashes different items in front of either the right or the left eye, and the subject tries to identify as many as possible. Nonverbal images such as dots (as opposed to words or letters) suggest some left-field (right-hemisphere) advantages for men, but here too the data vary a great deal. For example, many (but not all) studies show male left-eye advantages for perception of photographed faces, scattered dots, and line orientations, but no sex differences for the perception of schematic faces, depth, or color. In addition, the fundamental question of whether such tests have anything at all to do with brain lateralization continues to cloud the picture. . . .

Notes

1   These categories are based largely on Freedman and Clarke (1988).

2   These specific causes of misreading the prompt are the author's and not those of Ruth and Murphy.

3   Hamp-Lyons (personal communication) suggests that multitrait scoring could be referred to as a postmodern version of analytic scoring because of the common features that the two methods share.

4   The holistic scale is based on Hamp-Lyons (1991b), the analytic scale on the Jacobs, Zinkgraf, Wormuth, Hartfiel, & Hughey (1981) ESL Composition Profile, the primary trait scale on Freedman (1991), and the multitrait scales on the Michigan Writing Assessment Scoring Guide in Hamp-Lyons (1991b).

5   In an ESL context, it may be unreasonable to expect this to take place unless the learners are all or mostly from the same language and cultural background.

6   Actually, these drafts would be evidence of formative products before the summary one, and processes could be reflected in them.

7   Higher-level or superordinate idea units or statements.

8   It is also possible that Shohamy's summarization subtest was measuring some aspects of reading that the other subtests were not—for example, a more overall view of the text. But it was also probably measuring writing skills.

Chapter 10:
Taking Stock

Our intent in this volume was to broaden the scope of the material from the previous edition and also to provide more depth in certain areas. Our aim in the first edition was to write a testing book around the edges of other testing books—i.e., covering topics not covered in much depth elsewhere. The revised version has continued in this tradition to some extent, but it has also included more issues that other texts have discussed as well—now that there are so many more testing books available than when this book first appeared.

Another purpose of this edition was to focus on the needs of the classroom teacher on a daily basis. If a classroom teacher can read the preceding nine chapters and come away with some practical ideas, the book will have met one of its major objectives. However, we also wanted to provide material of interest to test constructors, researchers, and students who are not classroom teachers.

While on one hand we have been concerned with practical suggestions for assessment, we have also tried to include research findings when they may lend added significance to certain approaches to assessing language. As I started writing, I realized how prescriptive it would sound if I suggested that teachers do X or Y without giving them a rationale. Hence there are references to research, primarily contained within separate sections.

My personal view is that the classroom teacher can help in the research effort. For instance, consider the issue of test-taking strategies. Teachers can ask their students how they arrived at answers to items and procedures on quizzes and tests. One way to do this would be to have students work in pairs or in small groups after the quiz or test has been taken, taking turns reporting to the peer(s) how they produced an answer to a given item (e.g., their rationale or strategies). The peers can write down the answers or tick them on a checklist, and then the teacher along with the class can examine the data for the class as a whole. This is one way teachers and pupils can determine whether the assessment instruments are assessing what they purport to measure.

A question that kept going through my mind as I was writing this book was "to what extent does a second-language syllabus stimulate the development of assessment measures to match it, to what extent do tests themselves stimulate a particular line of teaching, and to what extent does the influence work both ways?" Over the years, a negative stigma has been attached to "teaching to the test." But if an assessment instrument really reflects the essence of a syllabus, and especially if this syllabus emphasizes skill-using or communicative ability, there is every reason to expect the relationship between teaching and assessment to be close, with a positive washback effect of assessment on teaching. For example, a measure of communicative speaking ability may itself stimulate types of classroom activities aimed at determining whether students have an ability to communicate orally. In fact, at times there may be little ostensible difference to the outside observer between a communicative task as a learning exercise and as a means for assessment.

I suppose that the issue is one of degree. When a particular assessment format on, say, a comprehensive matriculation exam dictates the teaching procedures for one or more courses, this is a situation in need of redress. At a far less comprehensive level, a clever assessment procedure may contribute one or more fresh ideas concerning **how** to go about teaching language and stimulating language learning, and such a spin-off would be all for the better. As pointed out in Chapter 2, determining the washback effects of an assessment instrument on teaching means looking not just at its effect on the content of instruction, but also its effects on **how** the content was taught, the pace of the instruction, the sequencing of material, the amount of material learned, and the depth of learning (Alderson & Wall, 1992). When we obtain answers to these questions, we are better able to speak to the effects of a given assessment instrument.

The following are some of the key issues emerging from the volume that a classroom teacher/test constructor would probably wish to consider:

1. It is almost easier to misuse a test than to use it wisely, so test users need to be wary about using a test for the wrong reasons.
2. As of the 1990s, it is difficult to talk assessment without referring to assessing the sociolinguistic and sociocultural competence of students. There is a growing trend in this direction.
3. Rather than labeling language assessment as an unauthentic assessment of language behavior, it is probably more fruitful to look at the ways in which a given assessment instrument **is** authentic.
4. Criterion-referenced testing continues to be an attractive means of assessment in that it assesses individuals according to their achievements.
5. Washback has a role to play in test validation, but one must assess all aspects of its role.
6. We can benefit from determining what test items and procedures are **actually** eliciting from respondents—both by close analysis of the items themselves and by gathering verbal-report data from the respondents.
7. The cognitive style and personality of the students can influence their responses on tests.
8. Test statistics can play a crucial role in informing the teacher/tester about the possible reliability and validity of the assessment instrument.

9. Test users can now draw on information from both traditional sources and from nontraditional sources (such as test-taking strategy data) regarding the strengths and weaknesses of assessment methods such as the storyline test, the cloze test, the C-test, reading passages with multiple-choice items, and summarization.

10. Test developers should give attention to the way items are constructed (e.g., to the elicitation and response formats) in order to make sure that they are consistent (e.g., having the input in a listening comprehension task be at the appropriate place along the oral/literate continuum).

11. The advent of the portfolio movement is a potentially beneficial one to the field of language assessment since the emphasis is on convergent and repeated measures over time rather than on single measures at one point in time.

12. There is a increasing interest in the nature of the actual discourse (e.g., its sociolinguistic characteristics) produced by interview sessions and other speaking measures.

13. Unambiguous and informative instructions are essential. Instructions that provide a mini-training in how to perform the given task can also be useful.

14. The way raters produce their scores needs to be an ongoing concern of testers, and the insights that emerge from this concern can help to make such ratings more reliable and valid.

15. Self-assessment provides a genuine opportunity for learners to become more involved in the assessment process, and it can take some of the responsibilities of assessment away from teachers, who have plenty of other things to do.

As I noted in the previous edition of this book, there is probably no ideal point at which to cease revising the manuscript of a book of this kind before publishing it. This is still true. In some ways, the field of assessment is moving so fast that even the focal issues change from one day to the next. This revised version makes an effort to deal with those issues that are currently in fashion. We have also noted that from time to time the pendulum swings back toward previous approaches to assessment, however much enlightened certain methods may now appear. In fact, it may not ultimately matter so much which type of items or assessment instruments we use, but rather what we **know** about these measures before we even give them, what we learn about how students produce answers to these tests, and what we do about evaluating these answers. A teacher/test constructor who can feel comfortable in these areas has nothing to fear about quizzing or testing students. In fact, such activities can even be seen as a welcome and stimulating challenge, both for the teachers and for the learners.

References

Aighes, B., et al. (1977). *Progress report on the BBN group*. BBN Report No. 3720, prepared for the National Institute of Education. University of Illinois at Urbana/Champaign & Beranek and Newman, 50 Moulton Street, Cambridge, MA 02138.

Alderson, J. C. (1978). *The use of cloze procedure with native and non-native speakers of English*. Unpublished doctoral dissertation, University of Edinburgh.

Alderson, J. C. (1983). The cloze procedure and proficiency in English as a foreign language. In J. W. Oller, Jr. (Ed.), *Issues in language testing research* (pp. 205–228). Rowley, MA: Newbury.

Alderson, J. C. (1987). *Innovation in language testing: Can the micro-computer help? Special Report No. 1: Language Testing Update*. Lancaster: Institute for English Language Education, University of Lancaster.

Alderson, J. C. (1993). Judgments in language testing. In D. Douglas & C. Chapelle (Eds.), *A new decade of language testing research* (pp. 46–57). Arlington, VA: TESOL.

Alderson, J. C., Krahnke, K. J., & Stansfield, C. W. (1987). *Reviews of English language proficiency tests*. Washington, DC: TESOL.

Alderson, J. C., & Lukmani, Y. (1989). Cognition and reading: Cognitive levels as embodied in test questions. *Reading in a Foreign Language, 5*(2), 253–270.

Alderson, J. C., & Wall, D. (1992). Does washback exist? Unpublished manuscript, Department of Linguistics and Modern English Language, Lancaster University.

Alderson, J. C., & Windeatt, S. (1991). "Learner-adaptive" computer-based language tests. *Language Testing Update, 9*, 18–21.

Alderson, J. C., & Windeatt, S. (1992). *Lancaster University Computer-Based Assessment System (LUCAS)*. Lancaster: Department of Linguistics and Modern English Language, Bowland College, Lancaster University.

Allan, A. (1992). Development and validation of a scale to measure test-wiseness in EFL/ESL reading test takers. *Language Testing, 9*(2), 101–122.

Allen, E. D. (1976). Miscue analysis: A new tool for diagnosing oral reading proficiency in foreign languages. *Foreign Language Annals, 9*(6), 563–567.

Allen, E. D., & Valette, R. A. (1977). *Classroom techniques: Foreign language and English as a second language*. New York: Harcourt.

Allwright, R. L. (1975). Problems in the study of the language teacher's treatment of learner error. In M. K. Burt & H. C. Dulay (Eds.), *New directions in second language learning, teaching and bilingual education* (pp. 96–109). Washington, DC: TESOL.

Alpert, R., & Haber, R. N. (1960). Anxiety in academic achievement situations. *Journal of Abnormal and Social Psychology, 61,* 207–215.

Anderson, N. J. (1991). Individual differences in strategy use in second language reading and testing. *Modern Language Journal, 75*(4), 460–472.

Anderson, N. J., Bachman, L., Perkins, K., & Cohen, A. (1991). An exploratory study into the construct validity of a reading comprehension test: Triangulation of data sources. *Language Testing, 8*(1), 41–66.

Anderson, R. C., & Freebody, P. (1983). Reading comprehension and the assessment and acquisition of word knowledge. *Advances in Reading/Language Research, 2,* 231–256.

Anderson, R. C., & Pearson, P. D. (1984). A schema-theoretic view of basic processes in reading comprehension. In P. D. Pearson (Ed.), *Handbook of reading research* (pp. 255–291). New York: Longman.

Arevart, S., & Nation, I. S. P. (1993). Adjusting fluency and grammar through repetition. In J. W. Oller, Jr. (Ed.), *Methods that work: Ideas for teaching languages and literacy* (pp. 297–308). Boston: Heinle.

Arndt, V. (1987). First and foreign language composing: A protocol-based study. In T. Bloor & J. Norrish (Eds.), *Written language* (pp. 114–129). British Studies in Applied Linguistics 2. London: Centre for Information on Language Teaching and Research (CILT).

Avery, P., & Ehrlich, S. (1992). *Teaching American English pronunciation*. Oxford: Oxford University Press.

Bachman, L. F. (1985). Performance on cloze tests with fixed-ratio and rational deletions. *TESOL Quarterly, 19*(3), 535–556.

Bachman, L. F. (1988). Problems in examining the validity of the ACTFL Oral Proficiency Interview. *Studies in Second Language Acquisition, 10*(2), 149–64.

Bachman, L. F. (1989). Language testing-SLA research interfaces. *Annual Review of Applied Linguistics, 9,* 193–209.

Bachman, L. F. (1990). *Fundamental considerations in language testing*. Oxford: Oxford University Press.

Bachman, L. F. (1991). What does language testing have to offer? *TESOL Quarterly, 25*(4), 671–704.

Bachman, L. F., Lynch, B., & Mason, M. (1993). Investigating variability in tasks and rater judgments in language tests. Paper presented at the Annual Conference of the American Association for Applied Linguistics, Atlanta, April 16–19, 1993. Los Angeles: Program in Applied Linguistics, University of California.

Bachman, L. F., & Palmer, A. S. (In press). *Language testing in practice*. Oxford: Oxford University Press.

Bachman, L. F., Purpura, J. E., & Cushing, S. T. (1993). *Development of a questionnaire item bank to explore test-taker characteristics*. Interim report submitted to the University of Cambridge Local Examination Syndicate. Los Angeles: Language Assessment Laboratory, Dept. of Applied Linguistics, University of California.

Barnett, M. A. (1989). *More than meets the eye: Foreign language reading: Theory and practice*. Englewood Cliffs, NJ: Prentice Hall Regents.

Basham, C. S. (1987). Summary writing as cultural artifact. Fairbanks, Alaska: Cross-Cultural Communications, University of Alaska.

Basham, C. S., & Rounds, P. L. (1986). A discourse analysis approach to summary writing. *Papers in Applied Linguistics-Michigan, 1*(2), 88–104.

Belanoff, P., & Elbow, P. (1986). Using portfolios to increase collaboration and community in a writing program. *WPA: Writing Program Administration, 9*(3): 27–39.

Ben Simon, A. (1988). Applying alternate response methods to reading comprehension tests. Presentation at the Annual University Teachers of English in Israel (ITELI) Conference. Jerusalem: National Institute for Testing and Evaluation.

Bensoussan, M., & Kreindler, I. (1990). Improving advanced reading comprehension in a foreign language: Summaries vs. short-answer questions. *Journal of Research in Reading, 13*(1), 55–68.

Berman, R. A. (1984). Syntactic components of the foreign language reading process. In J. C. Alderson & A. H. Urquhart (Eds.), *Reading in a foreign language* (pp. 139–159). London: Longman.

Bernhardt, E. B. (1991). *Reading development in a second language*. Norwood, NJ: Ablex.

Berry, V. (1991). Personality characteristics as a potential source of language test bias. Aichi, Japan: Nagoya University of Commerce & Business Administration.

Bialystock, E. (1990). *Communication strategies*. Oxford: Basil Blackwell.

Blanche, P. (1990). Using standardized achievement and oral proficiency tests for self-assessment purposes: The DLIFLC study. *Language Testing, 7*(2), 202–229.

Blanche, P., & Merino, B. J. (1989). Self-assessment of foreign-language skills: Implications for teachers and researchers. *Language Learning, 39*(3), 313–340.

Blau, E. K. (1982). The effect of syntax on readability for ESL students in Puerto Rico. *TESOL Quarterly, 16*(4), 517–527.

Block, E. (1986). The comprehension strategies of second language readers. *TESOL Quarterly, 20*(3), 463–494.

Bloom, B. S., et al. (1956). *Taxonomy of educational objectives: The classification of educational goals, handbook I: Cognitive domain*, New York: David McKay.

Blum-Kulka, S., & Olshtain, E. (1986). Too many words: Length of utterance and pragmatic failure. *Studies in Second Language Acquisition, 8*(2), 165–180.

Bonikowska, M. P. (1988). The choice of opting out. *Applied Linguistics, 9*, 169–181.

Bormuth, J. R. (1970). *On the theory of achievement test items*. Chicago: University of Chicago Press.

Bowen, J. D. (1972). Contextualizing pronunciation practice in the ESOL classroom. *TESOL Quarterly, 6*(1), 83–94.

Bowen, J. D. (1977). Practice effect in English proficiency testing. In H. D. Brown et al. (Eds.), *On TESOL '77* (pp. 295–308). Washington, DC: TESOL.

Brière, E. J. (1964). Testing the control of parts of speech in FL compositions. *Language Learning, 14*(1), 1–9.

Brière, E. J. (1967). Phonological testing reconsidered. *Language Learning, 17*(3,4), 163–171.

Brière, E. J. (1973). Cross-cultural biases in language testing. In J. W. Oller, Jr., & J. C. Richards (Eds.), *Focus on the learner: Pragmatic perspectives for the language teacher* (pp. 214–227). Rowley, MA: Newbury.

Brill, H. (1986). Developing a communicative test of reading comprehension and determining its effectiveness. Seminar paper, School of Education, Hebrew University, Jerusalem (in Hebrew).

Brindley, G. (1989). *Assessing achievement in the learner-centered curriculum.* Sydney, Australia: National Centre for English Language Teaching and Research, Macquarie University.

Brooks, N. (1967). Making your own language tests. In M. R. Donoghue (Ed.), *Foreign languages and the schools* (pp. 285–302). Dubuque, IA: W. C. Brown.

Brown, A. L., Campione, J. C., & Day, J. D. (1981). Learning to learn: On training students to learn from text. *Educational Researchers, 10*, 14–21.

Brown, A. L., & Day, J. D. (1983). Macrorules for summarizing texts: The development of expertise. *Journal of Verbal Learning and Verbal Behavior, 22*, 1–14.

Brown, G., & Yule, G. (1983). *Teaching the spoken language: An approach based on the analysis of conversational English.* Cambridge: Cambridge University Press.

Brown, J. D. (1988). *Understanding research in second language learning: A teacher's guide to statistics and research design.* Cambridge: Cambridge University Press.

Brown, P., & Levinson, S. (1987). *Politeness: Some universals in language usage.* Cambridge: Cambridge University Press.

Buck, C. (1973). Miscues of non-native speakers of English. In K. S. Goodman (Ed.), *Miscue analysis: Applications in reading instruction* (pp. 91–96). Urbana, IL: NCTE.

Buck, G. (1990). *The testing of second language listening comprehension.* Unpublished doctoral dissertation, Department of Linguistics and Modern English Language, University of Lancaster.

Buck, G. (1991). Expert estimates of test item characteristics. Unpublished manuscript. Department of Linguistics, University of Lancaster.

Buck, G. (1992). Translation as a language testing procedure: Does it work? *Language Testing, 9*(2), 123–148.

Byrnes, H., Thompson, I., & Buck, K. (1989). *The ACTFL oral proficiency interview: Tester training manual.* Yonkers, NY: ACTFL.

Canale, M. (1983). On some dimensions of language proficiency. In J. W. Oller, Jr. (Ed.), *Issues in language testing research* (pp. 333–342). Rowley, MA: Newbury.

Canale, M. (1984). Considerations in the testing of reading and listening proficiency. *Foreign Language Annals, 17*(4), 349–357.

Canale, M. (1985). Proficiency-oriented achievement testing. Toronto: Franco-Ontarian Centre and Curriculum Department, Ontario Institute for Studies in Education. Unpublished manuscript.

Canale, M. (1986). The promise and threat of computerized adaptive assessment of reading comprehension. In C. W. Stansfield (Ed.), *Technology and language testing* (pp. 29–45). Washington, DC: TESOL.

Canale, M., & Swain, M. (1980). Theoretical bases of communicative approaches to second-language teaching and testing. *Applied Linguistics, 1*(1), 1–47.

Cardelle, M., & Corno, L. (1981). Effects on second language learning of variations in written feedback on homework assignments. *TESOL Quarterly, 15*(13), 251–261.

Carré, C. (1981). *Language teaching and learning. 4. Science.* London: Ward Lock.

Carrell, P. L. (1988). Some causes of text-boundedness and schema interference in ESL reading. In P. Carrell, J. Devine, & D. Eskey (Eds.), *Interactive approaches to second language reading* (pp. 101–113). Cambridge: Cambridge University Press.

Carrell, P. L., & Eisterhold, J. C. (1983). Schema theory and ESL reading pedagogy. *TESOL Quarterly, 17*(4), 553–573.

Carroll, J. B. (1968). The psychology of language testing. In A. Davies (Ed.), *Language testing symposium: A psycholinguistic approach* (pp. 46–69). London: Oxford University Press.

Carroll, J. B. (1979). Psychometric approaches to the study of language abilities. In C. J. Fillmore et al. (Eds.), *Individual differences in language ability and language behavior* (pp. 13–31). New York: Academic.

Carroll, J. B. (1987). Book review: Klein-Braley, C., & Raatz, U. (1985). *C-tests in der Praxis. Language Testing, 4*(1), 99–106.

Carroll, J. B., Carton, A. S., & Wilds, C. P. (1959). *An investigation of "cloze" items in the measurement of achievement in foreign languages.* College Entrance Examination Board Research and Development Report, Laboratory for Research in Instruction, Harvard University, Cambridge, MA.

Cavalcanti, M. C. (1987). Investigating FL reading performance through pause protocols. In C. Faerch & G. Kasper (Eds.), *Introspection in second language research* (pp. 230–250). Clevedon, England: Multilingual Matters.

Celce-Murcia, M. (1974). Report of an informal classroom experiment on speedwriting with a suggestion for further research. *Workpapers in Teaching English as a Second Language, 8,* 63–69.

Chapelle, C. A., & Abraham, R. B. (1990). Cloze method: What difference does it make? *Language Testing, 7*(2), 121–146.

Chastain, K. (1976). *Developing second language skills: Theory to practice.* 2d ed. Chicago: Rand McNally.

Chaudron, C., & Richards, J. C. (1986). The effect of discourse markers on the comprehension of lectures. *Applied Linguistics, 7*(2), 113–127.

Chávez-Oller, M. A., Chihara, T., Weaver, K. A., & Oller, J. W., Jr. (1985). When are cloze items sensitive to constraints across sentences? *Language Learning, 35*(2), 181–206.

Chihara, T., Oller, J. W., Weaver, K., & Chávez-Oller, M. A. (1977). Are cloze items sensitive to constraints across sentences? *Language Learning, 27*(1), 63–73.

Child, J. (1988). Issues in reading proficiency assessment: A framework for discussion. In P. Lowe, Jr., & C. W. Stansfield (Eds.), *Second language proficiency assessment* (pp. 125–135). Englewood Cliffs, NJ: Prentice Hall Regents.

Chou Hare, V., & Borchardt, K. M. (1984). Direct instruction of summarization skills. *Reading Research Quarterly, 20*(1), 62–78.

Clapham, C. (forthcoming). Collected papers from the 1991 Language Testing Research Colloquium. Princeton, NJ: Educational Testing Service.

Clark, J. L. D. (1972). *Foreign language testing: Theory and practice.* Philadelphia: The Center for Curriculum Development.

Clark, J. L. D. (1977). *The performance of native speakers of English on the Test of English as a Foreign Language.* TOEFL Research Reports, Report 1. Princeton, NJ: Educational Testing Service.

Clement, R., & Kruidenier, B. G. (1983). Orientations in second language acquisition: The effects of ethnicity, milieu, and target language on their emergence. *Language Learning, 33*(3), 273–291.

Cohen, A. D. (1975a). English language placement testing: Separating foreign English from minority English. In R. Crymes & W. E. Norris (Eds.), *On TESOL '74* (pp. 189–199). Washington, DC: TESOL.

Cohen, A. D. (1975b). *A sociolinguistic approach to bilingual education.* Rowley, MA: Newbury.

Cohen, A. D. (1977). Successful second-language speakers: A review of research literature. *Balshanut Shimushit, 1,* iii–xii. ERIC ED 142 085.

Cohen, A. D. (1984). On taking language tests: What the students report. *Language Testing, 1*(1), 70–81.

Cohen, A. D. (1987a). Research on cognitive processing in reading in Brazil. *D.E.L.T.A.* (Journal of Brazilian Linguistics Association) *3*(2), 215–235.

Cohen, A. D. (1987b). Student processing of feedback on their compositions. In A. L. Wenden & J. Rubin (Eds.), *Learner strategies in language learning* (pp. 57–69). Englewood Cliffs, NJ: Prentice-Hall International.

Cohen, A. D. (1989). *Portuguese Speaking Test (PST). Language Testing, 6*(2), 233–237.

Cohen, A. D. (1990a). *Language learning: Insights for learners, teachers, and researchers.* New York: Newbury/HarperCollins.

Cohen, A. D. (1990b). The role of instructions in testing summarizing ability. In T. Shimaoka & Y. Yasukata (Eds.), *Studies in applied linguistics* (pp. 16–24). Tokyo: Liber.

Cohen, A. D. (1993). The role of instructions in testing summarizing ability. In D. Douglas & C. Chapelle (Eds.), *A new decade of language testing research* (pp. 132–160). Arlington, VA: TESOL.

Cohen, A. D. (In press). English testing in Brazil: Problems in using summary tasks. In C. Hill & K. Parry (Eds.), *Testing and assessment: International perspectives on English literacy.* London: Longman.

Cohen, A. D., & Aphek, E. (1979). *Easifying second language learning.* Research report under the auspices of Brandeis University and submitted to the Jacob Hiatt Institute, Jerusalem. Educational Resources Information Center, ERIC ED 163 753.

Cohen, A. D., & Fine, J. (1978). Reading history in English: Discourse analysis and the experiences of natives and non-native readers. *Working Papers on Bilingualism, 16*, 55–74.

Cohen, A. D., Glasman, H., Rosenbaum-Cohen, P. R., Ferrara, J., & Fine, J. (1979). Reading English for specialized purposes: Discourse analysis and the use of student informants. *TESOL Quarterly, 13*(4), 551–564.

Cohen, A. D., & Olshtain, E. (1993). The production of speech acts by EFL learners. *TESOL Quarterly, 27*(1), 33–56.

Cohen, A. D., & Robbins, M. (1976). Toward assessing interlanguage performance: The relationship between selected errors, learners' characteristics, and learners' explanations. *Language Learning, 26*(1), 45–66.

Cohen, A. D., Segal, M., & Weiss Bar-Siman-Tov, R. (1984). The C-test in Hebrew. *Language Testing, 1*(2), 221–225.

Cohen, A. D., & Tarone, E. (Forthcoming). Describing and teaching speech act behavior: Stating and changing an opinion. In L. Barbara & M. Scott (Eds.), *Reflections on language learning*.

Connor, U. M., & Carrell, P. L. (1993). The interpretation of tasks by writers and readers in holistically rated direct assessment of writing. In J. G. Carson & I. Leki (Eds.), *Reading in the composition classroom: Second language perspectives* (pp. 141–160). Boston: Heinle.

Cowan, J. R. (1976). Reading, perceptual strategies and contrastive analysis. *Language Learning, 26*(1), 95–109.

Cumming, A. (1990a). Expertise in evaluating second language compositions. *Language Testing, 7*(1), 31–51.

Cumming, A. (1990b). Metalinguistic and ideational thinking in second language composing. *Written Communication, 7*, 482–522.

Curran, C. A. (1976). *Counseling-learning in second languages.* Apple River, IL.: Apple River Press.

Curran, C. A. (1978). A linguistic model for learning and living in the new age of the person. In C. H. Blatchford & J. Schachter (Eds.), *On TESOL '78* (pp. 36–48). Washington, DC: TESOL.

Curtis, M. E. (1987). Vocabulary testing and vocabulary instruction. In M. G. McKeown & M. E. Curtis (Eds.), *The nature of vocabulary acquisition* (pp. 37–51). Hillsdale, NJ: Erlbaum.

Cziko, G. A., & Nien-Hsuan, J. L. (1984). The construction and analysis of short scales of language proficiency: Classical psychometric, latent trait, and nonparametric approaches. *TESOL Quarterly, 18*, 627–647.

Dailey, J. T. (1968). *Language facility test: Test administrator's manual.* Alexandria, VA: Allington.

Davidson, F., Hudson, T., & Lynch, B. (1985). Language testing: Operationalization in classroom measurement and second language research. In M. Celce-Murcia (Ed.), *Beyond basics* (pp. 137–152). Rowley, MA: Newbury.

Davies, A. (1990). *Principles of language testing.* Oxford: Basil Blackwell.

Davies, E., & Whitney, N. (1984). Study skill 11: Writing summaries. In *Study skills for reading: Students' book* (pp. 56–58). London: Heinemann.

DeAvila, E. A., & Duncan, S. E. (1978). *Research on cognitive styles with language minority children: Summary of pilot study design and data analysis.* Austin, TX: Southwest Educational Development Laboratory.

Des Brisay, M. (1984). Who knows best? A comparison of two placement procedures. *Institut des Language Vivantes Journal, 29*, 167–175.

Deyhle, D. (1987). Learning failure: Tests as gatekeepers and the culturally different child. In H. T. Trueba (Ed.), *Success or failure: Learning and the language minority student* (pp. 85–108). New York: Newbury/Harper.

DiPietro, R. J. (1987). Strategic interaction: Stepping outside the norm in second-language instruction. *Language Teaching Strategies, 2*, 1–9.

Dobson, B. K. (1974). Student-generated distractors in ESL tests. In R. Crymes & W. E. Norris (Eds.), *On TESOL '74* (pp. 181–188). Washington, DC: TESOL.

Doherty, C., & Ilyin, D. (1981). *A technical manual for ELSA (English language skills assessment)*. Rowley, MA: Newbury.

Dollerup, C., Glahn, E., & Rosenberg-Hansen, C. (1982). Reading strategies and test-solving techniques in an EFL-reading comprehension test—A preliminary report. *Journal of Applied Language Study, 1*(1), 93–99.

Douglas, D., & Selinker, L. (1985). Principles for language tests within the "discourse domains" theory of interlanguage: Research, test construction and interpretation. *Language Testing, 2*(2), 205–226.

Douglas, D., & Selinker, L. (1991). SPEAK and CHEMSPEAK: Measuring the English speaking ability of international teaching assistants in chemistry. Ames, IA: Department of English, Iowa State University.

Douglas, D., & Selinker, L. (1993). Performance on a general versus a field-specific test of speaking proficiency by international teaching assistants. In D. Douglas & C. Chapelle (Eds.), *A new decade of language testing research* (pp. 235–256). Alexandria, VA: TESOL.

Douglas, D., & Simonova, O. (1993). Testing spoken English ability in an agribusiness context. Ames, IA: Department of English, Iowa State University.

Ebel, R. L., & Frisbie, D. A. (1986). *Essentials of educational measurement.* 4th ed. Englewood Cliffs, NJ: Prentice-Hall.

Edmondson, W., & House, J. (1991). Do learners talk too much? The waffle phenomenon in interlanguage pragmatics. In R. Phillipson, E. Kellerman, L. Selinker, M. Sharwood Smith, & M. Swain (Eds.), *Foreign/second language pedagogy research* (pp. 272–287). Clevedon, England: Multilingual Matters.

Educational Testing Service. (1969). *Cooperative Primary Reading Test, Form 12 A.* Berkeley, CA: ETS.

Educational Testing Service. (1985). *SPEAK examinee handbook and sample questions.* Princeton, NJ: ETS.

Educational Testing Service. (1992). *TOEFL Test of Written English guide.* 3rd ed. Princeton, NJ: ETS.

Elbow, P., & Belanoff, P. (1986). State University of New York, Stony Brook: Portfolio-based evaluation program. In P. Connolly & T. Vilardi (Eds.), *New directions in college writing programs* (pp. 95–105). New York: Modern Language Association.

Ellis, R. (1990). *Instructed second language acquisition.* Oxford: Basil Blackwell.

Emanuel, E. (1982). The use of the cloze technique—regular cloze and discourse cloze—in the teaching of Hebrew as a mother tongue. Course paper, School of Education, Hebrew University of Jerusalem. (In Hebrew)

Ericsson, K. A., & Simon, H. A. (1980). Verbal reports as data. *Psychological Review, 87*(3), 215–251.

Faerch, C., & Kasper, G. (1983). Plans and strategies in foreign language communication. In C. Faerch & G. Kasper (Eds.), *Strategies in interlanguage communication* (pp. 20–60). London: Longman.

Faerch, C., & Kasper, G. (1987). From product to process—Introspective methods in second language research. In C. Faerch & G. Kasper (Eds.), *Introspection in second language research* (pp. 5–23). Clevedon, England: Multilingual Matters.

Fanselow, J. F. (1977). Beyond RASHOMON—conceptualizing and describing the teaching act. *TESOL Quarterly, 11*, 17–39.

Farr, R., Pritchard, R., & Smitten, B. (1990). A description of what happens when an examinee takes a multiple-choice reading comprehension test. *Journal of Educational Measurement, 27*(3), 209–226.

Feldman, U., & Stemmer, B. (1987). Thin___ aloud a___ retrospective da___ in C-te___ taking: diffe___ languages — diff___ learners — sa___ approaches? In C. Faerch & G. Kasper (Eds.), *Introspection in second language research.* Clevedon, England: Multilingual Matters, 251–267.

Fletcher, N. (1989). *CBELT—Does computer delivery make a difference in scores and attitudes?* Unpublished M.A. dissertation, Lancaster University.

Flower, L., & Hayes, J. R. (1984). Images, plans, and prose: The representation of meaning in writing. *Written Communication, 1*(1), 120–160.

Fowler, B., & Kroll, B. M. (1978). Verbal skills as factors in the passageless validation of reading comprehension tests. *Perceptual and Motor Skills, 47*, 335–338.

Fransson, A. (1984). Cramming or understanding? Effects of intrinsic and extrinsic motivation on approach to learning and test performance. In J. C. Alderson & A. H. Urquhard (Eds.), *Reading in a foreign language* (pp. 86–121). London: Longman.

Frederiksen, J. R., & Collins, A. (1989). A systems approach to educational testing. *Educational Researcher, 18*(9), 27–32.

Freedman, A., & Clarke, L. (1988). *The effect of computer technology on composing processes and written products of grade eight and grade twelve students.* Toronto: Queen's Printer.

Freedman, S. W. (1991). Evaluating writing: Linking large-scale testing and classroom assessment. Berkeley, CA: Center for the Study of Writing, University of California. Occasional Paper No. 27.

Gardner, R. C., & Lambert, W. E. (1972). *Attitudes and motivation in second-language learning.* Rowley, MA: Newbury.

Gattegno, C. (1972). *Teaching foreign language in schools: The Silent Way.* New York: Educational Solutions.

Gattegno, C. (1976). *The common sense of teaching foreign languages.* New York: Educational Solutions.

George, H. V. (1972). *Common errors in language learning: Insights from English.* Rowley, MA: Newbury.

Gimenez, R. N. (1984). Legibilidade de textos académicos em inglés da área de serviço social. M.A. thesis, Graduate Program in Applied Linguistics, Pontifícia Universidade Católica de São Paulo.

Goodman, K. S. (1967). Reading: A psycholinguistic guessing game. *Journal of the Reading Specialist, 6*, 126–135.

Goodman, K. S. (1969). Analysis of oral reading miscues: Applied psycholinguistics. *Reading Research Quarterly, 5*, 9–30.

Goodman, K. (1988). The reading process. In P. L. Carrell, J. Devine, & D. E. Eskey (Eds.), *Interactive approaches to second language reading.* Cambridge: Cambridge University Press, 11–21.

Goodrich, H. C. (1977). Distractor efficiency in foreign language testing. *TESOL Quarterly, 11*(1), 69–78.

Gordon, C. (1987). *The effect of testing method on achievement in reading comprehension tests in English as a foreign language.* Unpublished M.A. thesis. Ramat-Aviv, Tel-Aviv, Israel: School of Education, Tel-Aviv University.

Green, J. A. (1975). *Teacher-made tests.* 2d ed. New York: Harper.

Gregory, M. (1967). Aspects of varieties differentiation. *Journal of Linguistics, 3*, 177–198.

Grellet, F. (1981). *Developing reading skills: A practical guide to reading comprehension exercises.* Cambridge: Cambridge University Press.

Grice, H. P. (1975). Logic and conversation. In P. Cole & J. Morgan (Eds.), *Syntax and semantics 3: Speech acts* (pp. 41–58). New York: Academic.

Hadley, A. O. (1993). *Teaching language in context.* Boston: Heinle, 2nd ed.

Hambleton, R. K., & Eignor, D. R. (1978). Guidelines for evaluating criterion-referenced tests and test manuals. *Journal of Educational Measurement, 15*(4), 321–327.

Hamp-Lyons, L. (1989). Raters respond to rhetoric in writing. In H. W. Dechert & M. Raupach (Eds.), *Interlingual processes* (pp. 229–244). Tübingen: Gunter Narr.

Hamp-Lyons, L. (1991a). *Assessing second language writing in academic contexts.* Norwood, NJ: Ablex.

Hamp-Lyons, L. (1991b). Scoring procedures for ESL contexts. In L. Hamp-Lyons (Ed.), *Assessing second language writing in academic contexts* (pp. 241–276). Norwood, NJ: Ablex.

Hamp-Lyons, L. (1993). Components of portfolio evaluation: ESL data. Paper presented at the annual AAAL Conference, Atlanta, GA, April 16–19, 1993. Denver: Department of English and Applied Language, University of Colorado.

Hamp-Lyons, L., & Condon, W. C. (1993). Questioning assumptions about portfolio-based evaluation. *College Composition & Communication, 44*(2), 176–190.

Hamp-Lyons, L., & Prochnow, S. (1989). Person dimensionality, person ability, and item difficulty in writing. Paper presented at the Language Testing Research Colloquium, San Antonio, TX, March 4–5, 1989. Ann Arbor, MI: English Composition Board, University of Michigan.

Hamp-Lyons, L., & Prochnow, S. (1990). Prompt difficulty, task type, and performance. In S. Anivan (Ed.), *Current developments in language testing* (pp. 58–76). Singapore: SEAMEO/RELC.

Haney, W., & Scott, L. (1987). Talking with children about tests: An exploratory study of test item ambiguity. In R. O. Freedle & R. P. Duran (Eds.), *Cognitive and linguistic analyses of test performance* (pp. 298–368). Norwood, NJ: Ablex.

Harris, D. P. (1969). *Testing English as a Second Language*. New York: McGraw-Hill.

Hashkes, B., & Koffman, N. (1982). Strategies used in a cloze test. Course paper, School of Education, Hebrew University of Jerusalem.

Hatch, E., & Lazaraton, A. (1991). *The research manual: Design and statistics for applied linguistics*. New York: Newbury/HarperCollins.

Hawkins, B. (1985). Is an "appropriate response" always so appropriate? In S. M. Gass & C. G. Madden (Eds.), *Input in Second Language Acquisition* (pp. 162–178). Rowley, MA: Newbury.

Heaton, J. B. (1975). *Writing English language tests*. London: Longman.

Heaton, J. B. (1990). *Classroom testing*. London: Longman.

Hembree, R. (1988). Correlates, causes, effects, and treatments of test anxiety. *Review of Educational Research, 58*(1), 47–77.

Henning, G. H. (1978). Measurement of psychological differentiation and linguistic variation: A study of the relationship between field-dependence-independence, locus of control, hemispheric localization, and variations in the occurrence of syntactic classes in written language. Unpublished doctoral dissertation, University of California, Los Angeles.

Henning, G. (1984). Advantages of latent trait measurement in language testing. *Language Testing, 1*(2), 123–133.

Henning, G. (1987). *A Guide to Language Testing*. New York: Newbury/Harper.

Henning, G., Anbar, M., Helm, C. E., & D'Arcy, S. J. (1993). Computer-assisted testing of reading comprehension: Comparisons among multiple-choice and open-ended scoring methods. In D. Douglas & C. Chapelle (Eds.), *A new decade of language testing research* (pp. 123–131). Alexandria, VA: TESOL.

Herter, R. J. (1991). Writing portfolios: Alternatives to testing. *English Journal*, January: 90–91.

Hill, C., & Parry, K. (1992). The test at the gate: Models of literacy in reading assessment. *TESOL Quarterly, 26*(3), 433–461.

Holmes, J. L. (1986). Snarks, quarks and cognates: An elusive fundamental particle in reading comprehension. *The ESPecialist, 15*, 13–40.

Homburg, T. J., & Spaan, M. C. (1981). ESL reading proficiency assessment: Testing strategies. In M. Hines & W. Rutherford (Eds.), *On TESOL '81* (pp. 25–33). Washington, DC: TESOL.

Hosenfeld, C. (1977). A preliminary investigation of the reading strategies of successful and nonsuccessful second language learners. *System, 5*(2), 110–123.

Hosenfeld, C. (1979). Cindy: A learner in today's foreign language classroom. In W. C. Born (Ed.), *The foreign language learner in today's classroom environment* (pp. 53–75). Montpelier, VT: Capital City.

Hudson, T., & Lynch, B. (1984). A criterion-referenced measurement approach to ESL achievement testing. *Language Testing, 1*(2), 171–201.

Hughes, A. (1989). *Testing for language teachers*. Cambridge: Cambridge University Press.

Hughey, J. B., Wormuth, D. R., Hartfiel, V. F., & Jacobs, H. L. (1983). *Teaching ESL composition: Principles and techniques*. Rowley, MA: Newbury.

Huot, B. (1990a). The literature of direct writing assessment: Major concerns and prevailing trends. *Review of Educational Research, 60*(2), 237–263.

Huot, B. (1990b). Reliability, validity, and holistic scoring: What we know and what we need to know. *College Composition and Communication, 41*(2), 201–213.

Inbar, O. (1988). The effect of text and question-type on achievement in EFL listening comprehension. *English Teachers' Journal* (Israel), *37*, 45–48.

Ingram, E. (1974). Language testing. In J. P. B. Allen & S. P. Corder (Eds.), *Techniques in applied linguistics* (pp. 313–343). London: Oxford University Press.

Israel, A. (1982). The effect of guessing in multiple-choice language tests. Course paper, School of Education, Hebrew University of Jerusalem. (In Hebrew)

Jacobs, H. L., Zinkgraf, S. A., Wormuth, D. R., Hartfiel, V. F., & Hughey, J. B. (1981). *Testing ESL Composition.* Rowley, MA: Newbury.

Jenks, F. L. (1979). Homework assignments in the ESL class that work. *TESOL Newsletter, 13*(4), 11–12, 22.

Johns, A. M. (1985). Summary protocols of "underprepared" and "adept" university students: Replications and distortions of the original. *Language Learning, 35*(4), 495–517.

Johns, A. M., & Mayes, P. (1990). An analysis of summary protocols of university ESL students. *Applied Linguistics, 11*(3), 253–271.

Johnson, K. E. (1991). Modifying the SPEAK Test for international teaching assistants. *TESOL Matters, 1*(1), 8.

Johnson, R. E. (1970). Recall of prose as a function of the structural importance of the linguistic units. *Journal of Verbal Learning and Verbal Behavior, 9*, 12–20.

Johnson, Y. (1991). Proposal: ACTFL Oral Proficiency Interview role play items for the Japanese language. Minneapolis, MN: East Asian Languages and Literature, University of Minnesota.

Johnston, P. H. (1983). *Reading comprehension assessment: A cognitive basis.* Newark, DE: International Reading Association.

Joint Committee on Testing Practices. (1988). *Code of fair testing practices in education.* Washington, DC: American Psychological Association.

Jones, R. L. (1984). Testing the receptive skills: Some basic considerations. *Foreign Language Annals, 17*(4), 365–367.

Jonz, J. (1976). Improving on the basic egg: The M-C cloze. *Language Learning, 26*(2), 255–265.

Jonz, J. (1990). Another turn in the conversation: What does cloze measure? *TESOL Quarterly, 24*(1), 61–83.

Just, M. A., & Carpenter, P. A. (1987). *The psychology of reading and language comprehension.* Boston: Allyn and Bacon.

Kato, H. (1977). Some thoughts on oral examinations for advanced students in Japanese. *System, 5*(3), 181–186.

Kaya-Carton, E., Carton, A. S., & Dandonoli, P. (1991). Developing a computer-adaptive test of French reading proficiency. In P. Dunkel (Ed.), *Computer-assisted language learning and testing* (pp. 259–284). New York: Newbury/HarperCollins.

Kellerman, E. (1991). Compensatory strategies in second language research: A critique, a revision, and some (non-)implications for the classroom. In R. Phillipson et al. (Eds.), *Foreign/second language pedagogy research* (pp. 142–161). Clevedon, England: Multilingual Matters.

Kesar, O. (1990). *Identification and analysis of reading moves in completing a rational deletion cloze.* Unpublished M.A. thesis (in Hebrew). Jerusalem: School of Education, Hebrew University.

Key, M. R. (1977). *Nonverbal communication: A research guide and bibliography.* Metuchen, NJ: Scarecrow Press.

Kintsch, W., & van Dijk, T. A. (1978). Toward a model of text comprehension and production. *Psychological Review, 85,* 363–394.

Kirn, H. E. (1972). *The effect of practice on performance on dictations and cloze tests.* M.A. thesis, ESL Section, Department of English, University of California, Los Angeles.

Kleiman, A. B., Cavalcanti, M. C., Terzi, S. B., & Ratto, I. (1986). Percepçao do léxico e sua funçao discursivo: Algums fatores condicionantes. Campinas, Brazil: Universidade Estadual de Campinas.

Klein-Braley, C. (1981). *Empirical investigation of cloze tests: An examination of the validity of cloze tests as tests of general language proficiency in English for German university students.* Unpublished doctoral dissertation. Duisburg, Germany: University of Duisburg.

Klein-Braley, C. (1985). A cloze-up on the C-test: A study in the construct validation of authentic tests. *Language Testing, 5*(1), 76–104.

Klein-Braley, C. (1987). Fossil at large: Translation as a language testing procedure. In R. Grotjahn et al. (Eds.), *Taking their measure: The validity and validation of language tests* (pp. 111–132). Bochum, Germany: Brockmeyer.

Klein-Braley, C., & Raatz, U. (1984). A survey of research on the C-test. *Language Testing, 1,* 134–146.

Kleinmann, H. H. (1977). Avoidance behavior in adult second language acquisition. *Language Learning, 27*(1), 93–107.

Koike, D. A. (1989). Pragmatic competence and adult L2 acquisition: Speech acts in interlanguage. *Modern Language Journal, 73*(3), 279–289.

Kozminsky, E., & Graetz, N. (1986). First vs. second language comprehension: Some evidence from text summarizing. *Journal of Reading Research, 9,* 3–21.

Krapels, A. R. (1990). An overview of second language writing process research. In B. Kroll (Ed.), *Second language writing: Research insights for the classroom* (pp. 37–56). Cambridge: Cambridge University Press.

Krashen, S. D. (1977). Some issues relating to the monitor model. In H. D. Brown et al. (Eds.), *On TESOL '77* (pp. 148–158). Washington, DC: TESOL.

Krashen, S. D. (1982). *Principles and practice in second language acquisition.* Oxford: Pergamon.

Krashen, S. D. (1985). The din in the head, input, and the language acquisition device. In *Inquiries and insights* (pp. 35–54). Hayward, CA: Alemany.

Krypsin, W. J., & Feldhusen, J. F. (1974). *Developing classroom tests: A guide for writing and evaluating test items.* Minneapolis: Burgess.

Lado, R. (1964). *Language Testing.* New York: McGraw-Hill.

Lado, R. (1986). Analysis of native speaker performance on a cloze test. *Language Testing, 3*(2): 130–146.

Lantolf, J. P., & Frawley, W. (1988). Proficiency: Understanding the construct. *Studies in Second Language Acquisition, 10*(2), 181–195.

Larsen-Freeman, D. (1986). *Techniques and principles in language teaching.* Oxford: Oxford University Press.

Larsen-Freeman, D., & Long, M. H. (1991). *An introduction to second language acquisition research*. London: Longman.

Larson, J. W., & Madsen, H. S. (1985). Computerized adaptive language testing: Moving beyond computer assisted testing. *CALICO Journal*, March, 32–36, 43.

Larson, K. (1981). A study of student test-taking strategies and difficulties. Course paper, ESL Section, Department of English, University of California, Los Angeles.

Laufer, B. (1978). An experiment in teaching reading comprehension with written answers in the mother tongue. *System, 6*(1), 11–20.

Laufer, B. (1983). Written answers in Hebrew to English comprehension questions—Some advantages. *English Teachers' Journal* (Israel), *29*, 59–64.

Laufer, B., & Sim, D. D. (1983). To what extent is L2 reading comprehension a function of L2 competence rather than of reading strategies? Haifa, Israel: Department of English, Haifa University.

Laufer, B., & Sim, D. D. (1985). Taking the easy way out: Non-use and misuse of contextual clues in EFL reading comprehension. *English Teaching Forum, 23*(2), 7–19, 20.

Lee, J. F. (1986). On the use of the recall task to measure L2 reading comprehension. *Studies in Second Language Acquisition, 8*(2), 201–212.

Lehtonen, J. (1978). Problems of measuring fluency and normal rate of speech. Jyväskylä, Finland: Department of Phonetics and Linguistics, University of Jyväskylä. Unpublished manuscript.

Leu, D. J., Jr. (1982). Oral reading error analysis: A critical review of research and application. *Reading Research Quarterly, 17*(3), 420–437.

Levenston, E. A. (1975). Aspects of testing the oral proficiency of adult immigrants to Canada. In L. Palmer & B. Spolsky (Eds.), *Papers on language testing 1967–1974* (pp. 66–74). Washington, DC: TESOL.

Levenston, E. A., Nir, R., & Blum-Kulka, S. (1984). Discourse analysis and the testing of reading comprehension by cloze techniques. In A. K. Pugh & J. M. Ulijn (Eds.), *Reading for professional purposes* (pp. 202–212). London: Heinemann.

Lewis, H. E. (1974). *Learning Spanish in Jamaica: A study of errors caused by language transfer in a diglossic situation*. Unpublished doctoral dissertation, University of Toronto.

Lewis, J. (1990). Self-assessment in the classroom: A case study. In G. Brindley (Ed.), *The second language curriculum in action* (pp. 187–213). Sydney, Australia: National Centre for English Language Teaching and Research, Macquarie University.

Lieberman, D. A. (1979). Behaviorism and the mind: A (limited) call for a return to introspection. *American Psychologist, 34*, 319–333.

Lindvall, C. M., & Nitko, A. J. (1975). *Measuring pupil achievement and aptitude*. 2d ed. New York: Harcourt.

Liskin-Gasparro, J. E. (1984). Practical considerations in receptive skills testing. *Foreign Language Annals, 17*(4), 369–373.

Lloyd-Jones, R. (1977). Primary trait scoring. In C. Cooper & L. Odell (Eds.), *Evaluating writing* (pp. 33–66). Urbana, IL: NCTE.

Loughrin-Sacco, S. J. (1990). The reflections and confessions of an ACTFL Oral Proficiency Interview workshop participant. *The Canadian Modern Language Review, 46*(4), 706–713.

Low, G. (1985). Validity and the problem of direct language proficiency tests. In J. C. Alderson (Ed.), *Lancaster Practical Papers in English Language Education 6* (pp. 151–168). Oxford: Pergamon.

Low, G. D. (1986). Storylines and other developing contexts in use-of-language test design. *Indian Journal of Applied Linguistics, 12*(1–2), 15–38.

Lowe, P., Jr. (1988). The unassimilated history. In P. Lowe, Jr., & C. W. Stansfield (Eds.), *Second Language Proficiency Assessment: Current Issues* (pp. 11–51). Englewood Cliffs, NJ: Prentice Hall Regents.

Lowe, P., Jr., & Stansfield, C. W. (Eds.). (1988). *Second Language Proficiency Assessment: Current Issues.* Englewood Cliffs, NJ: Prentice Hall Regents.

MacKay, R. (1974). Standardized tests: Objectives/objectified measures of "competence." In A. V. Cicourel et al. (Eds.), *Language use and school performance* (pp. 218–247). New York: Academic.

MacLean, M., & d'Anglejan, A. (1986). Rational cloze and retrospection: Insights into first and second language reading comprehension. *The Canadian Modern Language Review, 42*(4), 814–826.

Madsen, H. (1960). *Laboratory versus traditional methods of teaching remedial English: An analysis and experiment.* Unpublished M.A. thesis, University of Utah, Salt Lake City.

Madsen, H. (1986). Evaluating a computer-adaptive ESL placement test. *CALICO Journal*, December, 41–50.

Madsen, H. (1991). Computer-adaptive testing of listening and reading comprehension. In P. Dunkel (Ed.), *Computer-assisted language learning and testing* (pp. 237–257). New York: Newbury/HarperCollins.

Malik, A. A. (1990). A psycholinguistic analysis of the reading behavior of EFL-proficient readers using culturally familiar and culturally nonfamiliar expository texts. *American Educational Research Journal, 27*(1), 205–223.

Mangubhai, F. (1990). Towards a taxonomy of strategies used by ESL readers of varying proficiencies while doing cloze exercises. *Australian Journal of Reading, 13*(2), 128–139.

Mann, S. J. (1982). Verbal reports as data: A focus on retrospection. In S. Dingwall & S. Mann (Eds.), *Methods and problems in doing applied linguistic research* (pp. 87–104). Lancaster: Dept. of Linguistics and Modern English Language, University of Lancaster.

Markham, P. L. (1985). The rational deletion cloze and global comprehension in German. *Language Learning, 35*(3), 423–430.

Marshall, J. C., & Hales, L. W. (1971). *Classroom test construction.* Reading, MA: Addison-Wesley.

Marzano, R. J., & Arthur, S. (1977). Teacher comments on student essays: It doesn't matter what you say. University of Colorado at Denver. ERIC ED 147 864.

McNamara, T. F. (1990). Item response theory and the validation of an ESP test for health professionals. *Language Testing, 7*(1), 52–76.

Meagher, R. S. (1987). Computerized adaptive testing: Innovative approach to determine language proficiency. ESOL/Bilingual Programs, Montgomery County Public Schools, MD.

Meara, P., & Buxton, B. (1987). An alternative to multiple choice vocabulary tests. *Language Testing, 4*(1), 142–154.

Mehan, H. (1974). Ethnomethodology and education. In D. O'Shea (Ed.), *The sociology of the school and schooling* (pp. 141–198). Washington, DC: National Institute of Education.

Meldman, M. A. (1991). The validation of oral performance tests for second language learners. In M. E. McGroarty & C. J. Faltis (Eds.), *Languages in school and society: Policy and pedagogy* (pp. 423–438). Berlin: Mouton de Gruyter.

Messick, S. (1988). Validity. In R. L. Linn (Ed.), *Educational measurement* (pp. 13–103). 3rd ed. New York: American Council on Education/Macmillan.

Messick, S., & Anderson, S. (1974). Educational testing, individual development, and social responsibility. In R. W. Tyler and R. M. Wolf (Eds.), *Crucial issues in testing* (pp. 21–34). Berkeley, CA: McCutchan.

Meyer, B. J. F. (1985). Prose analysis: Purposes, procedures, and problems. In B. K. Britton & J. B. Black (Eds.), *Understanding expository text: A theoretical and practical handbook for analyzing explanatory text* (pp. 11–64). Hillsdale, NJ: Erlbaum.

Morrow, K. (1981). Communicative language testing: Revolution or evolution? In J. C. Alderson & A. Hughes (Eds.), *Issues in language testing* (pp. 9–25). London: British Council.

Morrow, K. E. (1986). The evaluation of tests of communicative performance. In M. Portal (Ed.), *Innovations in language testing* (pp. 1–13). Berkshire, England: NFER-Nelson.

Munby, J. (1978). A problem-solving approach to the development of reading comprehension skills. Presentation at the Regional University Teachers of English in Israel (UTELI) Meeting, Jerusalem, Israel.

Munby, J. (1979). Teaching intensive reading skills. In R. Mackay, B. Barkman, & R. R. Jordan (Eds.), *Reading in a second language* (pp. 142–158). Rowley, MA: Newbury.

Murakami, K. (1974). A language aptitude test for the Japanese (GTT). *System, 2*(3), 31–47.

Murphy, S., & Smith, M. A. (1991). *Writing portfolios: A bridge from teaching to assessment.* Markham, Canada: Pippin.

Nagy, W. E., Herman, P. A., & Anderson, R. C. (1985). Learning words from context. *Reading Research Quarterly, 20*, 233–253.

Naiman, N., Fröhlich, M., Stern, H. H., & Todesco, A. (1978). *The good language learner.* Research in Education Series No. 7. Toronto: Modern Language Centre, Ontario Institute for Studies in Education.

Nation, I. S. P. (1978). Translation and the teaching of meaning: Some techniques. *English Language Teaching Journal, 32*(3), 171–175.

Nation, I. S. P. (1990). *Teaching and Learning Vocabulary.* New York: Newbury/Harper.

Nevo, N. (1989). Test-taking strategies on a multiple-choice test of reading comprehension. *Language Testing, 6*(2), 199–215.

Nickerson, R. S. (1989). New directions in educational assessment. *Educational Researcher, 18*(9), 3–7.

Nilsen, D. L. F., & Nilsen, A. P. (1973). *Pronunciation contrasts in English.* New York: Regents.

Norris, S. P. (1989). Can we test validly for critical thinking? *Educational Researcher, 18*(9), 21–26.

Nuttall, C. (1982). *Teaching Reading Skills in a Foreign Language.* London: Heinemann.

Oh, J. (1992). The effects of L2 reading assessment methods on anxiety level. *TESOL Quarterly, 26*(1), 172–176.

Oller, J. W., Jr. (1972). Dictation as a test of ESL proficiency. In H. B. Allen & R. N. Campbell (Eds.), *Teaching English as a Second Language* (pp. 346–354). 2d ed. New York: McGraw-Hill.

Oller, J. W., Jr. (1973). Cloze tests of second language proficiency and what they measure. *Language Learning, 23*(1), 105–118.

Oller, J. W., Jr. (1975). Cloze, discourse, and approximations to English. In M. K. Burt & H. C. Dulay (Eds.), *On TESOL '75: New directions in second language learning, teaching and bilingual education* (pp. 345–355). Washington, DC: TESOL.

Oller, J. W., Jr. (1976). Language testing. In R. Wardhaugh & H. D. Brown (Eds.), *A survey of applied linguistics* (pp. 275–300). Ann Arbor: University of Michigan Press.

Oller, J. W., Jr. (1979). *Language tests at school.* London: Longman.

Oller, J. W., Jr., & Jonz, J. (Forthcoming). *Cloze and coherence.*

Oller, J. W., Jr. & Tullius, J. R. (1973). Reading skills of non-native speakers of English. *IRAL, 11*(1), 69–80.

Olson, G. M., Duffy, S. A., & Mack, R. L. (1984). Thinking-out-loud as a method for studying real-time comprehension processes. In D. E. Kieras & M. A. Just (Eds.), *New methods in reading comprehension research.* Hillsdale, NJ: Lawrence Erlbaum, 253–286.

Oskarsson, M. (1980). *Approaches to self-assessment in foreign language learning.* Oxford: Pergamon.

Oxford, R. (1990). *Language learning strategies: What every teacher should know.* New York: Newbury/Harper.

Oxford, R. L., & Cohen, A. D. (1992). Language learning strategies: Crucial issues of concept and classification. *Applied Language Learning, 3*(1–2), 1–35.

Oxford, R. L., & Crookall, D. (1989). Research on language learning strategies: Methods, findings, and instructional issues. *Modern Language Journal, 73*(4), 403–419.

Oxford, R. L., Hollaway, M. E., & Horton-Murillo, D. (1993). Language learning styles: Research and practical considerations for teaching in the multicultural tertiary ESL/EFL classroom. *System, 20*(4), 439–456.

Ozete, O. (1977). The cloze procedure: A modification. *Foreign Language Annals, 10*(5), 565–568.

Pace, A. J., Marshall, N., Horowitz, R., Lipson, M. Y., & Lucido, P. (1989). When prior knowledge doesn't facilitate text comprehension: An examination of some of the issues. In S. McCormick & J. Zutell (Eds.), *Cognitive and social perspectives for literacy research and instruction* (38th Yearbook of the National Reading Conference) (pp. 213–224). Chicago: National Reading Conference.

Paribakht, T. (1985). Strategic competence and language proficiency. *Applied Linguistics, 6*, 132–146.

Paribakht, T. S., & Wesche, M. (Forthcoming). The relationship between reading comprehension and second language development in a comprehension-based ESL program. *TESL Canada Journal.*

Paris, S. G., Lawton, T. A., Turner, J. C., & Roth, J. L. (1991). A developmental perspective on standardized achievement testing. *Educational Researcher, 20*(5), 12–20.

Perrett, G. (1990). The language testing interview: A reappraisal. In J. H. A. L. de Jong & D. K. Stevenson (Eds.), *Individualizing the assessment of language abilities* (pp. 225–238). Clevedon, England: Multilingual Matters.

Pica, T. (1986). An interactional approach to the teaching of writing. *English Teaching Forum, 24*(3), 6–10.

Pikulski, J. J., & Pikulski, E. C. (1977). Cloze, maze, and teacher judgment. *The Reading Teacher, 30*(7), 766–770.

Pimsleur, P. (1966). Testing foreign language learning. In A. Valdman (Ed.), *Trends in language teaching* (pp. 175–215). New York: McGraw-Hill.

Poole, D. (1993). The social and curricular consequences of routine classroom testing: A sociolinguistic analysis. San Diego: Department of Linguistics, San Diego State University. Unpublished manuscript.

Popham, W. J. (1973). *Criterion-referenced instruction.* Belmont, CA: Fearon.

Popham, W. J. (1978). *Criterion-referenced measurement.* Englewood Cliffs, NJ: Prentice-Hall.

Popham, W. J. (1981). *Modern educational measurement.* Englewood Cliffs, NJ: Prentice-Hall.

Porter, D. (1976). Modified cloze procedure: A more valid reading comprehension test. *English Language Teaching, 30*, 151–155.

Poulisse, N. (1989). *The use of compensatory strategies by Dutch learners of English.* Doctoral dissertation, Department of Applied Linguistics, University of Nijmegen, the Netherlands.

Poulisse, N., Bongaerts, T., & Kellerman, E. (1986). The use of retrospective verbal reports in the analysis of compensatory strategies. In C. Faerch & G. Kasper (Eds.), *Introspection in second language research* (pp. 213–229). Clevedon, England: Multilingual Matters.

Pugh, A. K. (1978). *Silent Reading.* London: Heinemann.

Raatz, U. (1985). Tests of reduced redundancy—The C-test, a practical example. *Fremdsprachen und Hochschule* (pp. 14–19). Bochum, Germany: AKS-Rundbrief *13–14.*

Raatz, U., & Klein-Braley, C. (1982). The C-test—A modification of the cloze procedure. In T. Culhane, C. Klein-Braley, & D. K. Stevenson (Eds.), *Practice and problems in language testing 4* (pp. 113–138). Colchester: University of Essex.

Raatz, U., & Klein-Braley, C. (1985). How to develop a C-test. *Fremdsprachen und Hochschule* (pp. 20–22). Bochum, Germany: AKS-Rundbrief *13–14*.

Raffaldini, T. (1988). The use of situation tests as measures of communicative ability. *Studies in Second Language Acquisition, 10*, 197–216.

Rafoth, B. A., & Rubin, D. L. (1984). The impact of content and mechanics on judgments of writing quality. *Written Communication, 1*(4), 446–458.

Raimes, A. (1983). *Techniques in teaching writing.* New York: Oxford University Press.

Raimes, A. (1987). Why write? From purpose to pedagogy. *English Teaching Forum, 25*, 36–41, 55.

Ramírez, M., & Castañeda, A. (1974). *Cultural democracy, bicognitive development, and education.* New York: Academic.

Read, J. (1988). Measuring the vocabulary knowledge of second language learners. *RELC Journal, 19*(2), 12–25.

Ready-Morfitt, D. (1991). The role and limitations of self-assessment in testing and research. Ottawa, Canada: Second Language Institute, University of Ottawa. Unpublished manuscript.

Richards, J. C., & Rodgers, T. S. (1986). *Approaches and methods in language teaching: A description and analysis.* New York: Cambridge University Press.

Rickard, R. B. (1979). Exploring perceptual strategies and reading in a second language: Performance differences between speakers of different native languages. *TESOL Quarterly, 13*(4), 599–602.

Rigg, P. (1977). The miscue project. In H. D. Brown, C. A. Yorio, & R. Crymes (Eds.), *On TESOL '77: Teaching and learning ESL: Trends in research and practice* (pp. 106–118). Washington, DC: TESOL.

Rivers, W. M. (1968). *Teaching foreign-language skills.* Chicago: University of Chicago Press.

Rivers, W. M. (1981). *Teaching Foreign-Language Skills.* 2d ed., Chicago: University of Chicago Press.

Rivers, W. M. (1983). *Speaking in many tongues.* 3rd ed. Cambridge: Cambridge University Press.

Rivers, W. M., & Temperley, M. S. (1978). *A practical guide to the teaching of English as a second or foreign language.* New York: Oxford University Press.

Robbins, M. (1977). *Error explanations: A procedure for examining written interlanguage performance.* Unpublished M.A. thesis, ESL Section, Department of English, University of California, Los Angeles.

Rodríguez-Brown, F. V. & Cohen, A. D. (1979). Assessing Spanish reading: Criterion-referenced testing. In A. D. Cohen, M. Bruck, & F. V. Rodríguez-Brown, *Evaluating Evaluation* (pp. 23–39). Bilingual Education Series: 6. Arlington, VA: Center for Applied Linguistics.

Rolfe, T. (1990). Self- and peer-assessment in the ESL curriculum. In G. Brindley (Ed.), *The second language curriculum in action* (pp. 163–186). Sydney, Australia: National Centre for English Language Teaching and Research, Macquarie University.

Ross, S., & Berwick, R. (1992). The discourse of accommodation in oral proficiency interviews. *Studies in Second Language Acquisition, 14*(2), 159–176.

Rossier, R. E. (1975). *Extroversion-introversion as a significant variable in the learning of English as a second language.* Unpublished doctoral dissertation, University of Southern California, Los Angeles.

Rumelhart, D. E. (1980). Schemata: The building blocks of cognition. In R. J. Spiro, B. C. Bruce, & W. F. Brewer (Eds.), *Theoretical issues in reading comprehension* (pp. 33–58). Hillsdale, NJ: Erlbaum.

Russell, B. (1950). An outline of intellectual rubbish. In *Unpopular essays* (pp. 95–145). London: Allen & Unwin.

Ruth, L., & Murphy, S. (1984). Designing topics for writing assessment: Problems of meaning. *College Composition and Communication, 35*(4), 410–422.

Ruth, L., & Murphy, S. (1988). *Designing writing tasks for the assessment of writing.* Norwood, NJ: Ablex.

Rutherford, W. E. (1975). *Modern English.* Vol. 1, 2d ed. New York: Harcourt.

Sajavaara, K., & Lehtonen, J. (1978). Spoken language and the concept of fluency. *Kielikeskusuutisia, 1,* 23–57.

Sarig, G. (1987). High-level reading in the first and in the foreign language: Some comparative process data. In J. Devine, P. L. Carrell, & D. E. Eskey (Eds.), *Research in reading in English as a second language* (pp. 105–120). Washington, DC: TESOL.

Sarig, G. (1993). Composing a study-summary: A reading-writing encounter. In J. G. Carson & I. Leki (Eds.), *Reading in the composition classroom: Second language perspectives* (pp. 161–182). Boston: Heinle.

Savignon, S. J. (1972). *Communicative competence: An experiment in foreign-language teaching.* Philadelphia: Center for Curriculum Development.

Savignon, S. J. (1982). Dictation as a measure of communicative competence in French as a second language. *Language Learning, 32*(1), 33–51.

Scarcella, R. C. (1983). Sociodrama for social interaction. In J. W. Oller, Jr. & P. A. Richard-Amato (Eds.), *Methods that work* (pp. 239–245). Rowley, MA: Newbury.

Scarcella, R. C., & Oxford, R. L. (1992). *The tapestry of language learning.* Boston: Heinle.

Schachter, J. (1983). A new account of language transfer. In S. Gass & L. Selinker (Eds.), *Language transfer in language learning* (pp. 98–111). Rowley, MA: Newbury.

Schachter, J. (1984). A universal input condition. In W. E. Rutherford (Ed.), *Language universals and second language acquisition* (pp. 167–183). Philadelphia: John Benjamins.

Schlue, K. M. (1977). *An inside view of interlanguage: Consulting the adult learner about the second language acquisition process.* Unpublished M.A. thesis, University of California, Los Angeles.

Schmidt, R. W. (1990). The role of consciousness in second language learning. *Applied Linguistics, 11*(2), 129–158.

Schrafnagl, J., & Cameron, D. (1988). Are you decoding me? The assessment of understanding in oral interaction. In P. Grunwell (Ed.), *Applied linguistics in society* (pp. 88–97). British Studies in Applied Linguistics 3. London: Centre for Information on Language Teaching and Research (CILT).

Schulz, R. A. (1977). Discrete-point versus simulated communication testing in foreign languages. *Modern Language Journal, 61*(3), 94–101.

Scott, Mary Lee (1986). Student affective reactions to oral language tests. *Language Testing, 3*(1), 99–118.

Scott, Michael (1986). *The understanding to direct: Conscientização and reading.* Working Paper No. 18. Centro de Pesquisas, Recursos e Informaçao em Leitura, Pontifícia Universidade Católica de São Paulo, São Paulo, Brazil.

Semke, H. D. (1984). Effects of the red pen. *Foreign Language Annals, 17*(3), 195–202.

Serrano, N. S. de. (1986). *Reading in first and foreign language.* Unpublished M.A. Thesis, Trinity College, University of Dublin.

Shohamy, E. (1984). Does the testing method make a difference? The case of reading comprehension. *Language Testing, 1*(2), 147–170.

Shohamy, E. (1985). *A practical handbook in language testing for the second language teacher.* Ramat Aviv, Israel: Tel Aviv University.

Shohamy, E. (1988). A proposed framework for testing the oral language of second/foreign language learners. *Studies in Second Language Acquisition, 10*(2), 165–179.

Shohamy, E. (1990a). Discourse analysis in language testing. *Annual Review of Applied Linguistics, 11*, 115–131.

Shohamy, E. (1990b). Language testing priorities. *Foreign Language Annals, 23*(5), 385–393.

Shohamy, E. (1991). The validity of concurrent validity: Qualitative validation of the oral interview with the semi-direct test. Tel Aviv: School of Education.

Shohamy, E. (1992). The power of tests: A study of the impact of three language tests on teaching and learning. Paper presented at the Language Testing Research Colloquium, Vancouver, Feb. 28, 1992. Tel-Aviv: School of Education, Tel-Aviv University.

Shohamy, E., & Stansfield, C. W. (1990). The Hebrew speaking test: An example of international cooperation in test development and validation. *AILA Review, 7*, 79–90.

Silverman, R. J., Noa, J. K., & Russell, R. H. (1976). *Oral language tests for bilingual students: An evaluation of language dominance and proficiency instruments.* Portland, OR: Northwest Regional Educational Laboratory.

Simmons, J. (1990). Portfolios as large-scale assessment. *Language Arts, 67*(3), 262–268.

Skehan, P. (1989). *Individual differences in second-language learning.* London: Edward Arnold.

Smith, J. (1989). Topic and variation in ITA oral proficiency: SPEAK and field-specific tests. *English for Specific Purposes, 8*, 155–167.

Smith, J. (1992). *Topic and variation in the oral proficiency of international teaching assistants.* Unpublished doctoral dissertation, University of Minnesota, Minneapolis.

Solé, Dorothy. (1991). The big surprise: Multiple evaluations of oral presentations. Cincinnati, OH: ESL Program, Teachers College, University of Cincinnati. Unpublished manuscript.

Spaan, M. (1993). The effect of prompt in essay examinations. In D. Douglas & C. Chapelle (Eds.), *A new decade of language testing research* (pp. 98–122). Alexandria, VA: TESOL.

Spolsky, B. (1968). Language testing—The problem of validation. *TESOL Quarterly, 2*(2), 88–94.

Spolsky, B. (1985). The limits of authenticity in language testing. *Language Testing, 2*(1), 31–40.

Stanovich, K. E. (1980). Toward an interactive-compensator model of individual differences in the development of reading fluency. *Reading Research Quarterly, 16*, 32–71.

Stansfield, C. W. (1985). A history of dictation in foreign language teaching and testing. *The Modern Language Journal, 69*(2), 121–128.

Stansfield, C. W., Kenyon, D. M., Doyle, F., Paiva, R., Ulsh, I., & Cowles, M. A. (1988). *Portuguese speaking test: Official test manual.* 1988–89 edition. Washington, DC: Center for Applied Linguistics.

Stansfield, C. W., Kenyon, D. M., Paiva, R., Doyle, F., Ulsh, I., & Cowles, M. A. (1990). The development and validation of the Portuguese Speaking Test. *Hispania, 73*, 641–651.

Stemmer, B. (1991). *What's on a C-test taker's mind? Mental processes in C-test taking.* Bochum, Germany: Universitätsverlag Dr. N. Brockmeyer.

Stenson, N. (1974). Induced errors. In J. H. Schumann & N. Stenson (Eds.), *New frontiers in second language learning* (pp. 54–70). Rowley, MA: Newbury.

Stevenson, J., & Gross, S. (1991). Use of a computerized adaptive testing model for ESOL/bilingual entry/exit decision making. In P. Dunkel (Ed.), *Computer-assisted language learning and testing* (pp. 223–235). New York: Newbury/HarperCollins.

Stockwell, R. P., Bowen, J. D., & Martin, J. W. (1965). *Grammatical structures of English and Spanish.* Chicago: University of Chicago Press.

Strother, J. B., & Ulijn, J. M. (1987). Does syntactic rewriting affect EST (English for science and technology) text comprehension? In J. Devine et al. (Eds.), *Research in reading in English as a second language* (pp. 89–101). Washington, DC: TESOL.

Swaffar, J. K., Arens, K. M., & Byrnes, H. (1991). *Reading for meaning: An integrated approach to language learning.* Englewood Cliffs, NJ: Prentice Hall.

Swain, M. (1984). Large-scale communicative language testing: A case study. In S. J. Savignon & M. S. Berns (Eds.), *Initiatives in communicative language teaching* (pp. 185–201). Reading, MA: Addison-Wesley.

Swain, M. (1991). Second language testing and second language acquisition: Is there a conflict with traditional psychometrics? In J. Alatis (Ed.), *Georgetown University Round Table on Languages and Linguistics 1990* (pp. 401–412). Washington, DC: Georgetown University Press.

Tarone, E. (1977). Conscious communication strategies in interlanguage: A progress report. In H. Brown, C. Yorio, & R. Crymes (Eds.), *On TESOL '77* (pp. 194–203). Washington, DC: TESOL.

Tarone, E. (1983). On the variability of interlanguage systems. *Applied Linguistics, 4*(2), 143–163.

Tarone, E. (Forthcoming). Research on interlanguage variation: Implications for language testing. In L. Bachman & A. D. Cohen (Eds.), *Interfaces between SLA and language testing research.* Cambridge: Cambridge University Press.

Tarone, E., Cohen, A. D., & Dumas, G. (1983). A closer look at some interlanguage terminology: A framework for communication strategies. In C. Faerch & G. Kasper (Eds.), *Strategies in interlanguage communication* (pp. 4–14). London: Longman.

Tarone, E., & Yule, G. (1989). *Focus on the language learner.* Oxford: Oxford University Press.

TESOL. (1978). But how can you teach them English if you don't speak their language? *TESOL Newsletter, 12*(3), 13.

Thorndike, R. L., & Hagen, E. (1969). *Measurement and evaluation in psychology and education.* 3d ed. New York: Wiley.

Tucker, G. R., Hamayan, E., & Genesee, F. H. (1976). Affective, cognitive and social factors in second language acquisition. *Canadian Modern Language Review, 32*, 214–226.

Tuinman, J. J. (1973–74). Determining the passage dependency of comprehension questions in five major tests. *Reading Research Quarterly, 9*, 206–223.

Tullius, J. (1971). *Analysis of reading skills of non-native speakers of English.* Unpublished M.A. thesis. Los Angeles: ESL Section, Department of English, University of California, Los Angeles.

Tung, P. (1986). Computerized adaptive testing: Implications for language test developers. In C. W. Stansfield (Ed.), *Technology and language testing* (pp. 11–28). Washington, DC: TESOL.

Turner, C. E. (1989). The underlying factor structure of L2 cloze test performance in francophone, university-level students: Causal modeling as an approach to construct validation. *Language Testing, 6*(2), 172–197.

Ulijn, J. (1977). An integrated model for first and second language comprehension and some experimental evidence about the contrastive analysis hypothesis. *System, 5*(3), 187–199.

Ulijn, J. M. (1981). Conceptual and syntactic strategies in reading a foreign language. In E. Hopkins & R. Grotjahn (Eds.), *Studies in language teaching and language acquisition* (pp. 129–166). Bochum, Germany: Brockmeyer.

Ulijn, J. M., & Kempen, G. A. M. (1976). The role of the first language in second language reading comprehension—Some experimental evidence. In G. Nickel (Ed.), *Proceedings of the Fourth International Congress of Applied Linguistics.* Vol. 1 (pp. 495–507). Stuttgart: Hochschul-Verlag.

Ulijn, J. M., & Strother, J. B. (1990). What does efficient technical writing need: Writing or reading research? In *International Communication Conference Proceedings* (pp. 134–139). Gildford, England: YEEE YPCC.

Underhill, N. (1987). *Testing spoken language: A handbook of oral testing techniques.* Cambridge: Cambridge University Press.

Upton, T. A. (1993). *An examination of the influence of ESL reading proficiency on recall protocols of Japanese students.* Unpublished doctoral dissertation, University of Minnesota, Minneapolis.

Valencia, S., & Pearson, P. D. (1987). Reading assessment: Time for a change. *The Reading Teacher, 40*, 726–732.

Valette, R. (1969). *Directions in foreign language testing*. New York: Modern Language Association.

Valette, R. M. (1977). *Modern Language Testing*. 2d ed. New York: Harcourt.

van Dijk, R. A. (1980). *Macrostructures*. Hillsdale, NJ: Erlbaum.

Vaughan, C. (1991). Holistic assessment: What goes on in the raters' minds? In L. Hamp-Lyons (Ed.), *Assessing second language writing in academic contexts* (pp. 111–125). Norwood, NJ: Ablex.

von Elek, T. (1982). Test of Swedish as a second language: An experiment in self-assessment. (Work Papers 31) Molndal, Sweden: Language Teaching Research Center.

Weir, C. J. (1990). *Communicative language testing*. New York: Prentice Hall International.

Wesche, M., & Paribakht, T. S. (1993). Assessing vocabulary knowledge: Depth versus breadth. Unpublished manuscript. Ottawa: Second Language Institute, University of Ottawa.

White, E. M. (1985). *Teaching and assessing writing*. San Francisco: Jossey-Bass.

Wick, J. W. (1973). *Educational measurement*. Columbus, OH: Merrill.

Witbeck, M. C. (1976). Peer correction procedures for intermediate and advanced ESL composition lessons. *TESOL Quarterly, 10*(3), 321–326.

Wolfson, N. (1989). The social dynamics of native and nonnative variation in complimenting behavior. In M. R. Eisenstein (Ed.), *The dynamic interlanguage* (pp. 219–236). New York: Plenum.

Young, D. J. (1986). The relationship between anxiety and foreign language oral proficiency ratings. *Foreign Language Annals, 19*(5), 439–445.

Young, R., & Milanovic, M. (1992). Discourse variation in oral proficiency interviews. *Studies in Second Language Acquisition, 14*(4), 403–424.

Yule, G., Powers, M., & Macdonald, D. (1992). The variable effects of some task-based learning procedures on L2 communicative efficativeness. *Language Learning, 42*(2), 249–277.

Yule, G., & Tarone, E. (1990). Eliciting the performance of strategic competence. In R. C. Scarcella, E. S. Andersen & S. D. Krashen (Eds.), *Developing communicative competence in a second language* (pp. 179–194). New York: Newbury.

Zamel, V. (1985). Responding to student writing. *TESOL Quarterly, 19*(1), 79–101.

Zupnik, Y. (1985). A comparative study: English/Hebrew responses to open-ended reading comprehension test questions. Unpublished seminar paper, School of Education, Hebrew University of Jerusalem.

Index

ability, 47. *See also* speaking ability, writing ability
  communicative, 20–21, 283ff
    assessing, 281ff
    rating procedures, 291ff
  discourse, 20, 282
  grammatical, 20, 22, 179, 283, 286–287, 294ff
  sociocultural, 20, 21, 179, 282ff, 293ff, 360
  sociolinguistic, 21–22, 282–283, 285ff, 293ff, 360
  strategic, 20, 22, 120, 287ff
    components of, 288
  trait measurement, 226
Abraham, 235
Aighes, 123
Alderson, 2, 41, 48, 57, 139, 225, 236, 245–246, 249, 262, 360
Allan, 138
Allen, 32
Allwright, 17
Alpert, 78
American Council on the Teaching of Foreign Languages (ACTFL), 225, 300
  ACTFL Oral Proficiency Interview (OPI), 79, 268, 269
  ACTFL proficiency scale, 265ff
Anbar, 247
Anderson, 40, 43, 81, 123, 127, 134–135, 213, 243, 289
anxiety. *See* characteristics of test takers, and test anxiety
Aphek, 120, 146–147
Arens, 212, 241, 250
Arevart, 195, 277
Arndt, 306

assessment
  contexts, 13
  criterion-referenced, 8, 25–26, 28, 30, 48, 92, 100, 209, 360
  direct, 142ff, 161ff
  gatekeeping, 110
  indirect, 127, 161ff
  mastery vs. progress, 53
  minimal level, 30
  multiple means of, 196–197
  norm-referenced, 8, 25–26, 102, 104
  of listening skills. *See* listening skills
  of meaning, 219ff
  paralinguistics and, 323
  process approach to, 117ff, 308–309
  purposes, 22–25
  theoretical frameworks for, 24ff
Australian Occupational English Test, 333
authenticity, 3, 16, 18–29, 360
  and test method, 19
  of writing tasks, 20, 343
Avery, 174
Bachman, 3, 10, 11, 19, 22, 36ff, 82, 89, 101, 120ff, 139, 169, 236, 237, 267, 273, 283, 288–289
backwash effect. *See* washback effect
Barnett, 212
Basham, 343
Belanoff, 336–337, 339
Ben Simon, 232–33
Bensoussan, 345
Berman, 221
Bernhardt, 212, 239ff
Berry, 78
Berwick, 268, 269

387